Radical Reproductive Justice

Radical Reproductive Justice

FOUNDATIONS, THEORY, PRACTICE, CRITIQUE

EDITED BY

Loretta J. Ross, Lynn Roberts, Erika Derkas, Whitney Peoples, and Pamela Bridgewater Toure

FOREWORD BY DOROTHY ROBERTS

Published in 2017 by the Feminist Press
at the City University of New York
The Graduate Center
365 Fifth Avenue, Suite 5406
New York, NY 10016

feministpress.org

First Feminist Press edition 2017

This book was made possible thanks to a grant from New York State Council on the Arts with the support of Governor Andrew Cuomo and the New York State Legislature.

First printing November 2017

Cover and text design by Drew Stevens
Cover image © 2017 Mary Lee Bendolph / Artists Rights Society (ARS), New York

Library of Congress Cataloging-in-Publication Data
Names: Ross, Loretta, editor.
Title: Radical reproductive justice : foundation, theory, practice, critique / edited by Loretta J. Ross, Erika Derkas, Whitney Peoples, Lynn Roberts, and Pamela, Bridgewater Toure ; foreword by Dorothy Roberts.
Description: New York City : The Feminist Press at CUNY, 2017. | Includes bibliographical references and index.
Identifiers: LCCN 2017022896 (print) | LCCN 2017033227 (ebook) | ISBN 9781936932047 (E-book) | ISBN 9781558614376 (paperback)
Subjects: LCSH: Reproductive rights–United States. | Human reproduction–Law and legislation–United States. | Reproductive health–United States. | African American women–Health and hygiene. | Women's rights–United States. | BISAC: SOCIAL SCIENCE / Feminism & Feminist Theory. | SOCIAL SCIENCE / Discrimination & Race Relations. | SOCIAL SCIENCE / Women's Studies. | SOCIAL SCIENCE / Gender Studies.
Classification: LCC HQ766.5.U5 (ebook) | LCC HQ766.5.U5 R297 2017 (print) | DDC 305.420973–dc23
LC record available at https://lccn.loc.gov/2017022896

Contents

THEORY

POLICY, PRACTICE, AND ACTIVISM

POETRY

Foreword

Marking SisterSong's twentieth anniversary, 2017 is the perfect time to celebrate, explain, and illuminate what radical reproductive justice means. And this anthology—put together by SisterSong activists and others who believe in reproductive justice whose work has been critical to the reproductive justice framework and movement—is an ideal forum. The path-breaking vision and relentless organizing by SisterSong and other Indigenous and women of color organizations over the last two decades has been remarkably successful at increasing awareness of reproductive justice in activist and scholarly circles. Yet this very success in the face of intensifying oppression makes it more essential than ever to clarify the history and meaning of reproductive justice and to chart a path for the movement's future.

At the outset of my career as a law professor in the late 1980s, I was drawn from the academic world of researching reproductive oppression against black women into the burgeoning movement for their liberation. As I wrote my first book, *Killing the Black Body*, I found my engagement with women of color organizing for reproductive justice not only essential to my research but also my spirit. The dominant legal approach focused on the right to choose (which meant only the right to choose abortion) was completely inadequate to grasp the violations of black women's bodies I was documenting. The reproductive justice framework provided a radically different way to place reproductive health and rights in the context of the experiences of women of color and the struggle for equality, social justice, and human rights. The reproductive justice movement offered a radically different place for women of color to be in the leadership and to develop political strategies that could effectively contest the interlocking oppressions they faced, oppressions that had for centuries generated an unjust conception of reproductive freedom.

Soon after *Killing the Black Body* was published in 1997, I answered a call from Julia Scott, then president of the National Black Women's Health Project, to join the organization's board of directors. Over the next twenty years, I would share in the exciting work of SisterSong, along with other women of color organizations, to put the RJ framework into action. Serving on the plenary panel at SisterSong's first national conference in 2003, I felt the thrill of women of color activists coming together to stake a claim in the battle for reproductive freedom and make clear why our RJ movement mattered.

The critical importance of RJ became even clearer the following year, when SisterSong, Black Women's Health Imperative, the National Latina Institute for Reproductive Health, and the National Asian Pacific American Women's Forum brought an RJ approach to the leadership of the 2004 March for Women's Lives in Washington, DC, and helped to make it one of the largest of its kind in US history. Many victories grounded in RJ organizing followed. SisterSong's work with women of color organizations succeeded in staving off numerous racist and sexist assaults on reproductive freedom. For example, challenging antiabortion billboards accusing black women of perpetrating genocide against their own communities through abortion, and helping to defeat the Susan B. Anthony and Frederick Douglass Prenatal Nondiscrimination Act, introduced in Congress in 2012, that would have penalized abortions by Asian American and black women.

RJ's centering of women of color, social justice, and human rights provides a galvanizing moral reason for radical change and a concrete basis for building coalitions among organizations working toward a more humane society. RJ is a model not just for women of color, nor just for achieving reproductive freedom. RJ is a model for organizing for human equality and well-being. The world needs radical reproductive justice. This anthology tells us why and shows us how to get there.

—Dorothy Roberts
Philadelphia, 2017

Introduction

[We are] participating in the creation of yet another culture, a new story to explain the world and our participation in it, a new value system with images and symbols that connect us to each other and to the planet.

—*Gloria Anzaldúa,* Borderlands/La Frontera: The New Mestiza

Two decades after the creation of the reproductive justice framework, this timely anthology by members and supporters of SisterSong offers an overview of the scope and impact of the movement. At SisterSong, founded in 1997, we sought to explore whether reproductive justice was a sturdy enough concept to propel a growing movement of women of color activists from all parts of society and issues to fight for reproductive dignity. We knew the inadequate and imprecise pro-choice/pro-life dichotomy produced anemic political analyses that failed to offer the experiential and intellectual depth desired by the radical women of color collectively organizing. As Gloria Anzaldúa says in the epigraph, we needed a *new* story to explain the world of reproductive politics. We needed *new* language that would provide an analytical anchor to engage issues both within and beyond US borders to build strong connections between political organizing and theorizing by women of color. Women of color inhabit multiple worlds because of our gender, sexuality, race, spiritual beliefs, class, immigration status, abilities, and other identities, and embody what Anzaldúa called the "*mestiza* consciousness" from living in the borderlands, or interstices of rigid boundaries.

The RJ framework was created by black women in 1994, some of whom cofounded SisterSong. That innovative analysis provided a powerful tool for exploring issues of racial, economic, and social inequality by building on black feminist theory and applying those insights to reproductive politics. Reproductive justice is purposefully controversial in that it disrupts the dehumanizing status quo of reproductive politics. RJ centers the lives of communities of color instead of the middle-class white people on both sides of the abortion debate. SisterSong members from Asian American, Latina, Indigenous, Middle Eastern, and white communities expanded, improved, and propagated the RJ framework through organizing and scholarship, using it as a form of intellectual commons. Each historical experience informed the accounts of others.

In the ensuing decades, reproductive justice became an expansive and multilayered approach to the fight for reproductive freedom for all people. Consensus usage of the RJ framework by women of color has transformed reproductive politics in the United States through its power, elasticity, and opportunities for creative inquiry to illuminate connections of resistance to specific means of domination. RJ makes the power, agency, privilege, cultures, and histories of people visible by incorporating our diverse complexities and singularities. This anthology is a testament to our vision: that reproductive justice could create a culture shift in reproductive politics and bring fresh voices together to build an expansive vision for universal justice.

In realizing the power of the RJ movement, we move from the politics of inclusion to the politics of leadership. Instead of demanding that women of color be included in mainstream organizations—which often results in marginalization—women of color are ideologically leading the movement, centering ourselves, and transforming power relationships in the process. This is consistent throughout our history. Women of color helped build the US women's movement—from its inception centuries ago to major campaigns today to end violence against women—to combat poverty, racism, and the prison industrial complex, to defend reproductive and sexual freedom, to protect Mother Earth, and to achieve human rights for all. This is our collective history; we must learn about it and use it to challenge anyone who believes feminism is solely the property of middle-class white women. When that mythical (and racist) stereotype is internalized by women of color, we support our own subordination and diminish our foremothers' legacies, which are consistently underreported by the media and many historians. Women of color have always resisted white supremacy, settler colonialism, and gender injustice. To forget that legacy is to reshackle our souls, our spirits, our hearts, and our minds.

We hope that reproductive justice will help us build a human rights movement for the multigenerational struggle against white supremacy we have always faced. To paraphrase Dr. Willie Parker, it's at times like these we must remember it's always been times like these. Being "woke" is not an event; it's a lifetime commitment for which many people have sacrificed to give us the privilege of being able to march and protest.

Holocaust survivor Elie Wiesel said, "There may be times when we are powerless to prevent injustice, but there must never be a time when we fail to protest."

This book will illustrate the numerous intersections of reproductive justice and surprise those who believe it is simply a new name for pro-choice politics. People are sometimes confused about the relationship between pro-choice rhetoric and reproductive justice. Is RJ in tension with "choice" politics or does its theory and activism rest on an entirely different basis? Is RJ an attempt to make peace within the pro-choice and pro-life debate? Should women of color seek emulation, accommodation, assimilation, or separation? It is important to underscore here that RJ is neither an oppositional nor a peace-making ideology; it is an emergent radical theory that recasts the problem using the human rights framework.[1]

The artificial divide of pro-choice versus pro-life required a new vocabulary created and populated by women of color, as many are both pro-choice and pro-life, depending on the definition. Within SisterSong, pro-life members generally assert that while they would never choose an abortion for themselves, they would not interfere in other people's choices. Instead, they support them as people making the choices that make sense for them. Thus, debating pro-choice/pro-life politics has never been a threat to SisterSong's ability to work together, even as some of the US women's movement has become increasingly conservative and most radical feminist activism occurs on the margins.

SisterSong benefited from this unity because part of the power of reproductive justice is derived from its ability to provide a grounded theory that holds the shifting, intersectional ways that we define ourselves as human beings, without losing sight of the goals for which we strive: equity, dignity, and justice. Reproductive justice is for "[e]veryone who has wanted something more than criminalization, isolation, shame, self-hatred and invisibility," to borrow the words of disability rights activist Mia Mingus.

For RJ activists, it's not enough to speak about what we are *against*. We must use the human rights framework to articulate what we are *for*. We need elected officials who will uphold our human rights, who will make commitments about how many children they will send to college, debt free, rather than how many they will send to jail. Instead of railing against poor people, how about standing against poverty? We need an economic, political, and social system that understands healthcare is a human right, as are immigrants' rights, women's rights, and so on. Rather than only treating the symptoms of reproductive oppression, such as the excessive maternal mortality rate in Texas (the highest in the developed world), RJ activists address the causes—in this case, a political system led by conservative representatives who systematically closed over eighty women's health centers, violating women's rights to healthcare.[2] RJ examines the directionality of power relations, not just the means of power, such as voting rights which could have allowed for the election of a more balanced legislature in Texas. This is the vision of reproductive justice. Intersectionality is our process; human rights are our goal.

■ ■ ■

Reproductive justice is not difficult to understand. It is both a theoretical paradigm shift and a model for activist organizing centering three interconnected human rights values: the right *not to have children* using safe birth control, abortion, or abstinence; the right *to have children* under the conditions we choose; and the right *to parent the children we have* in safe and healthy environments. RJ activism is based on the human right to make personal decisions about one's life, and the obligation of government and society to ensure that the conditions are suitable for implementing one's decisions. In their analysis of the Atlanta HIV epidemic, the reproductive and sexual health organization SisterLove states, "We see Reproductive Justice as the conditions of liberation that will exist when all people have the power and resources necessary to make their own decisions about their bodies, health, gender, sexuality, relationships, families, and communities, to create and choose their families, and to reproduce their communities as a whole."[3] This creates a dialectical process in which individual, group, corporate, and government actions are interdependent to achieve reproductive freedom and control.

In particular, RJ draws attention to the current lack of physical, reproductive, and cultural safety. It focuses on structural oppression and the development of new theories and activism to create radical pathways of resistance and strategies for change that incorporate the complexities of our diverse economic, racial, gendered, cultural, and geographic locations. We understand how differences matter, and how we can account for power inequities to achieve our vision of justice. To obtain RJ, we must work on injustices in all arenas: social, economic, gender, racial, environmental, financial, physical, sexual, environmental, disability, and carceral. Since RJ includes the right *not* to have children, many advocates share an agenda with the pro-choice movement supporting sex education, birth control, abortion, and abstinence (if you can hang on!). RJ does not reduce the focus on abortion but contextualizes it within the larger matrix of oppression. This framework exposes the race- and class-based manipulations of abortion laws and availability to sculpt America's political landscape.

RJ posits that intersecting forces produce differing reproductive experiences that shape each individual's life. While every human being has the same human rights, our intersectional identities require different considerations to achieve reproductive justice. For example, a disabled, immigrant woman has multiple intersecting identities that affect her reproductive decision-making. Can she safely go to the hospital for a prenatal visit and tell the truth about her circumstances if she lacks documentation of her immigration status? Would she receive culturally appropriate treatment accounting for her disabilities? She does not have special rights; she has special needs that require an intersectional lens.

Since reproductive oppression affects our lives in multiple ways, multipronged approaches are necessary to fight this exploitation. There are three main frameworks for fighting reproductive injustices: *reproductive health* that deals with healthcare service delivery for individuals; *reproductive rights* that address the legal regime through the US Constitution, such as ending abortion restrictions and maintaining access to contraceptives; and *reproductive justice* that focuses on organizing resistance and movement building using global human rights standards.[4] Although the frameworks are distinct in their approach, they work in tandem to provide a complementary and comprehensive solution. Ultimately, as in any movement, all three components of service, advocacy, and organizing are crucial to advancement.

As Jessica Yee Danforth of the Native Youth Sexual Health Network states, "Actualizing [reproductive justice] beyond a hot, new buzzword still has a long way to go and it has to start with being honest about where we are at and what's really going on in terms of racism, sexism, classism, white supremacy, homophobia, transphobia, ableism and more—not just systematically, but what we ourselves are complicit in as well."[5]

For readers unfamiliar with reproductive justice, this book presents an opportunity to understand the history, origins, and definitions of the RJ framework, to explore its practical applications for radical and transformative feminist activism, and to broaden the theoretical possibilities of this groundbreaking political development in reproductive politics as it migrates from the community into the academy.

As the editors of this anthology, we are not claiming authorship of reproductive justice in an individualistic, privatized way nor claiming that we can describe all its innovative applications in a single book. The contributors to this anthology locate RJ in their own lives, experiences, places, and communities. As editors, we may not agree with every sentiment contained within but we believed that including a range of perspectives would offer an overview of the capacious potential of this framework, recognizing that some may view it as *too* inclusive. Reproductive justice is comprehensive, expansive, ambiguous, and demanding. We did not want an anthology of groupthink, but one that challenges our creativity and extends the conversation on the possibilities of RJ. The essays in this collection open windows to an emerging and powerful movement that provides an inclusive paradigm for thinking about reproduction and achieving universal justice both locally and globally. The topic of reproductive justice is so vast and contains a myriad of approaches and issues that one anthology cannot cover everything, but we hope this book may provide a platform for many others that further explore the framework.

We write with a sense of urgency. Some of us are elders; we might not be around to witness the full achievement of reproductive justice, but are honored to have been at its birth and seen its growth. Because the project was led by an activist, Loretta J. Ross, whose primary work was leading SisterSong until 2012, it took us many years to compile and edit this anthology, and we were constantly learning as we worked. As you will read, two of our authors, Aaronette White and Mary Krane Derr, have died since they sent in submissions, as did an important editorial team member, Pamela Bridgewater Toure.[6] Bernice Johnson Reagon, a founding member of the SNCC Freedom Singers, once said, "Most of the things that you do, if you do them right, are for people who live long after you are long forgotten. That will only happen if you give it away."[7] This reproductive justice anthology is our editorial team offering the universe our radical approach to reproductive politics. Our knowledge has been collectively developed and generously shared, and we trust readers will enjoy receiving this gift.

Defining Reproductive Justice

The reproductive justice movement was launched by twelve African American women in June 1994 in Chicago at a national pro-choice conference. This origin is discussed in Toni M. Bond Leonard's "Laying the Foundations for a Reproductive Justice Movement." It was the same year that many important changes occurred in anti-racist, anti-colonial, anti-fascist, and feminist politics worldwide, including the International Conference on Population and Development in Cairo and Nelson Mandela's election as president of South Africa.

That year was also significant as white supremacists gained massive influence in American politics by mainstreaming their hatred through the religious Right and ultraconservatives. The late Senator Jesse Helms, famously opposed to Civil Rights, had blocked ratification of the United Nations Convention on Elimination of All Forms of Discrimination against Women for almost two decades as chair of the Senate Foreign Relations Committee. He called LGBTQ people "degenerates" and "weak, morally sick wretches" in a *Newsweek* interview, demonstrating a clear link between racist antifeminist and antigay politicians.[8]

This political snapshot of 1994 underscores that reproductive justice opposes white supremacy as an ideology used to promote unequal laws, practices, and social outcomes. White supremacy is not a fact of genetics nor is it an accurate description of either a race of people or racial hierarchy. It is a totalizing system comprised of racism, sexism, homophobia, Christian nationalism, transphobia, ableism, and classism that differentiates who has access to institutionalized power. The ideology of the formal white-supremacist movement disgusts many people who identify as white, yet fewer understand white privilege is the practice of white supremacy.[9] It is white privilege to be able to ignore the role of race in reproductive politics.

These events informed the development and growth of the RJ framework. Black feminists understood how these issues intersected with our discussions on reproductive politics: apartheid and white supremacy, violence against women and abortion providers, and systematic economic underdevelopment in the US and the Global South. In the words of Chandra Talpade Mohanty:

> Poor women and girls are the hardest hit by the degradation of environmental conditions, wars, famines, privatization of services and deregulation of governments, the dismantling of welfare states, the restructuring of paid and unpaid work, increasing surveillance and incarceration in prisons, and so on. And this is why a *feminism without and beyond borders* is necessary to address the injustices of global capitalism.[10]

Unlike the mainstream pro-choice movement, black feminists could not, and would not, isolate discussions on reproductive healthcare from other critical global issues *because* our lives are interconnected and interdependent. Twelve black women decided to tell our truth and were awed by the results. By placing women of color at the center of our analysis and organizing, we recognized, in the words of the anti-violence organization INCITE!, that "there is no permanent center of organizing. Rather, by constantly shifting the center to communities that face intersecting forms of oppression, we have a more comprehensive view of the strategies to end all forms of violence."[11]

As activists we responded to the lack of appropriate language about the lived reproductive experiences of women of color. We had to account for racial, homophobic, and sexual violence, abortion murders, significant global events, and have these considerations in our mind at the same time we were listening to proposals for healthcare reform in 1994. The first antiabortion murder of a provider—Dr. David Gunn in 1993—serves as an example of the cross-over between white supremacist and antiabortion violence as his killer was assisted by a former member of the Klu Klux Klan. Some of us were working both in and outside a pro-choice movement that primarily focused on defending a woman's right to choose an abortion, while not necessarily advocating for an end to all reproductive injustices. For example, Andrea Smith's essay, "Beyond Pro-Choice Versus Pro-Life: Women of Color and Reproductive Justice," provides an analysis of the untenable myopia of the pro-choice/pro-life camps for women of color through a Native American lens.

We struggled within the pro-choice movement to have our intersectional lives acknowledged as women of color. We were tired of throwing our lived experiences up against the disbelief of white women, and sought to discover new ways of describing our realities. Our experiential and material bases formed a body of collective knowledge in which we could simultaneously center on our own experiences while coalescing with others situated within an oppressive society.

When we centered ourselves in Chicago, we recognized that we represented communities with few real choices. Black women spliced together the concepts of reproductive rights, social justice, and human rights to coin the term "reproductive justice" and launched a signature campaign to include the perspectives of African American women on healthcare reform policies being negotiated in 1994. We created a radical shift from "choice" to "justice" to locate women's autonomy and self-determination in international human rights standards and laws, rather than in the constitutionally limited concepts of individual rights and privacy. We challenged how liberal ideology misused the concepts of rights and justice to situate responsibility for health and wellness in individual choices, while ignoring the institutionalized barriers that constrict individual choices such as racism, homophobia, sexism, classism, ableism, or xenophobia, or more simply, lack of access to appropriate and comprehensive healthcare.

In reviewing the evolution of the RJ framework for this anthology, we realized that the language of reproductive justice is never static. It's like RJ has become a sort of open source code that activists have fleshed out, moving far beyond our original conceptualization in 1994. The RJ framework has significantly affected the organizing strategies of women working for reproductive health and rights as they adapt it to their own circumstances. More surprisingly because it was unintentional, it has profoundly shifted the focus of the pro-choice movement, proving the power of women of color to fundamentally impact strategies of the mainstream women's movement. Never has such a shift seemed so urgent or necessary.

Despite the success of RJ in ushering in a more radical framework, we also are concerned with the misappropriation and co-optation of RJ by those who ignore the realities of abuses of power and institutionalized inequality that circumscribe the reproductive experiences of vulnerable people. There may be those who seek to exploit our activist and intellectual work while ignoring our embodied realities and the genealogies that affected our journey from our critical standpoints.

Reproductive justice theory, strategy, and practices emerge out of the distinct historical realities of diverse communities. Because of the increasing popularity of the RJ analysis, leading many to adopt the term, a group of women of color embracing the framework met at the offices of the Moriah Fund in 2006 at a meeting facilitated by Inca Mohamed to set standards for what we would define as criteria for reproductive justice:

—Is intersectional
—Connects the local to the global
—Based on the human rights framework
—Makes the link between the individual and community
—Addresses government and corporate responsibility
—Fights all forms of population control (eugenics)
—Commits to individual/community leadership development that results in power shifts
—Puts marginalized communities at the center of the analysis

—Understands that political power, participation of those impacted, and policy changes are necessary to achieve reproductive justice
—Has its own intersectionality of involving theory, strategy, and practice
—Applies to everyone

By using these criteria, any organization may reformulate its mission and work within the RJ framework. This distinction has created some confusion in the pro-choice movement because some RJ advocates assert that mainstream organizations not led by women of color should not call themselves RJ organizations. As the multiracial team of editors of this anthology, we believe that reproductive justice is not an exclusive, essentialist race-based movement, but a movement for the human rights for all people.

Conditions Compelling a New Movement

It is significant that reproductive justice developed at the end of the twentieth century to offer a fundamental change in the underlying assumptions about how society should debate reproductive politics. As an organizing strategy, RJ helps knit together disparate movements such as civil rights, reproductive rights, Native American sovereignty, economic justice, civil liberties, disability rights, LGBTQ rights, environmental justice, and immigrant rights, among others. RJ is an inherently intersectional approach based on universal human rights that effectively counters the rise of the culture wars launched by conservatives attempting to roll back the progressive gains of the twentieth century.

These culture wars intentionally serve as distractions, effectively disguising how neoliberals abuse power by dismantling the welfare state, outsourcing jobs, attacking community self-governance, incarcerating millions, and privatizing or defunding public services in the pursuit of obscene profits through globalization. RJ compels us to critique, demystify, and resist all abuses of power. Individuals, organizations, governments, societies, and corporations may violate human rights, and these violations exacerbate economic, racial, and gender inequalities. A telling statistic regarding the relationship between national governments and corporations: of the world's largest economies, fifty-one are corporations, not countries, giving them disproportionate power over people's lives.[12] Since local or state agencies are no longer presumed responsible for social well-being or the protection of our communities, we are subject to the tender mercies of deregulated private corporations busily pursuing imperialist ventures.

Despite increased calls for billionaire business owners to be more socially responsible, a new breed of "philanthrocapitalists" cannot and will not give enough money away to correct the structural harms caused by the amoral pursuit of profits.[13] Few elected officials are brave enough to support increased taxation for the public good, despite an enormous national debt, impoverished state governments, disproportionately high unemployment in communities of color, and vanishing human services. As the Occupy protests pointed out, we have the rich people of the one percent instructing other rich people in the media to tell the middle class that everything is the fault of poor people.

Moreover, our opponents are in some ways often vexingly more culturally competent than our allies. Frequently, those opposed to human rights use people of color (often women) as spokespeople for conservative causes. They are also especially fond of the legitimated conservative mother as a defender of white traditional culture. They are the morality police poised to fight any number of progressive impulses toward protecting reproductive and sexual rights.

Complicating the assault from the Right, we also contend with a pernicious brand of neoliberal feminism promoted by a corporate-controlled mainstream media that ignores class (and often race) as a determining factor in women's lives. They naturalize capitalist values as if they are inevitable, and presume that any class power achieved by some women will lead to at least some lifestyle improvements for women with less power. In a subtle and passive victim-blaming approach, neoliberal feminist advertising has become a marketing ploy by some corporations supporting wealth accumulation while never challenging the economic exploitation of people globally. This is a sly neofeminist version of trickle-down economics. By claiming that we don't know how to speak up for ourselves as women without their sage corporate advice, they paper over the vast differences between women and feel absolved of responsibility when our demands for ideological and structural changes are ignored.

Equally problematic is the role of religious fundamentalists in denying the responsibilities of the state or religious institutions to provide economic, educational, or social opportunities for women. Fundamentalists deploy masculinist rhetoric against social justice movements, while inciting religious, ethnic, gender, anti-immigrant, and racial hatred. Religions that oppose women's rights offer little sustenance to those seeking self-determination over their lives and bodies. Religious leaders collude with the white supremacist/neoliberal alliance to define poverty, sexuality, lack of opportunity, and especially our fertility as sins (and crimes).

The Potential of Reproductive Justice

RJ offers everyone a way to claim ownership of their lives and stories through first-person narratives and storytelling as a vehicle for social and personal transformation—but not in a chatty self-help style that ignores the structural, historical, and political obstacles women of color face. A commercialized storytelling practice believes that the solutions to today's problems lie in a neoliberal market-based approach to structural problems that ignores corporate practices, endless wars, environmental degradation, gender and racial inequality, and the alienation of individuals as a response to collective oppression. The toxic mixture of white supremacy, xenophobia, Christian nationalism, racism, capitalism, patriarchy, and homophobia cannot be overcome simply through building our self-esteem. We cannot end reproductive oppression by learning to love ourselves.

According to historian Rickie Solinger, "The politics of the personal story insist that the reader consider the woman storyteller as real and whole, a person who must be heard."[14] Stories help us claim our dignity and respect to tell the truth of our lives. The Horatio Alger myth of lifting yourself up by your bootstraps doesn't work if you don't have boots, nor can you self-help your way out of neighborhoods like Flint, Michigan, poisoned by toxic drinking water in 2015. To illustrate, Laura Jiménez, Kierra Johnson, and Cara Page explore the intersections between environmental racism and reproductive justice in their collaborative essay in this book, "Beyond the Trees: Stories and Strategies of Environmental and Reproductive Justice."

Reproductive justice allows us to include all the real life intersections of our complicated lives by thinking and talking from a human rights perspective. This anthology especially lifts the reproductive injustices of the prison industrial complex. Rachel Roth's essay, "'She Doesn't Deserve to Be Treated Like This': Prisons as Sites of Reproductive Injustice," explores how the prison industrial complex violates the human rights of incarcerated women, such as shackling during childbirth. Along with

Dázon Dixon Diallo's contribution on HIV/AIDS and women, "HIV Prevention and Reproductive Justice: A Framework for Saving Women's Lives," these essays offer lenses for those marginalized by society to find their voices and rightfully demand inclusion in the RJ movement.

RJ enriches our analysis of where we come from, where we are, and where we will go. For those incorporating a radical, political, economic framework, it redefines the concept of "reproductive labor"—services provided for the benefit of others, often at the neglect of self—through the perspectives of women of color.

By building on previous black feminist theories, reproductive justice engaged the identity politics of the 1970s with intersectionality and the application of self-help from the black women's health movement in the 1980s to transform the reproductive rights movement in the 1990s. This family of ideas has produced flexibly inclusive theories. The authors in this anthology agree: the effects of reproductive oppression will be different for everyone and each community, but reproductive justice shares some of the basic characteristics of intersectionality: universality, simultaneity, and interdependence.

It is important to reiterate that although reproductive justice was created by African American women and popularized by women of color, it does not only apply to women of color. Everyone deserves the same human rights, and our intersectional identities inform how to honor them in specific ways based on our experiences and circumstances. It's not a matter of difference versus commonality, but difference as the pathway to fairer outcomes based on justice and equity. This book includes essays exploring the many ways others are using the RJ framework while resisting old habits of privileging their perspectives over those of marginalized women.

This anthology will explore some of the concepts encompassed by RJ as a positive approach tying together sexuality, health, and human rights and social justice movements by examining the larger context of the health and well-being of women, families, and communities. We believe that the ability of any person to determine their own reproductive destiny is directly linked to the conditions in their community, and these are not just a matter of individual choice and access. As Benita Miller explains in her essay, "Mothering While Poor: Utilizing the Reproductive Justice Framework to Build the Capacities of Young Mothers," women must routinely make individual decisions about their bodies in the midst of being members of communities whose rights are regularly violated. This in turn prevents individual women from fully accessing all their available and viable choices when making decisions about themselves and their families.

Reproductive Oppression

Reproductive oppression is genocide, or "reprocide," as Loretta J. Ross terms it. Women of color, who continuously face strategies of population control through eugenics-based ideologies, must fight equally as hard for the right to *have* children, thus highlighting the second tenet of RJ. The birth of our children of color is a cause for celebration, because, in the words of Audre Lorde, "We weren't meant to survive"—making our survival a direct challenge to reproductive injustices and white supremacy. RJ has spawned a separate movement for "birth justice," which includes the right to midwifery and nonmedicalized methods of birthing and parenting our children, however it is not privileged as the central goal. In "Tubes Tied, Truly Child-Free at Last!" Aaronette White offers her perspective as a black woman who is childless by choice, refuting the assumption that all women are meant to be biological mothers. Nor does RJ insist that only biologically defined women experience reproductive oppression. We recognize transgender people and the fight for bodily autonomy and sexual identity. Regardless of how we parent or of our legal or biological gender, we seek to create something new to celebrate our children, not as property, but as offerings to themselves.

Sexuality and motherhood rely on a system of racial and gendered ideology, replete with systemic cultural assumptions about and representations of race and gender through which individuals understand their relationships within the world. Mainstream elites who promote punitive policies to regulate the reproduction of people of color, such as family welfare caps that punish women for having additional children while receiving public assistance, perceive nonwhite women's bodies as inherently pathological or deviant. Similarly, many trans people are unable to obtain correctly gendered state-recognized identification or, when incarcerated, be housed among the prison population with which they identify without proof of cost-prohibitive or unwanted gender reassignment surgery.

In addition, RJ activists must pay careful attention to the multiple ways that Indigenous people and communities of color are constrained through a constellation of public policies. Because controlling the reproduction of a community is vital to the process of controlling its destiny, the nation-state places different values on different reproductive bodies. Katie O'Connell, for example, writes about disability rights using an RJ lens in "We Need to Talk about Disability as a Reproductive Justice Issue." Lucia Leandro Gimeno examines birth justice activism through a transmasculine femme lens in "The Reluctant Reproductive Justice Organizer and Birthworker." Indigenous women, women of color, immigrants, disabled people, and LGBTQ and gender nonconforming individuals are considered the racially and sexually constructed "other." Our bodies must be contained, constrained, and disdained.

Indigenous people experience reproductive oppression against the background of the history and struggles against colonization. White settlers committed genocide against Native Americans to seize their lands, ignored their sovereignty claims, denied their memories, and caused them to "reproductively disappear." Population control of Indigenous people requires not only destroying their spiritual and environmental practices but also constant management, manipulation, negotiation, and assimilation through a labyrinthine set of measures imposed by the Indian Health Service and the federal government.[15] Ironically, based on the treaties with the government, Indigenous people are the only people in the US guaranteed permanent healthcare delivered by the federal government under the Constitution, a core demand of RJ activists. Instead, white supremacist ideologies and institutions seek to manage Indigenous reproduction through inaccessible and incompetent services, the proliferation of alcohol and drug addiction, dangerous contraceptives, violence, sterilization abuse, kidnapping, abortion restrictions, inadequate funding for basic survival necessities, and weak punishments of non-Natives for crimes against Indigenous people.

The third pillar of RJ—the right to raise our children in safe and healthy environments—brings into the conversation recent events that are often neglected by the mainstream pro-choice and pro-life movements, such as Black Lives Matter. RJ makes white privilege visible when it comes to parenting. It analyzes the critical historical factors that affect our children's lives, or the downstream consequences of upstream racism. In Ferguson, Missouri, Michael Brown's mother is left wondering when women's reproductive rights will extend to having our children survive police brutality. Reproductive justice was relevant to Trayvon Martin's parents not only when their son was killed by a violent vigilante in 2012 but also when the criminal justice system allowed the murderer to go free. Gun control is a reproductive justice issue and as vital as the right to a clean environment or quality schools.

Feminism needs our RJ framework because we value the worth of children of color beyond birth, and understand that the struggle for justice is also a struggle against the violences of white supremacy. Reproductive justice advocates contend that "as necessary as racial slavery was for defining and ennobling whiteness and worthiness . . . [women and children of color are] crucial to the project of defining legitimate mothers, citizens, and voters. Their existence and treatment functions as tenebrous yet public messages regarding who has the right to education, the right to work, the right to just compensation, and the right to a roof over her head."[16] By emphasizing human rights and intersectionality, the RJ movement offers voice and representation to people whose experience of reproductive disciplining is affected by interlocked layers of oppression.

At its core, reproductive justice is about power. RJ faces white supremacy fearlessly. It allows us to analyze the intersectional forces that deny us our human dignity, and it enables us to determine how to work together across barriers to achieve the power necessary to protect and affirm our rights. Not all marginalized locations yield crucial knowledge of how to defeat the compounded power structures of white supremacy. As Cherríe Moraga says, "Oppression does not make for hearts as big as all outdoors. Oppression makes us big and small. Expressive and silenced. Deep and dead."[17] We as individuals cannot change the systemic reproductive injustices we face; rather, we must work together in alliances that use our lived experiences to theorize, strategize, and organize.

The Traveling Impact of Reproductive Justice

What has reproductive justice accomplished in the past twenty years to make it so remarkable and radical? It spurred the growth of women of color individuals and organizations leading and working on reproductive health and rights issues, producing legislative and policy victories at the state level in Colorado, California, New Mexico, and Georgia. The influence of RJ also reached beyond women of color in August 2014. A controversy erupted when a *New York Times* interview with Planned Parenthood Federation of America President Cecile Richards neglected to mention the critical work of women of color that affected Planned Parenthood's decision to discard the terms "pro-choice" and "pro-life." This erasure of the work the RJ movement has done to change the trajectory of reproductive politics in the US precipitated an admonitory open letter organized by Monica Simpson, executive director of SisterSong, and cosigned by thirty-eight organizations supporting reproductive justice.

This open letter was a line-in-the-sand moment for the RJ movement. We risked calling out an allied organization, even in these precarious times dominated by antiabortion policies. Two years later, when the *Washington Post* published another interview with Richards in August 2016, she quickly wrote a correction to chide them for omitting the impact of women of color in its coverage. According to Richards, the RJ movement has pushed the pro-choice movement toward more aggressive and radical campaigns to defend reproductive freedom. She wrote:

> As with any bold movement, ours is being fueled by a generation of activists and leaders—primarily women of color—who are challenging the country, and all of us, to be unapologetic champions for the rights of all people to access abortion and reproductive care with a lens of social justice. The roots of this supposedly newfound boldness lie in the reproductive justice movement, which formally began twenty-two years ago this November, and which generated the growth across the country of organizing primarily led by women of color that has turned conventional attitudes and organizations on their heads.[18]

The reproductive justice movement is not only contained within the United States, but is a true feminism without borders. For example, South Africa's Minister of Social Development, Bathabile Dlamini, spoke about reproductive justice to the UN General Assembly on September 19, 2014. She didn't speak in general language that could be interpreted to *suggest* reproductive justice; she used the specific term, acknowledging the role African American women played in gifting this theory and framework to the world. In addition to discussing sexual rights, reproductive health issues, and economic justice, she used the speech to explicitly embrace LGBTQ rights, serving as an important backstop against the rampant antigay legislation around the African continent fomented by the American evangelical missionaries.

Similarly, reproductive justice was the theme of remarks by Diakhoumba Gassama of Senegal, a human rights lawyer representing the international feminist organization Realizing Sexual and Reproductive Justice (RESURJ). She spoke at the UN on July 12, 2016, at the General Assembly's High-Level Thematic Debate on Human Rights about the role RJ has in correcting global and political inequities. This took place in the context of the fiftieth anniversary of the international human rights covenants and the thirtieth anniversary of the Declaration on the Right to Development.

Another exciting example was at the 22nd Harm Reduction International Conference that took place in Beirut, Lebanon, in 2011 when Joanne Csete, an associate professor at Columbia University's Mailman School of Public Health, gave an opening plenary address in which she explained the evolution of the concept of reproductive justice. She called upon the drug policy reform movement to follow suit and evolve into the drug policy justice movement. In an email to Loretta J. Ross, Lynn Paltrow, executive director of National Advocates for Pregnant Women, wrote, "It was thrilling to hear reproductive justice recognized in that setting and even more thrilling to have it so astutely used as a model for political action and human rights in the drug policy context."

Reading about how reproductive justice has made significant transformations in human rights dialogue and goals around the world, particularly in Africa, made us feel we had somehow issued a new iteration of the groundbreaking 1977 Combahee River Collective Statement.

Google metrics may help explain the impact of RJ. As Google didn't exist in 1994, there is no measurement for mentions of RJ, but we suspect there were none. Ten years later in 2004, there were seventeen thousand. Twenty years later in 2014, there were more than five million hits for the term "reproductive justice." It's as if we lit twelve candles and they lit others to eventually produce five million lights! RJ is viral and it has rocked our lives. This anthology is a tribute to the collective work our movement has achieved to forever change the movement against reproductive oppression in the early twenty-first century.

Organization of the Volume

This collection is divided into four parts with twenty-six essays total and includes poetry because culture is a critical pathway for collective resistance. Each section of the text works to map the history and growth of reproductive justice over the last twenty-three years. The book's innovation and dynamism stems, first and foremost, from its commitment to centering the experiences and work of US women of color in developing and growing the reproductive justice framework through innovative and consistent engagement. As the RJ approach has grown and increasingly circulated in ever-widening circles of advocacy and scholarship, the important work by women of color is often understated or erased. This anthology works to correct that erasure by featuring chapters by and/or about the experience of women of color fighting against reproductive oppression and for reproductive freedoms.

Radical Reproductive Justice provides an in-depth treatment of the history, theory, application, and new directions of reproductive justice, as well as an interdisciplinary and collaborative scholarship that bridges the divide between theory and practice. Each chapter analyzes and defines reproductive justice in a specific context, demonstrating the framework's expansive borders and ability to adapt to a diverse and wide-ranging set of social problems.

Part I of the book, Historical Context, explores the context for reproductive justice and the history of the movement, examines eugenics, and discusses personal intergenerational influences of the RJ movement. Part II, Theory, presents the intellectual claims of reproductive justice, particularly the framework's radical critique of pro-choice rhetoric for reproductive freedom. Part III, Policy, Practice, and Activism, demonstrates the practical applications of the RJ framework; for instance, the use of the reproductive justice framework to address the gendered impact of state institutions such as the blunt instruments of welfare and prison policies, trans RJ issues, immigration, electoral politics, and environmental justice.

As a dynamic and adaptive framework for social justice and reproductive freedom, reproductive justice resists easy and static explanations. This volume is not exhaustive in its treatment of reproductive justice, but it offers a more in-depth engagement than any other edited volume. This collection speaks to the need for a sustained engagement with the work and scholarship of reproductive justice advocates. *Radical Reproductive Justice* aims to rectify the silences and amplify the emerging voices, new directions, and novel applications of this groundbreaking framework.

Notes

1. Kimala Price, "What Is Reproductive Justice?: How Women of Color Activists Are Redefining the Pro-Choice Paradigm," *Meridians: feminism, race, transnationalism* 10, no. 2 (2010): 42–65.

2. Molly Redden, "Texas Has Highest Maternal Mortality Rate in Developed World, Study Finds," *The Guardian*, August 20, 2016, https://www.

theguardian.com/us-news/2016/aug/20/texas-maternal-mortality-rate-health-clinics-funding.

3. SisterLove, Inc., *Intersections at the Grassroots: A Reproductive Justice Analysis of Atlanta's HIV Epidemic* (Atlanta: 2017) 6, http://www.sisterlove.org/wp-content/uploads/2017/01/Executive-Summary_SisterLoveInc_Jan2017Report.pdf.

4. Asian Communities for Reproductive Justice, "A New Vision for Advancing Our Movement for Reproductive Rights, Reproductive Health and Reproductive Justice," Forward Together, 2005, http://strongfamiliesmovement.org/assets/docs/ACRJ-A-New-Vision.pdf.

5. Native Youth Sexual Health Network, "Reproductive Justice: For Me, for You, for Real, for Now," accessed May 15, 2017, http://www.nativeyouthsexualhealth.com/reproductivejustice.pdf.

6. Since these contributors are not present to tell their own stories, except through their writings, we have included their abbreviated obituaries on page 437.

7. Bernice Johnson Reagon, "Coalition Politics: Turning the Century," in *Home Girls: A Black Feminist Anthology*, ed. Barbara Smith (New York: Kitchen Table Press, 1983), 365.

8. The Convention on Elimination of All Forms of Discrimination against Women (CEDAW) was signed by President Jimmy Carter in 1979, but has never been ratified by the US Senate. The United States is the only industrialized country that has not ratified CEDAW. For Senator Helms's opposition to gay rights, see Garance Franke-Ruta, "How America Got Past the Anti-Gay Politics of the '90s," *The Atlantic*, April 8, 2013, http://www.theatlantic.com/politics/archive/2013/04/how-america-got-past-the-anti-gay-politics-of-the-90s/266976/.

9. See Loretta Ross, "White Supremacy in the 1990s," *Political Research Associates* (1995), http://www.publiceye.org/eyes/whitsup.html; and Loretta Ross, "Fighting White Supremacy and White Privilege to Build a Human Rights Movement," *Understanding & Dismantling Privilege*, 6, no. 1(2016): 1–11.

10. Chandra Talpade Mohanty, "'Under Western Eyes' Revisited: Feminist Solidarity through Anticapitalist Struggles," *Signs: Journal of Women in Culture and Society* 28, no. 2 (Winter 2003): 513–14. Emphasis added.

11. Andrea Lee Smith et al., "Introduction," in *The Color of Violence: The INCITE! Anthology* (Durham, NC: Duke University Press, 2016), 6.

12. Zillah Eisenstein, *Global Obscenities: Patriarchy, Capitalism, and the Lure of Cyberfantasy* (New York: New York University Press, 1998), 1.

13. See Matthew Bishop and Michael Green, *Philanthrocapitalism: How Giving Can Save the World* (New York: Bloomsbury, 2009).

14. Rickie Solinger, "Offending Women," *Women's Review of Books* 32, no. 3 (May/June 2015): 10.

15. See Barbara Gurr, *Reproductive Justice: The Politics of Health Care for Native American Women*, (New Brunswick, NJ: Rutgers University Press, 2015).

16. Solinger, "Offending Women," 11.

17. Cherríe Moraga, *Loving in the War Years: Lo Que Nunca Pasó por Sus Labios* (Brooklyn, NY: South End Press, 1983), 135.

18. Cecile Richards, "'The Recent *Washington Post* Article about the Boldness of the Abortion Rights Movement Didn't Actually Get the Story Right," *Medium*, August 17, 2016, https://medium.com/planned-parenthood-action-fund/the-recent-washington-post-article-about-the-boldness-of-the-abortion-rights-movement-didnt-6249e5c489a5#.jeurcj6kp. Richards attended SisterSong's celebration of the twentieth anniversary of RJ in November 2014, but the origination of the first RJ campaign was June 2014.

HISTORICAL CONTEXT

Gee's Bend: A Reproductive Justice Quilt Story from the South

MARY LEE BENDOLPH

Our cover design features a quilt by Mary Lee Bendolph, one of the legendary Gee's Bend quilter artists. Born in 1935, Bendolph's own reproductive story is a glimpse of reproductive justice theory as it intersects with and is vitalized by lived experience. Here is her story, in her words, drawn from an interview conducted by the Souls Grown Deep Foundation.

Families down here, we like to do together. See, we farm together, and the ladies in the family get together for quilting. In them days, they farm three months then when the lay-by time comes 'round the last of May, June they go to piecing quilts. August, go back to the field. October and November, up into December, and then after Christmas and New Year over with, back to piecing and quilting. Piece by yourself; quilt together.

When you go to quilt, you beat the cotton out on the floor, first thing, to get the dust out. Then sweep the floor, collect the cotton, spread the lining out and put the cotton back on the lining, beat it out, put the top on there, get your thread and needles and hook it in the quilting frame.

Most of the families down here did the same thing, piece by theirselves and come together to quilt. On my side, my family, we go fast, don't follow no patterns so close. Other families take more time, do slow work. They don't go out in the road much like us did. We just try to put it together and get it through with. We don't try to style it or nothing. Folks call some of this kind of stuff "crazy quilts"—don't know which-a-way it goin'. I never did go by a pattern. Didn't none us. I mostly take after my aunt Louella, but I never make a quilt altogether like anybody. I watch Mama back when she could work, but she was slow and careful more than me.

We got a big family spread out down here making quilts: Mama and her sister Louella Pettway, and Linda's daughters, Lucy Witherspoon and Gloria Hoppins; my mother-in-law, Indiana Bendolph Pettway. My sister Lillie Mae, she made real pretty quilts before she passed. Mama's first cousin Deborah Young could make beautiful quilts, and her daughter Arcola. My daughter, Essie, always been doing good work since she was little. She a very strong-minded person. Determination. She like to make things like I make, but she look at it and go home and do it better.

My daddy was Wisdom Mosely and my mama was Aolar Mosely. She was good at healing people. She was a lovely, caring person. She go down in the woods and pick some stuff—I missed out on that part, can't do none of that—and mix it up and give it to us, make us well. Only time we go to the doctor was with a toothache (she couldn't pull teeth) or if something was broke. She couldn't do that. My mother rubbed a lot of people and stopped they hurting. She always would be there for you. I don't care who need her. She say the Lord tell you to give. The more you give, the more you get. She say you got to always say you have it even if you didn't have it. Don't ever say you ain't got something. If folks think you ain't got nothing, you can't get nothing from them. If they think you got it, they give you some more.

Back then mamas didn't never tell they children about having babies. If she told me, I about wouldn't have had them. We didn't know nothing about how it happen. Mama would go to the doctor and come back with a baby. We think the doctor had give it to her.

One day, I got ready to go to school and Mama wouldn't let me go. I ask her why I couldn't go. She say, "You don't want to go." I kept asking her why I don't go. She say, "You big." That meant I was with a baby. I cried and prayed all day for the Lord to take it away from me, but he didn't. Nothing but made me big and fat. The first time I had sex my period came along. The next time I had sex, I got pregnant. I learnt the hard way.

I got to the sixth grade. When I got pregnant I had to quit. Mama knew the school wouldn't take you when you pregnant. They made you quit, and after you had the baby you couldn't go back to school. Soon as the school see you pregnant, you had to go home and stay. They say it was against the law for a lady to go to school and be pregnant, 'cause that influence the other children to get pregnant. Soon as you have a baby, you couldn't never go to the school again.

When Essie—she my only daughter—when she turn fourteen, I sat down and talk with her and the boys, the three that was older than Essie, and Beaver, he was right under her. And I told them I prayed to the Lord that he could let me know things so I can tell them, so they wouldn't go and grow up as stupid as I did. Some people not a breeding woman, but I was one. I was a fast breeder. I was little but I got grown 'fore time. I got a baby when I didn't need him. Dropped out of school. Fourteen years old. Didn't even finish the middle school. Just moved through life too fast. Even now I could sit down and relax, but I still moving too fast.

I prayed a whole lot during that time for the Lord to help show me. One night in my rest, I had this big dream the airplane and the helicopter was riding over our head—a lot of people on the ground—and when they lit down, people started to running—but I didn't run. Some white people and colored people, all mixed together, got off the plane and looked like they was having a meeting. I woke up and the dream wouldn't get off my mind. I told Mama, "Something coming here to this place."

I kept dreaming that dream about a helicopter—I always tell Mama 'cause she was good at telling me what the dreams mean, and she'd tell me to keep on praying, and the Lord will tell me things. And what I dreamed come to pass: Martin Luther King came to that big old church here in Gee's Bend, up on the hill, Pleasant Grove Baptist Church. He stood up and talked. I didn't miss nothing.

And when he went to Camden, I had to beg my husband to let me go, but I went. We rode on Monroe Pettway's truck, Bootnie's husband. I was in the group with Martin Luther King when he went up to drink the "white" water. He wanted us to know that the water wasn't no different and to let the white people know that we could all drink the same water. So, I went up to drink me some of it, and Lillie Mae, my oldest sister, caught hold to my coat. I put my arms back behind me and let that coat be pulled right off. I was on my way to that fountain to drink the white water. I got to it but she pulled me away, so I didn't get none of the white water that day. She thought they was going to hurt me. She was supposed to take care of me. She was so humble and sweet. I was the bad guy in the family. I always could be more straight out, didn't like holding back nothing. When I finally did get to drink that white water, it wasn't no different. I wondered what all of the fussing was about. I couldn't see why they would want to keep us from that water, unless they just thought we was dirty.

We have a good community. I thank the Lord for the peoples here. We hardly have a killing here. You don't have to worry about locking up things. When I first married and I locked up the doors, my husband say, "We don't have to lock up things here." We left the key in the truck all the time. Ain't nobody bothered it, year after year. I'm satisfied right here where I'm at. I'll go visit some place. But to live there? No.

I don't know enough to live in a city. I can't hear good enough to live in a city. Cars go too fast in a city. When I went to Connecticut, they was pretty good in the part I was in, but they don't do for each other. My son and I watched this white man trying to move a big old rock, and he had done dig around it until noon, and I told my son, "Go help that white man." And he say, "I ain't going nowhere help that man. Mama, you don't help nobody here; you ain't in the country." I went out there and say to the white man, "You want me to move that block?" And he say, "Naw, I can't let you do that." So I say, "You want me to sho you how?" And he say, "How you know about that?" And I say, "My mama taught me."

Laying the Foundations for a Reproductive Justice Movement

TONI M. BOND LEONARD

Birthing a Movement

In June 1994, twelve black women working in the reproductive health and rights movement gave birth to the concept of reproductive justice, creating a paradigm shift in what women of color termed their work to end reproductive oppression. Gathered for a conference in Chicago sponsored by the Illinois Pro-Choice Alliance and the Ms. Foundation for Women, the founding RJ mothers decided to draft a response to the Clinton administration's Health Security Act proposed in 1993. This plan, largely orchestrated by Hillary Clinton, brought healthcare reform to the national stage ahead of the 1994 midterm elections, but the proposed two-tier system was already a lived reality for many poor women of color in the United States. We believed that true healthcare for women needed to include the full range of reproductive health services, including abortion. We were standing at the brink of a pivotal moment for organizing and mobilizing black women around a policy issue with the potential to profoundly change all our lives.

Seizing a Political Moment

While the Clinton administration was lobbying the public for support, women's health advocates were simultaneously developing a women's health agenda to address the shortfalls within Clinton's proposal. A few of the founding mothers were connected with the Campaign for Women's Health, a national coalition of organizations formed in 1990. The Campaign had put together a "comprehensive 'model benefits package' for women" that included "primary, preventive, reproductive, and long-term care services in addition to services for the treatment of illness or disease."[1]

From the RJ founding mothers' perspective, even women's health advocates understated the unique concerns of those women most economically disadvantaged and facing some of the greatest health disparities. The black women at the conference decided to draft a statement offering recommendations to be included in any healthcare plan from the perspective of African American women, including coverage for abortions, contraceptives, well-woman preventive care, and pre- and postnatal care. We believed comprehensive healthcare for women of color and our families was a plan that, among other things, addressed those health issues that disproportionately affect women of color, such as fibroids, cervical and breast cancer, infant and maternal morbidity and mortality, intimate partner violence, and HIV/AIDS and other sexually transmitted infections. In addition to focusing on wellness and prevention, any healthcare plan would also include a strong educational component regarding sex and sexuality. Most importantly, it needed to be affordable.

Not satisfied with just the statement from the conference, we strategized a much larger effort, one that would reflect the voices of black women around the country. We wanted to send a message to federal legislators that black women understood what was at stake and held lawmakers responsible for making the right decisions on our behalf. Part of this strategy was to place a full-page signature ad in the *Washington Post* and *Roll Call*, a Washington, DC, newspaper covering Capitol Hill. Collectively, we raised the necessary funds from foundations, allies, and individual black women across the country. The Black Women's Health Imperative (BWHI), then called the National Black Women's Health Project (NBWHP), agreed to be our fiscal agent, keeping an accounting of all revenues and expenses. Cynthia Newbille—an RJ founding mother, former NBWHP executive director, and now Richmond City Council member—played a pivotal role in helping to raise the necessary funding for the signature ad.

There was still the question of exactly what we would name our collective effort because we represented multiple organizations and were not necessarily all authorized to speak for them. In Chicago, we decided on the name Women of African Descent for Reproductive Justice (WADRJ). It was a name that spoke to the injustices of the current health system that denied women of color full services due to compounded issues of race, class, and gender. It also referenced that not all of us were

African American, but from the African diaspora. We chose WADRJ because abortion access, while important, was but one of countless barriers to women and their families being healthy and living in healthy communities. Finally, the inclusion of "justice" in our name spoke to issues of fairness and the equitable distribution of resources. We recognized that "equality" within the context of rights oftentimes did not shift the imbalance of economic resources to favor the powerless, and that women of color, especially poor black women, were still disenfranchised. In simplest terms, we spliced together the concept of reproductive rights and social justice to coin the neologism "reproductive justice."

Within two months, we collected the endorsements of 836 black women nationally, including Alice Walker, Angela Davis, and Veronica Webb. On August 16, 1994, WADRJ took out our ad. It was titled "Black Women on Health Care Reform" because media advisors in Washington felt that offered a clearer, more succinct description of who we were rather than the more complex WADRJ name we had devised in Chicago.

We sponsored a press conference on Capitol Hill on August 17, 1994. Congresswomen Eleanor Holmes Norton, Maxine Waters, Carrie Meek, Cynthia McKinney, and Eva Clayton gave remarks. RJ founding mothers "Able" Mable Thomas (now a Georgia state legislator) and Newbille spoke on behalf of WADRJ and NBWHP. The full statement from the *Washington Post* follows.

Black Women on Health Care Reform

Dear Members of Congress:

Black women have unique problems that must be addressed while you are debating health care reform legislation. Lack of access to treatment for diseases that primarily affect Black women and the inaccessibility of comprehensive preventive health care services are important issues that must be addressed under reform. We are particularly concerned about coverage for the full range of reproductive services under health care reform legislation.

Reproductive freedom is a life and death issue for many Black women and deserves as much recognition as any other freedom. The right to have an abortion is a personal decision that must be made by a woman in consultation with her physician. Accordingly, unimpeded access to abortion as a part of the full range of reproductive health services offered under health care reform, is essential. Moreover, abortion coverage must be provided for all women under health care reform regardless of ability to pay, with no interference from the government. WE WILL NOT ENDORSE A HEALTH CARE REFORM SYSTEM THAT DOES NOT COVER THE FULL RANGE OF REPRODUCTIVE SERVICES FOR ALL WOMEN INCLUDING ABORTION.

In addition to reproductive health services, health care reform must include:

Universal coverage and equal access to health services. Everyone must be covered under health care reform. To be truly universal, benefits must be provided regardless of income, health or employment status, age or location. It must be affordable for individuals and families, without deductibles and copayments. All people must be covered equally.

Comprehensiveness. The package must cover all needed health care services, including diagnostic, treatment, preventative, long-term care, mental health services, prescription drugs and pre-existing conditions. All reproductive health services must be covered and treated the same as other health services. This includes pap tests, mammograms, contraceptive methods, prenatal care, delivery, abortion, sterilization, infertility services, STDs and HIV/AIDS screening and treatment. Everyone must also be permitted to choose their own health care providers.

Protection from discrimination. The plan must include strong anti-discriminatory provisions to ensure the protection of all women of color, the elderly, the poor, and those with disabilities. In addition, the plan must not discriminate based on sexual orientation. To accomplish this goal, Black women must be represented on national, state, and local planning, review, and decision-making bodies.

We, the undersigned, are dedicated to ensuring that these items are covered under health care reform legislation. As your constituents, we believe that you have a responsibility to work for the best interests of those you represent, and we request that you work for passage of a bill that provides coverage for these services.

Sincerely,
836 Black Women

That same year, WADRJ partnered with the Women of Color Partnership Program of the Religious Coalition for Reproductive Choice to republish the "We Remember" brochure from 1989, the first collective statement specifically in support of abortion rights by some of the most influential activist black women such as Dorothy Height (National Council of Negro Women), Byllye Avery (National Black Women's Health Project), Maxine Waters (Black Women's Forum), and Jewell

Jackson McCabe (National Coalition of 100 Black Women), in addition to Civil Rights leaders like Rev. Willie Barrow (Operation PUSH) and Ramona Edelin (National Urban Coalition), and mainstream leaders like Faye Wattleton (Planned Parenthood) and C. Delores Tucker (Democratic National Committee Black Caucus). The original statement was also endorsed by other nationally recognized black women, including Marcia Ann Gillespie (*Ms.* magazine), Jacqui Gates (National Association of Negro Business and Professional Women's Clubs), and the late Illinois congresswoman Cardiss Collins.

This landmark statement was in response to the US Supreme Court decision in *Webster v. Reproductive Health Services* to uphold a Missouri law that imposed restrictions on the use of state funds, facilities, and employees in performing, assisting with, or counseling on abortions. In *Webster* the Supreme Court allowed states to legislate in aspects previously thought to be forbidden under the original 1973 *Roe v. Wade* decision that legalized abortion. Donna Brazile, working with the National Congress of Black Women (founded by Shirley Chisholm), organized a conference call for black women leaders to express outrage about the decision, including RJ founding mother Loretta J. Ross. They decided black women around the country needed to know about their historical support for reproductive freedom, first suggested by Byllye Avery. "We Remember" gave black women permission to speak out openly in support of abortion rights, something many had been reluctant to do.

The republished brochure included endorsements by twenty-nine additional black women, including the twelve RJ founding mothers.[2] WADRJ issued two additional statements: a letter to former President Bill Clinton in support of Surgeon General Dr. Joycelyn Elders, who was fired in December 1994 for her public support of the distribution of contraception in schools, teaching youth about masturbation, and drug legalization; and the second in support of Dr. David Satcher as Elders's replacement.

After the successful ad campaign, some of us continued to think about and populate this intriguing new reproductive justice analysis. In September 1994, a month after the press conference, some of us attended the International Conference on Population and Development in Cairo, Egypt, at which the global women's health movement emphasized the ineluctable relationship between poverty, underdevelopment, and women's reproduction. We joined with our sisters from the Global South in resisting those forces endorsing strategies of population control, and learned from our international sisters who used the human rights framework to make stronger claims for women's full human rights that moved far beyond the limits of the US Constitution and the restrictive privacy framework.

No historical overview would be complete without placing reproductive justice within the context of a longer history of black women's reproductive health and rights activism. While the Chicago conference and universal healthcare were the policy vehicles that brought us together, it was just one of a myriad of concerns in our individual social justice activism. Black women's launching of the reproductive justice movement connects to the larger movement of women of color.

The Black Women's Health Imperative: Pioneering the Women of Color Health Movement

Byllye Avery cofounded the BWHI in 1984 following the first National Conference on Black Women's Health Issues in Atlanta in 1983. BWHI applied an intersectional lens to its body of work, recognizing that black women faced multiple forms of oppression such as race, class, gender, and poverty that affected their ability to lead healthy lives. Health educator Lillie Allen, also a BWHI cofounder, incorporated the components of dialogue and active listening she learned from a counseling technique called Re-evaluation Counseling to create BWHI's self-help method. This engaged black women in a process of examining their personal circumstances and connecting them to the sociopolitical conditions that made it impossible to exercise reproductive autonomy and realize true reproductive freedom. The self-help model grounded BHWI's work of building community among black women.

Other women of color who attended BWHI's founding conference went on to establish their own organizations. In 1986 Luz Alvarez Martinez developed the National Latina Health Organization, and Charon Asetoyer organized the Native American Women's Health Education Resource Center in 1988. Although Mary Luke was not at the BWHI conference, she organized Asian Pacific Islanders for Choice (now Forward Together) in 1989 after the *Webster* decision. Collectively, these organizations laid the foundation that would coalesce into the SisterSong Women of Color Reproductive Health Collective in 1997 (now the SisterSong Reproductive Justice Collective).

BWHI combined its self-help approach with an advocacy and public policy strategy. The organization utilized several creative mechanisms to educate black women, including *Vital Signs*, a publication on health issues written by and for black women; *On Becoming a Woman*, a video featuring mothers and daughters talking about menstruation; annual conferences; and its "Black and Female" and "Sisters and Allies" retreats.

The first health center devoted to the health concerns of black women, the Center for Black Women's Wellness (CBWW), was founded by BWHI in the Mechanicsville neighborhood of Atlanta. CBWW not only provided vital reproductive health services to low-income black women but it also made advocacy skills trainings available to them. CBWW also created "Plain Talk," a program designed to educate teenagers about pregnancy and other reproductive health issues.

Internationally, BWHI was an important participant in the 1985 UN World Conference for Women in Nairobi, Kenya, introducing its membership to the global health issues confronting women around the world. In 1986 BWHI endorsed both the East and West Coast March for Women's Lives, organized by the National Organization for Women in Washington, DC, and Los Angeles. BWHI played a critical role in building black women's support for abortion rights, including organizing meetings in response to the *Webster* decision. Its 1990 conference, Sisters in Session about Our Reproductive Health, crafted a black women's reproductive health agenda and organized the first face-to-face meeting of the signatories of the 1989 "We Remember" brochure. BWHI became the premier national advocate and expert on what it meant to authentically include black women's concerns in the mainstream reproductive health movement.

Abortion: Legal for All and Out of Reach for Many

Although the 1994 conference that brought the RJ founding mothers together was about the pro-choice agenda, the movement that ultimately manifested was greater than even its founders had imagined. The RJ cocreators understood that abortion was far too important an issue in the lives of black women to be excluded in any healthcare reform plan, and to that end repealing the Hyde Amendment was a top priority for them. Spearheaded by Illinois Representative Henry Hyde and passed in 1976, the Hyde Amendment ended Medicaid funding of abortions, effectively targeting poor women, young women, Indigenous women, and women of color. It was an annual attachment to the appropriations bill for the

Department of Health, Education, and Welfare (now the Department of Health and Human Services).[3] Although reproductive rights activists successfully obtained an injunction, it was lifted and the amendment was implemented in August 1977. Activists have made strides to chip away at the Hyde Amendment by expanding Medicaid access to abortion services for rape and incest survivors and to save the life of the mother, yet a full victory has not been won.

One of BWHI's most important policy initiatives was its 1994 Campaign for Abortion and Reproductive Equity (C.A.R.E.). Led by women's health activist Leslie Watson Malachi, the goal of C.A.R.E was to build a broad-based coalition to pressure Congress to repeal the Hyde Amendment. The campaign was extremely successful in galvanizing black women around this insidious legislation that unfairly impacted many of their own lives. Several years later, reproductive rights activists would resume the BWHI's effort to repeal the Hyde Amendment. This included the National Network of Abortion Funds' (NNAF) Campaign for Access and Reproductive Equity from 2000–2002 and Hyde—30 Years Is Enough! which ran from 2006–2008. The most recent effort is a collaboration of national and grassroots organizations working under the banner of All*Above All, including the NNAF and BWHI, continuing its legacy of ensuring that the voices and concerns of women of color are central in public policy issues.

The Original Intent of Reproductive Justice

A prevailing misperception is that black women were seeking to replace the abortion-focused pro-choice or reproductive rights frameworks based on the US Constitution with reproductive justice, which instead is based on the global human rights framework. Rather, our focus was on centering black women within the debate, moving our voices from the margins to the center of the discourse. There was and remains a level of intentionality behind the reproductive justice framework that recognizes women of color as the experts of our own lives. We connect personal experiences with the political reality of efforts to control the fertility of women of color through punitive legislation, dramatically affecting our ability to be self-determining about our bodies, and ultimately, our families and communities.

Reproductive justice never meant to replace the reproductive health or rights frameworks. This assumption promotes the myth that women of color are incapable of formulating theoretical analyses to successfully break the historical bonds over our embodied flesh. Instead, RJ was an intentional effort to shed light on the combined forms of oppression that threaten our bodily integrity and autonomy. The founding mothers, and the women of color who have broadened the framework over the years, invested in creating a meaningful paradigm centering the lived experiences of women of color, and formulated practical strategies of resistance leading to our liberation.

The Evolution of Reproductive Justice

While we had already put reproductive justice in practice for our advocacy work on healthcare reform, we needed to establish a theoretical base to explore the viability of RJ for building a movement of radical women of color and our allies. The year 1994 was significant for several other reasons. Three people were killed at abortion clinics that year; Nelson Mandela was elected president of South Africa; O.J. Simpson was arrested for the murder of his ex-wife, Nicole Brown Simpson; and, amid this news, the International Conference on Population and Development was held in Cairo. These events informed the development and growth of the RJ framework.

For the next several years, the concept of reproductive justice marinated in the hearts and minds of its originators but was never forgotten. I launched African American Women Evolving in Chicago in 1996, later renamed Black Women for Reproductive Justice. SisterSong organized in 1997 under the leadership of Luz Rodriguez. Many of the women of color health organizations founded in the 1980s and 1990s became SisterSong cofounding members. In 2004 the first book on reproductive justice, *Undivided Rights: Women of Color Organizing for Reproductive Justice*, was published and proved invaluable while writing this essay.

In the first six years, the SisterSong members prioritized their sustainability. In 2003 SisterSong organized its first national conference, inviting other women of color and white allies to build a concerted movement. The conference offered a plenary panel and workshops on the efficacy of the reproductive justice framework to challenge speakers to address these questions: What is reproductive justice? Could it serve as a new way for women of color to address reproductive oppression? Could it be used to build a more cohesive movement by and for women of color to address reproductive politics in the United States?

These questions launched what some might call the "proof of concept" phase of RJ. These inquiries became critical in terms of establishing reproductive justice as a theoretical and analytical framework, as well as an organizing practice. The questions explored at the conference came about because women of color were frustrated with the limitations of the privacy-based pro-choice movement that did not fully incorporate the experiences of women of color, and the failure of the pro-choice movement to understand the impact of white supremacist thinking on the lives of communities of color.

SisterSong was privileged to have in the plenary and workshops on reproductive justice great scholars and activists, including Dorothy Roberts, Jael Silliman, Byllye Avery, Malika Saada Saar, Rosalinda Palacios, Adriane Fugh-Berman, Eveline Shen, Barbara Smith, and Jatrice Gaithers. After receiving validation from the six hundred women at our first national conference, SisterSong decided to promote RJ as our central organizing strategy for work in the United States because it emerged as a unifying and popular framework among our base of women of color and Indigenous women. This was the national debut of the concept of reproductive justice as a strategy for building a movement of Indigenous women and women of color, not only to fight against reproductive oppression, but to offer a vision of what a society built on human rights and justice could look like.

SisterSong worked with its member organizations—Asian Pacific Islanders for Reproductive Health (APIRH), led by Eveline Shen, and the Abortion Access Project, led by Susan Yanow—to develop trainings for women of color on how to use the RJ framework. When APIRH renamed itself Asian Communities for Reproductive Justice (ACRJ) in 2004, it became the first SisterSong member organization to rebrand itself using the phrase "reproductive justice." In addition, Sujatha Jesudason, then working for ACRJ, deepened the original theoretical analysis in 2005 by coauthoring a manifesto, "A New Vision for Advancing Our Movement for Reproductive Health, Reproductive Rights, and Reproductive Justice," that distinguished between reproductive health (service delivery), reproductive rights (abortion advocacy), and reproductive justice (movement building). Soon other organizations used RJ in their names. African American Women Evolving became Black Women for Reproductive Justice, and California Latinas for Reproductive Justice was founded in Los Angeles. Several foundations, notably the Tides Foundation, created reproductive justice portfolios. Tides eventually launched the Groundswell Fund, under the leadership of Vanessa Daniels, to specifically fund reproductive justice activism around the country, both among women of color and mainstream groups.

While RJ was never originally intended to displace "choice" as a competing framework, it had that salubrious effect, particularly after the organizers of the 2004 March for Women's Lives changed its name from March for Freedom of Choice. The march drew more than 1.15 million participants, making it one of the largest protests in US history at that time. Within a short decade, reproductive justice began to challenge the pro-choice/pro-life logjam in capturing the imaginations of radical women of color and white women who wanted to revolutionize reproductive politics in the United States.

In November 2014, SisterSong celebrated the twentieth anniversary of the reproductive justice framework with a gathering in the founding city of Chicago. The previous two decades had proven the viability of the RJ framework and its success in laying a foundation for a new movement for human rights in the US and globally.

Notes

1. Carol Weisman, *Women's Health Care: Activist Traditions and Institutional Change* (Baltimore, MD: Johns Hopkins University Press, 1998), 211.

2. The text of the 1994 reissued brochure can be found online at https://www.trustblackwomen.org/2011-05-10-03-28-12/publications-a-articles/african-americans-and-abortion-articles/36-african-american-women-are-for-reproductive-freedom.

3. For an overview and history of the Hyde Amendment, see The Center for American Progress' five-part series *The Hyde Amendment*. Jessica Arons, et al., *The Hyde Amendment: 30 Years Is Enough*, Center for American Progress, October 6, 2006, https://www.americanprogress.org/issues/women/news/2006/10/05/2233/the-hyde-amendment-30-years-is-enough/.

A Brief Herstory of SisterSong[1]

RACHAEL STRICKLER and MONICA SIMPSON

In 1997, three years after the creation of the reproductive justice framework, sixteen women of color organizations came together to form the SisterSong Women of Color Reproductive Health Collective, the fifth and longest-lived national coalition of women of color in the reproductive rights/health/justice movements. Renamed the SisterSong Women of Color Reproductive Justice Collective in 2010, the organization was birthed at a time when there was considerable backlash against both the women's and Civil Rights movements as well as a severe lack of funding for creating and sustaining movement-based organizations. SisterSong was unique in its success. Brought together by a common belief in the right and responsibility of women of color to represent themselves and their communities, they were determined to create a space wherein women of color could have their voices heard and amplified through their collectivity.

Luz Rodriguez, then director of the Latina Roundtable on Health and Reproductive Rights in New York, organized a series of gatherings in 1997 and 1998, funded by Reena Marcelo, a Filipina program officer with the Ford Foundation. The original focus of the meetings was reproductive tract infections among women of color, but conversations quickly became about the need for a collective vision and coordinated efforts among women of color groups. With seed money provided by the Ford Foundation, a commitment to creating and maintaining a viable advocacy organization through the development of a collective identity, and the support of other women of color activists fighting for reproductive freedom, Rodriguez founded SisterSong, serving as its ideological midwife.

Project Azuka member and HIV/AIDS activist Juanita Williams, a founding member of SisterSong and to whom the name is attributed, said the collective hoped to reflect the commonality in the struggles of all racial and ethnic groups as well as to recognize the specificity of each community's needs in name and practice. At the second meeting, Williams noted that the individual organizations were all facing the same problems: few or no staff, nearly nonexistent or uncertain funding, distrust by the women's movement and communities of color, and having to meet large sets of needs with little infrastructure and/or capacity. She pointed out that if the individual organizations learned "not to sing the same song, but our individual songs together in harmony," they could build a strong national collective unified to work on behalf of women of color. Thus, SisterSong was born as a metaphor and a mission.

Coalesced, the original SisterSong members shifted the conversation about bodily autonomy away from the reductionist, privileged, and somewhat fictitious rhetoric of choice and toward one that recognized that choice is not always an option and is always made within a particular social context. These women sought a more intersectional movement and analysis that would align reproductive rights with social justice, and ultimately lead to the achievement of universal human rights. SisterSong found this in the theory and framework of RJ, which they understood as "the complete physical, mental, spiritual, political, social, environmental, and economic well-being of women and girls," based on the full achievement and protection of women's human rights.[2]

This assertion that reproductive rights are inherently human rights exemplifies the range of issues and individuals SisterSong hoped to bring together. Loretta J. Ross, one of the birth mothers of RJ and cofounders of SisterSong, stressed the intent to win concrete changes on the individual, community, institutional, and societal levels to improve the lives of women, families, and communities. By demonstrating the intersections of women's lives, identities, and experiences in conjunction with the oppressions and injustices they face, SisterSong successfully built a network of activists and organizations committed to real, lasting change.

Employing an intersectional analysis, SisterSong brought together women, their struggles, and their successes. Ross explains that

> in the process of making the reproductive justice framework effective in the world, we have shifted from individual resistance to proactive organizing with a new vision for political engagement. This shift transcends siloed single-issue identity politics. Rather, it connects multi-issue,

> multiracial, and polyvocal movements across borders, incorporates multiple and variable identities, and interrogates the structures below the surfaces of our sufferings.[3]

Through the leadership of Dázon Dixon Diallo, the founder of SisterLove, SisterSong was also greatly influenced by the organized efforts around women's health taking place in the Global South, particularly the emphasis on human rights and systemic underdevelopment of communities of color. Despite SisterSong's aspiration to transcend rights and move toward justice, they maintained a human-rights-based approach, incorporating strategies from women in the Global South. Choosing to adopt a human rights framework, rather than chafing under the limits of the US Constitution, they made the lives of those they were fighting for and with central to their work. This more holistic, inclusive framework is rooted in the early recognition among women of color organizers that they have a right to control their own bodies simply because they are human, and as social justice activists they have the obligation to ensure those rights are protected.

SisterSong utilizes this human-rights-based framework to emphasize and link women's reproductive health and lives to other movements for social justice. Moreover, the innate intersectionality of the human rights framework connects the dots in women's lives and does not isolate reproductive health issues from other social determinants of the quality of our lives like jobs, housing, childcare, education, violence, the environment, war, and crime. Shifting from a focus on *individual* rights based on privacy, the RJ framework invokes collective rights and collective responsibility for organizing our power and acting.

The unity guiding SisterSong's work is represented in the collective's motto: "Doing collectively what we cannot do individually." The founding members recognized that unity and survival were inextricably linked. As Audre Lorde states, "Divide and conquer must become define and empower."[4] The birth mothers of SisterSong were deliberate in the language they chose to use when naming and describing their organizing structure. The use of "collective" was intentional; it represented the founders' aspiration to build a coalition of activists and organizations who would work together to achieve lasting, sustainable change. For them, it was not merely about shifts in nomenclature or language but shifts in understanding and engagement.

SisterSong's desire to change the way people think about race, rights, and reproduction led them to organize from the margins to the center.

Laura Jiménez, then with the National Latina Health Organization and one of SisterSong's birth mothers, explains that part of the importance of SisterSong is how it provided a space for women of color to come together where they could talk about issues that were commonly understood, like intersectionality, because they were embodied in their real, lived experiences. SisterSong, she says, provided a much-needed space and analysis for these women, allowing them to see connections between themselves as well as the similarities between the past and present reproductive oppressions they faced as a direct result of their identities.

While RJ analysis centers women of color, it does not exclusively apply to them. Just as people and oppressions shift, so too does the center of the movement. RJ advocates felt that "constantly shifting the center to communities that face intersecting forms of oppression, we gain a more comprehensive view of the strategies needed to end all forms of violence."[5] The conversations and connections SisterSong wanted to foster spanned across both mainstream political organizations and marginalized groups. The founders recognized that to achieve the broad social change that drives the political and legal decision-making in our country, the analyses and movement must be inclusive so that the mainstream and the marginalized can find common ground.

SisterSong wanted to achieve change but realized it was not a foot race. They recognized that creating a sustainable movement, organization, and social change required them to break down social, political, and cultural boundaries that often seemed impenetrable. The first six years were spent expanding the capacity of their member organizations—purchasing computers, developing boards of directors, building their financial systems—while also working to strengthen the larger women of color movement. The human-rights-based framework helped them to connect with and demonstrate the minimizing nature of choice rhetoric. Ultimately, the framework would enable them to build a platform for larger social justice conversations as well as bring together people within and across movements and identities.

Upon its founding, SisterSong was comprised of four national anchor organizations, each representing what they understood as the four primary ethnic minority groups in the United States: African American, Latina, Asian/Pacific Islander, and Native American/Indigenous women. An anchor organization for each community was tasked with creating and managing a minicommunity of all the groups that identified as their ethnic group. It is important to note that SisterSong wanted to maximize diversity within their organization as well as within the smaller cohorts. This diversity spanned from the type and size of an organization to their priorities. In fact, some of the sixteen founding member organizations were pro-choice while others were pro-life. In the end, they united through their determination to achieve reproductive rights, health, and justice for all.

As they grew, SisterSong reconsidered their original organizing structure after the grant from the Ford Foundation ended. Members of SisterSong began to see the limits of the anchor structure, not just because of the disproportionate role and responsibility of anchor groups, but also because it restricted their membership base. In 2001 members decided to leave behind their original structure and create a multiracial Management Circle with a national coordinator that would more widely represent women across ethnic and racial identities. Laura Jiménez became the first national coordinator, and Loretta J. Ross succeeded her in 2005, with Jiménez becoming the deputy coordinator. Although the higher level of diversity led to challenges both within and without the organization, including a lack of funding at times, it was ultimately a successful strategy for expansion and increased impact.

SisterSong also hoped to bring established groups and newly emerging ones together, recognizing that one of the key problems was the lack of opportunities for women of color to meet collectively to focus on their own agendas, rather than as a subset of conferences or meetings by the pro-choice movement. The collective employed many avenues to fulfill these missions, such as capacity-building trainings, leadership development, and self-help sessions.

To this day the organization regularly hosts regional, national, and thematic membership meetings and conferences to connect, educate, and empower hundreds of individuals. In 2003 they sponsored their first national conference at Spelman College in Atlanta, the SisterSong Women of Color Reproductive Health and Sexual Rights Conference, that brought together six hundred activists to showcase the depth and diversity of women of color working on sexual rights and reproductive health issues. It was at this conference that the term "reproductive justice" was first publicly offered to the national pro-choice/reproductive rights/reproductive health movements. It became a focal point of their plenary, workshops, and conversations. Activists and organizations from all parts of the movement came together to explore the concept of RJ, and left with it as one of their central organizing strategies for work in the United States. This conference also signified SisterSong's success in building a sustainable, inclusive human rights agenda that connected reproductive rights and justice to broader issues of health, safety, and welfare.

SisterSong-sponsored conferences and meetings provided a space wherein women of color could collaborate and navigate their roles within the movement as well as—and to a certain extent because of—their capacity to share their work, lives, and stories. Another aspect of SisterSong, one of its most important and controversial aspects, is the utilization of a self-help model based on the pioneering work of the National Black Women's Health Project (now Black Women's Health Imperative) and the National Latina Health Organization. While it can be challenging to consistently practice self-help, it is also crucial for the sustainability of activists and organizations alike, and for the radical implementation of the RJ framework.

Unlike other organizations that have chapters, SisterSong wanted to spark new organizations. This was due in part to the desire to reflect their origins as a union of preexisting, autonomous women of color organizations. Because more of the 2003 conference attendees were not members of such organizations but individual white women and women of color, SisterSong revamped its membership structure, allowing individuals, men, and white allies to become members, growing the collective to eighty organizations within a few years.

The year 2004 was significant for SisterSong because of the upcoming national March for Women's Lives in April. Several organizational members—particularly the National Latina Institute for Reproductive Health (NLIRH), led by Silvia Henriquez—urged SisterSong to join the march, which was organized by the National Organization for Women, the Feminist Majority Foundation, Planned Parenthood Federation of America, and NARAL Pro-Choice America. After much debate, SisterSong decided to support the event, and Ross became the march codirector, working with Alice Cohan from the Feminist Majority Foundation as the march director. The Black Women's Health Imperative (BWHI), the NLIRH, and the American Civil Liberties Union joined the four original organizations on the steering committee. SisterSong provided funding to send buses of young women of color to the march and helped change the event organizing from exclusively focusing on abortion to the more expansive concept of RJ. The effort was overwhelmingly successful with more than 1.15 million people participating in the march.

Organizing for the march paid tremendous dividends for SisterSong and spurred new RJ organizing among women of color nationally.

For example, in 2004 participants from Pittsburgh organized SisterSong member organization New Voices Pittsburgh (now New Voices for Reproductive Justice) through the leadership of La'Tasha Mayes, Bekezela Mguni, Lois "Toni" McClendon, and Maria Nicole Smith. Original cofounding group Asian and Pacific Islanders for Reproductive Health renamed itself Asian Communities for Reproductive Justice (now Forward Together) in 2005, and California Latinas for Reproductive Justice was organized in 2005 by Rocio L. Córdoba. In 2006 in Chicago African American Women Evolving became Black Women for Reproductive Justice under the leadership of Toni M. Bond Leonard.

In 2006 SisterSong launched its Queer People of Color Caucus (QPOC) to incorporate into its work the intersection between LGBTQ rights and reproductive justice. In 2007 SisterSong also purchased its national headquarters in Atlanta, the Mother House, in partnership with SisterLove, Inc.—providing a permanent home for feminists of color organizing in the Deep South.

SisterSong organized its first Let's Talk About Sex Conference (LTAS) in Chicago in 2007, co-coordinated by Leonard, and it drew more than one thousand participants. The second LTAS was held in Miami in 2011 with the assistance of Erika Cordoba of MI LOLA and the Miami Workers' Center.

In 2012 Ross retired and Monica Simpson from the Charlotte Lesbian and Gay Community Center in North Carolina became the organization's executive director, which heralded another restructuring of the organization to face new challenges and changing members' needs, such as partnering the organization with the violence against women, anti-racist, and environmental justice movements. New projects, such as Artists United for Reproductive Justice, bring the RJ framework to new audiences and attract new members.

In 2014 SisterSong celebrated the twentieth anniversary of the development of the RJ framework in Chicago, bringing together a wide range of activists who use RJ as a national organizing practice. The SisterSong records are housed in the archives of the Sophia Smith Collection at Smith College in Northampton, Massachusetts.

SisterSong's commitment to education extends beyond its caucuses and conferences. They regularly host workshops, trainings, and webinars to provide information about the movement, and ways to successfully integrate RJ into activist pursuits as well as the day-to-day lives of individuals and member organizations. They also published a national newspaper, and now a webinar series, entitled *Collective Voices*, in which their staff, committee members, and other RJ organizers address issues of reproductive justice, such as building relationships between the Black Lives Matter movement and reproductive justice in 2015.

SisterSong endures as the only national membership organization that works exclusively around RJ. While other groups have come and gone, the collective has remained committed to providing the space and analysis necessary for women of color activists to theorize and organize. Many skeptics doubted the strength, durability, and determination of women of color to build their own movement for undivided justice in the United States. Yet in June 2017, three US Surgeons General called for an end to intersex surgery. One of the three, Dr. Joycelyn Elders, met an adult intersex woman of color activist at SisterSong's 2007 conference and that meeting was influential in changing her mind,[6] proving the organization's impact on public policy and leading healthcare decision makers.

Celebrating its twentieth anniversary in 2017 in New Orleans at its signature Let's Talk About Sex! Conference, SisterSong stands as a testament to the power and determination of women of color to build better futures for all people working to achieve human rights through reproductive justice.

Notes

1. This essay is based on 2015 interviews by Rachael Strickler with cofounding organizers of SisterSong Loretta J. Ross, Laura Jiménez, and Luz Rodriguez.

2. Asian Communities for Reproductive Justice, "A New Vision for Advancing Our Movement for Reproductive Rights, Reproductive Health and Reproductive Justice," 2005, 1. http://strongfamiliesmovement.org/assets/docs/ACRJ-A-New-Vision.pdf.

3. Loretta J. Ross and Rickie Solinger, eds. *Reproductive Justice: An Introduction* (Oakland: University of California Press), 114.

4. Audre Lorde, "The Master's Tools Will Never Dismantle the Master's House," *Sister Outsider: Essays and Speeches* (Berkeley, CA: Crossing Press, 1984), 110.

5. Andrea Lee Smith, et al., *The Color of Violence: The INCITE! Anthology* (Durham, NC: Duke University Press, 2006), 6.

6. Suzannah Weiss, "These Doctors Want Us to Stop Pathologizing Intersex People," *Refinery 29*, June 29, 2017, http://www.refinery29.com/2017/06/161533/intersex-surgery-surgeon-general-letter.

Trust Black Women: Reproductive Justice and Eugenics

LORETTA J. ROSS

On February 5, 2010, sixty-five billboards suddenly appeared in black communities around Atlanta, Georgia. From a distance, all I could see was a close-up of a black male toddler's face with the words "Black Children Are an Endangered Species." As an African American feminist leading SisterSong, a national reproductive justice organization headquartered in Atlanta, I felt compelled to investigate this strange fruit popping up without notice *only* in the black community. Were the billboards from a new group trying to help black women fight against white supremacy and reproductive oppression? Were they calling urgently needed attention to the numbing metronome of our endless tragedies when our children prematurely become ancestors at the hands of rogue cops? Did we have previously unknown allies who were willing to call attention to the fragility of black children's lives?

I have researched the white supremacist and neofascist movements in the US since the early 1990s. These are permeable movements, exchanging personnel and ideas between the margins and the mainstream depending on their perceived access to political power. I have studied diverse iterations of racism, anti-Semitism, sexism, and homophobia, especially in racial and antiabortion violence. I have written extensively about the white supremacist movement, white privilege, and the racialization of reproductive politics, historically and currently. My background in these fields made me skeptical that new, unknown champions for black lives would suddenly appear in my Atlanta neighborhood.

It can be exhausting to be a black person in a frightened, nihilistic America, where it is often easier to be illegal than legal when the law itself is lawless and cops enjoy an epidemic of impunity. In black, brown, Muslim, Asian, and Indigenous communities, the police are our domestic terrorists, financing themselves through for-profit policing. Being black is both a criminal act and an existential risk. The simple existence of blackness is a white trigger for rage, guilt, and fear. American society inventively contorts itself to constantly criminalize and profit off of our blackness, as our children either are valued only when they *produce* white wealth (for-profit prisons or professional athletes) or *protect* it (by joining the military and protecting corporate profits around the globe).

Black feminists launched the Black Lives Matter movement to respond to the staccato repetition of the deadly devaluation of black lives. It is horribly ironic to experience exotification and patronization simultaneously. The white gaze obsessively fixates on black bodies for profit culturally and economically, and yet the humanity of black people frequently gets ignored. We see it in the cultural appropriation of our music, our style, our cool, our grace, our forgiveness, our ideas. I call it the "Elvis effect," in which white people believe they have originated something they have actually stolen.

Superficially, these billboards appeared to cherish black children, but their appearance alarmed me because my lifelong work is foregrounded by generations of black feminists who felt the pressure to redefine their unique resistance to reproductive oppression according to their own needs and material circumstances. From the early black advocates for birth control like Anna Julia Cooper in the 1890s, Dorothy Ferebee in the 1930s, and Fannie Lou Hamer in the 1960s, black women have always fought to control their own fertility and achieve self-determination.

I fought against sterilization abuse in the 1970s after I was sterilized when I was only twenty-three. Sterilization of black, Puerto Rican, Mexican, and Native American women was more overt then. Women of color continue to organize to end such government-promoted eugenics practices. When these billboards appeared in 2010, women of color were already leading a movement for RJ in the context of an allegorical narrative of postracialism with the election of President Barack Obama as the first black president. Had America finally reached a new era in which it could put its slavery and genocidal history aside, proven by the election of President Obama as imagined racial progress? Were black children really valued, and was that the meaning of these billboards?

In the realm of reproductive politics, myths attach to our bodies about our alleged hyperfertility and wanton immorality. Sexual conservatives foist an image of primitivism derived from white supremacy onto black women's bodies, such as the frequent characterization of Michelle Obama and Serena Williams as animalistic. They believe they have the right and the obligation to dictate our reproductive choices. An unctuous religiosity imperfectly disguises their deep contempt and fascination for the sexuality of black people in general, and women accused of moral incompetence and failed motherhood.

I went to my office prepared to find out what this billboard campaign meant. I had hardly arrived at work when SisterSong received its first call from the *New York Times*. The reporter wanted to know what we thought about the billboards, since the architects of the publicity campaign thoughtfully sent out press releases to the media. With no time for preparation, investigation, or calling in consultants, we had to respond to multiple press inquiries once it became clear that the billboards were the first wave of publicity for an antiabortion legislative campaign pimping the African American community. The website at the bottom read, in small print, *toomanyaborted.com*, which provided a strong clue that our allies had not providentially provided the billboards.

In fact, it was the opening salvo of a campaign to racialize the abortion debate, tying a massive advertising campaign to state legislation. The ads piously claimed to protect black children while insultingly throwing shade at black women who choose to have abortions. Legislatively, the campaign sought to criminalize women's motives for ending pregnancies, something currently prohibited by law. According to the proposed legislation, if a woman seeks an abortion because of the race or the gender of the fetus, doctors must refuse to provide services or face sanctions. Currently doctors may ask, "When was your last menstrual period?" as the only salient medical question beyond general health issues. They are not supposed to ask why you are there in the first place. Women's motives are not their business, nor are they medically necessary or required for routine healthcare like abortions. This new assault on abortion rights offered false racial compassion from conservatives to permit judgmental abortion restrictions, purportedly to save children from abortion because of their race. The proponents didn't seem to realize that no black woman has an abortion because she's surprised that her baby will be black.

The billboards violated SisterSong's principles of RJ, attacked the agency and self-determination of black women, and claimed that abortion is a genocidal plan targeting the black community. The Endangered Species campaign resorted to a distorted history of the reproductive rights movement and deployed racist sexual stereotypes. Campaign materials traced an alleged direct progression from racist violence against freed slaves to state-sponsored sterilization by the eugenics movement to birth control campaigns by Margaret Sanger, the founder of Planned Parenthood. They argued that after the Civil Rights Movement discredited overt white supremacy, racists turned to legalizing abortion to continue their genocidal plan. Further, they inferred that the legalization of abortion justifies their racist accusations of rampant sexual irresponsibility, family instability, and poverty among black women today. Women would not be such sluts, they say, if abortion were illegal.

This race-based antiabortion strategy aroused fears of eugenics, as it depicts black women as victims of state-sanctioned population control policies by abortion providers; dupes of white elites who provide birth control and abortion; and destroyers of our own people through self-genocide. It denies our reality as racially conscious women with power and self-determination negotiating the circumstances of our sexual and reproductive lives. They criminalized our wombs, prefacing the cradle-to-prison pipeline challenged by prison abolitionist activists such as Deborah Small, who describes African Americans as preconditioned to accept monitoring and surveillance by the prison industrial complex through the entirety of their lives. This is no more than an extension of the alleged "fetal harm" movement that's attempting to outlaw all access to abortion.

This paper brings the agency of black women to the fore, refutes the "abortion as racist" narrative, and discusses the real history of eugenics. Using the Endangered Species campaign as example, I offer a brief history of RJ organizing among African American women from the early twentieth century to the present as we have struggled to gain control of our own bodies in the context of resisting white supremacist and state-sanctioned eugenics policies.

This paper will also present a case study of SisterSong's continuing fight against the antiabortion movement in communities of color as a testament to our passion, indignation, and agency. Our core organizing strategy channels individual storytelling into political analysis and collective action, such as the historic founding of the Trust Black Women (TBW) partnership. It will introduce a brief overview of eugenics ideology in the United States, and its impact on the reproductive rights activism of African American women. It will also examine some of the tensions around race, gender, and class within the pro-choice movement, which are challenged by an insurgent RJ movement led by women of color that is redefining the increasingly racialized terrain of the abortion wars.

Defining Reproductive Justice

Reproductive justice is a critical theoretical framework promoted by activist women of color to more effectively describe how the intersections of gender, race, class, ability, nationality, and sexuality influence reproductive politics in the United States to produce a complex matrix of reproductive oppression. This theoretical framework is based on discussions among activist women of color about sex, reproduction, and sexuality, originating with African American women in 1994. Oppression is defined as an "unjust situation where, systemically and over a long period of time, one group denies another group access to the resources of society."[1] As an expression of collective social trauma, reproductive oppression is experienced by women of color as the exploitation of our bodies, sexuality, labor, and fertility in order to achieve social and economic control of our communities and in violation of our human rights. A new theoretical framework for women of color was necessary because earlier analyses paid inadequate attention to our physical and emotional realities, and failed to analyze and criticize the immortalized eugenics ideologies and politics by which it is determined that some bodies matter and others do not.

In short, RJ has three core values: the right to have a child, to not have a child, and to parent the children we have in safe and healthy environments. As a departure from the privacy-based pro-choice framework, RJ activists recognize that in addition to supporting the pro-choice movement's goals of protecting abortion rights and securing safe and effective contraceptives, as people of color subjected to continuous population control strategies, we must fight equally as hard for the right to have children and to parent the children we have.

As people of color, we struggle for the recognition of our humanity against white prejudices not only through politics and economics but also through science, technology, and biomedicine. bell hooks posits that "the very concept of white supremacy relies on the perpetuation of a white race. It is in the interest of continued white racist domination of the planet for white patriarchy to maintain control over all women's bodies."[2] Racial and sociopolitical categories are "reproduced and reconstituted through techno-scientific practices that act on, with, and against human bodies."[3] These are additional sites of struggle around blood politics and the axes of domination that the predominantly white pro-choice movement either undervalues or understates. However, as women of color, our self-determination engages multiple dimensions of contention based on the intersections of race, gender, class, immigration, sexual orientation, gender identity, and religion. RJ asserts the human right to make personal decisions about one's life, and calls on the international legal regime and the norms and standards of the global human rights movement in our multi-issue, intersectionalized organizing strategy.

Black women had to ask, how did we become defined as the major threat to the health of our babies? Why was the womb the most dangerous place a child will ever inhabit, disregarding the invisible vulnerabilities and heightened precarity of our children's lives in a white supremacist society? Accused of being selfish, confused, potentially violent and incapable of making responsible choices, we were offered a platitudinous charge that said "innocent" fetuses needed to be protected from our selfish whims. These same people studiously deny the wider plateaus of risks our children face once born in a society allergic to their existence. We are accused of being progenitors of pathologies, mothers of superpredators.

Eugenics and African American Women

The fight against white supremacy and patriarchal state violence never ends, as the ongoing struggle against eugenics demonstrates. Eugenics is also popularly known as population control, and includes any number of nonbiological measures. To understand the impact of eugenics and white supremacy in reproductive politics, it is necessary to understand the ubiquitous nature of internalized racism and its dependence on misogyny that is disturbingly normalized in US society. In the words of Ruha Benjamin:

> Racism is . . . not simply ignorance, or a *not* knowing. It is also (at the very least) a logic, a reason, a justification, and a way of knowing the world and other human beings that is always violent, routinely deadly, and brilliantly codified in the very thing we would turn to for justice. Until we come to grips with the *reasonableness* of racism, we will continue to look for it on the bloody floors of Charleston churches and

> the dashboard cameras of Texas highways, and overlook it in the smart sounding logics of textbooks, policy statements, court rulings, science journals, and cutting edge technologies.[4]

Eugenics as a philosophy and practice depends on the intersections of racism, sexism, and nativism. Eugenics had its origins in manipulating human reproduction, but its philosophical tentacles spread throughout a society that was already deeply stratified by race, gender, region, class, and religion. Proponents of eugenics sought to affect nearly every area of human endeavor by assigning values to different births, engineering society toward perfectability, and designating the benefits of society based on elite racial and class preferences.

Eugenics was a formal movement launched in the early part of the twentieth century by people who believed they could improve humanity through "scientifically" selective breeding. The term "eugenics" was coined by British scientist Francis Galton in 1883, to mean "nobility of birth," at a time of British class upheaval due to industrialization. The middle and upper classes were determined to prevent revolutionary tendencies among the poor. Because elites benefited from the rapid industrialization, they did not perceive poverty and work dehumanization as an issue of social inequality, but rather one of heredity.

When elites migrated this ideology to the United States, they borrowed a "scientific" rationale for imposing limits on the births among populations they deemed undesirable, while they particularly encouraged white, middle- and upper-class Protestants to have more children. As part of a Victorian backlash against the growing sexual freedom of white women, religious and political leaders denounced birth control. The federal government had passed the Comstock Law in 1873 prohibiting the distribution of birth control information and devices, aiming to increase birth rates among white people. During this same period in the early twentieth century, thousands of African Americans fled the Jim Crow South and migrated to the North. These fast-paced demographic changes alarmed many nativist whites, who questioned birth control or sterilization for themselves but approved of it as a strategy of negative eugenics to contain people of color and immigrants. In contrast, northern European immigrants and their descendants were being encouraged to breed, as part of the positive eugenics ideology. Rapid population growth was one factor that helped overrun Native Americans, settle the West, and fulfill the mythical ideology of Manifest Destiny. The continuing sterilization of Indigenous women was a strategy of "reproductive disappearance."

It was in this context that Margaret Sanger began to campaign for women's birth control in the early 1900s. Sanger was a public health nurse who witnessed the tragic number of deaths in New York of women who sought to control their fertility using dangerous self-induced abortions or contraception techniques. She embarked on a personal and political crusade against maternal mortality to repeal the 1873 Comstock Law. To challenge the laws that unfairly punished sexually active women, she imported birth control information and devices from Europe and made it her personal mission to distribute them to poor white women. She opposed abortion, which at the time was unsafe due to prohibition and technological limitations, and believed contraception was the only practical way to decrease women's abortion mortality rates. She was arrested several times, but never desisted in her campaign to ensure that women could access birth control.

Sanger, eager to win the support of elites for her campaign, was endorsed by several leading eugenicists and permitted some of their articles to be printed in her magazine, *Birth Control Review*. The magazine contained a strange admixture of feminism, racism, and ableism. She has been accused by antiabortionists of promoting racialized genocide against African Americans, although she eventually repudiated the eugenics philosophy, largely because many eugenicists only supported birth control through a racist lens. Despite her distaste for eugenics, particularly after its association with Nazi philosophy, the damage to Sanger's reputation had already been done.

By also claiming genetic differences among races of people, eugenicists reinforced the justification for white supremacy as a politicized and publicly supported project. Indiana became the first state in 1907 to pass the first eugenically motivated sterilization law to promote the targeting of "confirmed criminals, idiots, imbeciles, and rapists." North Carolina was particularly aggressive in sterilizing African Americans: 65 percent of the procedures were performed on black women. By the 1970s, nearly one-quarter of Native American women in the United States had been sterilized.[5]

It was not ignorance about the humanity of poor people or nonwhite people that motivated these laws; it was indifference. Using the pseudoscience of eugenics, vulnerable people were targeted because of their race, mental and physical disabilities, economic status, ethnicity, immigration status, education level, religion, or age. It is important to point out that poor white women, particularly in Appalachia, were also targeted for forced sterilizations. Thus, eugenics was a race- and a class-based ideology of population control. Anyone whose freedom was impaired—

those in prisons, jails, detention centers, and mental health institutions; Native American's undergoing forced assimilation at boarding schools were especially vulnerable to this selective, "reasonable" state-sanctioned reproductive oppression.

People with disabilities were particularly singled out. Eugenics was as useful in defining disability as it was in defining race. People with disabilities were deemed inherently unfit to have and raise children, proving that parental capability was defined by social markers of disadvantage, not actual physical or biological characteristics. The definition of who should be sterilized expanded to include people who were homeless, alcoholics, or simply poor.

To promote the reproduction of self-defined "racially superior" people, eugenics proponents argued for both "positive methods," such as tax incentives and education for the desirable types, and "negative methods," such as sterilization, involuntary confinement, and immigration restrictions for the undesirables. The United States became the first nation in the world to permit mass sterilization as part of an effort to "purify the race." By the mid-1930s about twenty thousand Americans had been sterilized against their will, and most states had passed eugenics laws. Black people, Catholics, poor white women, and others such as the mentally or physically disabled were singled out for planned population reductions through both government and privately financed means.

The fiercest supporters of eugenics were not only the rabid haters in the Ku Klux Klan of the late nineteenth century, who practiced extra-legal executions like lynching but also mainstream white Americans troubled by the effects of urbanization, industrialization, and immigration—so that violent terrorism was enabled and shielded by public policies. After the Civil War, African Americans enjoyed a very brief period in which they could vote, participate in politics, acquire the land of former slave owners, start businesses, and use public accommodations. This aroused racist white panic throughout the country. Eugenics codified white American frenzy against African American progress during and after Reconstruction.

By the 1920s, more than five million white people openly belonged to the Ku Klux Klan, including several US Congressmen. President Theodore Roosevelt made dire predictions about "race suicide" in 1902 if the country continued to tolerate rising birth rates among black Americans and burgeoning "non-Yankee" immigration. Eugenics was endorsed by President Calvin Coolidge who said in 1924, "America must be kept American. Biological laws show . . . that Nordics deteriorate when mixed with other races."[6] Notably, state laws against miscegenation (or race mixing) increased after the Civil War until they were ruled unconstitutional by the Supreme Court in 1967.

In fact, the birth rate of African Americans was slower than that of whites after the Civil War and until World War II, but it suited the purposes of the white racial alarmists to distort the facts. At the height of the eugenics movement, thirty-two states enforced compulsory sterilizations through both legal and extralegal means. The United States was the first country in the world to undertake concerted compulsory sterilization programs, and inspired the Nazis during their genocidal reign of World War II.

Unfortunately, some notable people of color, including W. E. B. DuBois, also endorsed the false belief that humanity could improve through selective breeding. Despite the manifest widespread contempt for black women's fecundity, African American women have always fought the racist ideology and practices of the eugenics movement to assert our right to dignity, liberty, and personal autonomy as part of our struggle for human rights and against racism, sexism, and poverty.

The blood politics ideology of eugenics contaminated nearly every social policy in which racial and social inequalities became legitimized by cultural myths and pseudoscience. Today, such beliefs are called "neoeugenics" or "neo-Malthusianism" because they are partially derived from the 1798 theories of Thomas Robert Malthus, who asserted that unchecked population growth would threaten the survival of people on the planet because of food scarcity. Eugenics is a timelessly persuasive proposition, particularly for elites: if the economic, gender, and racial problems of society were genetically predictable and preventable, then society is relieved of the burden of addressing the real man-made causes of these problems. The futile search for a genetic rationale for social inequalities persists to this day, such as writers like Charles Murray and Richard Herrnstein, who wrote *The Bell Curve* in 1994, claiming that black people are genetically inferior. Murray sparked a 2017 uproar at Middlebury College when students protested his speech. These pseudotheories influence modern politicians who believe that social problems are genetically predetermined. In 2014 Russell Pearce, a former state senator in Arizona, declared, "You put me in charge of Medicaid, the first thing I'd do is get Norplant, birth-control implants, or tubal ligations. . . . Then we'll test recipients for drugs and alcohol, and if you want to [reproduce] or use drugs or alcohol, then get a job."

Because Sanger was the founder of Planned Parenthood Federation of America (PPFA), which provides most reproductive healthcare for poor and underserved communities in the United States, one hundred years after its founding, accusations of eugenics and genocide are still tossed at the organization and other abortion providers. RJ analysts believe, however, that the current campaign by ultraconservatives against Planned Parenthood is based more on fears about the demographic decrease in the white population in the US, because white women are intentionally having fewer children, rather than concern about protecting people of color from the alleged "genocide" of birth control and abortion. This is consistent with the "race suicide" fears expressed in the early twentieth century by Presidents Roosevelt and Coolidge. As Iowa Congressman Steve King tweeted in 2017, "We can't restore our civilization with somebody else's babies," earning the praise of former KKK member David Duke.[7]

As part of the billboard campaign in Atlanta, a black female spokeswoman alleged that the majority of clinics providing abortions are intentionally placed in African American neighborhoods. SisterSong's research revealed the actual facts: only three of the fifteen clinics in Georgia were in black neighborhoods. Given that African American women obtain about one third of the abortions in the US, for a variety of reasons, it could be argued that black communities are instead underserved rather than targeted, when states like Mississippi, where black people are 37 percent of the population, have only one abortion provider. The eugenics ideology is contradictorily hypocritical. White proponents believe there are too many black and brown babies and not enough white ones, but to disguise their racist motives, they pretend to care for all babies, even though their actions and policies that fail to support children of color once they are born clearly demonstrate they don't.

The concept of ideal children and races of people has not vanished. In the twenty-first century, perverse eugenics policies openly based on racial characteristics are modernized by new reproductive technologies promoted under a neoliberal logic that allows consumers to select "socially desirable" traits in their children. Sperm banks offer parents a chance to select for everything from health to intelligence. Either through egg harvesting from elite white women or *in utero* genetic modifications, it is not a stretch to believe that most people who can afford "designer babies" may not choose to parent the oversupply of African American children available from adoption agencies and foster homes. Biotechnological changes for enhancements in the genes of eggs, sperm, or early embryos would become inheritable genetic modifications and achieve laissez-faire eugenics. Science and technology seemingly neutrally deployed on a deeply racialized terrain facilitates the upgrading of racial inequality, just as cynical politicians misappropriate the language of racial and reproductive freedom for fetuses.

African American Women Resist Eugenics

Despite the dominance of eugenics ideology and practices, black women of the early twentieth century wanted to determine the number and spacing of their children. At the same time, they resisted government and privately funded antinatalist (antibirth) population control campaigns. This dual value system seeded an expanded vision of reproductive justice that guides the work of women of color today.

Early African American activists understood the complex nature of black womanhood and believed that fertility control was an essential part of the movement to rise from the brutal legacy of slavery. Sanger, through her passion to establish birth control clinics, touched a responsive chord in African American women, many of whom were middle-class. In 1918 the Women's Political Association of Harlem announced a scheduled lecture on birth control, Alice Dunbar Nelson endorsed birth control in an article in 1927, and Adam Clayton Powell Jr. spoke at public meetings sponsored by women's groups in support of family planning. The NAACP openly supported family planning. The "racial uplift" view of the times was that African Americans needed to control family size to integrate into the American mainstream through education and jobs.

The National Urban League asked Sanger to open a family planning clinic in the Columbus Hill section of the Bronx. In 1930 Sanger opened a clinic in Harlem that sought to enlist support for contraceptive use and to bring the benefits of family planning to women who were denied access to their city's health and social services. Staffed by a black physician and black social worker, the clinic was endorsed by the *Amsterdam News* (a powerful local newspaper), the Abyssinian Baptist Church, the Urban League, and the black community's elder statesman, W. E. B. DuBois.

Beginning in 1939, DuBois also served on the advisory council for Sanger's "Negro Project," which was a "unique experiment in race-building and humanitarian service to a race subjected to discrimination, hardship, and segregation"[8] designed to serve African Americans in the rural South. Sanger responded to requests by black women to offer services in the Deep South, which was most hostile to birth control, and where white people often discriminated against black women when they tried to obtain reproductive health services. Southern white men feared birth control access by white women, although they mostly masked their concerns in religious moralities rather than open racial animosity.

Other leaders of the African American community involved in the project included Mary McLeod Bethune, founder of the National Council of Negro Women, and Adam Clayton Powell Jr., pastor of the Abyssinian Baptist Church in Harlem. The Negro Project was also endorsed by prominent white Americans involved in social justice efforts at that time, including Eleanor Roosevelt, the most visible and compassionate supporter of racial equality in her era, and the medical philanthropists Albert and Mary Lasker, whose financial support made the pilot project possible. Funding for the project dried up in 1942 after Sanger clashed with the white men hired to run it. She had demanded African American doctors and nurses staff the project, but was denied.

Despite early missteps that resulted in her association with the eugenics movement, Sanger became a passionate opponent of racism. Sanger predicted in 1942 that the "Negro question" would be foremost on the country's domestic agenda after World War II. Her accomplishments on behalf of the African American community were unchallengeable during her lifetime and remain so today.

Charges of reproductive racism against Sanger are most often made by anti-choice activists unfamiliar with the history of black women's views on managing their fertility. They don't believe in the agency of black women and don't understand Sanger's collegial relationship with black leaders. Black women have never been dupes, but fierce defenders of our freedoms and our bodies, such as Fannie Lou Hamer calling sterilizations "Mississippi appendectomies" to protest sterilization abuse. The tangled fabric of lies and manipulation woven by anti-choice activists around the issues of class, race, and family planning continues to be embroidered today by the antiabortion movement using strategies like the antiabortion billboards, more than a century after the family planning movement began.

The Billboard Campaign and Republicans in the Age of Obama

When the antiabortion billboards first appeared in Atlanta in February 2010, it was not immediately apparent that they were part of a larger strategy to combine a national public relations campaign with legislation to establish a new front in the abortion wars. We learned from reporters our opponents wanted to wield race and gender as a weapon to undermine abortion rights as part of the Republican-led culture wars. As detailed in SisterSong's report, one of the first meetings to discuss this strategy occurred in late 2008 shortly after President Obama's election.

The black wing of the antiabortion movement had promoted the "abortion as racism" myth for the three decades prior with little success or financial support for changing the minds of black women. They believed, at best, that black women should be persuaded or guilt-tripped into not having abortions; at worst, that antiabortion laws should control us. It was ironic that the white conservative movement—which for a century had championed eugenics as a strategy for limiting the African American population—was suddenly financing these surrogates of color like the Radiance Foundation to "save" black babies from the "abortion industry," as they termed it.

In our opposition research, we learned what was both familiar and unique about this historical moment that forecast the resurgence of overt mainstreaming of white supremacy. Beginning in 2008 with the election of President Obama, Republicans sought ways to thwart the administration's agenda, particularly attempting to rehabilitate their public image on racism. The astonishing wave of antiabortion legislation around the country during his eight years in office was part of the predictable cyclical response of conservatives when they find themselves defeated at the ballot box and seek to regain political power by manipulating the latent and overt racism of white voters. The continuing battle over healthcare reform illustrates how the racism of most white voters can be cynically manipulated against their own interests because "Obamacare" is portrayed as unfairly benefiting poor people of color. Paradoxically, the states with the highest numbers of white people using Obamacare (or the Affordable Care Act as it is properly named) are the ones most energized in trying to repeal it. This contradiction is historically consistent when intersecting race with public welfare policies.

In the 1970s when Ronald Reagan was seeking the presidency, Republicans seized upon several cultural issues around which they could activate and mobilize their base, expanding a strategy crafted by Richard Nixon. Building on a core of dissatisfied white voters opposed to the civil rights gains of the 1960s, Republicans crafted a strategy that would meld together opponents of civil, women's, gay, workers', and immigrants' rights in a unified antigovernment political force mobilized by the religious Right to help them regain the presidency. In the process, they shifted most Southern white Democratic voters into aligning with the Republican Party. This strategy worked distressingly well in 1980 and was successfully repeated so often it has become known as the conservative "Southern Strategy."

A similar mobilization occurred after the election of President Bill Clinton in 1992 (remember Newt Gingrich's *Contract with America*?), and of course, was repeated by conservatives reinventing themselves as the Tea Party after the election of President Obama. Every Republican campaign for the presidency—and in many other elections—uses some version of this Southern Strategy to heighten racial, gender, antigay, and anti-immigrant tensions to mobilize their angry white voter base. Fears of alleged Muslim terrorists, nonwhite immigrants, queer people, feminists, and gun-control advocates added to this volatile mix to stoke the politics of fury and resentment.

After the success of the Civil Rights Movement in dismantling Jim Crow discrimination, African Americans witnessed how angry white men appropriated its moral mantle to lob charges of reverse discrimination and allege that the victims of racial injustice were its perpetrators. This echoes how, after this country was colonized by illegal white immigrants trampling the rights of Native Americans, they now want to racially profile the newest immigrants, claiming to do so in the name of reducing crime and fighting terrorism. After women fought hundreds of years for our freedom against the implacable forces of sexism, now we are accused of victimizing the fetuses we carry in our wombs. Such language coups disguise and distort reality while mobilizing a base of frustrated white men to reassert their dominion over American politics.[9]

Beginning in 2008, Republicans hoped to further the alliance between white and black conservatives in order to regain political hegemony, using religion and false compassion for black children to not only restrict abortion access for women but also split African American voters along gender and religious lines, thereby increasing black support for causes we traditionally have not supported. By using the fear of eugenics in African American communities to reinforce preexisting sexism, Republicans positioned anti-civil-rights conservatives as the champions of racial justice for the unborn, an irony that was not lost on black women. It was not an accident that the child in the original billboard was male. At the center of this strategy was a measured and relentless attack on African American women, a reliable voting base for the Democratic Party. A ginned up conspiracy theory that placed black women as the destroyers of the black family was used in previous approaches, like calling us welfare queens or hyperfertile women birthing superpredators. This character assassination of black women produces a predictable political and economic outcome: an increase in disabling poverty and instability for black women and our children.

A familiar tactic for white conservatives is the distortion of the meaning of civil and human rights. The Civil Rights Movement was about expanding freedom and opportunity for all people. It was not about limiting the rights of certain groups—unless one wanted to claim the right to discriminate. In a bizarre twist of logic, the antiabortion movement appropriates civil rights imagery, using tactics and rhetoric to "defend the rights of the unborn." They conveniently ignore one salient fact about biology: to defend the rights of fetuses, you must trample over the human rights of women, unless men suddenly become able to get pregnant. This has nothing to do with civil rights, but instead is privileging the rights of a fertilized ovum over the rights of living, breathing people who happen to be women.

To achieve antiabortionists' goal, women must be metaphorically reduced to mere birthing vessels, sacrificing our claims to equality. Sex and gender social constructions are used to create biological profiling, claiming that biology is destiny. The point is to control all people who can get pregnant. The antiabortion campaign is based on the racist and sexist stereotype that black women are "promiscuous, uncaring, and self-indulgent," in the words of Dorothy Roberts.[10]

The Legislative Campaign

Race- and gender-specific antiabortion legislation got its start in 2008 with Republican Representative Trent Franks from Arizona. Although Congressman Franks consistently fights every civil and human rights bill in both his state and Congress, he decided to introduce the offensively named Susan B. Anthony and Frederick Douglass Prenatal Nondiscrimination Act of 2008 (PRENDA). His corrosive cynicism propelled him to reintroduce the same bill in 2009. This federal bill claimed to prevent discrimination against fetuses in the womb, in other words, to save African American and Asian American fetuses from being aborted because of the race of the mother or gender of the fetus.

The basic logic of PRENDA legislation is flawed. One cannot save babies of color by discriminating against women of color. PRENDA legislation sets up women of color for racial profiling by abortion providers who are now compelled to question our motives for seeking abortions, something to which white women may not be subjected. This is legislatively mandated discrimination. It intrudes on doctor-patient confidentiality, increases barriers to abortion access and medical malpractice insurance costs, and is frankly unconstitutional, as it allows states to prohibit access to the federally protected right to an abortion.

While Franks's legislation failed at the federal level, it provided a model at the state level for abortion opponents to introduce bans on abortion access based on the race or gender of the fetus. When conservatives introduced Senate Bill 529 in Georgia in 2010 as the first combined race- and sex-selection state bill following the billboard campaign, they failed because our strong coalition of women's and civil rights organizations successfully fought them.

Arizona became the first state in the nation to make alleged sex- or race-selection abortions a crime. Governor Jan Brewer signed House Bill 2443 into law in April 2011, making it a felony for a doctor to perform an abortion based on the sex or race of the fetus. The Arizona law allows the father of an aborted fetus or, if the mother is a minor, the mother's parents to take legal action against the doctor or other health-care provider who performed the abortion. If convicted, physicians would face up to seven years in jail and the loss of their medical licenses. This unprecedented and predictably unconstitutional law would allow third parties to sue a doctor for performing a legal abortion for a woman who has signed ample consent forms. It makes providers vulnerable to other people who claim they were harmed by the abortion.

Other conservative states copied Arizona's example. Claiming to campaign against "reproductive racism," conservatives use the bizarre "abortion is racist" narrative that disregards the rights, wishes, and needs of women of color. Many more billboards appeared around the country to promote this national campaign, targeting Latinas and Indigenous populations as well.

When SisterSong decided to fight the antiabortion billboards and legislation popping up around the country, we did our homework and found that the sponsors of these billboards have millions of dollars to quickly spread their messages of hate, blame, and shame. Our opponents have nimbly institutionalized tokenism to thwart the pro-choice movement. Black surrogates cynically exploit the historical trauma of the black community to appear to speak seriously to our suffering by using genocidal arguments to decry abortions. Their white sponsors are particularly adept at using conservative African Americans as spokespeople for a racialized attack to make the whites for whom they work feel more comfortable in ignoring the structural racism that is central to reproductive oppression. Like other opponents of human rights and justice, the sponsors place highly visible people of color up front in defending ideas and programs that undermine racial, gender, immigrant, and queer justice.

We asked ourselves, what does it mean when in 2010 white conservatives with racist and sexist histories can recruit increasing numbers of African American leaders to support their campaigns against black women? In a sense, black leaders were not only surrogates in the attacks on President Obama but also pawns in a direct assault on Obama's largest and most loyal voting bloc. Was the pro-choice movement ready, and what could we as black feminists do to fortify African Americans against supporting a sexist and racist conservative agenda?

Our Opponents and Eugenics

Black feminists know we are up against formidable and well-funded opponents who believe they should control black women's reproduction like during slavery. Our opponents are manipulative, zealous, and immoral. They believe in population control and use false compassion for children to disguise their agenda by cynically using communities of color to attack abortion rights for all women. They lie, using deceptive religious language to coercively invoke guilt. They manipulate black history, our concerns about medical mistreatment, and our real collective pain around genocide and slavery to spin stories about black women as pawns of doctors, or as selfish women who do not care about our communities. While all of them may not be openly racist, they are at least racially challenged.

For example, Brian Follett, founder of Heroic Media, is a Texas-based millionaire who has also placed antiabortion ads on BET, MSNBC, and FOX. The Follett family earned its wealth from Anchor Foods, a manufacturer and supplier of frozen-food appetizers headquartered in Wisconsin. In 2000 it was sold to McCain Foods and H. J. Heinz Company with a reported $503 million in sales. The Folletts have created their own charity called Mercy Works Foundation. Funded through family tithing, Mercy Works reported $29 million in assets in 2008 and in that same year, gave $3.4 million to Catholic antiabortion groups. Follett said that Heroic Media's budget for 2011 was $5 million, and he projected growing the organization to an annual budget of $30–50 million within a decade.

Joining the racialized campaign was Priests for Life with a five million dollar war chest in 2010. They hired Alveda King, Dr. Martin Luther King Jr.'s niece, as director of African American outreach, trying to exploit the King name and legacy. They lavishly spent money on venues, publicity campaigns, buses, and salaries of their black surrogates, at a scale SisterSong could hardly match. But it doesn't take much money to start a media uproar. The Radiance Foundation, which launched the billboard campaign in Atlanta, was reported to have spent a mere $20,000 on the billboards that catapulted this antiabortion campaign into national prominence. It was estimated that this organization, incorporated in Georgia in 2009, raised more than $1 million for its campaigns from conservatives across the country in its first year of operations.

Another well-funded opponent was Life Dynamics, Inc. (LDI), founded in 1992 in Denton, Texas, by Mark Crutcher. PPFA has been the target of various "stings" by Crutcher, who claims to be gathering "intelligence" on abortion clinics and pro-choice organizations. LDI is accused of harassment and intimidation tactics by PPFA and the National Abortion Federation. LDI produced the film *Maafa 21*, a pseudo-documentary that misuses carefully selected facts about African American history to claim that the legalization of abortion was a plot to eliminate black people. The film has been distributed to all of Congress, as well as many colleges, universities, and civil rights organizations to promote the black genocide argument.

Conservatives, who apparently don't care to help children of color once they are born, are now claiming to be the champions of our children in the womb. At the same time, they are attempting to deny citizenship rights to the children born to undocumented women in the United States by pushing to exclude them from the Fourteenth Amendment as birthright citizens. They also oppose healthcare reform, controlling gun violence, environmental protections, immigration reform, marriage equality, gender-neutral bathrooms, public education, criminal justice reform, and other important human rights policy issues that determine the quality of life for children of color. As previously stated, these conservatives also falsely claim that abortion clinics are intentionally located in communities of color to eliminate us. They have used charges of black genocide or selling baby parts in the failed attempts to end Title

X federal funding and are continuing their efforts in state legislatures. They mount unceasing campaigns against PPFA, and black women are compelled to defend the organization even as we offer critiques of our relationships to it.

Racism in the Pro-Choice Movement

The paradox for African American feminists is not only from the Right but also the Left, or in other words, from the pro-choice movement that has yet to overcome its historical reluctance to confront accusations of racism and genocide. In fact, the pro-choice movement itself is a coalition of contradictory forces that support family planning for different reasons. The movement's better funded majority supports family planning as a strategy to achieve population reduction, often voiced as concern for overpopulation, environmental degradation, political instability, resource depletion, or fears of terrorism from "youth bulges" around the world. Feminist rhetoric about women's empowerment can obscure the neoeugenics philosophy in such approaches.

Radical white feminists and equally radical women of color have always asserted our right to control our own fertility as a goal in and of itself, in contrast to population control. We have challenged all utilitarian schemes for our bodies as a violation of our human right to self-determination and dignity, easily discerning the eugenical underpinnings of such apparently pro-woman approaches. As previously stated, we conceptualized the RJ framework to not only assert our right to access abortion and birth control along with the pro-choice movement but also to lift and highlight our human right to have and parent our children in safe and healthy environments. This is an aspect unique to the situation of women of color because of the enduring legacy of eugenics and its effects on public policies and resource allocation.

The pro-choice movement has blind spots that make it extremely vulnerable to accusations of racism. For example, black women may be used as mouthpieces for the pro-choice agenda, more so than looked to as leaders. Clearly black women can lead, as SisterSong and other RJ organizations demonstrate daily. Yet within the pro-choice movement, black women and other women of color sometimes serve largely as statistics for obtaining funding, as bridges—outreach workers—to low-income communities (who attract more funding), and as low-cost employee "help" (to stretch funding); crucial roles that further the missions of "progressive" nonprofits, in the words of SisterSong member Bani Hines Hudson.

This facilitates the tradition of white leadership, the custom of white women being "served," and a self-absorption that inhibits the sharing of resources or power. This is not a state of affairs peculiar to any specific pro-choice organization and is not meant to diminish the many important victories made by white women–led organizations that also benefit women of color. Planned Parenthood is an easy anti-choice target for antiabortionists, not only because it is the most recognizable and widespread family planning provider, but because of its Title X funding and the valuable services it provides women around the country, especially to vulnerable populations conservatives would rather ignore. Planned Parenthood and other pro-choice organizations have difficulty acknowledging their problematic histories that become distorted and exploited by the antiabortion movement. The silences of the pro-choice movement become opportunities for their critics. Failing to recognize how white supremacist ideology affects pro-choice organizations jeopardizes our collective ability to defeat our mutual opponents and weakens the entire movement.

The real question is whether pro-choice proponents can recognize this anti-black and anti-Asian strategy as a ruthless campaign to regain political power rather than just another gendered attack on abortion rights disguised as racial justice. If we fail to use an intersectional analysis to link this attack on abortion rights to other social justice wedge issues, we will inadequately respond to this all-out assault on human rights. It is not a coincidence that the sponsors of some of the billboards also fundraised for ultraconservative former vice presidential candidate Sarah Palin that same year. An intersectional response from African American women was urgently needed.

Trust Black Women

To defeat the billboards and the accompanying legislation, SisterSong decided on three primary strategies:

1. Redefine the campaign as an assault on black women's healthcare access, abortion rates, and underlying causes
2. Discredit opponents by revealing their anti-civil-rights agenda, and contrast them with historical and current evidence about

support for birth control and abortion in the African American community
3. Promote the power and agency of black women as leaders of the RJ movement

To achieve the first strategy, SisterSong used our interviews in the media to bring black women's voices into the foreground when accessing reproductive healthcare rather than have the focus be on pregnancies, abortions, and children. By pointing out the implied sexism and racism of the dual-pronged campaign, we could push the billboard proponents into a defensive posture. They tried to ignore the realities of black women's experiences, the unmet need for pregnancy prevention in African American communities, the complicated religious messages about black women's sexuality, and the social and economic drivers of the disproportionate abortion rates among black women. We framed abortion as a public health issue in which African American women face discrimination from a myriad of causes, not the least of which are the lack of support from black men in fighting against sexism and violence against women, and the fact that most black religious institutions are uncomfortable with addressing all issues of sex and sexuality. This strategy thwarted the opponents from only defining abortion as a moral issue of self-genocide. With this pivot, the campaign organizers were forced to proclaim their respect for black women, and became quite defensive when called out for ignoring the voices and perspectives of women who had abortions and others in the community who defended our rights to do so.

The second strategy required evidence. We decided that these newfound champions for black children had to be positioned against proven icons of the black community to provide a contrast, so that people could choose between believing Dr. Martin Luther King Jr. and W. E. B. DuBois or some lesser-known black people employed by a predominantly white antiabortion movement. We contacted Joyce Follet, an archivist at Smith College, and asked her to send us historical evidence documenting support for birth control and abortion from black historical icons. We presented the fact that Dr. King had received an award from Planned Parenthood, and Mary McLeod Bethune was on the Advisory Board of PPFA's Negro Project along with Adam Clayton Powell Jr. This strategy diminished the credibility of the billboard proponents, including one of Dr. King's nieces. It was difficult for the black antiabortionists to successfully claim that they cared more about the future of the African

American community than the legends we cited.

Another aspect of this strategy was to reveal the anti-civil-rights voting records of the antiabortion legislators, demonstrating their baked-in hostility to human rights. Proponents of states' rights, defiantly opposing all efforts to end racial discrimination and public policy measures that would benefit people of color, could not be trusted to suddenly care for the future of black children.

The final strategic prong was to demonstrate the national organizing power of black women to defend abortion rights. SisterSong organized Trust Black Women (TBW) in 2010 as a partnership of women from many different organizations, regions, and religious backgrounds to challenge antiabortion campaigns across the country targeting the African American community. TBW worked to establish a long-term response to racialized antiabortion attacks in the African American community. Our activism demonstrated that those who believe black women do not have the right nor the capacity to control our own bodies and defend ourselves stand on the wrong side of justice and human rights.

We launched TBW by bringing together black women's organizations and dozens of leading individual African American women to form, for the first time, a national coalition of black women expressly dedicated to protecting abortion rights through the RJ framework. We were young and older women, lesbian and straight, working together. Although SisterSong had both pro-choice and pro-life members, we never divided over the misleading debate on abortion. It was especially important to create a space for younger black women still in their fertile years to be visibly most of TBW's leadership. While African Americans have fought for reproductive control and autonomy for hundreds of years, explicitly forming a long-term coalition to fight race-based attacks on abortion rights was a new chapter in our ongoing struggle for human rights. In the words of one of our foremothers, Fannie Lou Hamer, "A black woman's body was never hers alone." We understand the wry sentiment underlying her reality.

We named ourselves Trust Black Women for several reasons. First, we wanted to honor Dr. George Tiller, an abortion provider who was assassinated in Kansas in 2009, but who always said to "trust women" to make their own reproductive decisions. Second, Byllye Avery, founder of the National Black Women's Health Project, arranged for the services of a first-class branding consultant to be donated to help select the best name for our aspirational, affirming, and complex work. Third, we wanted to speak to the reality that black women are not trusted by many in our society and, in fact, are unfairly blamed for many social problems. To demand that our society "Trust Black Women" boldly stated that we would let no one challenge our dignity, our human rights, and our self-determination without a strong response from empowered and organized African American feminists.

The TBW partnership took up the battle in the local communities in which the billboards appeared. We fought them in Atlanta, New York, Los Angeles, Milwaukee, St. Louis, and Chicago, among other locations. We helped black women and other women of color obtain the information and support to challenge these attacks. In states like Arizona, which fast-tracked the race- and gender-based antiabortion legislation, we worked to help local activists build quick multiracial response teams when billboards or legislation cropped up.

These billboards nearly always received national media attention in the *New York Times*, CNN, ABC News, and MSNBC, and generated dozens of stories based on the antiabortion myth that black women are either too stupid to make our own reproductive decisions or too selfish to be trusted. We were also featured on Oprah Radio and in many media stories about the billboards and campaigns. Only the progressive media covered the story fairly and enabled the full perspectives of black feminists to be heard.

Our strategies included community organizing, direct action, protests, speak-outs, storytelling, leadership development, media campaigns, and both opinion and opposition research. When the billboards appeared in a city, we helped organize local black women and allies to protest, wrote op-eds, organized coalitions that included allies, and exposed the organizations and motivations behind the campaigns. Our long-term goal was to build the capacity of black women's organizations across the country and provide permanent sites of resistance and local organizing to challenge the billboards and defeat any future race- and sex-selection legislation in the states. In short, we helped build a firewall of resistance to white conservatives using our bodies to divide the African American community and the pro-choice movement.

For example, TBW, SisterSong, and a coalition of allies protested when Priests for Life came to Atlanta in July 2010 with a so-called Pro-Life Freedom Bus that imitated the legendary Freedom Buses for voting rights in the 1960s. They staged a prayer service for the unborn at the tomb of Dr. King. This perverse strategy by the largely white antiabortion movement shamelessly attempted to claim moral superiority in caring about black children, and usurp the amazing grace of a black martyr killed by a white supremacist. What they ignored is Dr. King's actual history and legacy, because he and his wife, Coretta Scott King, were strong supporters of women's rights. Dr. King received a humanitarian award from Planned Parenthood in 1966, while Mrs. King unfailingly supported all human rights causes, including very strong support for LGBTQ issues. When the mostly white bus riders showed up in Atlanta, they were met by determined activists challenging their hypocrisy in claiming to save us from ourselves.

We also challenged the corporations that supported the billboards and the organizations that sponsored them like CBS, Lamar Advertising, and Dillard's department stores in Texas. We demanded that these corporations end their support of racist campaigns against black women. Although we can't be sure billboards won't be used again, we are sure that we will fight them everywhere they try. For example, we helped expose the fact that Heroic Media, the organization that paid for the New York and Chicago billboards, also supported ultraconservatives like Palin and Mike Huckabee. Pointing out this intersection mocked their claim to care about African American children.

The attacks also produced some wonderful support for TBW's work. Lionsgate Films gifted us tickets to advance premiere screenings of *For Colored Girls* by Tyler Perry as fundraisers in six cities. A documentary filmmaker, Charles Stuart, helped us produce a series of films on Laura Flanders's show *Grit TV* to lift the voices of African American women so that we could speak for ourselves on national television as activists, providers, clinic escorts, and everyday women. To expand the documentary and include the voices of more diverse black women and other women of color, SisterSong reedited the film and entitled it *We Always Resist: Trust Black Women.* SisterSong distributed thousands of free copies to students and community organizations around the country.

The NAACP, Reverend Al Sharpton's National Action Network, Operation PUSH, progressive black ministers, and other Civil Rights leaders and organizations began some valuable and overdue conversations about how African American men should not fall prey to this attempt to create a schism in our community around abortion rights to divide President Obama's voting base.

TBW also received support from some key foundations to conduct pioneering opinion research on what the African American community thinks about abortion rights and access. Although the pro-choice movement has more than forty years of opinion research on American attitudes about abortion, TBW found that the available data specifically on African Americans was scarce and disjointed. The result of this research was released in the summer of 2011.

The Future of Trust Black Women

In 2015 SisterSong's executive director, Monica Simpson, brought together new and former TBW members in Atlanta to recommit to the black feminist fight for abortion rights. "Trust Black Women" has become a rallying cry for thousands of RJ activists and students determined to challenge all who would deny African American women our agency, power, and self-determination. TBW expanded its work to support the domestic violence case of Marissa Alexander, who was unjustly imprisoned in Florida for defending herself against an abusive ex-husband. It also launched a strategic collaboration with the founders and members of the Black Lives Matter movement to emphasize the connections between reproductive oppression and racial violence.

TBW works with young people to counter attempts to enlist them in the antiabortion movement. Progressive students on high school, college, and university campuses are often blindsided when pictures, advertisements, and films suddenly appear that claim abortion is black genocide. Often, a predominantly white campus antiabortion or conservative religious group creates this uproar. Previously they used posters of bloody fetuses but found those grotesque images turned more people off than convinced folks to join them. Now they have found a more sensationalist tactic, inviting African American speakers to the school who falsely claim that abortion providers are deliberately seeking to eliminate the black race. When these lies are challenged, these purveyors of hate and misogyny claim it's a matter of academic freedom, like Holocaust deniers who trumpet their lies on college campuses under the guise of free speech.

Those of us in the RJ movement recognize that young people are on the frontlines in this struggle. It is a fight for the bodies of fertile young people, after all, in determining who gets to decide whether to have a child, receive factual sexual health information, and uphold the human right of young people to sex and sexuality. This is a war for bodily self-determination, and it may be the most important political fight of all because it affects whether young people have the freedom to make some of the most important decisions of their lives.

The leadership of African American women is vital in the fight against eugenics, as it has always been. We have a four-hundred-year-old history of fighting for liberty, reproductive autonomy, and self-determination that will succeed against those who would want to reenslave us through our wombs. When it comes to the intersection of race, gender, and abortion, African American women are among the most experienced with an anti-racist legacy going back hundreds of years. We can refute false charges of racism, xenophobia, and genocide in ways that are credible and passionate. We are the most trusted in telling the real and nuanced story about race, birth control, and Margaret Sanger. We are engaged in every aspect of the decision-making about this struggle against eugenics and for human rights, providing a context for our abortion decisions by telling our stories and validating the trust of our communities.

We always resist. Our opponents would do well to never forget that. Trust Black Women.

Notes

1. Patricia Hill Collins, *Black Feminist Thought: Knowledge, Consciousness, and the Politics of Empowerment* (New York: Routledge, 2000), 4.

2. bell hooks, *Feminist Theory: From Margin to Center* (Boston: South End Press, 1984), 52.

3. Ruha Benjamin, "Catching Our Breath: Critical Race STS and the Carceral Imagination," *Engaging Science, Technology, and Society* 2 (2016), 153.

4. Ibid., 148–49.

5. Kathryn Krase, "History of Forced Sterilization and Current US Abuses," Our Bodies Ourselves, October 1, 2014, www.ourbodiesourselves.org.

6. Alan L. Stoskopf, "Confronting the Forgotten History of the American Eugenics Movement," *Facing History and Ourselves News,* 1995, 7.

7. Avi Selk, "Rep. Steve King's reality is scarier than Stephen King's fiction, Seth Meyers says," *Washington Post*, March 15, 2017, https://www.washingtonpost.com/news/arts-and-entertainment/wp/2017/03/15/seth-meyers-rep-steve-kings-reality-is-scarier-than-stephen-kings-fiction/?utm_term=.4c85fc98fd30.

8. Ellen Chesler, *Woman of Valor: Margaret Sanger and the Birth Control Movement in America*, (New York: Simon & Schuster), 1992, 388.

9. See Jean Hardisty, *Mobilizing Resentment: Conservative Resurgence from the John Birch Society to the Promise Keepers* (Boston: Beacon Press, 1999); Leonard Zeskind, *Blood and Politics: The History of the White Nationalist Movement from the Margins to the Mainstream* (New York: Farrar, Straus

and Giroux, 2009); Chip Berlet and Matthew N. Lyons, *Right-Wing Populism in America: Too Close for Comfort* (New York: Guilford Press, 2000); Sara Diamond, *Spiritual Warfare: The Politics of the Christian Right* (Boston: South End Press, 1989).

10. Dorothy Roberts, *Killing the Black Body: Race, Reproduction, and the Meaning of Liberty* (New York: Vintage Books, 1997), 156.

Card-Carrying Marchers and Sister Travelers: Pro-Life Feminists and the Reproductive Justice Movement

MARY KRANE DERR

Editors' Note: This author uses reproductive justice in her argument for pro-life feminism, conveying the spectrum of opinions in the antiabortion movement. To showcase the broad applicability of the reproductive justice framework, we include this submission we received from the late Mary Krane Derr.

What Is Pro-Life Feminism? An Insider's View, from the Left

The reproductive justice movement already seeks to expand the abortion issue far beyond the rigidly individualistic us-versus-them stances of pro-life and pro-choice. These dogmatic stances ultimately do little or nothing to address grave, real-life human problems. The RJ movement, on the other hand, can comprehensively address and alleviate the root causes of abortion, especially if it enlists the insights and talents of activists with a wide variety of perspectives on whether and to what extent women have a right to abortion itself. Admittedly, I have a vested interest in discerning such promise in the RJ movement. Not only am I in my own way a long-time RJ activist, I have consciously identified myself for decades by the oft-disputed term "pro-life feminist."

Both encampments of the abortion war constantly tell pro-life feminists that such creatures as we profess to be simply do not and cannot exist by definition. This is, of course, offensive to us. But as much as pro-life feminists believe that we merit respectful consideration ourselves, we cannot get offended and indignant when others do not find our chosen description to be self-evident from the start. For one, the present cultural climate is so rife with stereotypes. Antiabortionists are thought to monolithically be ultra–right wing woman haters who believe that life begins at conception and ends at birth—and even then, it qualifies as life only when it is white. The other highly relevant stereotype is one of feminism as all about the obsession of racist, classist, well-off Anglo women to impose abortion on every possible occasion. So, the possibility of something called "pro-life feminism" can be baffling even to people who do not quite believe all this hype, whether they would ultimately find pro-life feminism persuasive.

As with anything else, there are as many takes on the phrase "pro-life feminism" as there are people who identify with the term. Alaska governor Sarah Palin—at this writing the 2008 Republican vice-presidential candidate—describes herself as a pro-life feminist. In a fashion that seems to elude many white, middle-class, pro-choice feminists, her biography may show that at least *some* egalitarian values have pervaded US culture, even supposedly unlikely sectors of it. However, I will leave it to conservative women to explain for themselves precisely what they mean when they call themselves pro-life feminists. I must register here my own vigorous and long-standing disagreement with such frequent aspects of US conservatism as:

— State-sanctioned, state-created, or state-perpetuated forms of violence such as war, the death penalty, and environmental destruction that fall hardest on the very people who have the least resources to protect themselves.
— An allegedly "colorblind" philosophy of "free markets" and "limited government," coupled with contradictory failures to separate "church" and state and to squander huge quantities of taxpayer dollars on the violent pursuit of global empire.
— "Traditional family values" that undermine women's, children's (born and unborn), and LGBTQ people's family lives and human rights.

How do such practices respect life before or after birth? Thus, I will focus here on pro-life feminism as I and others from the Left understand and practice it. At the same time, I acknowledge that, on any given point, some conservative pro-life women will agree and others will not; they are no more monolithic than any other group.

I approach this task of explaining pro-life feminism by addressing what, if anything, it has in common with the RJ movement. SisterSong identifies these three principles as the core of RJ. Every woman has the right to:

1. Decide if and when she will have a baby and the conditions under which she will give birth.
2. Decide if she will not have a baby and her options for preventing or ending a pregnancy.
3. Parent the children she has with the necessary social supports in safe environments and healthy communities, and without fear of violence from individuals or the government.

Pro-life feminists of diverse backgrounds heartily endorse and strive toward everything contained in these principles, with one exception. We identify abortion not as a right across all circumstances, but generally as a form of unjust violence against women and unborn children that arises from and perpetuates reproductive and other wrongs. "An injury to one is an injury to all," as the anti-apartheid slogan said. That is as apt a moral and political insight as ever. And so, we venture, RJ is less than it could be if it is not for all unborn and already born humans. Jennifer Ferguson, a former African National Congress activist and South African parliament member, arrived at these reflections in the long aftermath of a legal abortion and an illegal, backstreet attempt at one:

> If . . . we see abortion only as an issue of women's liberation, we have planted a seed of another cycle of oppression, one which neglects to hear that most silent voice of all, the voice of the unborn child. . . . We need a new way of seeing! We need to understand with empathy that abortion is a symptom not a solution. . . . I [am] searching for the third way, one that could compassionately embrace both mother and child. . . . In its deepest sense the abortion issue is a peace issue. . . . Abortion is a rejection of the innermost, but if we reject the rejectors we reject ourselves.[1]

While identifying abortion as violence that often has deeply negative repercussions for the pregnant woman as well as the fetus, pro-life feminists at the same time are not about blaming and shaming women who contemplate or have abortions. An analogy: opponents of militarization are not properly about heaping nasty judgments on people who join the military, for example, out of hope it will offer otherwise unavailable or hard-to-obtain education, employment, and/or public service opportunities. Pro-life feminists move beyond simply opposing the practice of abortion itself. We seek to address and relieve the difficult, deeply engrained cultural problems that so frequently disempower women and put them in situations where there appears to be no other or less bad choice than the (for many) grief, tragedy, and trauma of abortion. We connect these wide-scale problems of individuals, families, and communities most of all to pervasive sexism, and frequently to other enormous, institutionalized, overlapping, and mutually reinforcing injustices such as classism, racism, abelism, homo- and transphobia, the prison industrial complex, militarism, animal abuse, and environmental destruction. Regarding environmental justice, Katsi Cook notes in SisterSong's *Reproductive Justice Briefing Book*, "Woman is the first environment. . . . In pregnancy our bodies sustain life. Our unborn see through our eyes and hear through our ears. Everything the mother feels, the baby feels, too."[2]

Contrary to some prevailing views on both sides of the abortion debate, neither the pregnant woman nor the unborn child are insensate, inert bits of matter. As some people on both sides already grasp, the pregnant woman and fetus are *both* sentient, inherently valuable beings whose bodies and lives are profoundly, even inextricably, interconnected with one another, and simultaneously with the "seamless web" of all lives. Pro-life feminists like me systematically strive to advocate for both equally while and through sustaining and improving the larger ecology.

Although no one knows how many of us there are in the United States, let alone globally, we exist in substantial enough numbers to have created the anthology *Pro-Life Feminism Yesterday and Today, Second Expanded Edition*, which I coedited with Rachel MacNair and Linda Naranjo-Huebl. The volume includes, along with Ferguson's, the voices of such leaders as the Dalai Lama, ecofeminist Wangari Maathai, and the late Benazir Bhutto. Other contemporary articles, many from the US, deal with such vital subjects as sex-selective abortion, pro-life cases for LGBTQ and disability rights, bearing witness against all forms of violence, educating pro-lifers about feminism, being of service to pregnant women, and censorship of pro-life feminists. The volume also thoroughly documents the long herstory of (chiefly US-based) pro-life feminism, which I will discuss shortly. Earlier books in this vein include the North American–focused *Pro-Life Feminism: Different Voices,* edited by Gail Grenier Sweet, and *Swimming against the Tide: Feminist Dissent on the Issue of Abortion*, edited by Angela Kennedy, featuring activists from Ireland and Great Britain, including Mary McAleese, who soon after publication became the Irish president.

However, at present, little organizational support exists for a pro-life feminist approach to abortion as such. Thus, pro-life feminists are often united by stories of prolonged isolation from likeminded people. Although all of these US-based groups are small and have rather limited resources, some pro-life feminists do find open company and organizational backing in the likes of Consistent Life, the Pro-Life Alliance of Gays and Lesbians, and Feminists for Life of America (FFLA).

Founded in 1972, FFLA once had a broader, more radical vision of how to alleviate the root causes of abortion. It now focuses almost exclusively on mobilizing resources for pregnant and parenting students so they can continue their educations. As a long-ago pregnant and parenting-by-surprise student, and now the mother of such a student, I can attest to the persistent need for, and value of, such an effort. However, while it is not on record as opposing these vital measures, neither does FFLA today openly and straightforwardly stand up for all voluntary family planning methods, complete sex education, LGBTQ rights, and a comprehensive social welfare system.

Whether we as individuals find or do not find reasons to join or stay in these organizations, pro-life feminists talk among ourselves about what it might be like if we did not continually encounter such relentless processes of silencing, dismissal, and erasure. We would be blessedly free to seek conversation and cooperative action with people on both sides on reducing unintended pregnancies and abortion, as well as on a wide variety of other potentially shared RJ concerns. We already recognize fully that abortion rights supporting feminists are not motivated by some "selfish" desire for "convenience" but a profound ethical concern for women's suffering. We also recognize that not every antiabortionist is driven by some crazed lust to punish women for having sex but rather a concern for unborn children and even pregnant women. When the thoughtful, caring members of the various parties in the abortion debate learn to listen to and not demonize one another, everybody is that much closer to finding, standing, and acting together upon common ground, even while differing in critical ways.

No Easy or Single Answer: The Matter of the Law

Concerning the legal status of abortion itself, liberal-to-leftist pro-life feminists have different visions of collective responsibility in relation to the law. Pro-life feminists hail from all faiths and none, and often emphasize the need for separation of religion and state. To its advocates, pro-life feminism is not and must never be a sectarian-religious imposition. Sectarian religion is not the reason why *some* pro-life feminists advocate abortion regulations as a possible means of reducing abortion. Carol Crossed writes:

> Like reducing the need for the death penalty, reducing the need for abortion is necessary. But . . . while we are creating a society that values mothers and the unborn, let us build guardrails to protect them from abortion in the meantime. Which is better is not the issue. It is a question of how a community can do both.[3]

Personally, I do not have such a sanguine view of the law but rather a tortuously complex perspective that makes no one happy. But here goes. A mere legal ban on abortion can in fact sabotage any stated purpose of respect for fetal—let alone maternal—life. As far as I am concerned, any law concerning abortion needs to prove that it will actively protect both fetal and postnatal children and help rather than punish women. It can do this by writing *ample, comprehensive* support for women's right to make nonviolent (voluntary, nonabortion, or abortion-reducing) sexual and reproductive choices written right into and throughout it.

In part because such legal proposals are practically unheard of in the US, I personally focus my energies upon social welfare measures that will alleviate the root causes of abortion, whatever its legal status. I am deeply skeptical of the motives behind most proposed or enacted abortion restrictions within the United States. These tend to have the meat-stink of power-over, not the sweet blossoming fragrance of power-with. Though I bristle at the epithet "anti-choice," and ask pro-choicers to refrain from it, I do understand why this term arose.

At the same time, I must profess an equally deep skepticism about the *Roe v. Wade* decision. It is not exactly fragrant, either, at least to my nose. It was the product from on high of an all-male, privileged, mostly Euro-descended US Supreme Court. In his opinion, the late Justice Harry Blackmun dismissed concern for unborn life as no more than an unwarranted imposition of dour, moralistic religious sectarians. As I have argued elsewhere, this dismissal is based on an incomplete and distorted understanding of both ancient and modern religions. In addition—a very large addition—as Mary Ann Glendon notes, *Roe* "embodies a view of society as a collection of separate autonomous individuals" rather than as a network of ethically and politically affirmed and valued "connections among the woman, developing life, and the larger community."[4] Thus the privacy right it enshrines completely absolves US society of its public responsibility for substantive alternatives to abortion, including the fostering of men's collective and individual responsibility for the children they conceive, as well as for sex and family planning.

During the 1960s and 1970s, which I am old enough to remember, thoughtful woman-centered arguments for abortion rights were certainly part of the mix of forces toward mass ethical and legal acceptance of abortion. However, there were also some downright ugly and reactionary phenomena of backlash to growing civil rights movements for disabled persons, women, people of color, and the poor. During the early 1960s, many unborn babies became disabled in a rubella epidemic and others from their mothers' unwitting use of the drug thalidomide. These events stirred up the already great revulsion toward people of all ages with disabilities. Fear of a colorful planet and an interconnected dread of "uncontrolled" female sexual and reproductive power were also quite operative. As the pro-choice RJ advocate Rickie Solinger observes:

> By 1965 . . . the white unwed mother had been changed in the public consciousness from a species of mental patient into a sexual revolutionary. The black unwed mother was still portrayed as a participant in an aberrant culture of sexuality and as the taxpayers' nemesis . . . [and] increasingly as the triggering device attached to the Population Bomb, USA. The "sexual revolution" and the "population bomb" were racially specific metaphors of destruction. . . . By virtue of these tropes, unwed mothers . . . were assigned apocalyptic importance. . . . Abortion became an acceptable way to meet an old goal, that is, containing the social consequences of illicit female sexuality and fertility.[5]

I ignore this still (in many regards) enduring history at my own peril and that of individuals and communities I love profoundly. I am a multiply-disabled woman who hails from two immigrant, blue-collar, US subcultures, Polish and Irish, with considerable histories of colonization, genocide, and discrimination. For much of my life, although I received an excellent education by scholarship, I have been materially poor by US standards. Against a dominant culture which told me at every turn that I had no business doing this, I birthed and raised an unplanned daughter in conditions of hardship whose alleviation were beyond my individual control, but with the unexpected blessing of a responsible, loving, reciprocal male partner. I have long lived in a majority-black, working-class community that is now undergoing the outrageous upheavals of gentrification. My own close family is multiracial. My first, recently born, congenitally disabled grandchild is West African and Cherokee as well as Slavic, Celtic, and Germanic. He, too, was conceived unintentionally in difficult circumstances for his parents, and has from conception faced a world quite deeply hostile to the basic human rights of life and well-being for people like him and his family members. I understand others with parallel stories may form different conclusions about *Roe* and abortion in general. However, in part because of these particular life experiences, I personally cannot look upon *Roe* or a right to abortion as salvific foundations or touchstones of RJ.

When I happen to ride the bus past one of the abortion clinics in my city, I pray my decidedly interfaith prayers (I am not any one religion) for the safety of all the workers against violent attacks, for the women clients, their fetuses, and all touched by their situations, such as male partners, grandparents, friends. I pray for the relief of suffering and the causes of suffering. I brought together and publicized action alerts through the Nonviolent Choice Directory, a global directory of abortion-reducing resources that grew out of the *Pro-Life Feminism Yesterday and Today* anthology. I decidedly do not advocate turning the clock back to the horrific past that pro-choicers often invoke. Rather, it is way past time to turn the clock forward, as Jen Roth states in the very title of her eloquent pro-life feminist blog.

Whatever our disagreements may or may not be on abortion law itself, neither Carol Crossed, Jen Roth, nor I (nor any other pro-life feminists I know) seek to criminalize pregnant women ensnared in difficult situations and dilemmas, let alone subject them to the death penalty—a practice which, anyway, we generally oppose, and vigorously so. What sense does it make to defend unborn lives but sabotage the lives of the already born? We agree with this point that abortion-rights advocate Andrea Smith makes in her influential essay "Beyond Pro-Choice versus Pro-Life: Women of Color and Reproductive Justice."

> Criminalization [of women who seek abortion] individualizes solutions to problems that are the result of larger economic, social, and political conditions. Consequently, it is inherently incapable of solving social problems or addressing crime.
>
> Alternative social formations and institutions that can speak to these large-scale political and economic conditions are the appropriate place to address social issues, such as reproductive justice.[6]

The Need for Cooperative Action

Pro-life feminists agree with one another and abortion-rights advocates like Smith about creating and sustaining such "alternative social formations and institutions." Regarding reducing unintended pregnancies, abortions, and cases of grotesquely unsupported parenthood, the need goes greatly unmet. Unfortunately, Mary Ann Glendon's comparative legal observations from two decades ago are truer than ever. The United States publicly commits itself to far less support for birth control, maternity, and childrearing and consequently has much higher unplanned pregnancy and abortion rates than Western-European nations with similar material riches.[7] At the same time, US stinginess goes global, with lethal consequences, mostly for deeply impoverished women and children of color. For example, how many precious maternal, fetal, and newborn lives have been unnecessarily lost—killed—by the former president George W. Bush administration's withholding in the name of (all things!) "pro-life," of funds for nonabortion, abortion-preventing reproductive education and health services? This defunding does nothing to encourage, for example, the recent and most welcome global declines in the rates of abortion and already-born child mortality.

Cooperation across the spectrum of abortion views is vital for securing women's rights to agreed-upon sexual and reproductive health education and services: voluntary pregnancy prevention through the safe method(s) they personally prefer, whether contraception, fertility awareness, abstinence, outercourse, or same-sex relations; in the event of pregnancy, full access to nonabortion maternal and fetal health and social service care throughout the nine months; as well as desirable, generously supported choices in birthing, then parenting, adoption, guardianship, or foster care.

Antiabortion and abortion rights advocates of good will and otherwise shared RJ values can together ponder these questions regarding abortion, questions which I, for one, believe are ultimately much deeper and more decisive questions than the question of the law. The SisterSong motto of "doing together collectively what we cannot do individually" has meaning here, too.

Now, granting that not every woman necessarily experiences abortion in this way, why do so many women resort to abortion, especially when so many would much rather not? Especially when so many find abortion—not only those who now identify as pro-life—to be a real loss that brings immense suffering, suffering that might have been prevented by substantive abortion alternatives? What actions—at every level from the individual to the global—can be taken to ensure that women have the power to make voluntary, fully informed, and socially supported reproductive decisions other than abortion?

Herstorical Sources of Pro-Life Feminism

A number of SisterSong publications proclaim the importance of keeping and reclaiming RJ herstory. Pro-life feminists have a parallel sense of herstory and its immense value to today's activism. From the standpoint of promoting reciprocal understanding and cooperative action, RJ activists of all abortion perspectives may find it interesting and beneficial to learn more about their shared if not identical roots in particular constituencies and social justice struggles.

Although pro-life feminism as a term probably did not originate until the early 1970s, it provides apt shorthand for an approach to abortion that dates back centuries. Indeed, from the early nineteenth century through the 1960s, it was a majority view within US feminism, and has been a flourishing, if often ignored, minority ever since. No one knows when its life began, but here are some of its sources within modern times, particularly in the United States.

The Life and Work of Mary Wollstonecraft

Facing discrimination as a woman and a Unitarian, and occupying a precarious social and economic position, the Anglo-Irish intellectual and author Mary Wollstonecraft was acutely conscious of the need to thoroughly dismantle English society's rigidly stratified hierarchies. These were imposed most severely on its colonies but were nevertheless operative within England itself. Wollstonecraft had the power of imagination to envision a different and better world in part because of her bipolar disorder, which is often linked to creativity. Although she was dismissed as mad, Wollstonecraft's vision put her far ahead of her own time, and in some respects our own. In her *Vindication of the Rights of Woman*, Wollstonecraft advocated a form of voluntary, woman-controlled contraception whose current, scientifically based version is called the Lactational Amenorrhea Method and is up to 98 percent effective. Yet she opposed abortion on these terms:

> Women becoming, consequently, weaker, in mind and body, than they ought to be . . . have not sufficient strength to discharge the first duty of a mother; and . . . either destroy the embryo in the womb, or cast it off when born. . . . [M]en ought to maintain the women whom they have seduced . . . one means of . . . stopping an abuse that has an equally fatal effect on population and morals.[8]

Wollstonecraft's reproductive ethics were shaped by her own experience of conceiving, bearing, and raising her older daughter outside of legal marriage, followed by the vilification of her child as "illegitimate" and of herself as "wicked" (no word about her lover's abandonment of her and the child). Her life was cut short following the delivery of her second child, when she experienced overwhelming sepsis as the result of unwanted, invasive obstetrical interference in the birth process.

Both Wollstonecraft's daughters inherited her bipolar disorder. The younger daughter became Mary Wollstonecraft Shelley, the visionary author of *Frankenstein*. The older daughter, Fanny Imlay, committed suicide at age twenty-two, leaving an unsigned note that said: "The best thing I could do was to put an end to the existence of a being whose birth is unfortunate." She had struggled with her biological father's rejection, her mother's death, and a society that still, to say the least, did not listen to her purportedly insane mother's vision of welcoming every woman and child, before, during, and after birth, as innately valuable in their own right.

Along with her daughters, Mary Wollstonecraft left behind an incomplete novel, *Maria*. Maria is a middle-class Englishwoman whose husband forcibly commits her to an insane asylum for her questioning of his rule over her. Here Wollstonecraft anticipates a point made in the present-day feminist and disability rights movements about "madness," which is to some degree a social construction used to punish people perceived as dissident. Maria is sundered from her nursing infant, who thus may die. She becomes friends with Jemima, an asylum employee from the lower classes. Jemima eventually confides a horrific story from her time in domestic service, one of the few occupations open to her because of her working-class status and her illegitimate birth. Her employer sexually coerced her, then pressured and abandoned her to an abortion, despite her powerful sense of empathy for and identification with the unborn child. Feminists before and after Mary Wollstonecraft similarly linked abortion to a cycle of institutionalized violence against women and children from all walks of life.

The Haudenosaunee Six Nations, Ganeodiyo, and Matilda Joslyn Gage

Wollstonecraft's remarkable, unfinished life and work have gotten some credit for their profound influence on early US women's rights agitation. However, well before she wrote and lived, the Haudenosaunee of Upstate New York constructed a nearly feminist society. Perhaps the world's oldest continuing participatory democracy, the Haudenosaunee were and are a confederacy of Six Nations: Mohawk, Onondaga, Oneida, Cayuga, Tuscarora, and Seneca. Even after the severe upheavals and dislocations of European colonization, Haudenosaunee women fared better within their own culture than Anglo women did within theirs.

Haudenosaunee women continued to enjoy equal participation in government and religion and respect for their ingenious, ecologically sound farming methods, especially the "Three Sisters" way of cultivating the food staples corn, beans, and squash together. The very concept of illegitimacy was a European import and imposition that most Haudenosaunee resisted. Family descent was still traced through the mother. Women had their say in matters of property, marriage, divorce, and risking or minimizing their risk of conception. Pregnancy and birth were not considered pathological, but healthful, although evidently following colonization some women experienced additional fear of labor pains. Domestic violence and rape—still comparatively rare—were treated as truly grave offenses. Thus, Haudenosaunee women were remarkably free to enjoy voluntary motherhood.[9]

Today voluntary motherhood is often equated with an ethical and/or political right to abortion. However, among past- and present-day pro-life feminists, it was and is about the right to be *free from* abortion as well as unwanted sex, undesired pregnancy, and unsupported motherhood.

Haudenosaunee were encouraged by the oral religious teachings called the Gaiiwo, or "Good Message," which Euro Americans have called "the Code of Handsome Lake." The teachings were eventually translated from Seneca into English and put into writing by the Seneca anthropologist Gawasco Waneh, or Talking Leaves (also known as Arthur Caswell Parker). They came originally from visions that the Seneca prophet Ganeodiyo, also known as Handsome Lake, experienced around 1800. He then shared the visions as an antidote to growing demoralization and despair over religious and other forms of devastation wrought by European colonizers.

The Gaiiwo predicts the end of the world if environmental destruction continues. It also resonates with past and present social movements in its counsels against alcohol abuse, lack of hospitality to the poor, and violence and neglect of women and children, including the pregnant and the unborn. The Gaiiwo exhorts men to take responsibility toward the families they create and refrain from battering their wives. It directly challenges mistreatment of children with uncertain or nonmarital paternity. At the same time, while sympathetic to their motives, it counsels women who fear the pain of childbirth to refrain from abortion because "it is sad" and the Creator "created life to live."[10]

Many early European American feminists had significant ties with Upstate New York and the Haudenosaunee, including Lucretia Mott and her younger protégées in the "suffrage triumvirate" of Elizabeth Cady Stanton, Susan B. Anthony, and Matilda Joslyn Gage. In fact, the Wolf Clan of the Mohawk Nation adopted Gage and gave her the name Karon-ien-ha-wi, or Sky Carrier. Historian Sally Roesch Wagner argues eloquently for the tremendous influence of the Haudenosaunee over these Anglo feminists' ability to imagine women having their rights respected, including their right to choose whether and when to risk pregnancy.

Although Wagner does not mention this, Haudenosaunee views of abortion may have been part of this influence. Gage, the Anglo feminist who had the closest and most appreciative ties with Haudenosaunee people, described the Six Nations as preserving "reminiscences of the Matriarchate." Gage envisioned this once widespread, ancient culture of "Mother-Rule" as one in which

> all life was regarded as holy; even the sacrifice of animals was unknown. . . . The earliest phase of life being dependent upon [woman], she was recognized as the primal factor in every relation. . . . It is through a recognition of the divine element of motherhood as not alone inhering in the great primal source of life, but as extending throughout all creation, that it will become possible for the world, so buried in darkness, folly, and superstition, to practice justice toward women. . . . Both infanticide and prostitution with all their attendant horrors are traceable . . . to the [later] Patriarchate or Father-Rule.[11]

Among early US feminists, the term "infanticide" was widely understood to encompass both pre- and postnatal lifetaking, and was often used interchangeably with abortion and synonyms for it. Gage once wrote to the *Revolution*, the newspaper published by Stanton and Anthony, that abortion "touch[es] a subject which lies deeper down into woman's wrongs than any other" and that "most of this crime . . . lies at the door of the male sex." In the *History of Woman Suffrage*, she clearly identified the source of widespread pregnancy discrimination and abortion in US culture. "How completely demoralized by her subjection [woman] must be, who does not feel her personal dignity assailed . . . when she finds that which should be her glory—her possible motherhood—treated everywhere by men as a disability and a crime!"[12]

Gage did not romanticize the actual conditions under which so many women labored and faced heart-wrenching dilemmas about pregnancy. I will not attempt here to engage the question of whether Gage was archaeologically accurate in envisioning an ancient Matriarchate. However, I do affirm that Gage, and not one whit less the nineteenth-century Haudenosaunee who inspired her, present the US today with still-relevant questions and concerns about the practice of abortion, not to mention related reproductive injustices.

Slavery Abolition and Women's "Heart-Histories"

Many feminist-minded women participated in the multiracial abolitionist movement even before there was an organized push for women's rights in the United States. Matilda Joslyn Gage's home was a station on the Underground Railroad. The ethical and legal case for every woman's right to her own body took more shape through the challenges that emerging feminists of all races made to the sexual and reproductive abuses of enslaved black women. Sarah Grimké, a South Carolina slavemaster's daughter, was harassed and threatened with murder for her outspoken abolitionism, and was not the first or last feminist to identify male property claims over women, inside and outside of legal slavery, as a prime cause of abortion—nor to propose the right of voluntary motherhood as an antidote.

> Has [woman] not, too often, when thus compelled to receive the germ *she could not welcome*, refused to retain & nourish into life the babe, which she felt was not the fruit of a pure connubial love? . . . Surely as upon her alone devolves the necessity of nurturing unto the fullness of life the being within her & after it is born . . . she *ought* to have the right of controlling all preliminaries.[13]

Women's "heart-histories" moved early feminists of all races to regularly portray abortion and postnatal infanticide alike as desperate, violent acts to escape the enslaving conditions imposed on mothers from a wide range of backgrounds. One particularly horrific and galvanizing real-life story was that of Margaret Garner, a fugitive slave who killed her young daughter when they were threatened with capture. Although Garner left no account of her own, this incident was imaginatively reconstructed and retold by two prominent African American women writers—Frances Ellen Watkins Harper in the nineteenth century, and Toni Morrison in the twentieth and twenty-first.

Early feminists underscored the even more direct responsibility of white slaveholders for most acts of violence against black women and their children, before and after birth. As she describes in her slave narrative, Harriet Jacobs was subjected from age fifteen onward to the relentless sexual harassment of Dr. James Norcom, a physician of high social standing in Edenton, North Carolina. Desperately trying to resist, Jacobs became involved with another white man, future US Representative Samuel Tredwell Sawyer, whom she "at least did not despise." When Jacobs became pregnant by Sawyer, the jealous, resentful Norcom angrily reminded her of his societally sanctioned life-and-death power over her and her unborn child.

> He talked of the disgrace I had brought on myself. . . . He intimated that if I had accepted his proposals, he, as a physician, could have saved me from exposure. He even condescended to pity me. Could he have offered wormwood more bitter? . . . He came toward me, with ill-suppressed rage, and exclaimed, "You obstinate girl! I could grind your bones to powder. . . . You are blinded now; but hereafter you will be convinced that your master was your best friend. My lenity toward you is a proof of it. I might have punished you in many ways. I might have whipped you till you fell dead under the lash. But I wanted you to live.[14]

Jacobs may be speaking literally as well as metaphorically here of wormwood, a well-known abortifacient in her day. Called "gall" in the Bible Jacobs knew well, it was a powerful symbol of truncated lives. Although she did birth this particular child, Jacobs more than once contemplated taking her life and her children's, never imagining the freedom that they would one day win. The story of Harriet Jacobs and her children represented only one example of what, in an article published in the *Revolution*, Susan B. Anthony called the "dreadful volume of heart-histories that lies hidden in almost every family in the land!" She said this within an indictment of the sexual double standard and male responsibility for abortion and other wrongs.

Pioneering Women Physicians and Women's Heart-Histories

Along with slave narratives, feminists' careful, merciful attention to women's life stories owed much to pioneering women physicians. These doctors, in fact, may have coined the very term "heart-histories," meaning the inner experiences and emotions of women's own lives. Whether they originated the phrase, they prided themselves upon the healing nature of listening with deep empathy to patients and drawing out these personal narratives.

Many of the first officially credentialed woman doctors joined with other feminists in appealing to and mobilizing these personal stories to foster societal healing, for example, through the "moral education" movement. As William Leach notes, moral education societies offered women the opportunity "to safely, fully, and openly discuss . . . without intimidation from men"[15] the intimate, essential matters of sexuality, marriage, and birth control. Moral education leader Lucinda Banister Chandler identified the purpose of these groups as helping each participant achieve "the courage to assert the right to her own body."[16] Education in recent scientific findings about prenatal development was integral to this process. Women doctors worked to democratize this and other scientifically sound information about sexual and reproductive health, in part to prevent abortions. Eliza Bisbee Duffey fiercely advocated sex education and contraception after changing her belief from childhood that abortion constituted no harm. "Nor did I dream of questioning it, until in later years, I became thoroughly acquainted with sexual physiology, and comprehended . . . the generation and development of the human germ."[17] Although early feminist abortion opponents were deeply concerned about the threat abortions posed to women's lives and health, concern for developing life was clearly at the core of their beliefs.

Early feminist physicians resisted seemingly immovable social prejudices to pursue RJ for already-born and unborn people alike. Because I can describe only a few, I will focus here on three nineteenth-century women physicians who translated their own culturally disvalued selves and difficult life experiences into the pursuit of RJ for all. They were Maria Elżbieta Zakrzewska, Anandi Gopal Joshi, and Rebecca J. Cole.

Although well-trained as a midwife in Europe, Polish immigrant Maria Elżbieta Zakrzewska could at first only find ill-paid work as a seamstress when she immigrated to the United States. After she graduated from medical school at Case Western Reserve University, she, like her friend Dr. Elizabeth Blackwell, could not find rooms to rent in New York City for her obstetrician-gynecology practice. They were mistaken for abortion providers. The two doctors did not appreciate the confusion. Like Blackwell, who considered it a destruction of life and motherhood, Zakrzewska strongly opposed abortion.

When the two sought to challenge Madame Restelle, New York's most famous abortion provider, they were told to stop because Restelle was a "social necessity" defended by the rich and powerful and therefore beyond any challenge. Zakrzewska continued to challenge abortion through radical measures that made it less of a social necessity. Zakrzewska worked with Blackwell and her sister Emily, also a physician, after they started the New York Infirmary for Women and Children. The first entirely female-staffed US hospital, it was later chartered as a women's medical college. The Infirmary focused on service to the indigent. Elizabeth Cushier, a staff physician and Emily Blackwell's life partner, noted that the Infirmary was at the time the only haven in the city for single pregnant women. Elsewhere, while their babies' fathers were not called to account, single mothers themselves were moralistically deprived of aid before and after they gave birth, and even when they were in labor. Many ended up in prostitution because they had no other means of survival. The Infirmary was up against a widespread prejudice that anyone who helped single mothers was aiding and abetting immorality.

When Zakrzewska moved to Boston and founded the New England Hospital for Women and Children, she made maternity services for the poor and single an integral part of its services, and created the Temporary Infant Asylum. Zakrzewska drew much strength for her prejudice-dismantling, abortion-preventing work from her domestic partnership with Julia A. Sprague, and from their circle of pioneering professional women, many of whom were also lesbian couples. Zakrzewska was also moved by her own vivid memories of living as a poor immigrant herself. Although she eventually had a comfortable home, Zakrzewska never lost her "remarkable insight and sympathy" that allowed her to understand the lives of poor patients "from their own standpoint." She believed that instead of do-gooder charity, "it is *justice* to one another" that "we should cultivate and practice."[18] A suffragist and abolitionist, Zakrzewska called for an end to the sexual double standard. She warned the Moral Education Society of Massachusetts against consigning any women to "a class of *animal women*" who are treated as "legalized merchandise. . . . I say, therefore, that one of the laws of our moral code should be, 'Respect the *woman* in every woman.'"[19]

Grounded in such principles of moral education, female-oriented medical schools like Zakrzewska's could begin, however imperfectly and incompletely, to affirm the struggle for respect toward women and children of color and others of lower social status. Although professionally credentialed healers included few women to begin with, and even fewer women of color, they tended to be graduates of such institutions. For example, Joshi and Cole both graduated from an institution founded in Philadelphia by Quaker abolitionists, the Women's Medical College of Pennsylvania (WMCP).

Joshi, from the Indian state of Maharashtra, was the first Hindu and the first South Asian person to earn a medical degree in the United States, and the first female MD in her home country. As a girl of nine, she was married to a widower twenty years her senior. At fourteen, she birthed her only child. Ten days after delivery, the little boy died. His mother named medical inattention and incompetence as the cause of his death. Under British colonial rule, the social safety net had been shredded to bits, resulting, among other ills, in inadequate healthcare and high infant and maternal mortality rates among the Indian population. Joshi resolved to become a physician herself and spare other mothers and children from such preventable suffering. She dreamed of someday opening a women's medical college in India.

Fortunately, her husband backed her plans, although many in their community, including her own mother, reacted negatively. When Joshi made inquiries about medical education in the United States, she was offered help on the condition that she convert to Christianity. She refused to give up her religion. Because WMCP did not impose this condition, she matriculated there. As she went through the rigors of medical education in a very strange country, she struggled not only with her chronically poor health but the derision heaped on women doctors. Beyond that, even in the supposedly enlightened Anglo circles where she found friendship, she endured relentlessly scornful inspections of her "exotic" appearance and her "heathen" spirituality, including her resolute vegetarianism, an expression of her profound respect for all life.

In her thesis, Joshi reclaimed an ancient and advanced Indian obstetrical tradition that had become lost under colonialism. She described elements of this tradition that she felt still honored "the value of life and health." These include careful daily attentions to protect, "from the time of conception," the intertwined lives, health, and peace of the pregnant woman and the child equally. She also embraces the advice to physicians and midwives "that they are but second hands to Nature . . . in her wise work." Joshi does mention a surgical procedure for dismembering the fetus during labors complicated by tranverse presentation. However, the physician or midwife should first try manually maneuvering the fetus into correct place. If the baby is still alive, the knife should be avoided if possible, although it may "seldom" be necessary.[20] Joshi's embrace of both the pregnant woman and fetus expresses her own personal life experience and broad compassion, as well as Hindu devotion to the sacredness of all lives and its call to refrain from abortion except as a last resort to save the woman's life. Anandi Gopal Joshi never realized her dreams of educating other Indian women in a blend of this ancient wisdom with modern science. Soon after returning home to India, she sickened and died a month short of her twenty-second birthday.

Fortunately, Cole, the second African American woman to achieve a medical degree, had a fifty-year career in which to pursue her own dreams of RJ. Although sparse, the remaining records of her life speak of an enduring and inspiring commitment. After graduating from the Institute for Colored Youth and WMCP, Cole was appointed resident physician at the Blackwell sisters' medical school in New York City. She worked there as a "sanitary visitor" in the homes of indigent families, teaching them about hygiene as well as pre- and postnatal care.

Cole later directed a homeless shelter in Philadelphia. There she started the Women's Directory Center in 1873. The Center's mission was prevention of feticide and infanticide and the evils connected with baby farming by rendering assistance to women in cases of approaching maternity and of desertion or abandonment of mothers, and by aiding magistrates and others entrusted with police powers in preventing or punishing such crimes. It offered indigent women healthcare and legal representation at no cost. Eventually Cole moved to Washington, DC, to become matron at the National Association for the Relief of Destitute Colored Women and Children Home. The Home's annual report for 1900 praises her highly.

Cole also wrote and lectured on public health, even taking on W. E. B. DuBois. He explained the black community's high death rate in terms of individual ignorance about sanitation. Cole, on the other hand, pointed squarely to malpractice on the part of the white medical establishment.

Resistance to Eugenics and Its Lethal "Solutions"

Cole may have been reacting also to the then-ascendant philosophy of eugenics, which perniciously blamed the "defectiveness" of individuals in "inferior" groups for social problems, rather than attending to the structural inequalities these problems were rooted in. Thus, eugenic ideology concluded, the multiplication and even the very existence of the "unfit" must be curbed. During the late nineteenth and through the twentieth century, eugenics resulted in immigration restrictions that ultimately damned some Jews fleeing the Holocaust; laws forbidding interracial unions; laws forbidding people with disabilities to marry; rising persecution of LGBTQ persons; the forced removal of Native American children to boarding schools; the forcing of disabled persons into sexually segregated, poorly run institutions with high death rates from intentional medical neglect; calls for "mercy killing" of the disabled; and of course sterilization abuse. Eugenics also figured in the rising institutionalization and deployment of the death penalty and the incidence and visibility of lynching. The first person in the US to be executed by gas chamber was a Chinese immigrant. The gas chamber was developed by the US government's Chemical Warfare Service and modeled after the "lethal chamber," an 1880s invention for euthanizing abandoned animals with carbonic acid gas.

Although some shied away from it, outright, direct lifetaking "was always an option" for eugenicists, according to Edwin Black. "The lethal chamber, the permission of infant mortality, interference with antenatal life" were privately and publicly touted weapons for the cause.[21] Dr. William Josephus Robinson both performed abortions and recommended chloroform or potassium cyanide gas for the already-born children of the "unfit."[22] Pro-life feminist Mary Meehan examined archival records on the American Civil Liberties Union's early role in urging ethical and legal acceptance of abortion. Meehan convincingly argues that the "gloss of rights and freedom" the ACLU put on abortion quite knowingly served the calculated efforts of "eugenicists and population controllers . . . to suppress the birth rates of poor people and minorities."[23]

During the same time span Meehan studied, from roughly the early 1960s through the early 1970s, there were women of color activists who critiqued abortion in anti-eugenic, anti-population-control terms and in terms of human rights belonging to each individual pregnant woman and fetus. Fannie Lou Hamer was one of the most prophetic voices in this vein. An African American sharecropper from Sunflower County in the Mississippi Delta, Hamer served as secretary for the Student Nonviolent Coordinating Committee, moving spirit for the Mississippi Freedom Democratic Party, and cofounder of the National Women's Political Caucus, among other important social justice roles that sometimes led to attacks on her life. She vocally opposed the Vietnam War and worked for government programs to benefit the poor, especially Head Start.

Hamer openly testified about the incident that propelled her into activism: the act of forced sterilization committed against her in 1961. Such sterilization abuse was so common that it had a name, "Mississippi appendectomy." Hamer and her husband had endured two stillbirths, then adopted two girls, one handicapped by burns, the other the daughter of a single mother who could not care for the child. They had still hoped to add to their family through conception. Hamer channeled her feelings of powerlessness and outrage over this violation of her body and human rights into a vision of nonviolence and social justice for all.[24]

While the importance of the sterilization abuse to Hamer's activism is finally getting the attention it deserves, it is still relatively unknown that she also opposed abortion as an act of lifetaking and reproductive injustice. She passionately believed that if, instead of proffering abortion to their mothers, society gave poor black children a chance, "they might grow up to be Fannie Lou Hamer, or something else."[25] As a delegate to the 1969 White House Conference on Food, Nutrition, and Health, Hamer spent much of her time speaking up against both sterilization abuse and abortion as proposed antidotes to hunger and poverty.

One of her last public deeds as an activist was her expert testimony in a 1973 legal case brought by black single mothers against Sunflower County's segregated black school district. The young women were denied work as schoolteachers because they were bad moral examples for the students. Hamer had financially and morally backed one of the plaintiffs in her college education. Hamer strongly defended single mothers of all races and their children. She spoke of accepting her own daughter Dorothy Jean's nonmarital pregnancy. Dorothy Jean died during a second childbirth because of medical discrimination based on race. Hamer then adopted Dorothy Jean's babies herself. Standing conventional morality on its head, she said of nonmarital pregnancies:

> After these babies are born we are not going to disband these children from their families, because these are other lives, they are—God breathed life into them just like He did into us. And I think that these children have a right to live. And I think that these mothers have a right to support them in a decent way. . . . I think of what would have happened to Virgin Mary if she walked into [the local school], what would have happened if Christ had been born in that school.[26]

Another prophetic voice that deserves a hearing is that of Graciela Olivarez. Olivarez became a founding member of the National Organization for Women, the first woman to graduate from the University of

Notre Dame Law School, and a leader in such groups and agencies as the Urban Coalition, Food for All, the Arizona Office of Economic Opportunity, and the Mexican American Legal Defense Fund. She directed the Community Services Administration during the Carter administration. Olivarez also pioneered in Spanish-language broadcasting, where she had as a young woman found her activist start as host of a call-in "action line" radio program. She quickly realized from this experience that individual problems originate in institutionalized problems and therefore demand collective solutions.

Olivarez brought this consciousness to bear on the issue of abortion. At the 1971 Conferencia de Mujeres por La Raza in Houston, she directly linked the emphasis on virginity for young Latina women and sexual activity for young Latino men to their difficulties with facing the prospect of unplanned pregnancy and guarding against it with contraception. Thus, she pointed out, young women end up having panic-stricken abortions and sustaining a heavy blow to their bodily and mental health. The next year, as vice chair of the Presidential Commission on Population and the American Future, Olivarez registered a strong dissent from other commissioners on abortion, while calling for wide-scale distribution of voluntary contraceptives. She asked, "[What] kind of future [do] we all have to look forward to if men are excused either morally or legally from their participation in the creation of life?" Even more pointedly, she said:

> Many of us have experienced the sting of being "unwanted" by certain segments of our society. . . . Human beings are not returnable items. Every individual has his/her rights, not the least of which is the right to life, whether born or unborn. . . . [Yet] in this affluent nation of ours, pregnant cattle and horses receive better health care than pregnant poor women.[27]

Do these insights of Hamer and Olivarez not ring true today, all these decades later?

Where to Go from Here?

Across the whole spectrum of RJ advocates, this rich herstory can lead to reflection; it is and is not still very much with us. It can present the questions: What to take for the journey, what to leave behind? This herstory can also inspire the sort of rethinking that Andrea Smith asks from other abortion rights supporters. She calls for leaving behind "simplistic analyses of who our political friends and enemies are in the area of reproductive rights. That is, all those who call themselves pro-choice are our political allies while all those who call themselves pro-life are our political enemies."[28]

Whether they do, or would, identify themselves as pro-life feminists, there are already open dissenters from customary pro-choice beliefs within the RJ movement. For example, Alice Skenandore, a Native American midwife and member of SisterSong's Management Circle, talks beautifully about what it is like to be "an anti-abortionist surviving in the pro-choice movement."[29] Quite possibly other dissenters have been pressured away or never thought to join at all. Because of my own take on abortion, it took me many years to realize I myself was already a card-carrying member of the RJ movement. Even before I learned the term "reproductive justice," that is precisely what I sought. Other pro-life feminists have reported similar journeys to this.

So, I call upon reproductive justice activists who support abortion rights—those who have not graciously and generously done so already—to make room for abortion dissenters, whether we go by the name of pro-life feminist, or something else. Please remain ever alert to the possibility that you may find other card-carrying RJ activists, or at the very least sister (if not brother) travelers, among the ranks of those who question or even outright oppose an abortion-rights position in some sense.

Over a century ago, Dr. Maria Elżbieta Zakrzewska (incidentally a religious freethinker) told the Moral Education Association of Massachusetts:

> I fully believe that this world . . . is constantly improving. . . . Yet I feel that we are far from being what we might become if each one of us would carry out fully, all the time, daily and hourly, the precepts of the Golden Rule. In order to attain such a state of perfection, workers are constantly needed who, with deeper insight or stronger conviction or warmer hearts, shall lift the banner high over all our heads, and thus summon followers from all directions.[30]

Even though many members will not agree completely with pro-life feminists, hopefully the RJ movement can welcome us. After all, there are already pro-life feminists and somewhat likeminded activists marching under the banner of reproductive justice. And there are more to be invited in, from all directions, accompanied by the spirits of foremothers and forefathers.

Notes

1. Jennifer Ferguson, "Abortion Issue Is One of Peace," in *Pro-Life Feminism Yesterday and Today, Second Expanded Edition*, ed. Mary Krane Derr, Rachel MacNair, and Linda Naranjo-Huebl (Kansas City, MO: Feminism and Nonviolence Studies Association, 2005), 330–32.

2. Katsi Cook, "Environmental Justice: Woman Is the First Environment," in *Reproductive Justice Briefing Book: A Primer on Reproductive Justice and Social Change*, ed. Rickie Solinger and Loretta J. Ross, Pro-Choice Education Project/SisterSong Women of Color Reproductive Health Collective, last updated 2007, 62, http://protectchoice.org/downloads/Reproductive%20Justice%20Briefing%20Book.pdf.

3. Carol Crossed, "The Law's Role in the Consistent Life Ethic," in *Consistently Opposing Killing: From Abortion to Assisted Suicide, the Death Penalty, and War*, ed. Rachel M. MacNair and Stephen Zunes (Westport, CT: Praeger, 2008), 150.

4. Mary Ann Glendon, *Abortion and Divorce in Western Law: American Failures, European Challenges* (Cambridge, MA: Harvard University Press, 1989), 35.

5. Rickie Solinger, *Wake Up Little Susie: Single Pregnancy and Race before Roe v. Wade* (New York: Routledge, 1992), 206.

6. Andrea Smith. "Beyond Pro-Choice Versus Pro-Life: Women of Color and Reproductive Justice," *NWSA Journal* 17, no. 1 (2005): 123.

7. Glendon, *Abortion and Divorce*, 2.

8. Mary Wollstonecraft, *A Vindication of the Rights of Woman with Strictures on Political and Moral Subjects* (Dublin: James Moore, 1792), 180.

9. Sally Roesch Wagner, *Sisters in Spirit: Haudenosaunee (Iroquois) Influence on Early American Feminists* (Summertown, TN: Native Voices, 2001).

10. Arthur Caswell Parker (Gawasco Waneh), *The Code of Handsome Lake, the Seneca Prophet* (Albany: New York State Museum at Albany, 1913).

11. Matilda Joslyn Gage, *Woman, Church, and State* (Chicago: Charles Kerr, 1893), 43–48.

12. Elizabeth Cady Stanton, Susan B. Anthony, and Matilda Joslyn Gage, eds., *History of Woman Suffrage, Volume One*, (New York: Fowler and Wells, 1881), 466.

13. Sarah Grimké, "Marriage," in *The Female Experience: An American Documentary*, ed. Gerda Lerner (New York: Oxford University Press, 1992), 90–91.

14. Harriet Jacobs, *Incidents in the Life of a Slave Girl, Written by Herself* (Boston: NP, 1861), 91.

15. William Leach, *True Love and Perfect Union* (New York: Basic Books, 1980), 85.

16. Lucinda Banister Chandler, "The Courage to Assert the Right to Her Own Body," in *Pro-Life Feminism Yesterday and Today, Second Expanded Edition*, 81.

17. Eliza Bisbee Duffey, "The Limitation of Offspring," in *The Relations of the Sexes*, Eliza Bisbee Duffey (New York: Wood and Holbrook, 1876).

18. Marie Zakrzewska, *A Woman's Quest: The Life of Marie E. Zakrzewska*, ed. Agnes Vietor (New York: D. Appleton and Company, 1924), 180.

19. Ibid.

20. Anandibai Joshee, *Obstetrics among Aryan Hindoos* (DM thesis, Women's Medical College of Pennsylvania, 1886).

21. Edwin Black, *War against the Weak: Eugenics and America's Campaign to Create a Master Race* (New York: Four Walls Eight Windows, 2003).

22. "Reproductive Wrongs unto Death," in *Pro-Life Feminism: Yesterday and Today*.

23. Mary Meehan, "ACLU v. Unborn Children," pp. 363-370 in *Pro-Life Feminism: Yesterday and Today*, 368.

24. Jennifer Nelson, *Women of Color and the Reproductive Rights Movement* (New York: NYU Press, 2003), 68.

25. Fannie Lou Hamer, quoted in Kay Mills, *This Little Life of Mine: The Life of Fannie Lou Hamer* (New York: Dutton, 1993), 274.

26. Hamer's testimony is excerpted *Pro-Life Feminism: Yesterday and Today*, 206–12.

27. Olivarez's dissent is excerpted *Pro-Life Feminism: Yesterday and Today*, 214–18.

28. Smith, "Beyond Pro-Choice," 132.

29. Alice Skenandore, "An Anti-Abortionist Surviving in the Pro-choice Movement," SisterSong, Summer 2004, http://www.sistersong.net/publications_and_articles/AntiAbortionist_Surviving.pdf.

30. Zakrzewska, *A Woman's Quest*, 420–22.

On Becoming and Being a Mother in Four Movements: An Intergenerational View through a Reproductive Justice Lens

LYNN ROBERTS

I am third in a cycle of black women who became mothers of four children, each of us having two daughters and two sons. Both my daughters had declared their intent to break the cycle, my eldest by having two sons and the younger a daughter. This intertwined herstory of how motherhood, specifically black motherhood, has played out in my family reveals both our glorious triumphs and our significant challenges in overcoming the racism, sexism, classism, violence against women, and plain ignorance we experienced all at once in an immediate, noncompartmentalized, intersectional—as in the personal is *always* political—kind of way. As June Jordan reminds us, "To tell the truth is to become beautiful, to begin to love yourself, value yourself. And that's political, in its most profound way."[1] These are the stories we black womenfolk often hesitate to or dare not talk about in the "mixed company" of our menfolk (it would shame too many, enrage a few, and distance others), let alone with our white sisters (most, but thankfully not all, of whom would miss some of the subtlety and complexity). So we might figure, "what would be the point?" but if we are lucky enough, we do dare to share our truths with other black women and other women of color who, all too often, have their own stories to tell.

The First Movement: My Maternal Grandmother (1930s)

My maternal grandmother, Coretha Flack Lovell, married my grandfather, Walter Raleigh Lovell Sr., when she was twenty-three years old. He was thirteen years her senior and their union would be his second of three marriages. Coretha's mother died when she was a young girl, so with the help of assorted female relatives, Coretha practically raised herself into her young womanhood. Given her modest upbringing, she was considered fortunate to have caught the eye and become the wife of her former teacher and a prominent minister in the African Methodist Episcopal Zion Church. In addition to raising their four children and managing her household responsibilities while her husband traveled the country as a "church builder,"[2] Coretha served on several church and community volunteer boards. On occasion, she hosted a virtual who's who of black intelligentsia and entertainers performing on the Chitlin' Circuit who were unable to receive accommodations elsewhere in the Jim Crow South. Trained from an early age in music and oratory, my mother and her brothers and sister were frequently called upon to perform for the famous guests—including Louis Armstrong and Earl "Fatha" Hines—who passed through their Charlotte home.

In 1951 Coretha learned that her absentee father had died in Los Angeles, and made plans to travel across the country for the funeral. At that time, it was uncommon for women to travel alone without their husbands. On the day she embarked on her journey, my grandfather asked to kiss her goodbye and bit down hard on her lip until it bled. Her oldest son, my uncle Walter, grabbed his father's shotgun and held him at bay until she could safely leave their home. Realizing that it was unsafe for a woman to travel alone cross-country, she dressed in a man's suit and hat and set off for California in her Ford Falcon with her youngest son, my uncle Jesse, in tow. With her child-rearing years nearly over and no interest in returning to a husband who disrespected her, she decided to make a new life in Los Angeles, where she worked as a domestic while studying to become a licensed practical nurse. She eventually returned to Charlotte where she worked as a nurse at the height of the Asian flu epidemic of 1957–1958 and later in rehabilitation services. After divorcing my grandfather, she became a persona non grata within the church community, especially among the other women, but she had discovered a new spiritual community in the Bahá'í Faith while in Los Angeles. Her new faith expanded and reinforced a vision of a world community that upholds the equality of all humankind, irrespective of race, gender, nationality, or class. She continued to dedicate herself to worthy causes like petitioning the local authorities to install a stop sign after several accidents, including a fatal one involving a young child.

I only met my grandmother once during my childhood, and her visit in the summer of 1966 would become one of my fondest memories. She and I shared my single bed with a thin mattress that could be folded up and rolled in or out of a closet upon short notice. This bed had wheels, and in the room I shared with my older sister that made it very convenient for me to pull it closer to her stationary bed whenever I had nightmares and would, to her annoyance, inveigle her to hold my hand under the covers. Until my grandmother's arrival, it had never been used for company. When my grandmother and I slept in my bed together on those hot summer nights, with her feet at my head and mine at hers, I was ever mindful not to toss and turn for fear of kicking her in the chest as I found comfort in the sweet-and-sour smell of her feet. With a simple flourish of a few blueberries, my grandmother lovingly transformed my breakfast cereal into the most heavenly ambrosia, far superior to any box of Lucky Charms I had ever coveted on the grocery shelf. She left with me two gifts: a strong impression of what a spirituality grounded in love and goodness looks like in a living, breathing person and a yellow, hardcover Bahá'í children's prayer book. The cherished talisman was lost years later during a family move, but her loving human spirit was permanently etched upon my five-year-old soul.

Less than a year later my grandmother would die alone in her Charlotte apartment at age sixty-four when an aneurysm burst in her brain. It may have been the result of her untreated pica—a nutritional disease characterized by developmentally inappropriate craving and eating of nonnutritive items such as dirt, clay, starch, and chalk, historically associated with pregnant, poor, and rural women—which I would later learn about while a student at Howard University. My grandmother was known to consume large quantities of cornstarch and blocks of magnesium, even long after she was of child-bearing age. That the medical research on pica and its long-term consequences is rather scant might have something to do with who is most affected by it: poor women of color around the globe and through the ages. Whatever the exact cause of her death, my beloved grandmother did not live to enjoy her retirement and never received any Social Security benefits. Without realizing it at the time, she was the first woman warrior for justice, albeit a quiet one, I had ever met.

The Second Movement: My Mother (1950s–1970s)

More than a decade before that summer visit, my grandmother had tried to discourage my mother, née Constance Garnet Lovell, from marrying my father, Robert Wakefield Roberts; at least not before earning her college degree. Her eldest daughter, my aunt Ida, had previously dropped out of Howard University to marry her college sweetheart. My grandmother considered an education the best insurance against her daughters having to engage in menial work such as cleaning toilets, a job my mother once performed to augment her college scholarships. My grandmother's high aspirations for her daughters were grounded in not wanting either of them to ever be dependent on a man. Convinced that her sons could always find work without an education, or at least join the military, she urged both daughters to earn college degrees and become self-sufficient. To her point, Uncle Walter joined the Marines and later completed a correspondence course in architecture and engineering, and depending on whom I speak to, her younger son, Uncle Jesse, either just attended courses or earned a college degree from UCLA. While still a student at Hollywood High School in Los Angeles, Jesse fathered twin boys who, as infants, became child actors in the 1957 film *Something of Value*. My grandmother was the only one who kept in touch with the young mother and her first grandsons. There is a photo of the twins perched on the lap of a white Santa Claus in my mother's family scrapbook. I may never know the story behind that photo—whether my grandmother took the boys to see Santa or if their mother sent the photo to my grandmother as a thank you for her support or to beseech my uncle for his. What I took away from this photo is that my grandmother claimed them as hers. Knowing that she did not deny them would matter to me when I became a mother and grandmother in nontraditional and socially unaccepted ways.

My parents first met as children when she was nine and he was thirteen—my grandfathers were close friends who worked in the post office while also serving as AME Zion ministers. They met again as young adults, and married in a civil ceremony during her junior year at Howard University in June 1952. According to my mother, their first child, my eldest brother Michael, was conceived on her graduation day in June 1953 and born the following March in Philadelphia, where my mother had gone to stay with her sister-in-law, my aunt Bettyelee, and her husband, Bishop Cameron Chesterfield Alleyne. Bishop Alleyne was a close friend with the famed orator, actor, singer, and freedom fighter Paul Robeson. Indeed, one of our family's most prized possessions is a photo of Robeson holding Michael during a visit that fell somewhere between his travels to Russia.

Racial segregation and discrimination in hospitals were common during this period. The laws were slowly changing in the decade leading up to the landmark *Simkins v. Moses H. Cone Memorial Hospital* case in 1963 that would prohibit segregation of hospitals receiving Medicare funds. Nonetheless, although my mother ultimately delivered all four of her children in hospitals in the nominally integrated North, she was sometimes treated with neglect or such contempt that she might have had similar or even better birth experiences in the more segregated South. It was through my parents' connections to Bishop Alleyne that Dr. Helen Octavia Dickens, the first African American woman admitted to the American College of Surgeons, was chosen as my mother's obstetrician. While Dr. Dickens would later serve a long tenure on the staff of the integrated Woman's Hospital of Philadelphia and as professor emeritus at University of Pennsylvania, in 1954 she was denied admitting privileges to the Woman's Hospital, thus was not able to attend to my mother during the delivery. Instead my mother was forced to self-admit to the hospital where she gave birth to her first born under the gaze of gawking interns. Indeed, because of Dr. Dickens's stellar reputation and dedicated service in the black community, she had barely had enough time to see my mother during her pregnancy (my mother recalls having only one prenatal visit with her), but it was an even greater disappointment for her own doctor to not even be allowed to be present in the delivery room. It would be at another integrated hospital in Pennsylvania, St. Luke's Hospital in Bethlehem, while screaming in pain during a difficult labor prior to my cesarean birth, that my mother vividly recalls a white nurse slapping her harshly in the face and telling her to just be quiet, and further suggesting that she should suffer silently "like a good nigger."[3]

My father had previously interrupted his own studies at Lincoln University to enlist in the Eighty-Second Airborne of the US Army. Upon his discharge in 1954 and at the behest of his father, he became an ordained minister. In 1955 the young family moved to Gettysburg, Pennsylvania, where my father resumed his studies at Lincoln University while serving his first pastorate. Needing to supplement the modest salary provided by the church and with my father focusing on his studies, my mother was turned down for a factory job for having too much education; the owner explained to her that the white women who worked there would be offended if an educated (translate: uppity) black woman was paid more than they were.

Appalled by the meager living conditions provided by the church, my maternal grandfather insisted that my mother and brother temporarily return to Charlotte with him. He appealed to the church leadership to arrange for another assignment for my father, and in 1956 the young family moved to Bethlehem, Pennsylvania, where my father assumed the pastorate of St. John's AME Zion Church. Once again, my father terminated his studies, and ultimately would never complete his degree, despite his eligibility for the GI Bill. The new parsonage had sufficient space, a backyard, and they were now able to afford a washer and dryer with the additional income my father earned as a shipping clerk at the local textile mill. Three more children would follow: my brother Gary in 1957, my sister Pamela in 1958, and then me in 1961, just one year after the first oral contraceptives were approved by the Food and Drug Administration and four years before the *Griswold v. Connecticut* decision established a married couple's right to contraception. With two toddlers still at home, my mother was not prepared to have a fourth child; in fact, none of her pregnancies had been planned. Her only method of contraception was to douche after sex. Emphatic that she never considered an illegal abortion, my mother recalls privately praying for a miscarriage and attempting to naturally abort me by walking up and down stairs and lifting heavy things during her pregnancy, to no avail.

Although many others had applied in the decade before her, my mother was not hired by the Bethlehem Area School District as the first negro teacher until June 1963. That same month, President John F. Kennedy gave his radio and television address "Report to the American People on Civil Rights," proposing that sweeping legislation be drafted to ensure equal rights and protection of all citizens regardless of their race.

Having spent nearly ten years as an at-home mother, she entered the classroom that fall and I would become my mother's first and only child to attend preschool. This was to the relief of my grandmother, who, according to family folklore, had chastised my mother for, in her mind, not making better use of her education, saying, "I did not work hard to send you to college to have all these babies." My grandmother might have been projecting her own regret that her education was interrupted by an early marriage and child-rearing, and it might also have been a reflection of her increasing awareness and support of women's rights as she embraced her new religion.

In the year 1964 a lot was happening nationally, locally, and within my family. The nation was still healing from the assassination of President Kennedy, and just as Bob Dylan declared with his epic album *The Times They Are A-Changin'*, the newly sworn-in President Lyndon B. Johnson signed the most sweeping civil rights legislation since Reconstruction into law. By that time, both my parents had become significant community leaders in the Lehigh Valley. It was in 1964 that the Bethlehem US Junior Chamber honored my father by naming him "Young Man of the Year" for his strong record of community service and civic engagement. He cofounded the Bethlehem Community Civic League, a multiracial and interfaith organization that strove to advance equal opportunity and mobilized to desegregate housing and investigate discriminatory hiring and advancement practices within Bethlehem Steel, one of the most significant employers in the area, indeed the nation.

There were other significant events that year. The first Christmas I can recall was spent with virtual strangers. In what can only be described as a desperate act fueled by the despair of learning that my father was having an affair with a white woman and she was allegedly pregnant with his child, my mother deliberately turned the gas stove to full blast on Christmas Eve in an attempt to end her life and those of her four children. Fortunately, my father returned home in time, and my mother was subsequently institutionalized in the local state psychiatric hospital for the holidays while my siblings and I were dispersed to relatives and, in my case, the mercy of my father's friends. These events would be replayed again and again in arguments between my parents over the course of their marriage, and I would string together fragments suggesting that either the "other woman" was planted by the FBI to disrupt my parents' marriage and derail their activism (my mother's preferred version) or that the affair was my father's only recourse when my mother's attention was increasingly devoted to her career and the care of her children (my father's preferred version). Neither explanation—my mother's quite plausible conspiracy theory nor my father's likely self-serving rationalization—was pleasing to my childhood ears, but both would inform my understanding of how systemic racism and patriarchy intersected and combusted in the lived experience of our family.

After my mother's "treatment and recovery" at Allentown State Hospital, my parents reconciled enough to purchase a new home and move us from a working-class, ethnically mixed neighborhood on the south side of Bethlehem to an all-white, newly annexed suburb across town. I do not believe my mother was ever treated, at least not with compassionate care, at this hospital, a foreboding institution known then for its abuses. And how can someone ever fully recover from the trauma of being led to a despair deep enough to want to end their life and those of their children? To my knowledge, the white woman and the alleged love child were never seen nor heard from again—she may have gotten an illegal abortion with the help of my parents' friends. In other words, she disappeared as quickly as she had arrived; the damage to my parents' marriage was done and the sanctity of our family forever changed. During the summer of my beloved grandmother's visit in 1966, she went for a ride with my father in his sporty little red MG. According to my mother, my grandmother, who was not known for raising her voice, cautioned my father while holding a pot of hot grits in her hand, "If you don't want her, then I will take her with me!" Privately, she told my mother, "If you have elected to stay with him, then learn to keep your mouth shut!" Based on my observations during wakeful nightly vigils spent listening at their bedroom door, my mother never learned nor opted to do that.

I must have heard every accusation, every shout, every whisper exchanged between them. I witnessed domestic violence on multiple levels and in both directions: from the physical abuse of my father holding his .32 revolver to my mother's head and playing Russian Roulette or my mother throwing an entire bottle of rubbing alcohol in my father's face to the emotional abuse of my mother belittling my father's sexual prowess or my father calling my mother a whore and denying one of my brothers was his. There were the daily rituals of presenting to the outside world that everything was all right in our home by camouflaging my mother's physical bruises with stylish clothes and drowning her emotional ones with alcohol, and redirecting my father's anger to the indulgence of cigarettes and flashy sports cars and resolving his educational insecurities with avid model railroad and electronics hobbies. Theirs became a loveless, thankless marriage preserved at high costs to both of them, and for the sake of us children.

With all the challenges in their marital lives, my parents continued to thrive in their respective professions, at times seemingly in competition with each other. My mother became a highly regarded and respected teacher and sang in the esteemed Bach choir. My father left his pastorate shortly after his father's death to become the executive director of the local War on Poverty programs for the Lehigh Valley, and later headed the Pennsylvania Council of Farmworkers in Harrisburg and the Afro American Cultural Center in Allentown.

It would be another decade before my mother heeded her mother's words, and like her mother before her, she eventually opted, at my urging, to leave my father, her home, and her job. I was sixteen and the last of her children still living at home. I thought it was the best move for her to make at that time. I told her that I feared for her safety; if she did not leave I was certain it would be only a matter of time before someone got seriously hurt, perhaps even killed. She asked me if I wanted to come with her, but I chose to stay with my father. I cannot say my motives were all pure. My mother had been the strict disciplinarian in our home, in stark contrast to the permissive parenting style of my father. I was dating a young man three years older than me at the time, and like many teens, I often sought opportunities to be away from my mother's constant gaze. Spending time with friends and a boyfriend provided refuge from my parents' loveless and often volatile marriage and emptying nest. I also knew my father, with whom I had always been close, would need someone to keep him company—we could not both leave him. Besides, my mother had met someone, a soft-spoken gentleman who treated her well. After years of verbal, emotional, and physical abuse, she confided in me that she had fallen in love, and it was the first time I had *ever* seen her happy. She left our home in the midst of a teachers' strike in fall 1977, cashed in her retirement, and moved to Washington, DC, where she stayed with an aunt. She never returned to our home.

My mother was not only fleeing the anguish of a very troubled marriage; she was also escaping a legacy of institutional racism that had always simmered beneath the surface during her years in the Bethlehem Area School District. As she told an interviewer at an NAACP banquet honoring her in 2009, "It was not easy being a token!" It all bubbled up in a pivotal moment when my mother overheard her immediate colleague refer to her as "that n-word" after a faculty meeting in which my mother was defending a bright black female student's right to remain in the classroom despite a tendency to get into physical and verbal fights with teachers and other students. In an era when public school teachers across the nation were increasingly lamenting their need to become "social workers in the classroom," my mother earned her master's degree in guidance just so that she could be a better advocate for the black and brown students like this unapologetically black girl named Penny. Feeling defeated at work and at home, it was as if my mother surrendered and lost any will to fight the twin oppressions of racism and sexism that permeated her world and denied her dignity. She would never return to the classroom.

The Third Movement: Me, Myself, and I (1970s–Present)

As a mother, I have had four movements of my own, which I will call submovements.

I. Preamble to Motherhood

The first leg of my maternal journey began even before I became a mother during my adolescent years in the Lehigh Valley. When I was seven years old, just before my beloved grandmother died, I sacrificed the innocence of my childhood to become the only one of my siblings to keep vigil at my parents' door as they battled each other every night. I thought if I kept watch, they would not say or do anything to hurt each other. I heard and saw things no child should be exposed to at such a tender age. I became a confidante to both my parents—they told me what they could not tell each other. I grew up much too quickly and became a parentified child, a psychological term I later learned about in college. Between the ages of nine and eleven, I served as a "parent helper" for two preschool-aged girls in the neighborhood whose mother, a stay-at-home white woman, was overwhelmed with their care. Like my brother had done for me, I taught the girls to speak clearly and to read. So even before I became a parent, myself, I often acted in loco parentis to others. The extent to which black children are socialized at young ages to assume adult roles and responsibilities has been well documented, but few have theorized about the root causes of this more explicitly than Joy DeGruy:

> Post Traumatic Slave Syndrome (PTSS) is a condition that exists when a population has experienced multigenerational trauma resulting from centuries of slavery and continues to experience oppression and institutionalized racism today. Added to this condition is a belief (real or imagined) that the benefits of the society in which they live are not accessible to them.[4]

II. Becoming a Teen Mom (1979–1988)

After my mother's departure/escape to Washington, DC, my father sold our house and the two of us resettled into a two-bedroom apartment on the west side of town, within walking distance of the same state psychiatric hospital where my mother had her already wounded spirit broken. At fifteen, I took my first job working the seven-to-three shift at a nursing home every Saturday and Sunday. I also cleaned the apartment, did the grocery shopping, and cooked meals. My father was the executive director of a popular cultural center in nearby Allentown that held dances until 2:00 a.m. every Saturday night, and this is where I met and fell hard for Donald, a young man who exemplified everything both my parents might have warned me against had they been paying closer attention. Ever since his first heart attack at age forty-eight, my father was beset with medical problems, including prostate cancer and complications from an untreated military injury that resulted in a colostomy. Whenever my father was hospitalized, which was frequently, I took responsibility for managing the household and ensuring the bills were paid on time. I felt grown and, in many respects, I was. I would later come to realize that I should not have had that much freedom or responsibility and that I surely could have used a lot more guidance from the adults in my life.

I felt entitled to explore the rights and privileges of adulthood, including driving a sporty car (my father's red MG now replaced with a gold Pontiac Trans Am) and the pleasures of sex with my boyfriend, who, being three years older than me, could already be considered an adult. Unfortunately, my junior high sex education was limited to *Cosmopolitan* and the minimally mandated instruction from a male health teacher who was also my mother's colleague so, naturally, I assumed any probing questions I asked in class would be reported to her. I also knew about Planned Parenthood, as did all of my close girlfriends in high school—all of whom, by that time, were black and Latina—so we educated ourselves and sought services about sex and birth control and, when necessary, abortion.

Despite the abrupt end of my childhood innocence, my parents also managed to sprinkle the joys of learning, a passion for music and the arts, and their commitment to social justice and service on behalf of others throughout my childhood. This sense of social justice was one of several factors that drew me to the young man who would become the father of my first child. First and foremost, I was drawn to his undeniably black masculine sex appeal (think Idris Elba at eighteen) that sparked immediate chemistry the moment he spotted me on the dance floor. When I discovered he was one of ten children born into an extended family of former migrant farm workers who had "settled out of the stream" in the Lehigh Valley, I recognized him and his people as the same folks my parents were always defending. I fell for him hard and quickly and also slowly fell out of love with school as the center of my adolescent world.

By the time I entered high school in 1976, my interest in being educated exclusively by white teachers had already waned, but as someone who had always made the honor roll, I quickly lost my respect for any and all school systems that ignored or passed along mostly black and Latino students like my boyfriend, Donald, who at eighteen could barely read or write. Any prior sense I had of my parents' and my suffering as black people in the United States paled in comparison to what I witnessed Donald's family experience being black *and* poor. I saw no value in living a black middle-class life in a predominantly white community that did not accept us, however accomplished we were. If my mother with all her degrees could be seen as "that n-word," then what was the point of aspiring for anything in a system that did not value black people?

It would be two years of dating with heavy making out before Donald and I became sexually active. He was not my first boyfriend, but he was my first lover. I was not his. I never felt pressured to have sex before I was ready, but when my father was hospitalized for long periods of time, it was convenient and comforting to have him spend the night. I was clear that I did not want to use birth control, the pill, for fear that it would harm my body, and condoms were not readily accessible nor any more popular with young males in the years before HIV/AIDS than they are today. I felt confident I knew when I was ovulating and tried to time our intercourse accordingly or at least immediately after my period ended.

By my seventeenth birthday in July before my senior year of high school, we were pregnant. I kept this a secret for five months before my family found out and before receiving any prenatal care. During that time, Donald and I discussed our options. He was adamant about not wanting me to have an abortion. Most of the time, I was scared, confused, and alone. I sometimes spent hours in the tub and contemplated ways to self-abort. I avoided going to Planned Parenthood myself although I had accompanied girlfriends who had the procedure. I continued to work every weekend at the nursing home, which involved lifting patients, some of whom were much heavier than I was. One day I experienced a bout of morning sickness at school and went to the nurse's office. My father was called and when they could not determine what was wrong with me, I was sent home with him. To this day, I am not sure if the school nurse suspected I was pregnant, but I was certain my father was clueless. That would be my only contact with a medical professional until I was sent to live with my mother in DC—a decision made quickly by my parents as soon as my father discovered I was pregnant. It also relieved me being pregnant in the community where I expected to be shamed and ostracized like other young, unwed pregnant girls had been. By the time I was first seen by a doctor I was past twenty-six weeks. An abortion was no longer an option, and my mother briefly explored the possibility of sending me to a home "for unwed mothers" where I could give birth and then place the child for adoption. I felt like I had brought shame to the family and she wanted me to be hidden away so no one else had to know this ever happened. Being separated from Donald left me with mixed feelings of anger, abandonment, and hurt as I realized that this was my problem and he was not there to form a united front with me, but also some relief that he could not interfere with any decision I made on my own. In short, I was an emotional mess and I did not have any one to talk to about it.

Although her disappointment was palpable, my mom provided support the best way she knew how. She connected me to prenatal healthcare and social services and enrolled me in the neighborhood high school where I arrived with enough credits to graduate. I quickly learned what it meant to be regarded as what Joseph A. Califano Jr., then Secretary of Health, Education, and Welfare, called "one of the most serious and complex social problems facing our nation."[5] In March 1979, less than one month before my daughter was born, a report appeared in the Congressional Research Quarterly (CRQ) declaring teen pregnancy an epidemic with dire consequences:

> The birth of a child usually is an occasion of great joy. But for thousands of teenagers, especially those who are unmarried, childbirth can usher in a dismal future of unemployment, poverty, welfare dependency, emotional stress and health problems for mother and child. "The girl who has an illegitimate child at the age of 16 suddenly has 90 percent of her life's script written for her," population expert Arthur A. Campbell has written. "Her choices are few and most of them are bad."[6]

Prior to this CRQ report, the Carter administration had previously convened a task force to explore the problem of teenage pregnancy and introduced legislation in response to concerns that teen parents and their babies were at high risk for pregnancy and birth complications, dropping out of school, facing unemployment, and being a long-term burden to tax payers. This political rhetoric has continued to this day.

Of course, I was unaware of these reports or their implications at the time, but I saw the news and magazine headlines on grocery store racks, and heard the whispers and felt the stares as I traversed the corridors at school or sat in waiting rooms without a ring on my finger, and heard the deafening silence of my family members. The one solace I found was in a classroom at Eastern High School with other pregnant and parenting mothers and a supportive teacher—a black woman—who did not shame, blame, or demonize us as "babies having babies" but rather treated us as young women becoming mothers in need of a little help. I made two friends in the class, another pregnant student named Jackie and her friend Mark, who voluntarily took the class to show his solidarity for her and other girls in our "situation." They formed a united front and became my shield in the cafeteria at lunchtime and whenever I walked the stairwells—where rumor had it pregnant girls had been intentionally pushed. Their friendship made up for the lonely nights spent wondering how painful the labor pains would be, or the stress of being snowbound for a week after an unprecedented blizzard, or the massive task of figuring out the future. Nothing quite prepared me for what happened when I awoke at 5:35 a.m. on April 9 with my first labor pains. After describing what I felt to my mother, she determined this was it and called my obstetrician's answering service as I got showered and dressed. She drove me to Howard University Hospital, where, after I was examined, the nurse told her she could go on to work and they would monitor me and call her as things progressed. I spent the next several hours on a gurney in a hallway waiting for an X-ray to ascertain my pelvis size to determine if I would require a C-section because the baby was too large. My attending physician, Dr. Lennox Westney, was also the Chief of Obstetrics and considered an expert on high-risk pregnancies at a time when DC had one of the highest infant mortality rates in the country. Apparently no one considered that a first-time mother (of any age!) might benefit from having someone at her bedside before going into major surgery. Exactly ten hours after my early morning wake-up call, my daughter was delivered by C-section, but I would not get to see or hold her for another twenty-four hours due to a mild fever. I was not greeted by a lactation specialist extoling the benefits of and providing instruction on breastfeeding. Instead, I was given a shot of something to stop my lactation and samples and coupons for infant formula. As a young patient, I was expected to accept whatever was done to me without question. I recall being disappointed that my doctor performed a vertical incision on my abdomen instead of the more common horizontal cut along the pubic area, known as the "bikini-cut" most favored by young women. I suspected his choice of incision might have been a paternalistic way to discourage me from baring my midriff in public, and thus controlling my body and sexual expression rather than a medical necessity. While I was thrilled to be treated by a black doctor in a historically black college and university (HBCU) hospital predominantly staffed by black people, I did not escape the patriarchal norms of the medical profession.

Patriarchy would also hit me closer to home. Donald wanted to get married and for me to move back to the Lehigh Valley. When I informed him I had plans to go to college, he was taken aback. He had no framework to conceive that my going to college would be preferable to being married and taken care of by my man "like a queen." Unlike my own and those of most others in his extended family, Donald's parents were still married although they struggled, through thick and thin, to take care of all ten of their children without ever relying on welfare. I had no framework with which to conceive being a kept woman and not pursuing a fulfilling career even while raising a family. All the women in my family worked outside of the home, with the exception of my paternal grandmother, who had raised seven children, and one of my aunts who married a dentist but did not have any children. We had reached an impasse and would never speak about this again.

When I tried to call Donald to share the news that our daughter was born, I learned he was in jail and I was heartbroken. I had known that he smoked weed, but it was not something he did when we were together. I admired him because he was always working, taking any construction job he could find as an unskilled day laborer with the equivalent of a third-grade education. It was a disappointment, but not surprising, that he was supplementing his sporadic income by selling weed.

My daughter and I were discharged on Easter morning, and I spent those early days applying all I had learned about parenting a newborn from my teacher at school and guidance from my mom. I found a babysitter in the neighborhood from the bulletin board in the local AME Zion Church, and three weeks later I returned to school, and graduated with honors and plans to enter American University as a business major in the fall. These plans changed at summer's end upon realizing that I was not prepared to leave my daughter to focus on school full-time. I requested a deferral at American and became a stay-at-home mom while receiving a modest (since I lived with my mom) welfare check. During that period I was recruited to participate in a research study on teen parents conducted by Howard University, having been identified through my hospital record, and I agreed out of curiosity and for the stipend. During the interview, I was asked all kinds of questions that I would eventually learn were measuring my self-esteem, locus of control, and self-efficacy related to my sexual behaviors, reproductive health, and family life. By the end of the interview I was intrigued enough to ask the graduate student about her program of study and decided to apply to their undergraduate program in human development. I was accepted and enrolled the next fall.

I arrived on Howard's campus excited to be in a stimulating learning environment that centered blackness for the very first time and proud to be the third generation in my family to attend a revered HBCU. This is also where I first became formally radicalized. I learned from fellow students and scholars in the Pan-African movements sweeping the country and globe. My reproductive justice lens developed under the tutelage and mentorship of radical black women scholars like social anthropologist Beverlee Bruce, a human rights advocate who later served as chair of the International Women's Rescue Committee; gerontologist Jacqueline Johnson Jackson, who coined the term "ethnogerontology" and with a joint appointment at Duke flew in weekly to teach us about black aging; and I did my work-study assignment as an assistant to child psychologist Ura Jean Oyemade, chair of the Department of Human Development and principal investigator in the teen-parent study in which I was first a subject and later ended up coding the data.

As a commuter student with a toddler, I was very focused on my studies but also found time to make a few friends and occasionally date. For the most part, I was enjoying my college experience up until the time I was raped during my senior year. I could say he was an acquaintance, but he was really a stranger. We met one afternoon in the student center and he invited me on a date that evening to hear some jazz. After we left the club, he drove me to his apartment where he locked the door behind us, opened up a sofa bed in his living room, and without either of us saying a word, no kissing, no foreplay, we had sex. I was terrified to say no since I had no viable means of escape. Afterward, he closed up the couch and drove me home as if nothing had ever happened. I never told my mother for fear she would not believe me or blame me for going out on a date with someone I had just met, for not resisting, for not keeping my legs shut, for everything! I showered and crawled into the bed I shared with my daughter. The stranger had not used a condom, and since I did not have my diaphragm with me, I spent the next weeks waiting and praying my period would come. Thankfully, it did.

I graduated magna cum laude and applied to several graduate schools because with my love of learning reignited, I wanted my independence and thought having a graduate degree would increase my chances, and knew I needed to leave my mother's home and to raise my daughter on my own terms. I still needed her support, but I realized if I stayed in her home, I would be stifled and prevented from living the life I wanted for myself and for my daughter. When I went to the DC welfare office to have my case closed, my white caseworker was incredulous upon learning I was heading to Cornell University. He said to me, "I didn't know you could do that!" While there were no prohibitions (like "workfare") against attending college while on welfare, there were also few incentives and no caseworker had ever encouraged me to do so. Indeed, I had to learn about my welfare rights by taking classes in public policy and administration where we analyzed how Aid to Families with Dependent Children (AFDC) went from being an entitlement program for the deserving widows and children of white war veterans to a punitive means-tested program for unwed mothers and children falsely presumed to be black, lazy, and unworthy. I considered my diploma from Howard and my scholarship to Cornell as a small victory in the War against the Poor that had been waging as the meager gains of the War on Poverty were being replaced by Reagonomics. Becoming a teen mother *and* getting my radical black education at Howard had saved me from a life of mediocrity and despair that engulfed me as a result of the racism in the Lehigh Valley. These were the two things I knew could not be taken away from me as I prepared to leave the oasis of the "Chocolate City" for another enclave of whiteness in Ithaca, New York.

III. Becoming a Married Mother with Children (1988–2000)

During my first year at Cornell, my daughter and I lived on campus in student family housing where we were warmly embraced by an international community of mostly married students with children who supported each other with childcare and potluck dinners. I originally went to Cornell to get a master's degree and received a tuition scholarship and living stipend for my first year. The summer afterward I worked as a research assistant, but had no clue how I could continue to pay for my studies in the fall. I quickly enrolled in an MS/PhD program after learning from one of my black professors that there was funding available. Even with a fellowship, it was a challenge to make ends meet while raising my daughter. I applied for Section 8 and moved into an off-campus apartment. It was in Ithaca that I became immersed in a vibrant Bahá'i community and bonded with a fellow graduate student who was also a single parent with a young daughter.

It was also in Ithaca that I met and married my husband. Chris was getting his master's in healthcare administration and we were both part of the same social circle. Our first date was a picnic with my daughter during which he made clear his desire to be married and have a family. Eventually we became lovers, but I was still more interested in my studies than marriage, although he provided a lot of practical and financial support during times when having an alcoholic parent (even at a distance) became emotionally draining. When I spent weeks living in a migrant farm labor camp on the border of Canada to collect data for my dissertation, he stepped up to help care for my daughter in my absence. Despite his awkwardness with parenting, his consistency in being there for the two of us eventually wore me down and we easily agreed on a few core principles of marriage: I would not change my last name, we would both pursue careers of our choosing, and we would share equally in all aspects of rearing children and household responsibilities. To my mother's chagrin and against my beloved late grandmother's advice, we got married on a beautiful day in June 1988 overlooking Cayuga Lake when I was ABD (all but dissertation)—in other words, *before* completing my doctoral degree. We moved to New York City where he had already landed a job. We were what could be described in more ways than one a blended family comprised of a third-generation African American Baha'i, a brilliant free-spirited nine-year-old daughter, and a self-described white Irish-Scottish Protestant with agnostic tendencies.

All the while, my eldest brother, Michael, was dying of HIV/AIDS in an era when people did not live long past their diagnosis. I got a job as a research interviewer on an NIH-funded study on HIV and fertility decision-making where I learned first-hand that women were impacted by HIV/AIDS in ways that were not being presented to the general public. I became immersed in the fight against AIDS, which led to a job with the state Department of Health coordinating HIV-prevention and support programs for women and youth. When my brother died of AIDS complications in January 1990 on the eve of his thirty-sixth birthday, I had lost my early protector, my first teacher, so I channeled my grief into completing my dissertation—an ethnographic study of migrant farm-worker families in upstate New York—and earned my doctorate exactly one year later on the anniversary of his death.

My privilege of earning an Ivy-League doctoral degree in human service studies and my exposure to the inner workings of the government and not-for-profit worlds fast-tracked me to an opportunity that I could not resist. At the recommendation of a former boss, I was invited to become the director of a new program in Harlem to support women and families impacted by the crack cocaine epidemic that had gripped impoverished black and brown neighborhoods of New York, the same communities who were rapidly dying from the stigma and neglect that accompanied HIV/AIDS. In the First Steps program, we created an oasis for mothers, their children, their partners (both men and women), and sometimes their parents to heal and grow together. As an outpatient drug treatment program licensed by the state and funded by the city welfare agency, we provided individual and group counseling that we augmented with home visits, case management and a full range of supportive services. Our staff of eighteen women and men, queer and straight, from across the African- and Latin-descended diaspora were carefully chosen to reflect, but more importantly embrace, the families we served and protected. While the mainstream media was busy demonizing mothers and labeling their children "crack babies," we were busy engaging in the revolutionary act of "mothering—creating, nurturing, affirming, and supporting life" as described most recently and fiercely by Alexis Pauline Gumbs, China Martens, and Mai'a Williams in their book *Revolutionary Mothering*.

Between 1990 and 1995, First Steps and nineteen other programs collectively known as the Family Rehabilitation Program (FRP) spread throughout NYC neighborhoods (there were five in Harlem alone). They had been on the budget chopping block each year during the David Dinkins administration, but were spared through the advocacy of then NYC Councilwoman C. Virginia Fields and Manhattan Borough President Ruth Messinger, our patron godmothers. Within one year of Rudolph Guliani's first term as mayor, the city funding was cut entirely from several programs, including First Steps, despite mounting evidence that these programs not only preserved families but also saved money. All eighteen staff members and I were without jobs, but more tragically, fifty-five Harlem families and many more citywide were left without a safe harbor. Refusing to close our doors without a celebration, we gathered and raised the roof of Riverside Church in honor of *all* the families who had taken their first steps to recovery with us. To my knowledge, there has not been a city initiative since FRP that centers low-income black and Latina women and their families and provided support rather than punishment for their drug use.

Three years prior to the closing of First Steps, Chris and I contemplated whether to have more children. Our teenage daughter was increasingly independent and had a social life that rivaled the two of us combined, so we decided to refill our emptying nest. Sadly, my first and only planned pregnancy ended prematurely as the result of an ectopic pregnancy that required two surgeries. While recovering we made the decision to adopt, and before the child we had conceived would have been born, we welcomed our first chosen child, a two-and-a-half-year-old boy, to our family. Two years later we would welcome our second chosen child, a four-year-old girl, who was the same age as our son. They were both removed from the care of their birth mothers due to substance use and alleged neglect. Our son's birth mother was using multiple substances during her pregnancy and cared for him for his first five months while living in a shelter. Our daughter's birth mother used cocaine while parenting her and an older sister and was also living with HIV/AIDS. She lost her parental rights, and while she was engaged in choosing adoptive parents for both her daughters, the sisters were separated because the state agency reasoned that the older girl was acting as a parentified child by caring for her sister. The agency placed our daughter in foster care and the older sister was placed with members of their birth mom's church family. The adoptive mother chosen by our daughter's birth mom changed her mind just weeks after the placement. Our daughter's birth mom died shortly after our adoption was completed and the only knowledge she has of her birth mom are the stories passed on by her older sister. Both our children's birth moms reflect the stories of the countless women programs like First Steps were designed to help. For far too many of them, their stories will never be told.

IV. Becoming a Divorced Mother with Children (2000–present)

Chris and I did not have a perfect marriage, but it was working up until I no longer felt he supported me as a mother. Parenting our three children together had always presented challenges to us. Our eldest daughter never fully embraced Chris as her stepfather, and when she was twelve, she told me she wanted to know her father. I found a phone number for Donald's mother in an old address book and she was able to connect me with his family. He was married with two children and a stepson. I reached out to his wife, and she was very receptive to having our daughter visit for family reunions and took her and her half siblings to visit their father who was incarcerated in a Pennsylvania state prison. As her relationship with her father was rekindled, albeit from behind bars, the distance between her and Chris only widened. Chris placed all of his energies into being a father to our son, but his approach was markedly different than mine.

Our chosen children each grappled differently with being separated from their birth families. Our son had no interest in knowing his birth siblings (all of whom were being raised by their paternal grandparents) while our younger daughter delighted in having regular visits with her birth sister. We went through a brief honeymoon period with each of them, but eventually the signs of primal loss manifested in behaviors that school psychologists and other therapists were quick to label as "oppositional defiance," and, for our son, the catch-all diagnosis of the decade, ADHD. Chris and I could not agree on the best approach to parenting or treatment; he was a permissive parent and more comfortable with pharmaceutical cures whereas I preferred to ride it out with firm but loving discipline and talk and play therapy as needed. The joys of parenting far outweighed any of the challenges, but I was not prepared for the toll it would take on our marriage to battle each other in addition to the various systems that intersected our children's lives.

When our eldest daughter was halfway through her senior year of high school, Chris made the decision to get a vasectomy—our nest was full— and the surgery was scheduled for early March, after Valentine's Day. As it turned out, we were too late. I discovered we were pregnant in February. Although it was unplanned, I wanted to have this child for several reasons: unlike with my first pregnancy, I had the means to support a child; I was older and more prepared as a parent; and being married, I looked forward to sharing the experience of pregnancy and childbirth with a supportive partner and without the societal shame. Initially, Chris assured me that he would support whatever decision I made, but once I made it, it was evident that he did not want to have *this* child as much as he had wanted the pregnancy we lost five years earlier. He did not think we could afford the expense of caring for an infant while sending our daughter off to college, and was concerned that our two chosen children would be negatively impacted by our having another child, especially a birth child. While I shared some of his concerns, I wanted to continue this pregnancy. Despite his feeble attempts to be supportive, my husband of nearly ten years was emotionally absent the entire pregnancy, including the delivery. For the second time, I had an unplanned pregnancy and still went through it alone. I was devastated, and on top of all the other challenges of our raising a family together, I could not forgive him for that. It was the beginning of the end of our marriage.

My only consolation was that my older sister was pregnant at the same time with twins that she and her husband had gone to great lengths and tremendous debt to conceive through in vitro fertilization (IVF). It was their second IVF pregnancy; my first nephew was born the same summer we adopted our son. Black women like my sister who experience infertility are seldom discussed in the context of reproductive technology, yet they, too, can experience shame and disappointment within themselves and their families and often suffer in silence. In the end, my sister and I have both raised children who are not biologically related to us, albeit under different circumstances, different choices.

The Fourth Movement: My Daughters (2002–present)

Both of my daughters are now mothers, and between the two of them I have been blessed with two grandsons and two granddaughters (the cycle resumed). My daughters have become pregnant and mothers in both planned and unplanned ways, with and without the support of partners, and each of them for varying reasons considered the reproductive choices before them: to have an abortion, to continue their pregnancy, to place a child for adoption, or to become a stepparent. During each of their decisions and beyond, I have done my best to be the supportive parent I wish I had had when I was younger, and do not want anyone else (including the state) to interfere with the choices that are theirs and theirs alone to make. While their choices may not have been as constrained as those of my grandmother, my mother, my sister, nor myself, each generation continues to face significant obstacles to reproductive justice. With both of them coming of age in New Jersey and one now living in Maryland, neither of my daughters has had to worry about having access to a safe and legal abortion unlike their counterparts in numerous states across this country. Had the Affordable Care Act that extended my health insurance coverage to my twenty-something children not been passed and upheld, it is likely that one of my daughters would have died during her pregnancy as a result of a gestational condition known as HELLP syndrome that she developed without any warning. Despite these modest gains in public policy and their middle-class privilege, both daughters have had to struggle with choosing between childcare and making ends meet (one daughter's partner gave up his full-time job while she worked because they could not afford day care, while the other daughter was fired twice from part-time jobs because she did not have a reliable source of day care); with having medical procedures delayed (a preferred private gynecologist has a six-month wait for a primary care nonemergency appointment) or denied due to insurance gaps (our local Planned Parenthood in New Jersey does not charge a copay for a pap smear exam but requires Medicaid patients to pay two hundred dollars for the lab kit); and with restricted or coercive contraceptive access (one daughter experienced tremendous pain with an IUD, but her complaints were ignored and she had to change doctors in order to have it removed).

Across all four generations of motherhood in my family, black women have had to struggle to become mothers, to not become mothers, to mother the children we birthed, to mother the children other mothers were denied their right to mother, and to mother other mothers. I share our stories as testimony to our individual and collective strength and perseverance, our resistance, and to prepare a way forward and toward reproductive justice for *all* of us who mother whether it be our own or someone else's child, each other, or ourselves.

Notes

1. June Jordan, *Some of Us Did Not Die: New and Selected Essays of June Jordan* (New York: Basic Books, 2002), 280.
2. A church builder is a pastor who is skilled at fundraising to have new churches built, often by giving rousing sermons that inspired congregations to dig deep and often into their pockets, and is designated by the church leadership to travel to various communities for this specific purpose.
3. Constance Garnet Lovell, in conversation with the author, April 2014 and August 2016.
4. Joy DeGruy, *Post Traumatic Slave Syndrome: America's Legacy of Enduring Injury and Healing* (Portland, OR: Uptone Press, 2005), 125.
5. Alan Guttmacher Institute et al., *11 Million Teenagers: What Can Be Done About the Epidemic of Adolescent Pregnancies in the United States* (New York: Alan Guttmacher Institute, 1976).
6. Sandra Stencel, "Teenage pregnancy," *Editorial Research Reports 1979 (Vol. 1)* (Washington, DC: CQ Press, 1979), http://library.cqpress.com/cqresearcher/document.php?id=cqresrre1979032300.

Moving SisterSong Forward

MONICA SIMPSON

When SisterSong was founded in 1997 by sixteen women of color organizations and radical mothers, we knew we had the power to make history with fierce determination, hard-fought unity, and revolutionary vision for a better future for our communities and families. SisterSong founding mothers were from four ethnic communities of color, urban and rural locations, and of various ages, gender identities, and sexual preferences. Some were pro-choice while others were pro-life, and they worked on a variety of reproductive health and rights issues as they built the national collective to organize and represent the voices of women of color.

I'm proud to be the third formal leader of SisterSong, following in the footsteps of Laura Jiménez and Loretta J. Ross. We stand on the shoulders of Luz Rodriguez and Reena Marcelo, who dreamed that women of color could and would build a powerful movement for reproductive justice. I want to tell my story so that you can understand that we offer a sisterhood, a home, and an opportunity for those who always resist injustice and oppression and believe we are stronger together. In SisterSong, we don't all sing the same song; we sing our individual songs in harmony with each other.

I knew from the first day I pulled into the driveway of what I now know as the Mother House that I was home. I will never forget the feeling when I walked into the conference room and saw three beautiful women of color waiting to interview me. I had been organizing professionally for well over a decade before coming to SisterSong, and not once had I worked for an organization led by a woman or person of color.

Ross spoke first. Her voice sent what felt like an electrical current through my body. She was no longer just a person whose words I read.

She was sitting right in front of me. She wore beautiful African-print garb and her long dreadlocks fell to one side. I asked myself, "Is this real? A movement being led by women who look like me?"

I didn't feel like I had to censor myself or any parts of my story to make the team feel comfortable. We understood each other. They wanted to hear about me, not just my work experience. And for the first time in my activist life I felt like I was a part of a movement where all parts of me were accepted.

As we talked, my connection to the work of the movement through SisterSong became more and more clear. I wasn't just applying for a job; I was experiencing an awakening that was leading me into one of the most transformative phases of my life.

A few days later I got a call from Loretta. She asked me the question that still makes me smile today: "So you ready to come work for SisterSong?"

Seven years ago I said yes to Loretta and to SisterSong. Since then I have transitioned from the development coordinator to the deputy coordinator, and from the interim executive director to executive director in 2013. I have helped guide us through the organization's first major leadership transition. I have worked with our new board of directors to formulate our strategic focus areas where we are working to build Southern synergy, expand our training program across movements and beyond borders, implement innovative culture-shift strategies by empowering art-activists across mediums, and strengthen our movement and build a pipeline for more leaders as a national convener.

I have experienced SisterSong at its pinnacle as well as at its lowest point, when closing the doors seemed inevitable. So many people asked me to quit. So many people asked me if it was really worth all of the heartache and stress. But what people did not understand is that, for me, failure was never an option.

Very soon after accepting the role, I decided that my job as ED would not be to close an organization—especially not SisterSong. Because over my many years in the movement I realized that I'm not the only one transformed by this work.

Whether it was in our trainings or at our convenings, there was always someone who would come up to me to say how grateful they were for the work of SisterSong. I learned about the countless women of color who are leading this movement and how SisterSong created opportunities for them to do their work.

With the creation of our Queer People of Color Caucus in 2006,

SisterSong has continued to become more LGBTQ inclusive, and my leadership as the first lesbian director has led to SisterSong amplifying this intersection more by emphasizing bodily and sexual autonomy as a foundational pillar of RJ. Since I came to SisterSong as an artist, I have created Artists United for Reproductive Justice to implement culture-shift strategies and help move the RJ framework into wider populations.

We are a portal that must remain open for the people drawn to this movement—just as I was seven years ago. SisterSong will continue to be radical and real. We will continue to amplify the voices of Indigenous women and women of color, and people of all gender identities and races. We will continue to push radical reproductive justice farther and wider. And we will always stay committed to collective action.

As we celebrate twenty years, we are excited to look back at SisterSong's evolution and to envision big for the future. Membership is open to all who believe in reproductive justice at SisterSong.net. Join us and celebrate yourself!

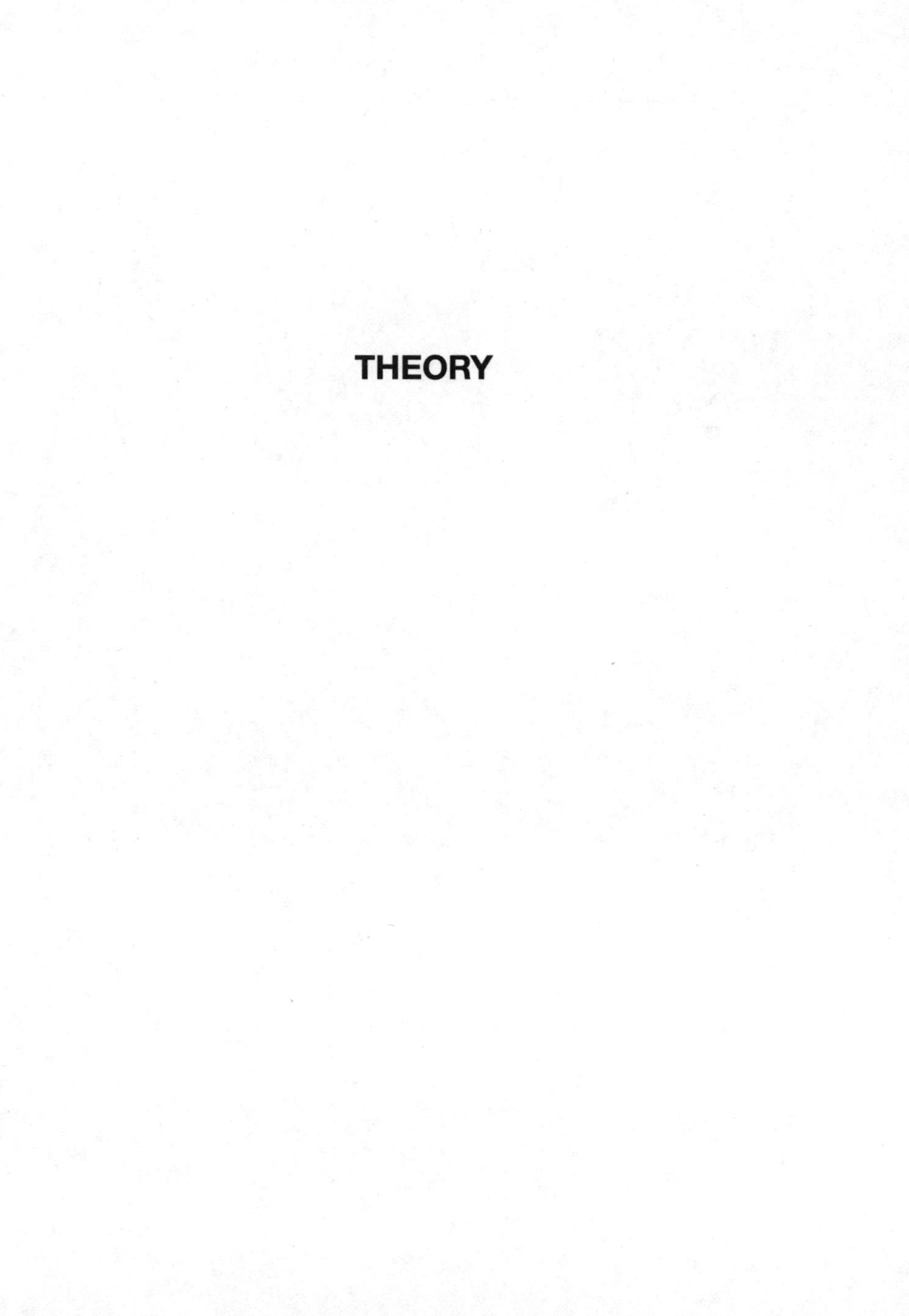

THEORY

Reproductive Rights Activism after *Roe*

MARLENE GERBER FRIED

This article describes the major activist trends after 1973, focusing primarily on those that have been less visible. Documenting feminist-activist history allows us to draw inspiration and important lessons for the future and understand the transition from reproductive freedom to reproductive rights to reproductive justice. The article provides a snapshot of recent activist victories for reproductive rights, reflecting a powerful breadth of activity. It demonstrates that reproductive rights advocacy continues to be shaped through countering antiabortion initiatives. Since *Roe v. Wade* legalized abortion in 1973, those dedicated to decriminalizing abortion have waged a multifront, sometimes violent, battle. There have been direct legal challenges to *Roe* itself, but the dominant strategy has been to restrict the availability of abortion. More than forty years later, opponents have severely curtailed a person's options through the passage of hundreds of laws and policies and the appointment of antiabortion justices and judges; campaigns that stigmatize abortion, those who have them, and those who provide care; and criminal attacks on providers and clinics. As a result, the legal right to abortion stands, but obtaining a safe and legal abortion is not an option for many who need one.

These attacks on abortion rights have been in the forefront of a broad conservative agenda, targeting all aspects of reproductive and parenting rights. The consequences have been devastating, especially for those whose race, age, legal, or economic status makes them targets of discrimination. At the same time, these threats have galvanized activism. Since *Roe*, there has been tremendous growth in the number of organizations and coalitions working to protect abortion rights, and advocating a broader reproductive rights, health, and justice agenda. In addition to the ongoing work of advocacy organizations, there have been several mass mobilizations in the face of the most high-profile threats to abortion rights. Examples include the efforts in the seventies and eighties to add a Human Life Amendment to the federal constitution, the murders of eight people involved in abortion care, and widespread blockades of clinics.

Following are some examples of post-*Roe* activism that has made an exciting difference in reproductive politics in the US.

Trust Black Women is a partnership of organizations founded in 2010 by SisterSong and other black feminist organizations after nearly two hundred antiabortion billboards were displayed in New York City, Atlanta, Jacksonville, Austin, Los Angeles, and other cities. They successfully challenged the racist billboard campaign depicting women of color as the most dangerous threat to their children and mobilized the defeat of proposed legislation in Georgia in 2010 restricting abortion based on the race of the fetus. They were up against tremendous odds in a red state dominated by anti-choice Republicans. Some of the billboards targeted African American women with the message: "The most dangerous place for an African American is in the womb." Similar billboards targeted Latinas. Disguised as expressions of concern for communities of color, these campaigns not only conflated abortion and genocide but also scapegoated women of color. Although it is true that African American and Latina women have disproportionately higher rates of abortion than white women, such campaigns distract from the real causes, which include lack of access to high-quality and culturally appropriate reproductive healthcare. That women of color led one of the few defeats of antiabortion legislation in the country in 2010 was cause for celebration and recognition that new power from women of color representing reproductive justice organizations is arising in the struggle for abortion rights.

Amid massive protests, the Susan G. Komen Foundation for the Cure was forced to reverse its decision not to fund breast cancer screenings at Planned Parenthood clinics, after a fierce battle to preserve contraception coverage was won through the Affordable Care Act (ACA). After five years, in February 2012 the Komen Foundation announced that it would no longer fund breast examinations at Planned Parenthood clinics. Although the stated reason was that Planned Parenthood Federation of America (PPFA) was under investigation, it was widely believed that the real reason was opposition to abortion within Komen's national leadership. In February 2012, Komen also announced it would no longer make grants to organizations that were under local, state, or federal investigation. Planned Parenthood, which received more than $600,000 annually from Komen to perform breast examinations and conduct breast health education at nineteen of its centers, was facing an investigation into whether the organization had violated a prohibition against using federal funds for abortion services. The public outcry against the Komen decision was swift and massive. They were criticized for politicizing women's health, and many people threatened to stop supporting the foundation. Proving the power of the reproductive rights movement, millions of dollars in new donations poured into PPFA, many redirected from the Komen Foundation who eventually rescinded its decision.

Thousands of women without economic means have been able to obtain an abortion with financial assistance from grassroots abortion funds included in the National Network of Abortion Funds (NNAF). This has been necessary because the Hyde Amendment passed by Congress in 1976 prohibits the use of federal funds to pay for abortions. The Hyde Amendment was attached to the Departments of Labor and Health, Education, and Welfare Appropriation Act. As originally offered by Representative Henry Hyde, the proposal would have prohibited the funding of all abortions, but a compromise was eventually achieved, providing that "none of the funds contained in this act shall be used to perform abortions except where the life of the mother would be endangered if the fetus were carried to term." In subsequent years, the Hyde Amendment was sometimes reworded to include exceptions for rape and incest or long-lasting damage to the physical health of the mother. However, from the Ninety-Seventh Congress until recently, the language has been identical to the original enactment, allowing only an exception to preserve the mother's life. During the first year of the Clinton Administration in 1993, coverage under the Hyde Amendment was expanded to again include cases of rape and incest. This means that people whose healthcare is provided by the federal government (women on welfare, in the military or the Peace Corps, in federal prisons, and on Indian reservations) face discriminatory restrictions on abortion care and funding. Such antiabortion measures especially burden poor women, women of color, young women, and rural women.

With the call to "Fund Abortion, Build Power," NNAF builds an active grassroots base of people directly affected by barriers to abortion access by working to distribute information and implement necessary cultural and political change. Founded in 1993, NNAF has expanded its fund membership to seventy funds operating in forty states, defying the government's prohibitions and fearlessly organizing donors to help those in need.

Pro-Choice Defense of *Roe*

Immediately following *Roe*, the antiabortion movement gained momentum. It became part of the burgeoning New Right, which, with the election of President Ronald Reagan, consolidated its power. At the same time, abortion rights advocacy declined. Thinking the question of legalization had been settled, activists hoped they could now shift their attention to making abortion services affordable and accessible, as well as to other women's rights issues. The radical movement that framed abortion rights in the broader context of women's liberation had fragmented, and there was diminishing activism at the grassroots level. In the 1980s, when a visible abortion rights movement did reemerge on the national scene, it was on the defensive and responded by narrowing its vision and conservatizing its language.

Mainstream abortion rights organizations dedicated themselves to defending *Roe v. Wade* under the rubric of "choice." They appealed to the right to privacy that was at the core of the Supreme Court decision. They did not prioritize the threats to access, and deliberately moved away from talking about women's rights, sexuality, and abortion. These were strategic decisions, taken with the belief that this approach would appeal to the broadest constituency of voters. Until recently, this limited notion of choice has remained the dominant framing for abortion rights advocacy.

Since legalization, mainstream pro-choice groups have been the voice of the movement in Congress and to the general public. Their strategies have focused on holding on to the rights secured by *Roe*, concentrating their efforts on the legislative arena and messaging. Although the legal right to abortion has been preserved, the pro-choice movement has been ineffective in stopping the ongoing attacks on and erosion of access. In fact, polls show a decline in support for abortion rights. Currently, there is general agreement within the movement about the need to reframe abortion rights and reproductive choice, but no agreement on the frame itself.

Simultaneously, throughout the post-*Roe* period, other approaches have arisen. Women of color and their allies have advocated placing the rights and needs of women of color and low-income women at the center of a broad reproductive justice agenda. Other advocates have primarily focused on expanding abortion access. Providing reproductive health services, including abortion, has been an important approach, predating *Roe*, as has monitoring and changing health policy.

Prioritizing Women of Color in the Agenda

The reproductive lives of women of color have been shaped by a long history of abuses, and these experiences are central to the ways in which women of color think about reproductive rights. In their activism, they have kept a dual focus on racial and reproductive justice, and have worked to integrate the two. For women of color, *Roe* was a victory to be viewed with caution, according to the National Council of Negro Women in 1973:

> Bitter experience has taught the Black woman that the administration of justice in this country is not colorblind. . . . We must be ever vigilant that what appears on the surface to be a step forward, does not in fact become yet another fetter or method of enslavement.[1]

Indeed, women of color sustained the first major blow to abortion access after *Roe*, when, in 1976, Congress passed the Hyde Amendment banning federal Medicaid funding for abortion. A majority of the states followed suit by banning state aid, and poor women, disproportionately women of color, saw their abortion access evaporate. The subsequent failure of mainstream pro-choice groups to marshal a large-scale response to Hyde was a second blow. However inadvertently, the pro-choice movement had sent a message that the dilemmas of women of color and low-income women were not its priorities. This charge was compounded by the fact that some leading pro-choice organizations did not support efforts to pass federal guidelines to prevent sterilization abuse.

In the 1970s, the Committee for Abortion Rights and Against Sterilization Abuse (CARASA) was one of the first and largest of groups working to end sterilization abuse and supporting abortion rights. CARASA was a cofounder of the Reproductive Rights National Network and also worked with the Committee to End Sterilization Abuse cofounded by the late Dr. Helen Rodriguez Trias, to publicize sterilization abuses and successfully advocated for guidelines to protect women. Activists proposed and lobbied for guidelines to regulate sterilization in New York City in 1973, and in 1979 the federal Department of Health, Education, and Welfare adopted federal guidelines. Planned Parenthood, Zero Population Growth (now Population Connection), and the Association for Voluntary Sterilization were among the pro-choice groups who opposed the guidelines. Some of the opposition was based on a population-control perspective whereas others objected on grounds that the guidelines interfered with an individual woman's choice, were unnecessary and paternalistic, and interfered with the doctor-patient relationship.

Although lesbians played major roles in many reproductive rights organizations, they were often not out within these groups, nor was the connection between reproductive rights and sexual liberation made explicit at the time, except by the 1977 black feminist statement of the Combahee River Collective.

Beginning in the eighties, women of color formed their own organizations and coalitions to advocate for the reproductive rights and health needs of women in their communities. The 1984 founding of the National Black Women's Health Project (now the Black Women's Health Imperative) was the catalyst for other organizations that emerged at the grassroots and national levels. These organizations articulated new definitions of reproductive rights affirming each woman's right to make her own reproductive decisions.

The concept of reproductive justice initially emerged at a black women's caucus in June 1994. They placed the right to have a child or not and the right to parent one's existing children on equal footing and stressed that legal rights alone are not adequate. This was the definition propagated by SisterSong at its first national conference in 2003. Women must have the resources necessary to turn their rights into realities. Thus, access to health, education, and employment all became part of the reproductive rights agenda, and an individual woman's rights and health were linked to that of her community.

In 2005 Asian Communities for Reproductive Justice expanded this perspective when it published its definition of reproductive justice:

> We believe reproductive justice is the complete physical, mental, spiritual, political, economic, and social well-being of women and girls, and will be achieved when women and girls have the economic, social, and

> political power and resources to make healthy decisions about our bodies, sexuality, and reproduction for ourselves, our families, and our communities in all areas of our lives.[2]

This crucial paradigm shift locates women's autonomy and self-determination in human rights, rather than in individual choice or privacy.

Reproductive Rights Politics

Many activists who had been involved in the Civil Rights and women's liberation movements of the 1960s and 1970s were also mobilized by the passage of the Hyde Amendment. These activists shared the agenda and understanding of reproductive rights put forth by women of color. They formed new organizations to resist Hyde and to reject the population-control politics present not only in public policy but also within the pro-choice movement. By adopting the language of reproductive rights, activists signaled their broader vision and distinguished themselves from pro-choice politics. Feminism and sexuality were in the foreground of their activism and analysis, which included raising the visibility of LGBTQ politics.

Reproductive rights activists also differed from the mainstream pro-choice movement over how best to build a large movement. They saw the need for grassroots activism, public education, public demonstrations, and disseminating radical analyses. Instead of targeting existing voters, RJ activists sought to draw in new constituencies who did not find pro-choice and mainstream political approaches appealing.

The Woman's Health Approach

A woman's health movement had also developed in the 1960s to address the discrimination and disempowerment women faced in medical settings. It too was focused on the lack of affordable and women-centered care for women from marginalized populations. Central to this approach was the belief that giving women the ability to get the care they need and deserve was about empowerment. A primary strategy was to ensure that women had knowledge about their bodies, especially in the areas of reproduction and sexuality. Women's health activists challenged the top-down model of service provision and demanded acknowledgment and respect for women's expertise, and worked to change the medical establishment and also created alternative institutions. The Jane Collective, a Chicago-based group of laywomen trained to provide abortions before *Roe*, put these tenets into practice.

For some activists, the post-*Roe* attacks on abortion further underscored the need for women to take control of abortion care. The Federation of Feminist Women's Health Centers (FWHC) continued, as it had before *Roe*, to teach self-examinations and menstrual extraction abortions. FWHCs provided a model of women-centered care. The Our Bodies Ourselves Collective (initially known as the Boston Women's Health Book Collective), started in 1969, provided updated knowledge through wide dissemination and frequent updating of their book, *Our Bodies, Ourselves*. Along with other groups, including the Committee to End Sterilization Abuse and the National Women's Heath Network, they focused on monitoring and changing health policy. Successes in this area include winning federal guidelines for sterilization, packaging that provides women with better information about the risks of the birth control pill, and raising awareness about the potential dangers of estrogen replacement therapy and the risk of toxic shock syndrome from tampons. The National Women's Health Network, Raising Women's Voices, the National Latina Institute for Reproductive Health, the Black Women's Health Imperative, and the National Asian Pacific American Women's Forum have all been active in championing the concerns of women of color and low-income women in the debate over national healthcare reform.

A Focus on Abortion Access

After the 1992 election of President Bill Clinton, who openly claimed to be pro-choice, the attacks on abortion access escalated, including the murders of abortion practitioners and clinic workers, and ongoing criminal assaults on abortion services with bombings, chemical attacks, and intimidation of clinic staff. In response, for the first time since *Roe*, the focus of abortion rights activism shifted to access. Groups who had been advocating to prioritize access were joined by new organizations working to address all aspects of the problem including supporting and increasing the number of providers, countering Targeted Regulation of Abortion Providers (TRAP) laws, advocating for integration of abortion into medical- and nursing-school curricula, providing direct financial assistance to women needing abortions, and advocating to restore public funding of abortion.

The Future

In addition to continuing the work described previously, there are other priorities that cut across the different trends.

Youth-Focused Advocacy and Leadership

There is a generational divide within the movement, and this divide has extended to influence and power within the movement. Younger women were counted on to swell the numbers at demonstrations but not called to the decision-making tables. But for these women, abortion is only one of many issues that define their reproductive lives.

Several organizations have been created to build the leadership of young women and bring their issues to the foreground. These groups have been promoting youth leadership throughout the movement. Organizations dedicated to advancing youth issues and leadership include URGE (formerly Choice USA), Third Wave Fund, Young Women's Empowerment Project, the Civil Liberties and Public Policy Program at Hampshire College, Young Women United, Advocates for Youth, and the Feminist Majority Foundation.

Safe, Legal Abortion as a Public Health Issue

It is ironic that the fact that maternal morbidity and mortality rates from legal abortion are so low that its importance as a public health issue is obscured. Recent debates excluding abortion and contraceptive coverage from the ACA highlight the need to recapture this ground, and public health professionals have played a historic role in this battle. After *Roe*, the American Public Health Association was among only a handful of national medical organizations to affirm its support for legal abortion. Continuing to promote advocacy within the health professions is a crucial activist strategy.

The public health field has also been a clear voice for evidence-based public policy. Over the years, the antiabortion movement has increasingly moved away from grounding its claims in established science. Instead, it uses its own religiously based scientific "experts" to support claims that abortion causes breast cancer, that teaching abstinence is the only effective form of sexuality education, that women who have abortions suffer from "Post Abortion Syndrome"—a form of post-traumatic stress disorder—and that rape-induced pregnancies are rare. Organizations dedicated to producing legitimate research and analysis and dispelling myths that masquerade as science play a critical role. The Guttmacher Institute and Ibis Reproductive Health are two of the leading organizations doing this work.

Combating Silence and Stigma

The antiabortion movement has been trying to show that it cares about women, not just fetuses. However, contempt and distrust for women is a recurrent theme. Conservative radio host Rush Limbaugh called law school student Sandra Fluke a slut because she advocated the inclusion of birth control coverage in the ACA. In September 2012, Fluke was not allowed to speak to an all-male Congressional Republican panel on contraception coverage, and subsequently was invited to testify at a hearing convened by Congressional Democrats. Limbaugh's comments revealed the misogyny that has pervaded the Right's attacks on women's reproductive rights and sexuality. Todd Akin, a Missouri Republican then running for Senate, said in an August 2012 television interview: "If it's a legitimate rape, the female body has ways to try to shut that whole thing down."[3] Akin's remarks echo the 1976 Congressional debate over the Hyde Amendment when Silvio Conte opposed an exception for rape and pushed to have the language changed to "forced rape," arguing that without that stipulation, "any woman who wants an abortion under Medicaid could go in and say, 'I'm raped,' and there could be a lot of perjury."[4]

Countering the demonization of women—especially those who are poor, young, and of color—is an ongoing priority for the reproductive justice movement. Women telling their own stories has been one of the most powerful strategies. How abortion and reproductive rights are framed is also relevant. Many of the leading advocacy voices in Congress and the public continue to talk about abortion in ways that perpetuate stigma. Arguing that abortions should be rare, prevention is the most important goal, and banning public funding is an unchageable policy all imply that abortion is a necessary evil. Alternative framings of abortion as a matter of justice, human rights, survival, and public health provide positive ways of inspiring future activism.

Conclusion

The ongoing threats to reproductive rights are wide-ranging. Within the reproductive rights movement there continues to be a lack of agreement over priorities and strategies, which weakens the ability both to withstand attacks and be proactive. Nonetheless, I think there are reasons for optimism about the future. There is a greater diversity of organizations and leadership, as well as more strategic convergence, now than at any other time since *Roe*. There is a widespread acknowledgment that while abortion rights have been at the forefront, the conservative agenda is challenging *all* aspects of women's human rights, and there is agreement about the need to counter these activities with new ways of framing, advocating, and collaborating.

Important efforts are underway that provide models for working together across organizations. For example, advocates for low-income women and women of color have come together to create and implement a long-term plan for prioritizing affordability of abortion care for those who have been denied access. They created the All* Above All campaign, the first reproductive justice effort to increase the political power of women to lift bans through restoring public insurance coverage of abortions. The first abortion speakout was held in New York City in 1969 when the state legislature was considering abortion law reform. Since that time, feminists have used this format as an important political tool both through publishing collections of women's stories and organizing live speakouts. Reproductive rights advocates have also developed websites that provide women with the opportunity to speak about their abortion experiences in their own words. Spearheaded by the National Network of Abortion Funds and the National Latina Institute for Reproductive Health, many organizations are part of this effort.

There is a strong and growing network dedicated to supporting new and diverse leadership and drawing in new constituencies among reproduction justice organizations. The New Leadership Networking Initiative, a project of the Civil Liberties and Public Policy Program at Hampshire College, has more than three hundred organizational members. There is also an effort underway to foster greater collaboration and long-term strategizing by the CoreAlign Initiative based at the University of California at San Francisco.

Most important, reproductive justice—led by women of color, younger women, and their allies—has breathed new life into the movement and is becoming the dominant framework. Placing reproductive rights in the struggle for social justice and human rights has global resonance and is a compelling, expansive, and inclusive vision for US activists who may be daunted by the challenges facing them today, but are determined to protect people's human right to abortion.

Notes

1. National Council of Negro Women, *Black Woman's Voice* 2, no. 2 (Jan/Feb 1973).

2. Asian Communities for Reproductive Justice, "A New Vision for Advancing Our Movement for Reproductive Rights, Reproductive Health and Reproductive Justice," Forward Together, 2005, http://strongfamiliesmovement.org/assets/docs/ACRJ-A-New-Vision.pdf, 1.

3. John Eligon and Michael Schwirtz, "Todd Akin Provokes Ire with 'Legitimate Rape' Comment," *New York Times*, August 19, 2017, http://www.nytimes.com/2012/08/20/us/politics/todd-akin-provokes-ire-with-legitimate-rape-comment.html.

4. Marlene Gerber Fried, "The Hyde Amendment: 30 Years of Violating Women's Rights," Center for American Progress, October 6, 2006, https://www.americanprogress.org/issues/women/news/2006/10/06/2243/the-hyde-amendment-30-years-of-violating-womens-rights/.

Beyond Pro-Choice versus Pro-Life: Women of Color and Reproductive Justice

ANDREA SMITH

Once, while taking an informal survey of Native women in Chicago about their position on abortion—were they pro-life or pro-choice—I quickly found that their responses did not match up with these neatly media-mandated categories.

Example 1:

Me: Are you pro-choice or pro-life?

Respondent 1: Oh I am definitely pro-life.

Me: So you think abortion should be illegal?

Respondent 1: No, definitely not. People should be able to have an abortion if they want.

Me: Do you think then that there should not be federal funding for abortion services?

Respondent 1: No, there should be funding available so that anyone can afford to have one.

Example 2:

Me: Would you say you are pro-choice or pro-life?

Respondent 2: Well, I would say that I am pro-choice, but the most important thing to me is promoting life in Native communities.

These responses make it difficult to categorize the Native women queried neatly into pro-life or pro-choice camps. Is Respondent 1 pro-life because she says she is pro-life? Or is she pro-choice because she supports the decriminalization of and public funding for abortion? I would argue that, rather than attempt to situate these respondents in pro-life or pro-choice camps, it is more useful to recognize the limitations of the pro-life/pro-choice dichotomy for understanding the politics around reproductive justice. Unlike pro-life or pro-choice advocates who make their overall political goal the criminalization or decriminalization of abortion, the reproductive justice frameworks these Native women are implicitly articulating are based on fighting for life and self-determination of their communities. The criminalization of abortion may or may not be a strategy for pursuing that goal.

In previous works, I have focused more specifically on Native women and reproductive justice. Here, I am using these Native women's responses to questions about abortion to argue that the pro-life versus pro-choice paradigm is a model that marginalizes women of color, poor women, and women with disabilities. It reifies and masks the structures of white supremacy and capitalism that undergird the reproductive choices women make, and narrows the focus of our political goals to the question of the criminalization of abortion. Ironically, I will contend, while the pro-choice and pro-life camps on the abortion debate are often articulated as polar opposites, both depend on similar operating assumptions that do nothing to support either life or real choice for women of color. In developing this analysis, I seek to build on previous scholarship that centers women of color as well as reflect on my more than two decades as an activist in the reproductive justice movement.

Pro-Life Politics, Criminalization of Abortion, and the Prison Industrial Complex

The fetus is a life—but sometimes that life must be ended.
—Jeanette Bushnell, Seattle-based Native health activist

The pro-life position maintains that the fetus is a life, hence abortion should be criminalized. Consequently, its position is situated around moral claims regarding the sanctity of life. In a published debate on pro-life versus pro-choice positions, Gary Crum, former vice president of South Carolina Citizens for Life, argues that the pro-life position is "ethically pure."[1] Because of the moral weight he grants the protection of the life of the fetus, Crum contends that abortion must be criminalized. Any immoral actions that impact others should be a "serious crime under the law."[2] The pro-choice position counters this argument by asserting that the fetus is not a life, and hence policy must be directed toward protecting a woman's ability to control her own body. To quote sociologist Thelma McCormack's response to Crum: "Life truly begins in the . . . hospital room, not in the womb."[3] Gloria Feldt, former president of Planned Parenthood, similarly asserts that if the fetus is established as a life, the principles of *Roe v. Wade* must necessarily be discarded.

Jeanette Bushnell's statement that "the fetus is a life—but sometimes that life must be ended"[4] suggests, however, a critical intervention in the pro-life argument. That is, the major flaw in the pro-life position is *not* the claim that the fetus is a life but the conclusion it draws from this assertion: that because the fetus is a life, abortion should be criminalized. In this regard, reproductive rights activists and scholars could benefit from the analysis of the anti-prison movement, which questions criminalization as an appropriate response to social issues. As I shall demonstrate, assuming a criminal justice regime fails to address social problems or to adjudicate reproductive issues, and results in further marginalization of poor women and women of color. To make this connection, I must first provide a critical history of the failures of the prison system to deal effectively with social problems.

The anti-prison-industrial-complex movement has highlighted the complete failure of the prison system to address social concerns. In fact, not only do prisons not solve social problems but they are more likely to increase rather than decrease crime rates. Most people in prison are there for drug- or poverty-related crimes. Prisons do not provide treatment for drug addiction, and it is often easier to access drugs in prison than on the outside. For people who are in prison because of poverty-related crimes, a prison record ensures it will be that much more difficult for them to secure employment once released. Consistently, study after study indicates that prisons do not have an impact on decreasing crime rates. For instance, the Rand Corporation found that California's three strikes legislation, which requires life sentences for thrice convicted felons, did not reduce the rate of "murders, rapes, and robberies that many people believe to be the law's principal targets."[5] In fact, changes in crime rates often have more to do with fluctuations in employment rates than with increased police surveillance or incarceration. In addition, as documented by prison activist groups such as the Prison Activist Resource Center, government monies are siphoned away from education and social services into prisons, thus destabilizing communities of color and increasing their vulnerability to incarceration.

The failure of prisons is well known to policymakers. In fact, John Dilulio, a prominent right-wing analyst who was one of the major advocates for the build-up of the prison industrial complex, later renounced his position and came out in support of a prison moratorium. Given that this failure is well-known, it then becomes apparent that the purpose of prisons has never been to stop crime. Rather, as a variety of scholars and activists have argued, the purpose has been in large part to control the population of communities of color. As Michael Mancini and Angela Davis point out, the racial background of the prison population prior to the Civil War was white. After the Civil War, the Thirteenth Amendment was passed, which prohibits slavery—except in punishment for a crime. The slavery system was then essentially replaced by the convict leasing system, which was often even more brutal than the former. Under slavery, slave owners at least had a financial incentive to keep slaves alive. In the convict leasing system, no such incentive existed—if a prisoner died, she or he could simply be replaced by another. The regime of the prison was originally designed to "reform" the prisoner by creating conditions for penitence (hence the term "penitentiary"). After the Civil War, however, the prison adopted similar regimes of punishment as those found in chattel slavery, which coincided with the reenslavement of black communities into the convict leasing system. As Davis argues, "Racisms . . . congeal and combine in prisons"[6]; they exist to maintain the capitalist and white supremacist underpinnings of US society. The continuing racism of the prison system is evidenced by who is in prison. In 1994, for instance, one out of every three African American men between the ages of twenty and twenty-nine was under some form of criminal justice supervision. Two-thirds of men of color in California between the ages of eighteen and thirty have been arrested according to statistics in 1996. Six of every ten juveniles in federal custody are American Indian and two-thirds of women in prison are women of color.

In a statement that also applies to the criminalization of abortion, Davis further argues that it is critical to disarticulate the equation between crime and punishment because the primary purpose of punishment is not to solve the crime problem.

> "Punishment" does not follow from "crime" in the neat and logical sequence offered by discourses that insist on the justice of imprisonment, but rather punishment—primarily through imprisonment (and sometimes death)—is linked to the agendas of politicians, the profit drive of corporations, and media representations of crime. Imprisonment is associated with the racialization of those most likely to be punished. . . . If we . . . strive to disarticulate crime and punishment . . . then our focus must not rest only on the prison system as an isolated institution but

> must also be directed at all the social relations that support the permanence of the prison.[7]

Prisons simply are not only ineffective institutions for addressing social concerns, they drain resources from institutions that could be more effective. They also mark certain peoples, particularly people of color, as inherently criminal, undeserving of civil and political rights—thus increasing their vulnerability to poverty and further criminalization.

Davis's principle of disarticulation is critical in reassessing the pro-life position. That is, whether one perceives abortion to be a crime, it does not therefore follow that punishment in the form of imprisonment is a necessary response. Criminalization individualizes solutions to problems that are the result of larger economic, social, and political conditions. Consequently, it is inherently incapable of solving social problems or addressing crime.

Alternative social formations and institutions that can speak to these large-scale political and economic conditions are the appropriate place to address social issues, such as reproductive justice. As Davis argues: "Prison needs to be abolished as the dominant mode of addressing social problems that are better solved by other institutions and other means. The call for prison abolition urges us to imagine and strive for a very different social landscape."[8] Thus, even if we hold that a top social priority is to reduce the number of abortions, there is no evidence to suggest that involving the criminal justice system will accomplish that goal, given it has not been effective in reducing crime rates or addressing social problems. In addition, increased criminalization disproportionately affects people of color—and in the case of abortion, women of color and poor women. An interrogation of the assumptions behind the pro-life movement suggests that what distinguishes the pro-life position is not so much a commitment to life (since criminalization promotes death rather than life, particularly in communities of color and poor communities) but rather a commitment to criminal justice interventions in reproductive justice issues.

An assessment of recent debates within the anti-domestic-violence and anti-sexual-assault movements further illustrates this argument. As I, and others, have argued, the anti-violence movement, as it became increasingly funded by the state, began to rely on criminal justice interventions. Domestic violence and sexual assault agencies formed their strategy around the slogan that sexual and domestic violence *is a crime*. The response then of activists was to push for increased criminalization of sexual and domestic violence through mandatory arrest policies, no-drop prosecution policies, and longer sentencing. Sadly, the result of this approach was that not only did it not reduce violence rates, it often contributed further to women's victimization. For instance, under mandatory arrest laws, the police often arrest the women who are being battered. In fact, the *New York Times* recently reported that the impact of strengthened anti-domestic-violence legislation is that battered women kill their abusive partners less frequently; however, batterers do *not* kill their partners less frequently, and this is truer in black than white communities. Thus, ironically, laws passed to protect battered women are actually protecting their batterers! While prisons currently are not filled with batterers and rapists, this approach contributed to the growth of the prison industrial complex by implicitly buying into a criminal justice regime on which the prison system depends. Legislators attach violence-against-women provisions (such as the Violence Against Women Act) to repressive anticrime bills, and by doing so legislators can then rely on anti-violence activists to support the legislation as a whole.

Similarly, the pro-life position implicitly supports the prison industrial complex by unquestioningly supporting a criminal justice approach that legitimizes rather than challenges the prison system. As Davis argues, it is not sufficient to challenge the criminal justice system; we must build alternatives to it. Just as the women of color anti-violence movement is currently developing strategies for ending violence, a consistent pro-life position would require activists to develop responses to abortion that do not rely on the prison industrial complex. Otherwise, these pro-life activists will continue to support policies that are brutally oppressive, particularly to communities of color and poor communities.

Interestingly, this critique of the prison system is prevalent even within conservative evangelical circles. For example, Charles Colson, a prominent Christian Right activist, and former attorney with the Nixon administration, served time in prison for his role in the Watergate break-in. Following his imprisonment, Colson began to work on prison reform, founding the Prison Fellowship and its associated lobbying arm, Justice Fellowship. Many platforms implicitly or explicitly supported by both the Prison and Justice Fellowship could be used to question the wisdom of the criminalization of abortion: decarceration for drug offenders; minimum wage compensation for prison labor; decarceration of all nonviolent offenders; prison construction moratoriums; eradication of mandatory sentencing; suffrage for convicted felons; and expansion of community sentencing programs. In fact, Colson argues that 50 percent of people in prison today should be released immediately. To quote Colson:

> The whole system of punishment today is geared toward taking away people's dignity, putting them in an institution, and locking them up in a cage. Prisons are overcrowded, understaffed, dirty places. Eighty percent of American prisons are barbaric—not just brutal, but barbaric. . . . Prison as a punishment is a failure. Mandatory sentences and longer sentences are counterproductive. . . . The tougher the laws, I'm convinced, the more lawless and violent we will become. As for public safety, it can hardly be said that prisons contribute to public safety. . . . Prisons obviously are not deterring criminal conduct. The evidence is overwhelming that the more people we put in prison, the more crime we have. All prisons do is warehouse human beings and at exorbitant cost.[9]

Yet, despite his sustained critique of the failure of the prison system, Colson never critiques the wisdom of criminalization as the appropriate response to abortion. In the name of promoting life, the pro-life movement supports one of the biggest institutions of violence and death in this society. But given that this critique of criminalization is not inaccessible to large sectors of the pro-life movement, there should be opportunities to make anti-criminalization interventions into pro-life discourse. A commitment to criminalization of social issues necessarily contributes to the growth of the prison system because it reinforces the notion that prisons are appropriate institutions for addressing social problems rather than causes of the problems. Given the disproportionate impact of criminalization on communities of color, support for criminalization as public policy also implicitly supports racism.

In addition, I am suggesting that those committed to pro-choice positions will be more effective and politically consistent if they contest the pro-life position from an anti-prison perspective. For instance, increasingly, poor women and women of color are finding their pregnancies criminalized. As Dorothy Roberts and others have noted, women of color are more likely to be arrested and imprisoned for drug use because—as a result of greater rates of poverty in communities of color—they are more likely to be in contact with government agencies where their drug use can be detected. While white pregnant women are slightly *more* likely to engage in substance abuse than black women, public health facilities and private doctors are more likely to report black women than white women to criminal justice authorities. Meanwhile, pregnant women who would like treatment for their addiction can seldom access it because treatment centers do not meet the needs of pregnant women. One study found that two-thirds of drug treatment centers would not treat pregnant women. Furthermore, the criminalization of drug use is more likely to drive pregnant women who are substance abusers from seeking prenatal or other forms of healthcare for fear of being reported to the authorities. Roberts critiques communities of color for often supporting the criminalization of women of color who have addictions and for failing to understand it as another strategy of white supremacy that blames women for the effects of poverty and racism. Lisa Maher and Rickie Solinger note that a simple choice perspective is not effective for addressing this problem because certain women become marked as women who make "bad choices" and hence deserve imprisonment.

Similarly, Elizabeth Cook-Lynn argues in her essay "The Big Pipe Case" that at the same time Native peoples were rallying around Leonard Peltier, no one stood beside Marie Big Pipe when she was incarcerated on a felony charge of assault with intent to commit serious bodily harm because she breastfed her child while under the influence of alcohol. She was denied both services to treat her substance abuse problem and access to abortion services when she became pregnant. Not only did her community not support her, but it supported her incarceration. Cook-Lynn argues that in doing so, the community supported the encroachment of US federal jurisdiction on tribal lands for an issue that would normally be under tribal jurisdiction. Cook-Lynn recounts how this demonization of Native women was assisted by the publication of Michael Dorris's *The Broken Cord* in 1989, which narrates his adoption of a Native child who suffered from fetal alcohol syndrome. While this book has been crucial in sensitizing many communities to the realities of fetal alcohol syndrome, it also portrays the mother of the child unsympathetically and advocates repressive legislative solutions targeted against women substance abusers. Thus, within Native communities, the growing demonization of Native women substance abusers has prompted tribes to collude with the federal government in whittling away their own sovereignty.

In the larger society, Barbara Harris started an organization called Children Requiring a Caring Kommunity (CRACK) in Anaheim, California, which gives women two hundred dollars to have sterilizations. Their mission is to "'save our welfare system' and the world from the exorbitant cost to the taxpayer for each 'drug addicted birth' by offering 'effective preventive measures to reduce the tragedy of numerous drug-affected pregnancies.'"[10] Some of CRACK's initial billboards read, "Don't let a pregnancy ruin your drug habit."[11] The organization has since opened chapters in several cities across the country, and has changed its name to Project Prevention to present a less inflammatory image. Nonetheless, its basic message is the same—that poor women who are substance abusers are the cause of social ills and the conditions that give rise to poor women becoming substance abusers do not need to be addressed.

Unfortunately, as both Roberts and Cook-Lynn point out, even communities of color (on either side of the pro-life/pro-choice divide) have supported the criminalization of women of color who have addiction issues. The reason for this is because the focus is on what they perceive to be the moral culpability of women of color for not protecting the life of their children. If we adopt an anti-prison perspective, however, it becomes clear that even on the terms of moral culpability it does not follow that the criminal justice approach is the appropriate way to address this social concern. In fact, criminal justice responses to unwanted pregnancies and/or pregnant women with addiction issues demonstrate an inherent contradiction in the pro-life position. Many pro-life organizations have been ardent opponents of population control programs and policies—advocating against the promotion of dangerous contraceptives or the promotion of sterilization in developing countries. Yet, their position depends on the prison industrial complex as an institution of population control for communities of color in the United States.

Meanwhile, many pro-choice organizations, such as Planned Parenthood, have supported financial incentives for poor and criminalized women to be sterilized or to take long-acting hormonal contraceptives. As I will discuss later, part of this political inconsistency is inherent in the articulation of the pro-choice position, but another reason is that many in the pro-choice camp have also failed to question criminalization as the appropriate response for addressing reproductive health concerns. The pro-choice camp may differ from the pro-life groups regarding which acts should be criminalized, but it does not necessarily question criminalization itself.

The Pro-Choice Position and Capitalism

The pro-choice camp claims a position that offers more choices for women making decisions about their reproductive lives. A variety of scholars and activists have critiqued the choice paradigm because it rests on essentially individualist, consumerist notions of free choice that do not take into consideration all the social, economic, and political conditions that frame the so-called choices that women are forced to make. Solinger further contends that in the 1960s and 1970s, abortion rights advocates initially used the term "rights" rather than choice; rights are understood as those benefits owed to all those who are human regardless of access to special resources. By contrast, argues Solinger, the concept of choice is connected to possession of resources, thus creating a hierarchy among women based on who can make legitimate choices. Consequently, since under a capitalist system, those with resources are granted more choices, it is not inconsistent to withdraw reproductive rights choices from poor women through legislation such as the Hyde Amendment, which restricts federal funding for abortion, or family caps for Temporary Assistance for Needy Families (TANF) recipients. In 1960 Planned Parenthood commissioned a study which concluded that poor and working-class families lacked the rationality to do family planning, and that this lack of "rationality and early family planning as middle class couples" was "embodied in the particular personalities, world views, and ways of life"[12] of the poor themselves. As Solinger states:

> "Choice" also became a symbol of middle-class women's arrival as independent consumers. Middle-class women could afford to choose. They had earned the right to choose motherhood, if they liked. According to many Americans, however, when choice was associated with poor women, it became a symbol of illegitimacy. Poor women had not earned the right to choose.[13]

What Solinger's analysis suggests is that, ironically, while the pro-choice camp contends that the pro-life position diminishes the rights of women in favor of fetal rights, the pro-choice position actually does not ascribe inherent rights to women either. Rather, women are viewed as only having reproductive choices if they can afford them or if they are deemed legitimate choice-makers.

William Saletan's history of the evolution of the pro-choice paradigm illustrates the extent to which it is a conservative one. Saletan contends that pro-choice strategists, generally affiliated with National Abortion and Reproductive Rights Action League (NARAL), intentionally rejected a rights-based framework in favor of one that focused on privacy from *big government*. That is, government should not intervene in the woman's right to decide if she wants to have children. This approach appealed to those with libertarian sensibilities who otherwise might have had no sympathy with feminist causes. The impact of this strategy was that it enabled the pro-choice side to keep *Roe v. Wade* intact—but only in the narrowest sense. This strategy undermined any attempt to achieve a broader pro-choice agenda because the strategy could be used against a broader agenda. For instance, the argument that government should not be involved in reproductive rights decisions could also be used by pro-life advocates against federal funding for abortions. Consequently, Saletan argues, "Liberals have not won the struggle for abortion rights. Conservatives have."[14]

Furthermore, this narrow approach has contributed to some pro-choice organizations, such as Planned Parenthood and NARAL, often developing strategies that marginalize women of color. Both supported the Freedom of Choice Act in the early 1990s, which retained the Hyde Amendment. The Hyde Amendment, besides discriminating against poor women by denying federal funding for abortion services, discriminates against American Indian women who largely obtain healthcare through Indian Health Services, a federal agency. One of NARAL's petitions stated: "The Freedom of Choice Act (FOCA) will secure the original vision of *Roe v. Wade*, giving *all* women reproductive freedom and securing that right for future generations."[15] Apparently, poor women and Indigenous women do not qualify as women.

Building on this analysis, I would argue that while there is certainly a sustained critique of the choice paradigm, particularly among women of color reproductive justice groups, the choice paradigm continues to govern much of the policies of mainstream groups in a manner that sustains the marginalization of women of color, poor women, and women with disabilities.

One example is the extent to which pro-choice advocates narrow their advocacy around legislation that affects the one choice of whether to have an abortion without addressing all the conditions that gave rise to a woman needing to make this decision in the first place. Consequently, politicians, such as former president Bill Clinton, will be heralded as pro-choice if they do not support legislative restrictions on abortion regardless of their stance on other issues that may equally impact the reproductive choices women make. Clinton's approval of federal welfare reform that places poor women in the position of possibly being forced to have an abortion because of cuts in social services, while often critiqued, is not viewed as an anti-choice position. On Planned Parenthood's and NARAL's websites, there is generally no mention of welfare policies in these organizations' pro-choice legislation alerts.

A consequence of the choice paradigm is that its advocates frequently take positions that are oppressive to women from marginalized communities. For instance, this paradigm often makes it difficult to develop nuanced positions on the use of abortion when the fetus is determined to have abnormalities. Focusing solely on the woman's choice to have or not have the child does not address the larger context of a society that sees certain children with disabilities as undesirable and provides inadequate resources to women who may otherwise want to have the child. As Martha Saxton notes, "Our society profoundly limits the 'choice' to love and care for a baby with a disability."[16] If our response to disability is to simply facilitate the process by which women can abort fetuses, we never actually focus on changing economic policies that make raising children with disabilities difficult. Rashmi Luthra notes, by contrast, that reproductive advocates from other countries such as India, who do not operate from this same choice paradigm, are often able to develop more nuanced political positions on issues such as this one.

Another example is the difficulty pro-choice groups have in maintaining a critical perspective on dangerous or potentially dangerous contraceptives, arguing that women should have a choice of contraceptives. Many scholars and activists have documented the dubious safety record of Norplant and Depo-Provera, two long-acting hormonal contraceptives. In fact, lawsuits against Norplant have forced an end to its distribution. In 1978 the FDA denied approval for Depo-Provera on the grounds that dog studies confirmed an elevated rate of breast cancer; there appeared to be an increased risk of birth defects in human fetuses exposed to the drug; and there was no pressing need shown for use of the drug as a contraceptive. In 1987 the FDA changed its regulations and began to require cancer testing in rats and mice instead of dogs and monkeys, and Depo-Provera did not cause cancer in these animals, but major concerns regarding its safety persist.

Also problematic is the way these contraceptives are frequently promoted in communities of color and often without informed consent. Even with formalistic informed consent, the danger warnings offered women are understated or omitted altogether. Full disclosure of short- and long-term dangers should be made by providers but often is not. Yet none of the mainstream pro-choice organizations have ever seriously taken a position on the issue of comprehensive informed consent as part of their agenda. Indeed, Gloria Feldt, former president of Planned Parenthood, equated opposition to Norplant and Depo-Provera as opposition to choice in her 2004 book, *The War on Choice*. Previously,

Planned Parenthood and NARAL opposed restrictions against sterilization abuse, despite the thousands of women of color who were being sterilized without their consent, because they saw such policies as interfering with a woman's right to choose.

Particularly disturbing has been some of the support given by these organizations to the Center for Research on Population and Security, headed by Stephen Mumford and Elton Kessel, which globally distributes quinacrine, a form of sterilization which is used to treat malaria. It is inserted into the uterus where it dissolves, causing the fallopian tubes to scar, rendering the woman irreversibly sterile. Family Health International conducted four in vitro studies and found quinacrine to be mutagenic in three of them. It, as well as the World Health Organization, recommended against further trials for female sterilization, and no regulatory body supports quinacrine. However, the North Carolina–based Center for Research on Population and Security (CRPS) has circumvented these bodies through private funding from such organizations as the Turner Foundation and Leland Fykes organization (which incidentally funds pro-choice *and* anti-immigrant groups). It has been distributing it for free to researchers and government health agencies. There are field trials in eleven countries, with more than seventy thousand women sterilized. In Vietnam, one hundred female rubber plant workers were given routine pelvic exams during which the doctor inserted quinacrine without their consent. Thus far, the side effects linked to quinacrine include ectopic pregnancy, puncturing of the uterus during insertion, pelvic inflammatory disease, and severe abdominal pains. Other possible concerns include heart and liver damage and exacerbation of preexisting viral conditions. In one of the trials in Vietnam, many cases that had serious side effects were excluded from the data.

Despite the threat to reproductive justice that this group represents, Feminist Majority Foundation featured the CRPS at its 1996 Feminist Expo because, I was informed by the organizers, they promoted choice for women. Then in 1999, Planned Parenthood almost agreed to sponsor a quinacrine trial in the US until outside pressure forced it to change its position. A prevalent ideology within the mainstream pro-choice movement is that women should have the choice to use whatever contraception they want. This position does not consider that a choice among dangerous contraceptives is not much of a choice; the millions of dollars pharmaceutical companies and the medical industry have to promote certain contraceptives, compared to the few resources women's advocacy groups have to provide alternative information on these same contraceptives; and the social, political, and economic conditions in which women may find themselves are such that using dangerous contraceptives may be the best of even worse options.

One reason that such groups have not taken a position on informed consent in the case of potentially dangerous contraceptives is due to their investment in population control. As Betsy Hartmann has argued, while contraceptives are often articulated as an issue of choice for white women in the first world, they are articulated as an instrument of population control for women of color and women in developing nations. The historical origins of Planned Parenthood are inextricably tied to the eugenics movement. Its founder, Margaret Sanger, collaborated with eugenics organizations during her career and framed the need for birth control in terms of the need to reduce the number of those in the "lower classes." In a study commissioned in 1960, Planned Parenthood concluded that poor people "have too many children"; yet something must be done to stop this trend in order to "disarm the population bomb."[17] Planned Parenthood is particularly implicated in this movement as can be seen clearly by the groups it lists as allies on its website: Population Action International, the Population Institute, Zero Population Growth, and the Population Council. A central campaign of Planned Parenthood is to restore US funding to the United Nations Population Fund (UNFPA). In addition, it asserts its commitment to addressing *rapid population growth*. I will not repeat the problematic analysis, critiqued elsewhere, of this population paradigm that essentially blames women in developing nations for poverty, war, environmental damage, and social unrest without looking at the root causes of all these phenomena (including population growth)—colonialism, corporate policies, militarism, and economic disparities between poor and rich countries.

As Hartmann documents, the UNFPA has long been involved in coercive contraceptive policies throughout the world. The Population Council produced Norplant and assisted in Norplant trials in Bangladesh and other countries without the informed consent of the trial participants. In fact, trial administrators often refused to remove Norplant when requested. These population organizations intersect to promote generally long-acting hormonal contraceptives of dubious safety around the world. Of course, Planned Parenthood provides valuable family planning resources to women around the world as well, but it does so through a population framework that inevitably shifts the focus from family planning as a right in and of itself to family planning as an instrument of population control. While population control advocates are increasingly more sophisticated in their rhetoric and often talk about ensuring social, political, and economic opportunity, the *population* focus of this model still results in its advocates working to reduce population rather than to provide social, political, and economic opportunity.

Another unfortunate consequence of uncritically adopting the choice paradigm is the tendency of reproductive rights advocates to make simplistic analyses of who our political friends and enemies are in the arena of reproductive rights. That is, all those who call themselves pro-choice are our political allies while all those who call themselves pro-life are our political enemies. An example of this rhetoric is Feldt's description of anyone who is pro-life as a "right-wing extremist."[18] As I have argued elsewhere, this simplistic analysis of who is politically progressive versus conservative does not actually do justice to the complex political positions people inhabit. As a result, we often engage uncritically in coalitions with groups who, in the words of anti-violence activist Beth Richie, do not pay us back. Meanwhile, we often lose opportunities to work with people with whom we may have sharp disagreements, but who may, with different political framings and organizing strategies, shift their positions.

To illustrate: Planned Parenthood is often championed as an organization that supports women's rights to choose with whom women of color should ally. Yet, as discussed previously, its roots are in the eugenics movement and today it is heavily invested in the population establishment. It continues to support population control policies in the developing world, almost supported the development of quinacrine in the US, and opposed strengthening sterilization regulations that would protect women of color. Meanwhile, the North Baton Rouge Women's Help Center in Louisiana is a crisis pregnancy center that articulates its pro-life position from an anti-racist perspective. It critiques the Black Church Initiative for the Religious Coalition for Reproductive Choice for contending that charges of racism against Sanger are scare tactics. It also attempts to provide its services from a holistic perspective—it provides educational and vocational training, GED classes, literacy programs, primary healthcare and pregnancy services, and child placement services. Its position: "We cannot encourage women to have babies and then continue their dependency on the system. We can't leave them without the resources to care for their children and then say, 'Praise the Lord, we saved a baby.'"[19]

It would seem that while the two organizations support some positions that are beneficial to women of color, they both equally support positions that are detrimental to them. If we are truly committed to reproductive justice, why should we presume that we should necessarily work with Planned Parenthood and reject the Women's Help Center? Why would we not instead position ourselves independently from both approaches and work to shift their positions to a stance that is truly liberatory for all women?

Beyond Pro-Life versus Pro-Choice

To develop an independent position, it is necessary to reject the pro-life versus pro-choice model for understanding reproductive justice. Many reproductive advocates have attempted to expand the definitions of either pro-life or pro-choice depending on which side of this divide they may rest. Unfortunately, they are trying to expand concepts that are inherently designed to exclude the experiences of most women, especially poor women, women of color, Indigenous women, and women with disabilities.

If we critically assess the assumptions behind both positions, these camps are more similar than they are different. As I have argued, they both assume a criminal justice regime for adjudicating reproductive issues, although they may differ as to which women should be subjected to this regime. Neither position endows women with inherent rights to their body—pro-life pits fetal rights against women's rights whereas pro-choice argues that women should have freedom to make choices rather than possess inherent rights to their bodies regardless of their class standing. They both support positions that reinforce racial and gender hierarchies that marginalize women of color. The pro-life position supports criminalization, which depends on a racist political system that will necessarily impact poor women and women of color who are less likely to have alternative strategies for addressing unwanted pregnancies. Meanwhile, the pro-choice position often supports population control policies and the development of dangerous contraceptives that are generally targeted toward communities of color. And neither position questions the capitalist system—they focus solely on the decision of whether a woman should have an abortion without addressing the economic, political, and social conditions that put women in this position in the first place.

Consequently, it is critical that reproductive advocates develop a framework that does not rest on pro-choice versus pro-life. Such a strategy would enable us to fight for reproductive justice as a part of a larger social justice strategy. It would also free us to think more creatively about who we could work with in coalition while simultaneously allowing us to hold those who claim to be our allies more accountable for the positions they take.

To be successful in this venture, however, it is not sufficient to simply articulate a women of color reproductive justice agenda—we must focus on developing a nationally coordinated women of color movement. While there are many women of color reproductive justice organizations, relatively few focus on bringing new women of color into the movement and training them to organize on their own behalf. And to the extent that these groups do exist, they are not generally coordinated as national mobilization efforts. Rather, national work is generally done on an advocacy level with heads of women of color organizations advocating for policy changes, but often working without a solid base to back their demands. Consequently, women of color organizations are not always in a strong position to negotiate with power brokers and mainstream pro-choice organizations or to hold them accountable.

As an example, many women of color groups mobilized to attend the 2004 March for Women's Lives in Washington, DC, to expand the focus of the march from a narrow pro-choice abortion rights agenda to a broader reproductive rights agenda. While this larger agenda was reflected in the march, it became co-opted by the pro-choice paradigm in the media coverage of the event. My survey of the major newspaper coverage of the march indicates that virtually no newspaper described it as anything other than a pro-choice or abortion rights march. To quote New Orleans health activist Barbara Major, "When you go to power without a base, your demand becomes a request."[20]

Base-building work, which many women of color organizations are beginning to focus on, is very slow work that may not show results for a long time. After all, the foundation of the Christian Right did not become publicly visible for fifty years. Perhaps one day, we will have a march for women's lives in which the main issues addressed and reported will include repealing the Hyde Amendment; stopping the promotion of dangerous contraceptives; decriminalizing women who are pregnant and have addictions; and ending welfare policies that punish women, in addition to other issues that speak to the intersections of gender, race, and class in reproductive rights policies.

At a meeting of the United Council of Tribes in Chicago, representatives from the Chicago Pro-Choice Alliance informed us that we should join the struggle to keep abortion legal or else we would lose our reproductive rights. A woman in the audience responded, "Who cares about reproductive rights; we don't have any rights, period." What her response suggests is that a reproductive justice agenda must make the dismantling of capitalism, white supremacy, and colonialism *central* to its agenda, and not just as principles added to organizations' promotional material designed to appeal to women of color, with no budget to support making these principles a reality. We must reject single-issue, pro-choice politics of the mainstream reproductive rights movement as an agenda that not only does not serve women of color but actually promotes the structures of oppression which keep women of color from having real choices or healthy lives.

Notes

1. Gary Crum and Thelma McCormack, *Abortion: Pro-Choice or Pro-Life?* (Washington, DC: American University Press, 1992), 54.

2. Ibid., 28.

3. Ibid., 121.

4. Jeanette Bushnell, in discussion with the author, May 21 2004.

5. Samuel Walker, *Sense and Nonsense about Crime, Drugs, and Communities* (Belmont, CA: Wadsworth Publishing Company, 1998), 139.

6. Angela Davis, *Are Prisons Obsolete*? (New York: Seven Stories Press, 2003), 26.

7. Ibid., 112.

8. Angela Y. Davis and Dylan Rodriguez, "The Challenge of Prison Abolition: A Conversation," *Social Justice* 27, no. 3 (2000): 215.

9. Charles Colson, quoted in Andrea Smith, *Native Americans and the Christian Right: The Gendered Politics of an Unlikely Alliance* (Durham, NC: Duke University Press, 2008), 9.

10. Theryn Kigvamasud'Vashi and Communities Against Rape and Abuse, "Fact Sheet on Positive Prevention/CRACK (Children Requiring a Caring Kommunity)," last updated February 12, 2002, https://users.resist.ca/~gidget/repro/fact%20sheet%20CRACK.pdf.

11. Ibid.

12. Lee Rainwater, *And the Poor Get Children* (Chicago: Quadrangle Books, 1960), 5, 167.

13. Rickie Solinger, *Beggars and Choosers: How the Politics of Choice Shapes Adoption, Abortion, and Welfare in the United States* (New York: Hill and Wang, 2001), 199–200.

14. William Saletan, "Electoral Politics and Abortion," in *The Abortion Wars*, ed. Rickie Solinger (Berkeley: University of California Press, 1998), 114.

15. NARAL (National Abortion and Reproductive Rights Action League), "Freedom of Choice Act (FOCA)," last updated January 1 2017, https://www.prochoiceamerica.org/wp-content/uploads/2016/12/4.-Freedom-of-Choice-Act.pdf.

16. Martha Saxton, "Disability Rights," in *The Abortion Wars*, 375.

17. Rainwater, *And the Poor Get Children*, 2, 178

18. Gloria Feldt, *The War on Choice* (New York: Bantam Books, 2004), 5.

19. Sheryl Blunt, "Saving Black Babies," *Christianity Today*, 47 (February 2003): 23.

20. Barbara Major, "Keynote Address" (speech delivered at National Women's Studies Association National Conference, New Orleans, Louisiana, June 2003).

Conceptualizing Reproductive Justice Theory: A Manifesto for Activism

LORETTA J. ROSS

Silhouettes unknown
Momentarily colorless
Will reveal themselves
—*Jerome Koenig*

Reproductive Justice Theory: Keisha's Story

In 2010 a twelve-year-old girl named Keisha (a pseudonym) needed an abortion and traveled to Atlanta from Chicago. I was her abortion escort and I met her at the airport. Her mother, two-month-old baby sister, and the mother's boyfriend came with her. Keisha traveled to Atlanta because, at the time, the state of Georgia offered twenty-four-week abortions and she was in her twenty-third. Illinois only provided abortions up to twenty weeks. Toni M. Bond Leonard, founder of Black Women for Reproductive Justice (BWRJ), contacted my organization SisterSong and asked me to escort Keisha to the Feminist Women's Health Center for her two-day procedure.

Keisha was a baby still sucking her thumb. I saw her obvious signs of distress. I understood why her mother was there; she had to provide permission and Keisha's birth certificate, but why did the boyfriend come? After all, they had solicited financial help from BWRJ to fly to Atlanta, pay for the abortion, and stay at a hotel. Who paid for the boyfriend? I spent three days with this family and felt some uncomfortable vibes. The mother obviously was still in shock that her twelve-year-old daughter was pregnant and needed an abortion. Quite possibly, in dealing with her own fifth pregnancy, the mother hadn't paid enough attention to her oldest child. The way the boyfriend hovered around the mother and the girl gave me the creeps; he did not seem supportive as much as monitoring.

After the abortion and waiting period to make sure everything was medically safe, the clinic offered the mother and daughter several free options for birth control. Sadly, the mother turned them down. All I could do was quietly escort them back to the airport and hope that Keisha stopped sucking her thumb before she became a mother.

Keisha's story illustrates why black women needed a new theoretical framework to move beyond the mired debates on abortion. The tragedy wasn't that Keisha *had* an abortion but that she *needed* one. How can Keisha protect her body when it is vulnerable to reproductive violence at any time? Neglecting the violence committed against girls and women weakens all attempts to achieve reproductive freedom and autonomy.

For complicated lives like Keisha's, black women activists invented reproductive justice in 1994 based on our shared legacy of feminist theories and organizing. We wanted to close the gap between an alarmingly routine story like Keisha's and the activists who helped her. We needed new language to ground moments like these in our own understanding of the vulnerability of an unprotected young black girl enmeshed in a pervasive rape culture. Reproductive justice is a real and present embodied activism by women of color pushing against a conservative, racist, and misogynist antisex society that devalues our lives, our partners, and our children.

Reproductive justice centers on three interconnected values based on human rights: the right *not* to have children by using safe birth control, abortion, or abstinence; the right to *have* children under the conditions we choose; and the right to *parent* the children we have in safe and healthy environments. In addition, reproductive justice demands sexual autonomy and gender freedom for every human being. For the past two decades, RJ has served as an important model for activist practices and movement building. It provides a prism through which I can refract Keisha's story.

This essay will offer an overview of the growth and impact of reproductive justice theory (RJT). It will examine its disruptive challenges to the pro-choice/pro-life abortion binary and the role of white allies; critique neoliberalism and white supremacy; explore the process of knowledge production (epistemology) using black feminist, critical race, and critical feminist theories; and incorporate classic feminist standpoint theory. It will also briefly analyze the pre-Enlightenment philosophy of Ubuntu as a philosophical foundation for this emerging RJT, and discuss RJ underpinnings of self-help, intersectionality, and human rights.

This essay communicates only some of the transformative potential of RJT as a synthesis of theory, strategy, and practice. This manifesto is for readers interested in movement building, feminist studies, black women's theories, and women of color activist practices to gain new perspectives on organizing and reproductive politics. RJT explores the complex relationship between lived experiences and knowledge production by challenging false binaries and false solutions through what feminist theorist Judith Butler calls "intellectual promiscuity" to synthesize theories from many disciplines. RJT has become a family of ideas generated by black women and other women of color who have transformed feminist theory and practice, moving from the margins to the mainstream.

Reproductive Justice Flowers in the Compost of the Pro-Choice Movement

Twelve black women created the concept of RJ in the summer of 1994 in Chicago at a conference sponsored by the Illinois Pro-Choice Alliance and the Ms. Foundation for Women. After the first day, black women met to analyze healthcare reform proposed by President Bill Clinton's adminstration. We believed that the proposals, while tiptoeing around abortion rights, inadequately addressed the range of intersectional reproductive health concerns in the African American community.

In abortion debates of privacy, women's rights, fetuses, and the law, the isolation of abortion from other social justice issues like violence against women fails to incorporate the intersecting issues that actually determine how a pregnant woman makes the decision to have a baby. She may base her decision on available healthcare, housing, violence, age, finances, her partner, education, immigration status, or other considerations. Combinations of social and economic issues matter.

Remember, Keisha had to travel from Chicago to Atlanta to have her abortion. Her mother had to ask for funds to pay for it as well as provide permission for her to have the procedure. Obviously Keisha was not old enough to work or be financially self-sufficient, and lacked the education, maturity, and other resources to be a successful parent. That she survived childhood sexual abuse was obvious; whether she would receive effective mental health counseling to help her cope with her experiences was doubtful. Even if she had the capacity to provide informed consent, she could not even make the independent decision to obtain and use birth control. Needing an abortion was a symptom of Keisha's situation, not the cause. Terminating her pregnancy did not solve other problems in her life.

This is why both the pro-choice and the pro-life movements incompletely address the complexity of black women's lives and decision-making. "White women's feminisms still center around *equality*," writes Brittney Cooper. "Black women's feminisms demand *justice*. There is a difference." Cooper continues, "One kind of feminism focuses on the policies that will help women integrate fully into the existing American system. The other recognizes the fundamental flaws in the system and seeks its complete and total transformation."[1] As feminist philosopher Chandra Talpade Mohanty says, "My insistence on the specificity of difference is based on a vision of equality attentive to power differences within and among various communities of women."[2] Black women felt the need to disengage from the abortion binary to create a more holistic framework for understanding our lives before, during, and after our pregnancies. When we centered ourselves in our lens, we understood how intersectional paradigms could reframe historical inequalities and differences in power and opportunities that affect our reproductive behaviors. Rather than accommodating ourselves in a pro-choice paradigm, we chose to transform the model itself.

To end the artificial isolation of abortion from other social justice issues, the twelve women in Chicago spliced together the concepts of reproductive rights and social justice to create the term "reproductive justice." We decided to call ourselves the Women of African Descent for Reproductive Justice in order to launch a campaign in July 1994 to influence healthcare reform. A few months later, some of us attended the International Conference on Population and Development in September 1994 in Cairo, Egypt, where the global women's health movement emphasized the relationship between poverty, underdevelopment, and women's reproduction. We joined sisters from the Global South to critique strategies of population control and learned from our sisters internationally who used the human rights framework to make stronger, more positive claims for women's full human rights that moved far beyond the limits of the US Constitution and the restrictive privacy framework.

Analyzing white supremacy is a cornerstone of reproductive justice. Failures to criticize it produce sterile theories and practices that are, in fact, complicit with white supremacy by airbrushing it to soften its lethality. It is important to underscore that white supremacy is an ideology used to promote unequal laws, practices, and social outcomes, such as differential, racially structured access to power. White supremacy is not a fact of genetics or an accurate description of either a race of people or the hierarchy of all races. The ideology and tactics of the formal white supremacist movement disgust many people in the US who identify as white. White supremacy is an ideology; white privilege is the practice.

Including an analysis of the observable historical factors that determine the worth of the lives of people of color, or the downstream consequences of upstream racism, required a new theory by African American women. Just as critical social theory "constitutes theorizing about the social in defense of economic and social justice,"[3] RJT analyzes intersectional reproductive politics in pursuit of human rights. Intersectionality is the process; human rights are the goal.

Keisha's life was obviously at the intersection of gender, age, sexual violence, race, class, neglect, mental health, and a host of other mutually reinforcing issues I could not explore with her. I could have asked what happened, but that would have been objectionable and objectifying. Keisha did not have to satisfy my curiosity, and I did not have the right to impose my need on her story. However, she lingers in my heart as I write this essay. Helping Keisha helped me. I had my own experiences with childhood sexual abuse, unhealed trauma, and abortion. Simply debating whether Keisha could or should have an abortion clearly overlooks the avalanche of other issues in her life.

Reproductive justice is based on the human right to make personal decisions about one's life, and the obligation of government and society to ensure that the conditions are suitable for implementing one's decisions. Individual and state actions are interdependent to achieve reproductive freedom and bodily autonomy. In particular, RJ draws attention to the lack of physical, reproductive, and cultural safety for vulnerable people. It does not privilege the production of babies as the only goal of women's biology, but also includes sexual freedom and autonomy, bodily self-determination, and the complex interdynamics between an individual and their communities.

RJ is collective and interdependent by definition, in contrast to the individualistic, atomistic worldview of liberals or the alienated, selfish worldview of ultraconservatives. Scientific racism that claims people of color are genetically and intellectually inferior to white people is part of an ideology that propelled Iowa Representative Steve King to tweet in March 2017, "We can't restore our civilization with somebody else's babies."[4] Both conservatives and liberals support the neoliberal, cowboy capitalism and soft eugenics so hazardous to our bodies and communities both domestically and globally. Reproductive justice is needed because underdeveloped analyses of the impact of white supremacist ideas on reproductive politics are insufficient to offer a radical new vision for the future.

Keisha's life is not just a story about the pro-choice/pro-life debate. The African American community has difficulty honestly discussing issues of sex and sexuality because of shame and religious beliefs. Maybe it is a remnant of respectability politics through which we try to dispute racialized sexual stigmas. Some black women fiercely seek to establish ourselves as respectable women deserving the same regard as other people in society, regardless of our dress, language, or religion. Black women are accused of sexual irresponsibility and hyperfertility in the media, in public policy debates, and in our homes. Internalizing such myths creates self-inflicted soul wounds leading to low self-esteem and intense discomfort about our human right to sexual pleasure. Overidentifying with the stereotypes may produce seemingly rebellious displays of blatant sexuality to reclaim our power. Regardless, we get slut shamed and often believe that only by following the moral compass of the conservative wing of the black church or mimicking a mythologized white society can we redeem our honor and respectability.

Leonard, one of the RJ cocreators, is a religious scholar developing a theology of reproductive justice. She writes that the black community needs "a discourse that would begin to examine and erase the lasting remnants of White culture's reproductive violation and degradation of Black women and inhumane portrayal of Black men as nothing more than sexual predators during slavery."[5] She references the work of noted scholar and theologian Kelly Brown Douglas, who calls for a "sexual discourse of resistance" as a way to "expose the manifold impact White culture has on Black sexuality."[6] Douglas's excellent scholarship asserts that the sexual exploitation of black women and men has not only damaged the self-esteem of the community but creates a particularly grave injustice for African American women. The majority-female population keeps the black church thriving while the church ignores black women's sexual and reproductive needs. While recognizing that the church is not monolithic when sex, sexuality, and reproduction are mentioned, it is often in a judgmental and condemnatory way, rather than with love and support because our collective sexual consciousness has been warped by misogyny, slavery, and colonialism.

Byllye Avery, founder of the National Black Women's Health Project (NBWHP), calls this a "conspiracy of silence." If the black church seeks to heal not hurt, failing to acknowledge the amazing gift of sexual expression every human is entitled to enjoy is unacceptable. Some religious leaders believe that merely talking about sex is a sin, and actually having sex is the pathway to spiritual damnation for those not in monogamous, heterosexual marriages. A sexually conservative black church abandons its responsibility to black men, women, children, and gender nonconforming people when it is condemnatory. What's a child like Keisha to do, much less her mother, when all conversations on sex and sexuality are religiously verboten?

RJT is an example of Douglas's sexual discourse of resistance that challenges both the conspiracy of silence around sex and sexuality that stifles black church culture and inhibits African American communities, and the respectability politics that bolster that silence. We have difficulties talking about sex, sexual abuse, abortion, HIV/AIDS, sexism, gender identities, violence against women, and a host of key issues that affect the lives of black women. Keisha's story offers an important lesson: we cannot keep our children safe if we cannot talk about sex. We cannot proceed out of this morass of silence without a new way of thinking about reproductive politics.

We must affirm the worth and fragility of our children and our black communities to bring epistemic and political processes together because of the importance that knowledge plays in empowering oppressed peoples to analyze sites of domination and resistance. For example, racism and capitalism together cause premature deaths among African Americans in the United States. According to Ruha Benjamin, an "estimated 83,570 excess deaths each year could be prevented if this black-white mortality gap could be eliminated. To put it more starkly, that's the equivalent of a major airliner filled with black passengers falling out of the sky every single day, every year."[7] Breaking endlessly reproducing cycles of oppression demands dismantling interlocking systems of disadvantage and privilege, and reimagining a world in which autonomy, dignity, and freedom are available to everyone globally. We envision liberation and justice from within our dynamic realities. As Olga Villa-Parra said, "We are always hungry for understanding, we engage in the eternal human search for reason, for grouping things together so we can make sense of them. We want to understand what drives us in life."[8]

Because it places vulnerable people in the center of our lenses, RJT helps people understand the relationship between white supremacy and white privilege. Most white people justifiably deny that they subscribe to the ideology of white supremacy, but all do benefit from white privilege. For example, white privilege is not necessarily special treatment, but it means that white people do not have to worry about many things people of color do, like racist police brutality or racial profiling. Special treatment based on racist stereotypes is what people of color routinely experience, especially black and brown victims like Michael Brown, Sandra Bland, Manual Diaz, or Terence Crutcher, who were unjustly killed by law enforcement. Or, like James Means or Jordan Davis, they may be assassinated by angry, entitled white men with guns. Special treatment is housing discrimination or higher mortgage interest rates because of race, such as brilliantly described by Ta-Nehisi Coates in his incisive "The Case for Reparations" article in the *Atlantic* in June 2014. Special treatment is to be seen with a fearful gaze before one's humanity is acknowledged, so that a twelve-year-old black child like Tamir Rice is killed within seconds by Cleveland police who say they mistook a toy gun for a real one, even in an open-carry state.

Black feminists reject the belief that quotidian repetition and legalistic rituals should numb us to the violence of these injuries. It is cowardice not to draw attention to this through feigned innocence. Moral cowards flee responsibility for threats and deaths based on white supremacist ideologies and traditions. A complex reality is not an excuse for silence.

In a sense, reproductive justice simply finds new words for old ideas. There is admittedly little original about RJ; black women have used an intersectional analysis to fight racism since Sojourner Truth declared, "Ain't I a Woman?" to an 1851 women's rights convention that ignored racial justice issues. Frederick Douglass protested the lynching of a black man in 1858 using the term "human rights" and Anna Julia Cooper wrote about the unique situation of black women in the United States in 1892. What is fresh about RJ is that women of color are leading the way in applying the global human rights framework to reproductive politics in the US, to move beyond the limits of the Constitution by continuing our historical resistance to white supremacy.

By the beginning of the twenty-first century, two decades after reproductive justice was created, we understood that this expanding RJT was a logical next step in the tradition of the intellectual history of women of color. Like our foremothers, each generation of women of color RJ activists has built new conceptual expansions of pioneering work by black feminists from the 1960s forward. These decades were particularly important for the emergence of seminal race/gender/class/sovereignty/immigrant/queer intersectional approaches. Each writer fiercely pushed against the devaluing of our lives. Audre Lorde so eloquently stated: "I am not free while any woman is unfree, even when her shackles are very different from my own."[9] RJ emerged as a theory and a movement to reimagine what reproductive freedom could look like for all people.

The novelty of the RJ framework makes it attractive, but its primary influence may be because many people want to move beyond the stalemate of abortion politics. Perhaps the pro-choice/pro-life binary has outlived its shelf life in the past forty years, becoming obsolete. Planned Parenthood Federation of America (PPFA) reported in 2014 that it would no longer describe itself as a pro-choice organization. I guess it was providential that RJ came along twenty years before that announcement. Problematizing the pro-choice/pro-life deadlock may be a matter of timing and attention span, or possibly women of color have pivoted to a new, more radical consciousness attractive to some on both sides of the debate. Only time will tell if RJ is a sustainable concept.

The framework of reproductive justice was populated and popularized because women of color, not just African American women, needed a "theory that explains how we articulate or otherwise express our bodies, experiences, and affects, all of which are fluid and energetic, in some form of meaningful signification so that we can communicate."[10] Activism by women of color provided the scaffolding for RJ for many years as we attempted to strengthen the pro-choice movement. We recognized that the lack of appropriate language imprisoned our souls and frustrated our alliances. We were not offering to colorize an existing pro-choice framework by merely adding women of color and stirring, but to shake it up and offer our own radical paradigm that could account for the differential impacts of white supremacy and incorporate intersectionality. This led us to explore new ways of describing our realities, producing multiple voices in dialogue as part of a movement conversation between activists and the state. We sought to investigate how linguistic practices can either reproduce or transform the very structures that shape them. As scientific historian Evelynn M. Hammonds says, "Investigating how medicine and public health structure power relationships that construct gendered, 'raced,' and 'classed' identities must be at the center of our work."[11]

An example is how the language of choice based on the concept of privacy reinforced the subordination of poor women through the Hyde Amendment that prohibits using federal funds for abortions. This legislative prohibition first passed in 1976 and has been attached to appropriations bills ever since. Although there are legal exceptions for rape, incest, and threats to the life of the mother, many states have used Hyde as an excuse to restrict abortion even further than the federal law requires. Hyde prohibits federal funding for abortions for anyone whose healthcare is provided by the federal government, including impoverished people on Medicaid, those within the Indian Health Service, people in the military and the Peace Corps, etc. The privacy framework used by the Supreme Court to affirm Hyde says that if abortion is a private decision, then the government has no obligation to pay for this private decision, laying the groundwork for making an exception for abortion coverage as if it is not a routine part of reproductive healthcare for women. This inferred interpretation of the right to privacy—which is not actually in the Constitution—was rationalized by the Supreme Court in the 1973 *Roe v. Wade* decision legalizing abortion, as well as other decisions decriminalizing the use of birth control. The danger lies in its tenuous foundation lacking a constitutional basis: what the Supreme Court giveth, the Supreme Court can taketh away. Feminists pay careful attention to the vulnerability of the liberal/conservative ratio of the court because we recognize the frailty of the legal protections for abortion rights and birth control. Abortion presented as a choice became a co-opted neoliberal frame that denied government responsibility for providing healthcare.

Hyde discriminated against people trapped in poverty, and the mainstream pro-choice movement largely failed to analyze the impact of white supremacist thinking on tax policies. Black women, of course, pointed out that white Americans are particularly resistant to public policies that appear to help people of color in general and African Americans in particular. Hyde was disguised as concern for fetuses, and became yet another public policy to be rejected or attacked because of racial politics. For example, in 1978 California voters passed Proposition 13 as a thinly disguised property-tax-relief measure that had the net effect of decreasing funding to California's public schools, colleges, and universities. Because publicly funded education benefited the increasingly diverse California student population, a tax-disguised dog whistle joined the list of publicly beneficial policies opposed by the majority of white voters who believe undeserving people of color take advantage of public systems like education, welfare, and healthcare while "hard working white people" unfairly foot the bills. These types of enraged, race-based producerist diatribes against education and healthcare, in particular, have had severe consequences in every avenue of political discourse.

Black women led campaigns to remove the Hyde restrictions on abortion beginning in the early 1990s. The first campaign was initiated by the NBWHP from 1993 to 1996, according to Leslie Watson Malachi, the C.A.R.E. campaign director. NBWHP understood the desperate conditions of many impoverished black women who needed abortion coverage. They protested that low-income women on Medicaid, many of whom are women of color, could not use their public insurance coverage for an abortion, whereas middle-class women with private insurance faced few or no restrictions. Some mainstream organizations financially supported C.A.R.E. but most did not, believing that taxpayers could not be persuaded to subsidize abortions. This passive acceptance of antitax and antiabortion rhetoric that singularly punished poor women using racist dog-whistle politics infuriated black women. Even without the political power at the time to revoke the legislation, black women insisted that Hyde would provide a slippery slope to undermine abortion rights and healthcare as opponents cascaded even more restrictions. History has proven our point.

Becoming an RJ Activist by Building a Theoretical Home

> *We know things with our lives, and we live that knowledge, beyond what any theory has yet theorized.*
>
> —*Catherine MacKinnon*

I have been active in the black feminist movement since the 1970s, when I was sterilized at age twenty-three. Now, I'm a passionate writer creating change through my experience, unapologetically using my heart to guide my words. My educational background in chemistry, physics, and women's studies paralleled my feminist activism for the past five decades. I've been a scientific researcher, an antirape organizer, a professional feminist, a human rights educator, and an analyst of fascism and white supremacy. As a bridge-builder who delights in ambiguous borderlands in the tradition of Gloria Anzaldúa, I've become deeply attuned to both the community and the academy simultaneously while working with an inadequate theoretical language to better convey my growing understanding of the transformative power of RJT.

Reproductive justice has become a free and safe conceptual love zone for integrating my subjective and objective experiences as an African American woman hoping to connect feminist theory with political organizing. Synthesizing this emergent RJT is an honor while standing on the shoulders of black feminist scholars who influenced me like Dorothy Roberts, Toni Cade Bambara, Beverly Guy-Sheftall, Stanlie James, Angela Davis, Patricia Hill Collins, Audre Lorde, Paula Giddings, bell hooks, and Kimberlé Crenshaw, among others. They have written about asserting our body autonomy, sexual expressions, and reproductive rights as African American women, creating conceptual space for my ruminations. bell advised me to write about black women in the anti-rape movement in 1981 while I was at the DC Rape Crisis Center and organized one of her lectures on black feminism. Nevertheless, I felt very insecure about my lack of academic credentials to do so, at the time lacking even a bachelor's degree.

Crenshaw first encouraged me to write this essay on RJT. I attended a conference on critical race theory in 2009 seeking an academic scholar who could do justice populating this concept. Among my targets was lawyer and activist Crenshaw, who coined the term "intersectionality" that will be discussed further in this essay. I believed she was the most appropriate person to further develop a radical theory of reproductive justice. When I asked if she would write for this anthology, Crenshaw threw the ball back into my court, insisting that theorizing on RJ was best done by the very activists who created the framework. I was intimidated by her response and taken aback by her belief that I could adequately transmit my heartfelt belief in the theoretical capacity and power of reproductive justice. When I investigated the artificial binary between the activist and scholar communities, I spoke of my fears to scholars like my Agnes Scott women's studies professors Elizabeth Hackett and Isa Williams, and my Emory University professor Rosemarie Garland-Thomson. Gloria Steinem, who recommended the excellent book *Disciplining Feminism*, helped me feel empowered to live up to the courage of my instincts to write this essay. In the words of Zora Neale Hurston, "I had knowledge before its time."[12]

As feminist biologist Banu Subramaniam explains, I have learned through my activism that feminism moves

> beyond a focus on women, to how material bodies, institutions, and structures are gendered. Feminists also recognize that woman is not a universal monolithic category, but always intertwined with other social categories such as gender, sexuality, race, ethnicity, class, and nation since women's experiences are shaped by their multiple social locations and identities. Thus, "feminist" means not just exploring women or gender, but recognizing the co-constituted meanings of categorizing human populations. We need to focus on the process of knowledge production, not just the content.[13]

Fortunately, there is a rich body of scholarship available to help me flesh out a capacious theory of reproductive justice. I developed my feminism in the company of other black women in Washington, DC, in my formative years, so I came to my understanding of the intersection of feminism and white supremacy long before I had to armor it against the reservations of white women. Instead, many women of color first learn feminist theoretical concepts outside of their natal communities and struggle to articulate their own analyses of oppression through intersectional lenses. As an African American woman who relies on the scholarship of black feminists to evolve this manifesto, I recognize that is part promising theory and part polemic against injustices. This does not deny the other amazing seminal influences of other women of color, white women, and men who influence me and who may further theorize reproductive justice through their own lenses. I choose to use the register that I am most comfortable with (just as I am with dangling prepositions and split infinitives!).

Because my activism and advocacy seek to create change in the present and lay a foundation for alternative futures as an RJ cocreator, I'm glad reproductive justice was an intersectional activist practice long before it was theory. Reproductive justice also confronts the presumed objectivity, neutrality, and certitude of the rapacious white supremacist system that violates the human rights of black women and girls. America's legal, economic, and even academic systems are not racially or gender neutral, nor objective. These metasystems have built-in biases against all who are not white, heterosexual males, proven daily through economic or academic statistics, news reports, elections, and popular culture. Such systems only value knowledge derived from privileged sites of power. Reproductive justice organizes grassroots knowledge into words and experience into theory to counter this false narrative of objectivity and certainty, i.e., that heterosexual white men are best qualified to develop laws and policies governing women's reproduction.

In contrast, RJ is the effort "to bridge the gap between the actualities of our lives and the consciousness of our oppressor,"[14] to transcend the too simplistic dualism of victim and oppressor. It investigates the social constructions of race, gender, class, sexual identity, and sexual preference, and how socially imposed boundaries affect our reproductive decision-making. We explore how ideologies of motherhood are an intersectional locus with which to analyze gendered and racial concepts of citizenship, as well as the right to sexual agency and sexual desire and pleasure. RJ challenges the stereotypes of black women as inferior beings without agency, without the power to think for ourselves or make decisions about our lives and bodies. RJT helps fill the relative paucity of black feminist theorizing about the sexual body. As I reflect on Keisha's situation and her presumed choices, I will speculate on what we, as black feminists creating new theory, have to offer Keisha as she grows and copes with difficulties common for vulnerable black girls.

Black feminist theorizing generally avoids jargon and the reliance on obscure theorists in a language that is difficult to acquire and understand, an elite mark of status. Black feminists write about the intimate connection between the production of knowledge and the power relations in our society. As activists writing about theory, we endure accusations of philosophical naïveté because our writings are not dense, opaque, or mystifying. The goal is communication, not self-presentation. As Patricia Hill Collins writes,

> Theory of all types is often presented as being so abstract that it can be appreciated by only a select few. Though often highly satisfying to academics, this definition excludes those who do not speak the language of elites and thus reinforces social relations of domination. Educated elites typically claim that only they are qualified to produce theory and believe that only they can interpret not only their own but everyone else's experiences.[15]

I hope RJT can both use feminist theoretical language and make it accessible. I want to have all such tools at our disposal to deploy them in a new way using our lives as the intellectual centers of our inquiries. At the same time, I seek to avoid the opaqueness of high theory (assuming I'm even qualified to speak passably about postmodern theories without confusing myself in convolutions). My interpretation of RJT does not seek to present a singular, unified view of the entire RJ field, but rather to explore its diversity, depth, and flexibility. I most want to offer pathways for future scholars and activists. The goal is not to arrive at consensus or cohesion but to establish a foundational set of analyses to counter racial and "biological determinism, [presumed] scientific objectivity, and assumptions about value neutrality, reproduction, and the labor of women."[16]

The kind of knowledge a society has reflects the kind of society it is. Thinking about when Isaac Newton named gravity is illustrative. He did not invent gravity, but he observed that objects always fall down not up, and he named theories of gravity, motion, and inertia. It was not possible for the concept of gravity to emerge without the rise of scientific inquiry because it had to counter religion-based explanations of physical phenomena. The social conditions had to be ripe for rethinking how the universe works, and the social relations had to be favorable for Newton not to be executed by the church for offering his novel theory about invisible physical forces. While not presuming to compare RJT to profound scientific discoveries, RJ is a theory about social and economic forces and reproductive politics whose time had come for African American women.

Reproductive justice theory is the logical next step in the tradition of black women's intellectual history, to bring the work of black feminists into focus when we assert our leadership in reproductive politics. We can help prevent more tragedies for girls like Keisha. If she goes to college in a few years, I hope we can explain RJT to Keisha in a way that is clear and helps her own this knowledge and her body.

Why Is Reproductive Justice Theory Needed?

Reproductive justice theory is needed because many earlier theories about reproduction pay inadequate attention to the physical, socioeconomic, and emotional realities of Indigenous women, poor women, trans women, and women of color. Such theories fail to thoroughly analyze and critique the system of white supremacy that determines which bodies matter and which do not. Any theory that does not work for or include marginalized cis and trans women does not adequately describe gender relations. Analyzing the relationships between people who are reproductively privileged and those who are disadvantaged is key to understanding the systems of difference and inequality and to illuminate the experiences of each group of people (and the individuals within them) who seek to control their destinies. To comprehend how the American empire uses and misuses bodies, especially the bodies of people of color, is part of my mission with this essay.

It is important for RJT to go beyond affirming the right *not* to have children and pivot to emphasize the right to *have* children under the conditions we choose. Women of color and Indigenous women live in communities constantly under siege by forces promoting and enacting policies of privatized eugenics and population control, so applications of RJT must account for the politics of white supremacy. Debates about desirable and undesirable bodies have been a site of scientific and social inquiry for centuries, bolstered by white fears of miscegenation, disabilities, and the fertility of people of color. The government has historically used women's bodies as sites of population and community control to build an exclusive national identity based on ideas about who was appropriately white, heterosexual, able-bodied, and middle class. In her book *Pregnancy and Power*, historian Rickie Solinger calls this the "racialization of reproductive politics." RJT challenges the perception that the racialized female-identified body is uniquely suitable for regulation by the state and private parties. As transgender writer Katherine Cross says, "I cannot indulge the false premise that women are born to be oppressed—a very different notion from saying we are born into a world that oppresses us."[17]

The construction of the hierarchies of white supremacy depended on preserving white racial "purity" as a political, not biological, category as well as the separating and subjugating of Indigenous peoples and enslaved Africans. hooks posits that "[t]he very concept of white supremacy relies on the perpetuation of a white race. It is in the interest of continued white racist domination of the planet for white patriarchy to maintain control over all women's bodies."[18] Indigenous scholar Andrea Smith argues that this domination required the "constant purification and elimination of racialized enemies within the state."[19] White men in power have erected and continue to reinforce racial boundaries by placing the regulation of reproduction and policing of all sexual relations at the center of their project, leading to "reproductive disappearing" of Indigenous people, and perpetrating racist beliefs about the sexual and reproductive behaviors of all people of color, but particularly black women and men.

As people of color, we are engaged in an ongoing struggle against white supremacy because the history of the United States is thick with racism, one of the manifestations of white supremacy. White supremacy is also a patriarchal war against the feminine, especially for women of color and trans women, for whom state violence is political currency to maintain the status quo. The disproportionate violence against trans women proves that violence against women includes gender subordination without having been assigned a female label at birth. Who is vulnerable to violence depends on the male supremacist need for domination, identity, and destruction of others.

Population control measures, also called eugenics, focused primarily on the biological control of people, and included sterilization abuses, dangerous contraceptives, and separation of family members. These policies sought to manage reproduction in communities of color as well as among others, such as poor white people and mentally or physically disabled people. Racialized population engineering processes continue today through sterilization abuse, promotion of long-term contraceptives that providers refuse to remove or carry exorbitant removal costs, overincarceration, and environmental racism. More blatantly, the assaults on sex education, abortion, and birth control are attempts to compel white women to have more children through promoting a culture that normalizes breeding (i.e., *19 Kids and Counting*) while at the same time punishing women of color through myths about our reproductive recklessness in order to maintain the system of white supremacy. For example, a pseudo-documentary entitled *Demographic Winter: The Decline of the Human Family* is popular among those who fear white "demographic suicide" through reduced births. There is also a new phenomenon reproductive technology has made available, persuading privileged (and mostly white) women to freeze their eggs as incentivized by Apple and Facebook (now a twenty-thousand-dollar employee benefit). These are just two examples of racialized reproductive engineering.

The policies are working. Despite the stereotype of teen pregnancy as a black, Indigenous, or Latina phenomenon, white teenage pregnancy rates are rising in states that mandate the toughest restrictions on sex education, birth control, and abortion access. While the national teen pregnancy rate in 2010 was thirty-eight per one thousand teens, the most conservative states with the most stringent restrictions had much higher rates, forty-eight per one thousand teens, and higher. These states resist providing the kinds of resources that would reduce teen pregnancy, concentrating instead on disproven abstinence-only programs. In addition, states that offer the stingiest welfare state benefits also experience a decrease in life expectancy.

Biological strategies can control entire communities, but they are not the only method. A privatized modern form of population control, neo-Malthusianism—based on perceptions of resource scarcity, safety fears, and regurgitated racism—is sophisticated ideological glue that binds together many disparate issues that affect reproductive politics such as security, climate change, religious nationalism, white supremacy, resource scarcity, public health, and family planning.

Population control critiques through an RJ lens go far beyond abortion and sterilization abuse to broaden the picture and show how oppressions are interrelated. Policies that at first glance appear disconnected have implications for reproductive decision-making.[20] Fighting police brutality, gun violence, or tainted water supplies so our children can survive is as equally urgent as fighting for bodily integrity and self-determination. I coined the term "reprocide" to describe when genocide is primarily committed through reproductive control. These political crimes of reprocide occur in full view of the American public, yet there is no accountability. RJT offers a lens through which we examine the various ways in which social stigmas and public policies affect black women's sexuality, reproduction, children, and labor during stages of economic expansion and contraction, as well as shifts in engagement with the ideology of white supremacy and the practices of white privilege.

Black women know population control ideologies morph over time, but are never totally abandoned. Sociologist Nicole Rousseau writes, "As Black women's relationship with the United States begins with her role in a forced labor pool, it stands to reason that her continued position in society, even in the years following slavery, would remain connected with her labor location."[21] Rousseau explores the relationship between the shifts in the tools and technology of capitalist wealth creation and how these means of production correlate to the shifts in the demand for black women's forms of labor: productive, reproductive, and biological.

Ironically, we can also add political labor to this list. During the 2016 presidential election, 91 percent of college-educated black women voted against Trump, while non-college-educated black women more eagerly opposed him at 95 percent. At the same time, 45 percent of college-educated white women voted for Trump, and 62 percent of non-college-educated white women did so. Averaged out, 53 percent of white women voted for Trump. While some mainstream media pundits have described the crisis in white masculinity that animated the angst in Trump's base, few recognize that affirming white supremacy also reassured conservative white women about the immutability of gender relations to protect their own perceived privileges as white women. Black women drove the gender gap, not the white women who privileged race over gender, or said another way, asserted white racial identitarian politics as the best protection for their gender, despite the evidence to the contrary.

The passionate activism and theories of black feminists excavates the nightmare of America's history and explains the legacies of settler colonialism, xenophobia, and enslavement. I've tried to talk to my friends who are progressive but completely underestimate the power of white supremacy as a body of ideas that is affirmed daily in thousands of ways: The feminists who believe that gender should have kept Trump out of office. The economic radicals who believed that a class analysis should have prevented this political moment. My LGBTQ friends who thought we turned the corner with marriage equality. And so on. White supremacy is not a resurgent, anachronistic characteristic or symptom of America, but its DNA. Not every marginalized social location provides a sturdy or even particularly insightful analysis of how to deconstruct white supremacy and build a better future for the world. Will the progressive movement ever listen to progressive black women who understand this probably better than anyone ever has?

Black feminists gifted the concepts of identity politics, intersectionality, and now reproductive justice to the progressive movements, and witnessed the transformative power of our ideas to build social justice movements for human rights. Yet misogynoir still contaminates every radical political discussion, and our allies keep getting continuously surprised by the resilience of white supremacist ideas. Black feminist scholar Moya Bailey termed this ingrained habit of dismissing the knowledge of black women "misogynoir," referring to hatred of women or misogyny directed toward black women that can be conscious or unconscious. She describes the unique experiences of black women when anti-blackness and misogyny combine to malign African American women.

It is okay to be optimistic but dangerous to be naive. White supremacy determines what one knows or chooses not to know. We concur with James Baldwin when he said, "People are trapped in history and history is trapped in them."[22] The impact of this history reflects the politics of our time, and the least prepared people to deconstruct white supremacy are perhaps not the best to lead the struggle against it within reproductive politics.

Reproductive justice theory challenges the effects of white supremacy on our minds and bodies in what African philosopher Frantz Fanon called "epidermilization," or the imposition of race on the body. Black feminists had to create alternative modes of analysis based on neglected or understated intellectual influences and foundations that accounted for the ideology of white supremacy and its handmaiden, white privilege. It is impossible to fully understand reproductive politics and build a movement for reproductive justice without comprehending the politics of population control and the ideology of eugenics underlying such thinking.

The human right to birth or to parent in the RJ framework addresses a system that is constantly trying to manage or pathologize communities of color. Institutionalized racism, sexism, and xenophobia within the medical-industrial complex distort our reproductive experiences. Different axes of identity, location, and circumstance are manipulated by economic and social forces, creating a chain of "-isms" too tiresome to endlessly repeat. An emerging field of birth justice activists comprised primarily of midwives and doulas who use the RJ framework understand how, according to Patricia Hill Collins, "these forces collide, often violently, in determining the sexual and reproductive trajectories of entire communities," and offer radical birth work to humanize people's reproductive experiences.[23]

The right to mother is never and has never been uncontested for black women in the United States. Motherhood here has meanings and assumptions about racial differences, gender roles, work-force participation, and masculinity. Controlling black women's sexuality maintains race, class, and gender inequality. Slavery created the interpretations of racial differences that underpinned capitalist development and expansion. The pursuit of white racial purity created a hierarcy of subordination continuously affecting laws, public policies, economics, and social relations.

Our children's lives are a battleground in which a black women's standpoint on the human right to mother and have our children survive in a system that devalues their existence has generated a radical set of ideas and social practices in dialogue with each other. Black women pursuing justice are becoming more radicalized through the deaths of our children. We organized the Black Lives Matter movement, for example, to challenge the monstrous appetite of white supremacy that chews up black lives. In the words of Thandisizwe Chimurenga, "We have a shared victimization by white supremacy. As we transform society, we also heal ourselves."[24] Assata Shakur, a legendary political exile in Cuba, asserts, "It is imperative that we, as black women, talk about the experiences that shaped us; that we assess our strengths and weaknesses and define our own history."[25] Black women have to determine for ourselves our meanings for motherhood through the RJ framework. We resist accusations of failed femininity or failed motherhood when we are stereotyped as hypersexualized and promiscuously fertile, or overmasculinized and desexualized.

We stand accused as black women of being incapable of speaking for ourselves, and much less capable of composing our own cultural and historical narratives and theories, yet we have offered a different kind of knowledge production based on black feminism. As Mai'a Williams says in the brilliant anthology *Revolutionary Mothering*, we are black women determining the meaning of motherhood for ourselves "who believe in themselves and their children, in the future and the ancestors so fiercely they will face down the ugly violence of the present time and time again."[26] Alexis Pauline Gumbs continues, "Those of us who nurture the lives of children who are not supposed to exist, who are not supposed to grow up, who are revolutionary in their very beings are doing some of the most subversive work in the world."[27] We dare to imagine an America in the future that is not violent toward the marginalized bodies of people of color. That America has never existed before.

Neoliberalism and Reproductive Justice

Through reproductive justice theory, we need to challenge conceptual practices of the pro-choice movement that not only understates issues of intersectionality and white supremacy but also offers no radical alternatives to neoliberal capitalism and its emphasis on rights and choices. Liberal feminism also inadequately explains the lived experiences of all women and the differences between them.

As reproductive justice activists, we need to "think about ideologies of family, sexuality, and reproduction as animating imperial and racial projects" in the context of our victimization by white supremacy, according to Laura Briggs, who writes about the colonization of Puerto Rico through militarism and reproductive abuses.[28] White supremacy attempts to eliminate or at least contain the racially constructed other through differentiated values for reproductive bodies. It simultaneously claims our bodies and our sexuality, while erecting undisputable barriers of exclusion through legal and political subordination.

Attacks on the reproductive behaviors of women of color are necessary to disguise the neoliberal capitalist system's manipulation of racial politics to hide its class warfare against poor and middle-class people. The system generates endless recyclable myths of the undeserving mother—poor, immigrant, queer, disabled, or a woman of color—accused of reproductive recklessness. Conservatives claim we put our sex lives ahead of our social responsibilities. The sexuality of women must always be hidden or punished. The visible products of this sexuality, our children, must also suffer from having been born. From Ronald Reagan's rants against "welfare queens" to Tyre King's murder in Ohio, the white supremacist rallying cry is that the world must be saved from our wanton sexual desires because women of color—and our children—are held responsible for all the ills of society, from environmental degradation to the 2007 collapse of the mortgage industry.

Most liberals and conservatives assume poverty results from our reproductive behaviors, and is not the inevitable consequence of the unjust distribution of wealth and opportunities in the United States. These myths about our alleged lack of morals and individual responsibility prop up the austerity justifications used by the 1 percent and the politicians who serve them as excuses to decimate the welfare, unemployment, and social security systems, and demonize what they characterize as the dependency culture pitting the makers against the takers. This highly individualistic, producerist worldview is inherently and manipulatively antithetical to our competing worldview based on human rights and human interdependence. In this neoliberal worldview, care for the social good is no longer the responsibility of local and federal governments and agencies. It is left, rather, to the biases of private corporations, charities, and the discretionary impulses of uneven global capitalists.

In response to the economic and demographic changes of the twenty-first century that will produce a nonwhite diverse demographic, white supremacy rearranges its power relations. Examples include claiming that white people are the principal victims of reverse racism, that women feminize men by having too much power, or that trans people have unfair advantages over cisgender people, such as the legislative battles over bathroom access.

The Great Recession of 2007–2008 is similar to the Great Depression in that it deepened a crisis in white masculinity with the disappearing of economic futures for white men without a college education. Economic upheaval was defined not as a consequence of unregulated laissez faire capitalism but rather the result of the loss of male authority within families, as presciently described by Ruth Feldstein. Both of these economic crises are characterized by a backlash against anti-racist efforts and misogynist policies designed to push women out of the workforce to reassert white male power and control. Trumpism may reaffirm older ideas about the role of women as mothers to rebuild the prominence of white patriarchal values and distract from the privatized, neoliberal policies at the root of the economic collapse of the white working and middle-class.

A central oppressive feature is white men reasserting the power to name and define the identities and realities of marginalized people, and for these accounts perceived as objective and authoritative, eclipsing our perspectives as black women. As part of this rearrangement, increasing numbers of conservative people of color seduced by white supremacist ideologies deny the persistence of racism, sexism, imperialism, transphobia, etc. They cynically thwart progressive movements, spending their best efforts keeping others down, without offering viable economic or racial justice solutions.

Reproductive justice is our answer to the myriad forms of such interlocked oppressions because justice-centered feminist ethics are needed. Reproductive oppression is the exploitation of our bodies, sexuality, labor, and fertility in order to achieve social and economic control of our communities and in violation of our human rights, according to Asian Communities for Reproductive Justice (now Forward Together). This expansive definition provides many possibilities for reproductive justice analyses, particularly for women.

Knowledge Production through Reproductive Justice Activism

As black feminists, we cannot consider the question of what to do before we examine the question of how we think. Otherwise, we risk settling for false solutions that reproduce the existing system of inequalities. The most important work must be epistemological, an inquiry into how we know what we know, and how what we know makes us think. "I am therefore I think" could be a fresh expression of this embodied knowledge production based on our lived experiences. We are not disembodied as thinking subjects. How the body acts and is acted upon affects why, how, and what we think.

Incorporating the fluidity of social constructs describing and defining bodies is among the possibilities of reproductive justice theory that invests in shifting meanings, accounting for the gender continuum and the artificiality of racial boundaries. Reproductive justice will never be a linear narrative. It has leaps, chasms, circumlocutions, subversions, and conundrums that transform relationships of perceived difference into possibilities for concerted social change. In many ways, it is a decentered, polyvocal, and cocreated theory of justice applicable to all. It offers a theory, strategy, and practice with which to challenge dominant narratives about the power and experiences of marginalized people.

For example, this emergent theoretical framework is based on discussions among women of color and Indigenous women about sex and sexuality and how current practices and norms fail to meet the needs of our communities and our lives. Perhaps Keisha's situation could have been avoided if she had received age-appropriate evidence-based sex education and protection from the violence of a male predator. Although she probably was not responsible for her pregnancy, we live in a society that blames young women for their pregnancies, regardless of cause. Our society is especially scornful of and unhelpful to young mothers, passing judgment on their perceived reproductive misbehavior.

RJT is a new addition to feminist epistemology and activist practices. "From its inception, radical feminism in particular emphasized the importance of sexuality, not simply as the ground of women's oppression, but equally as the take-off point for an account that valorized bodily difference,"[29] according to theorists Janet Price and Margrit Shildrick. Radical feminist theories call for a "dissolution of subject and object, of observer and observed" even in academic settings that have "vivisected a vibrant world into sterile disciplinary formations."[30] RJT, like most advanced feminist theories, uses disciplinary and interdisciplinary resources to challenge masculinist incorporeal abstraction theories because of the validity of the lived experiences foregrounded by women of color. The false dichotomy of mind versus body generates a default otherness for subordinated people accused of the physical malfeasance of caring for and nurturing the life forces of humanity. Denial of the corporeal impacts of embodiment disregards the process of wealth creation in the United States for which that materiality is vital for explaining the importance and endurance of reproductive oppression experienced by black women. This subject has been undertheorized by most traditional theorists. "Indeed, understanding intersectionality as a process emerging through the institution of science and the material production of different bodies has not been adequately explored or theorized," according to Subramaniam.[31]

As a positive theorization, RJT presents an immediate acknowledgment of the centrality of bodies by resisting the artificial hierarchies determined by abstract individualistic universalism, but RJT also avoids a biological essentialism that centers sexual, gender, and racial subordination. RJT radically reconceptualizes the politics of reproduction by speaking not only to how bodies are gendered but how they are racially and sexually identified to analyze hierarchical reproductive relations imposed by the ideology of white supremacy. RJT actively engages theories of embodiment that account for racial, class, ability, gender identity, and citizenship (among an infinite array of differences), and examines the specific focused and rigorous contexts in which bodies exist. In this sense, RJT builds on French feminist theorist Luce Irigaray's project of rewriting sexual difference beyond the static masculine-feminine binary, and challenges the alienation from the maternal and material body, disputing widely accepted binary theories. Differences based on artificial binaries are too conventional and mechanical to adequately account for the porousness of the fabric between knowledge production and embodiment which is an epistemological ecosystem rather than yet another dichotomy in reproductive justice theory.

RJT developed outside of the formal settings of an academic institution or an organization. Theoretical works by marginalized women or groups are often delegitimized by the academy because they are accessible, not written in jargon, and lack obscure references. This sets up "unnecessary and competing hierarchies of thought which re-inscribe the politics of domination by designating work as either inferior, superior or more or less worthy of attention."[32] Some theories that originate in the academy have erected barriers even as they offer new meanings and explanations of the world. Theories are necessary, sometimes productive, in the ways they enable tools and scholarship. Conversely, they may bind or restrict new knowledge through institutional and intellectual biases and structures.

The construction of countertheory by women of color feminists is a complex process and emerges from engagement with collective oral and written history sources rather than individual scholars. This is dismissively seen as "folk knowledge" by self-appointed elite traditional theorists who reinforce institutionalized power and privilege. "Indeed, the privileged act of naming often affords those in power access to modes of communication and enables them to project an interpretation, a definition, a description of their work and actions, that may not be accurate, that may obscure what is really taking place," writes hooks.[33]

Reproductive justice theory uses historical folk knowledge as intellectual fodder: memories of the enslavement of Africans, the forced breeding of black people, and the selling and murdering of our children. This knowledge is in our emotional and spiritual DNA, and black women offer our own facts and theories to counter worldviews that dismiss our realities. Black women's bodies are not only a place of vulnerability but also a place of power and affirmation giving sustenance to an ethos of caring, relationality, and mutual responsibility that is the essence of human rights practices upon which RJT is foundationally based.

According to scholars Wendy Kolmar and Frances Bartkowski:

> Knowledge is that body of information, facts and theories through which a society or culture defines what is true and important, what constitutes its past, and how it understands the complexities of the natural and so-

> cial worlds. To be excluded from these bodies of knowledge and the sites and processes of knowledge production [epistemology] as women of color and other marginalized groups have been, is to live in a "reality" not of one's own making.[34]

To speak up is to ask many epistemological questions about knowledge and beliefs in our society, and explore why inequalities persist through time and repetition. Speaking about knowledge formation from lived experiences, South African legal scholar Tshepo Madlingozi writes that epistemicide is "the repression and marginalization of the knowledge system and cosmologies of the historically colonized group."[35] Our knowledge comes from the way we keep our memories. Black women had to develop our own pathways to knowledge, and lifting our voices paved the way.

In RJT, we created an accessible theory that was both rigorous and powerful that bridged the language of the academy. Theory is important, as black theorist Barbara Christian argues, but disconnected from activism it becomes prescriptive and limited. Black women activists are not alienated from our communities. Instead, communities are launch pads for our activist and scholarly explorations, allowing both objective and subjective perspectives. We did not want to reinforce social relations of domination but instead understand our realities by incorporating diverse theoretical traditions. Without a new theory to explain our lived experiences, the reality of reproductive violence, such as sterilization abuse targeting incarcerated women, becomes a contested concept: a theoretical playground for those not experiencing reproductive oppression every day.

This radical RJT does not offer arcane abstractions that preoccupy some recent feminist theorizing that is not only inaccessible to those not versed in European philosophical norms but relatively useless in effecting social change in the material world of economics, politics, and public policy. Feminism was a practice in the women's movement before it was theorized. As legal scholar Catharine MacKinnon observes:

> The postmodern version of the relation between theory and practice is discourse unto death. Theory begets no practice, only more text. It proceeds as if you can deconstruct power relations by shifting their markers around in your head. Like all formal idealism, this approach to theory tends unselfconsciously to reproduce existing relations of dominance, in part because it is an utterly removed elite activity.[36]

We ground RJT by creating a way of understanding reproductive relationships in the world that has practical applications and promotes constructive social change: in other words, praxis. For example, SisterLove, an HIV/AIDS organization, uses the RJ framework to assess state legislatures and Congressional actions on reproductive health through the lens of black women. SisterLove fought and won the protection of certain Medicaid-covered antiretroviral prescriptions that were due to be defunded in Georgia, including medications that many women prefer who use contraceptives.

All human knowledge is learned and conveyed through economic, social, and cultural processes, but most scholarship on black women focuses on our work as victims and activists, not as producers of knowledge. RJT affirms that radical new insights emerge when black women reimagine the status quo. For example, when an African American woman, Mechelle Vinson, established in 1986 that sexual harassment was sex discrimination under civil rights law, she believed that she had the human right to employment without fear of sexual exploitation by her supervisor. Her case changed the theory of sex discrimination for all women.

Just as Vinson's case changed laws on sex discrimination, feminist and LGBTQ activists and scholars have pushed the boundaries of thinking about sex, gender, and the law, and this expansion informs RJT. In her best-known work, *Gender Trouble*, Judith Butler argues that the insistence on sex as a natural category is itself evidence of its very unnaturalness. She points out that sex as well as gender are culturally produced categories, and the definitions change over time. While multiple gender identities are increasingly accepted by society, legal systems remain ill-equipped to address the gender continuum legitimated by science. RJT affirms gender fluidity as described by Butler but also confirms that while categories such as gender and race are socially contrived, they are also embodied sites of reproductive oppression. The esoteric, dense language of some feminism theorizing cannot account for, or counter, the material realities of embodiment, as Butler also points out.

Reproductive justice advocacy and theorizing are not just expressions of simplistic understandings of identity politics. This dismissal describes black women's lives as essentialist sources of limited knowledge production. Epistemological and embodied politics intersect through reproductive justice, and knowledge production by black feminists demonstrates universalist connections. RJT recognizes that the epistemological constraints are different when they arise from the best practices of activists in the field as we reconfigure subjects (knowledge producers) and objects (those about whom knowledge is produced). Through RJT, we can envision layers of meanings and unpack the dominant narratives that devalue our lives.

People's life choices occur in a context of racialized and gendered notions of morality and normalcy. For example, Lillian Garland went to court in 1987 to establish that guaranteeing unpaid leaves for pregnant women by law is not discrimination on the basis of sex, but is a step in *ending* discrimination on the basis of sex. An African American woman, Garland's resistance to her employer, the California Federal Savings and Loan Association, fortified sex-equality law away from its previous alleged neutrality that, in fact, discriminated against all women. As an example of lived experiences contouring new understandings of law and reproductive theory, her case signaled that reproduction is an issue of sexual equality, something conservative courts are reluctant to admit even while they permit the narrowing of abortion rights, especially through bans on alleged race- and sex-selective abortions.

RJ functions as a belief system that aids in understanding the objective and subjective conditions in which we live that attempt to repress our consciousness, restrain our reproduction, and reduce our human potential. Black feminists underscore that categories of race or gender are not functionally or analytically equivalent because the definitions are structured to produce different risks and benefits.

Theoretical Roots of Reproductive Justice

Reproductive justice theory rests on an intellectual inheritance in which we are rooting our new framework. Black feminist theory provides an affirmation of our voices and lived experiences, and arises not from the academy, but from activist places that help us understand our world and ourselves. Self-help theory describes the art and power of telling and owning our stories to heal from internalized oppression and take action to change our objective circumstances. Critical race and critical feminist theory explain the social customs, laws, and legal practices that disadvantage nonwhite and nonmale people in society while providing the framework for understanding intersectionality. Human rights theory provides internationally recognized standards, norms, and a legal regime for articulating a vision for what we demand and deserve as fully embodied persons with inherent and inalienable rights. Standpoint theory validates our multifaceted perspectives, ambiguities, and subjectivities as African American women when we center ourselves in the lens. Womanist ethics and religion theory empowers us to imagine the female as spiritual, and enables us to converse with liberation ethicists like Katie Cannon, who deconstructs the religious legitimization of a society based on the contradictions between liberalism and white supremacy.

Just as importantly, Latinas/Chicanas such as Gloria Anzaldúa and Cherríe Moraga offered breakthrough concepts such as borderlands, bridges, and ambiguity that help flesh out RJT. Indigenous women such as Connie Uri and Ingrid Washinawatok linked bodily self-determination to Native sovereignty and domestic land struggles to the United Nations, invoking the human rights framework that is foundational in RJ. In *Fertile Matters*, Elena Gutiérrez writes about Mexican American women, immigration, and sterilization abuse through an RJ lens. While my essay focuses predominantly on African American women, I hope others will offer more analyses that further explore the expansive theoretical influences in RJT.

Using these influences in tandem, black women as both insiders and outsiders to the pro-choice movement and the academy created RJT to describe the rich density and varied textured meanings of the reproductive politics of the world we experience by trusting in our personal and cultural biographies. Our black feminist "ideas are necessarily produced in dialogue with lived experience," and always affected by "the social facts [constructions] of race, class, and gender."[37] We desired a theory that would help us examine multiple and intersecting oppressions and change the world for the better using knowledge-affirming criteria we established as worthy of our dignity. Reproductive justice theory is not externalized knowledge we acquire, but instead emerges organically from our lived experience and describes our relationship to the world, the same way we resonate with Keisha's story.

Black Feminist Theory

African American women are responsible for three of the most widely disseminated and applied feminist theories in the last half century: identity politics, intersectionality, and reproductive justice. This required thinking between and beyond colonized spaces to discover new knowledges from the pain of our bodies and from the multigenerational dislocations we experienced as people of the African Diaspora. This section will also more fully explore the black feminist origins of reproductive justice, including the African concept of *ubuntu* as it intersects with the human rights framework. This lifts the philosophy and language of the oppressed—the ignored African American subject—in defiance to the deliberate and debilitating amnesia and alleged objectivity of white supremacy. At the core of black feminist thought is a "specialized knowledge created by black women . . . [that] provides a unique angle of vision on self, community and society," according to Collins.[38]

Our theories explain things most people can't see. Our concepts of resistance, subversion, and transgression have both embodied as well as aesthetic dimensions. We build upon our traditions and legacies the same way we consult with the ancestors for guidance while pouring libations for the spirits. When we theorize, we not only recover ourselves and our voices but we move forward in building an active, inclusive, and liberatory movement that benefits all people. As Toni Cade Bambara wrote, the standpoint of African American women

> means a sense of community with individuals and groups here and throughout the world who are poised for the light, who work daily to rescue and ransom us all from amnesia and fear, who work sometimes wearily—most times joyously—to encourage and equip us to train for the future as sane, whole, governing people.[39]

Black feminists were urgently compelled to "unmask the power relations of their world."[40] Reverend Pauli Murray, a black lesbian cofounder of the National Organization for Women (NOW), spoke about the intersection of race and gender for African American women:

> [I] must be involved with and necessarily concerned with racial liberation. But I must also personally be concerned with sexual liberation, because as I often say, the two meet in me, the two meet in any individual who is both woman and a member of an oppressed group or a minority group. . . . [R]acism and sexism have been closely interrelated historically, especially in the American South, but they have not been exactly parallel. Rather we should recognize them as interstructural elements of oppression within the overarching system of male domination.[41]

Ubuntu and Reproductive Justice

> *Sometimes a breakdown can be the beginning of a kind of breakthrough, a way of living in advance through a trauma that prepares you for a future of radical transformation.*
>
> —*Cherríe Moraga*

Reproductive justice theorizing invites a closer examination of pre-Enlightenment ideologies to imagine alternative futures for society. There is no genetic or inherent way of thinking for any race of people, but there are different philosophical traditions beyond the individualism of the Enlightenment that can serve as foundations for deconstructing the Western worldview to enable the reconstruction of a value-system more in harmony with life and human dignity for all peoples. Ideologies cohesively control relationships, pattern behaviors, direct activities, and mold personalities. White supremacy is an ideology whose meanings are constantly recreated and affirmed, defining all who are not white, male, and heterosexual as Others, and promoting the cultural nationalism and dominance of Western thought that has colonized all forms of knowledge about the world.

It is possible, however, to recognize influences of the Enlightenment without bowing to its presupposed philosophical dominance. Reproductive justice theorizing can explore patriarchal consciousness and the degradation of the feminine in the binaries, tensions, and polarities of reason versus emotion, objectivity versus subjectivity, holism versus reductionism, linear versus cyclical thinking, science versus spirituality, etc. Reviving non-European philosophies may offer another way of disrupting the general trends in the history of Western civilization. These trends include the concentration of power and wealth in the hands of the few; rapid industrialization that exploits rather than harmonizes with nature; and increasingly abstract and linear thinking at the expense of holistic thinking. They also include rigid gender roles and expressions that deny the gender continuum; religious intolerance and evangelism in the propagation of those abstract and linear ideas at the expense of the religions of other cultures; and attacks on the people who oppose such absolutes. In the words of Chandra Talpade Mohanty, they use the "universal to erase the particular or positing an unbridgeable gulf between the two terms."[42]

Instead, I hope future RJ scholars examine the philosophical profundity of other cultural understandings. In the Jewish tradition, for example, there is a worldview that declares, "My spiritual needs are my neighbors' material needs," indicating the innate interdependence of human relations. One cannot be spiritually whole if one is selfish toward others in this philosophical tradition. Other philosophical traditions, such as Confucianism with its particular emphasis on the importance of social harmony and the family, may also be explored to counter the sterility of alienated, individualistic philosophies.

As a black feminist, I am intrigued by Ubuntu, an African, humanist philosophical tradition of collective caring that has pre-Enlightenment roots. The cultural, spiritual, and physical trauma of enslavement and the postcolonial struggles on the African continent also gave rise to a radical revisiting of our African history and practices. This reclamation of a different philosophical foundation to counter the individualistic, competitive theories of Western thought is an important shift in understanding the full transformative power of reproductive justice. Relatively little work has been done on African philosophies or African theorists within Western feminist scholarship, yet Ubuntu offers a philosophical belief in the universal bond of sharing that connects all humanity.

Stated most simply, Ubuntu is an expression of the concept "I am because We are." It recognizes that societies determine the sanctity of humanity, and that social relationships imply a shared human subjectivity that promotes a community's good through an unconditional recognition and appreciation of individual uniqueness and difference. As transgender software designer Audrey Tang says:

> Ubuntu implies that everyone has different skills and strengths; people are not isolated, and through mutual support they can help each other to complete themselves. This emphasis on complementing and completing each other, and through it, helping people to self-actualize, is a South African cultural value.[43]

In terms of reproductive justice, Ubuntu offers another way of envisioning collective mothering and fathering, for example, because children are never orphans depending on a single individual or nuclear family to raise them. Instead, children are the links to our ancestors, and responsibility for their health, education, safety, and well-being rests with the community. Modern evidence of an Ubuntu practice is in the concept of radical mothering offered by Alexis Pauline Gumbs, discussed earlier. Ubuntu also offers possibilities for restorative rather than retributive justice to transform practices of crime and punishment within societies. It focuses on redemption rather than exile of people who transgress against the community.

Instead of viewing different people as potentially malignant others threatening rigid kinship and homogenous cultural boundaries, Ubuntu offers a striking counter to individualism, alienation, and atomism dominant in Western philosophy. This is an important philosophical shift because much of our current cultural interpretations about who we should reasonably care for depends on proximity, kinship, or nationalism. For example, many people fighting oppression believe we can best counter it by getting to know each other better, and considerable time is spent endeavoring to help white people understand what it means to be black, for men to understand what it means to be a woman, for Americans to understand other countries, etc. The key word is *understanding* because this kind of empathy is predicated on knowledge and propinquity, which are by definition limited. Instead, through an Ubuntu lens, one can care about bombs dropped on Syria even if one has never met an actual Syrian or knows nothing about the country. The question is not what you know about others but what you know about yourself in relationship to others. Historian Michael Onyebuchi Eze states:

> "A person is a person through other people" strikes an affirmation of one's humanity in the recognition of the "other" in his or her uniqueness and difference. It is a demand for a creative intersubjective formation in which the "other" becomes a mirror (but only a mirror) for my subjectivity. This idealism suggests to us that humanity is not embedded in my person solely as an individual; my humanity is co-substantively bestowed upon the other and me. Humanity is a quality we owe to each other. We create each other and need to sustain this *otherness* creation. And if we belong to each other, we participate in our creations: *we are because you are*, and *since you are, definitely I am*. The "I am" is not a rigid subject, but a dynamic self-constitution dependent on this *otherness* creation of relation and distance.[44]

Ubuntu clearly offers another conception of ethics, caring, the law, economics, and being human in community with everyone else on the planet. South African Archbishop Desmond Tutu further explains a bold vision of spirituality that contrasts with Western concepts of religion:

> A person with *ubuntu* is open and available to others, affirming of others, does not feel threatened that others are able and good, for he or she has a proper self-assurance that comes from knowing that he or she belongs in

a greater whole and is diminished when others are humiliated or diminished, when others are tortured or oppressed.[45]

Given the current political moment in which we find our world besmirched by the overt resurgence of white supremacy, I believe that RJT framed as an Ubuntu practice presents an invitation for us to better understand the social identities within us as individuals. We resist the totalizing and universalizing theories of alienation and harsh individualism to offer a critique of the kinds of debilitated knowledge that limit our actions as embodied, politically conscious, and interconnected human beings. We are capable of creating a just society in which all people have their human rights respected and protected.

Self-Help: Reproductive Justice Theory in Practice

We tell our stories and reflect each other. I am not the enemy; I am the answer. If you silence my voice, then what happens to my behavior?

—Juanita Williams, AIDS survivor and SisterSong cofounder

Storytelling is a crucial part of reproductive justice theory, an act of reclamation and resistance, because our theories grow from our activist locations. Our black feminist ideas emanate from our lived experiences affected by the social constructions of race, class, and gender. As Rachel Kaadzi Ghansah states, marginalized women are "structurally denied the ability to tell our stories."[46] Silence was a strategy of agency that was both individual and collective, and by which black women honored their ability to think critically within a culture that denigrated them.

The role of oral history and storytelling is vital to our survival, and the complexities of our silences speak many meanings. Silence is not absence of thought. It may be a survival mechanism, such as slaves singing songs to express their pain when reading or talking back had deadly consequences. Yet our silence does not really protect us, in the immortal words of Audre Lorde. If one does not understand our silences, it may be even harder to understand our words. Because it may be dangerous to lift our voices individually to tell our truths no matter how much we are dying inside, women of color often work together collectively for strength and safety, such as the SisterSong motto of "doing collectively what we cannot do individually." As bell hooks says, "Moving from silence into speech [is a] revolutionary gesture" in which we tell our own stories and determine what they mean.[47] Echoing this political practice, Rickie Solinger writes:

> The politics of personal story insist that the reader consider the woman storyteller as real and whole, a person who must be heard . . . as necessary as racial slavery was for defining and ennobling whiteness and worthiness. . . . [Women of color are] crucial to the project of defining legitimate mothers, citizens, and voters. Their existence and treatment functions as tenebrous yet public messages regarding who has the right to education, the right to work, the right to just compensation, and the right to a roof over her head.[48]

This section will discuss the black feminist definition of self-help, discuss why storytelling practices are necessary, and what they achieve in building the RJ movement. It is a critical aspect of healing from trauma and crucial in developing the stamina to withstand the percussive impacts of multiple forms of reproductive and sexual oppression. Thus, self-help is vital to the realization of RJ, not as an expression of individualism, but as a way to link personal stories to collective experiences to form a platform for shared political action.

In practice, RJ involves changing personal and collective behaviors as a statement of philosophy in which processes of self-help from the black feminist movement and conflict resolution from peace studies are intentionally incorporated to assist in helping diverse people work better together. hooks states, "When our lived experience of theorizing is fundamentally linked to processes of self-recovery, of collective liberation, no gap exists between theory and practice. Indeed, what such experience makes more evident is the bond between the two—that ultimately reciprocal process wherein one enables the other."[49]

Self-help as used in this context is a storytelling-based, peer-support process introduced as a black feminist practice by the National Black Women's Health Project (NBWHP) organized by Byllye Avery and Eleanor Hinton-Hoytt in 1983 in Atlanta, Georgia. NBWHP trainer Lillie Allen adapted Re-evaluation Counseling theory, called it self-help, and offered her popular self-help workshops at the first National Conference on Black Women's Health Issues. Lisa Diane White, former NBWHP staffer, describes how "[s]elf-help became a strategy for me and other women to actively pursue our wellness by supporting each other in addressing emotional, spiritual, mental and physical health concerns in our lives."[50] In the practice of RJ, self-help is available as a strategy for appreciating and managing our diversities and the internalized oppressions we bring to the struggle. Without such a process or one similar, it is difficult to imagine how diverse movements will flourish in unity and power. We have to learn how to transform our pain into medicine, like turning winter into spring, to heal our battered selves. Storytelling is a crucial part of RJT, an act of reclamation and resistance, because our theories grow from our activist locations and practices.

Anticolonialist psychiatrist and scholar Frantz Fanon's studies of the psychology of racism and the dehumanization it produces demonstrated both the possibility and the necessity for creating new values, ideas, and practices in order to resist the subjugation of the spirit, the mind, and the body. Reproductive justice is an emancipatory projection of our ideals and the dialectics between consciousness, oppression, and activism, but also transcends inherent dualistic contradictions by producing a tridimensional resistance process. In this way, theory is directly applied to activism to transform not only the thinking but also the strategies and practices of activism, incorporating both reason and emotion. Instead of reason and emotion existing in relational opposition, they exist in conversation. Theories that prerequisite an allegedly apolitical and objective stance thwart the very project of producing liberatory consciousness, theory, and practice working together to end all forms of oppression.

In 1981 hooks wrote in *Ain't I a Woman: Black Women and Feminism* about the devaluation of black women. In concluding that chapter, she wrote:

> Widespread efforts to continue devaluation of black womanhood make it extremely difficult and oftentimes impossible for the black female to develop a positive self-concept. For we are daily bombarded by negative images. Indeed, one strong oppressive force has been this negative stereotype and our acceptance of it as a viable role model upon which we can pattern our lives.[51]

Black women work ceaselessly to end the devaluation of our lives and experiences in the workforce, in the media, in communities, and in relationships. African American women—no matter how rich or famous—face a barrage of negativism. It can happen through the incredible caricatures of shows like the *Real Housewives of Atlanta*, the belittling of scholar and media analyst Melissa Harris-Perry by MSNBC when she refused to alter her show's depth to suit the racist perspectives of the station, or even the disbelief Anita Hill faced when she reported Clarence Thomas's sexual harassment during his confirmation hearing to the Supreme Court.

The rates of domestic violence and childhood sexual abuse in the African American community are staggering for a variety of factors. The number-one killer of African American females, ages fifteen to thirty-four, is domestic violence; we comprise only 8 percent of the population but are 20 percent of the homicide victims at the hands of a partner or ex-partner.[52] Approximately 40 percent of black girls report coercive contact or childhood sexual abuse by age eighteen.[53] Sadly, suicides are disproportionately high among young girls who are slut shamed, and black girls deserve more from society than neglect and blame. We stand accused of being sexually irresponsible, hyperfertile overbreeders birthing superpredatory children who white society must fear and imprison. We are not safe as children or adults, yet black women refuse to accept the white supremacist perception that the African American community is more pathologically violent than the white community.

We are not oversensitive when we organize to stop this devastation; the devastation is not over. African American women organize against the tropes of white supremacy, against an antifeminist backlash in the black community, against judgmental religious institutions that preach that we deserve our fate because of the alleged story of Adam's fall from grace due to Eve's curiosity, and against a feminist movement that views us as an afterthought, one beat too late. Our stories of freedom and dignity constantly challenge the lies told about us, our partners, and our children, often in the face of incredible dangers like rape, murder, and punitive social policies.

We always resist. We use an RJ analysis to intersect the myriad of issues affecting our sexuality and reproductive decision-making. Yet we also internalize these ceaseless negative messages about our beauty, anger, bodies, or reproductive and sexual behaviors. Many of us develop low self-esteem even as we work collectively to unlearn self-hatred. To counter these stereotypes, black women may rely on practices of self-knowledge, self-recovery, and self-determination. We apply these practices to the project of achieving reproductive justice, exploring its theoretical, strategic, and healing potential.

As an action strategy, reproductive justice requires working across social justice issues by bringing together diverse issues and people "based not upon expediency, but upon our actual need for each other," in the words of Barbara Smith.[54] Instead of working together based on shared victimization, we acknowledge that we all suffer in some way from white supremacy and population control, but we do not suffer in the same way, nor are we all equally oppressed. In fact, some of us have the ability to oppress others because of our own privileges within the social construct, a victimized-violator stance that requires rejecting monolithic experiences, good/bad dichotomies, and essentialized definitions.

Of course, black women are not alone in valuing the power of building a movement through introspective storytelling. Revealing one's subjective self and standpoint increasingly is treasured in ethnography as well as the reproductive justice movement because we actually challenge the omnipresent, allegedly neutral voice that distances itself from the objects of the discourse. This is a distinct project from those who claim that structural constraints only exist in our minds and the ideal solutions are mostly found in our determination to overcome them. As we said in the NBWHP, you can't self-help yourself out of a toxic neighborhood. Poverty is not caused by low self-esteem.

More recently, I have witnessed younger activists use the art of telling their stories as a strategy for healing from internalized trauma, especially students of color at predominantly white colleges and universities, such as Weaving Voices at Smith College. Smith students of color share stories through storytelling and monologues "to celebrate and honor the labor and struggles that it took to survive" within an elite, predominantly white college. At the same time, they seek to "pass on their lived experiences as knowledge to future generations," noting "that there are other ways to live—past survival, past isolation." While this practice may not be a formal descendant of the self-help practices of the black women's health movement, it can be effective in ensuring everyone's voice is heard, and loving attention is paid to each person to create social transformation in a community.

We question those who believe they can co-opt the concept of reproductive justice without embracing the necessity for engaging in what dismissively is called the "touchy-feely" self-help and/or storytelling work of introspection, self-disclosure, and emotional discharge. According to Lisa Diane White, self-help enables use to become "more aware of the impact of oppression on our lives. These oppressions are interlocking and affect all of us, even when we believe ourselves to be surviving and thriving in our personal and working lives."[55] Self-help and storytelling affirms our experiences as women of color and supports us as we become more aware of the oppressive systems we face within the broader social/political/economic context that is our reality. Self-help allows us to take control of our lives and support each other to do the same. This means that we "acknowledge that we are divided and must develop strategies to overcome fears, prejudices, resentments, competitiveness, etc."[56] Absent a process of self-help or a similar liberatory practice such as conflict resolution, strategic efforts to bring people together while respecting differences and commonalities may be virtually impossible to sustain.

When we try to become what others expect us to be, we divide ourselves and then self-police the divisions in case we transgress, in the Foucauldian sense of manipulated consent. Without structured storytelling practices, the constant shifting of our consciousness and languages can produce madness and anxiety, sometimes genius, sometimes insight, but often suicidal internalizing of oppressive ideas within ourselves. When we conform to a system of internalized white supremacy, we lose sight of who we really are. We sometimes wear the masks of conformity so completely, so endlessly, that we can even forget we are wearing them in the first place. Through policing and internalizing, we become our own intellectual and emotional jailers. As Patricia Hill Collins says, "Suppressing the knowledge produced by any oppressed group makes it easier for the dominant groups to rule because the seeming absence of dissent suggests that subordinate groups willingly collaborate in their own victimization."[57]

We are forming our own processes of self-recovery and self-care. As Indigenous women and women of color, we have had to create our theories from our struggles as diverse peoples experiencing multiple and intersecting forms of oppression. In doing so, we not only recover ourselves and our voices but we move forward in building an active, liberatory reproductive justice movement that benefits all people. What is most evident at this time is that our multiplicity of voices and perspectives, our polyvocality, breaks the chains of a world that insists on marking us as one-dimensional, subject to only one truth—theirs—and insisting that to be heard, we must speak their language, use their references, and only exist in their limited, linear, finite gaze. Storytelling gives us new meanings for our experiences and helps black women develop a collective sense of order and direction for social change.

Critical Race and Critical Feminist Theories

Reproductive justice theory also incorporates earlier pioneering work on critical race and critical feminist theories (CR/CFT) from legal academia by scholars such as Derrick Bell, Mari Matsuda, Kimberlé Crenshaw, Patricia Williams, Adrien Katherine Wing, and Richard Delgado, who speak of multiple levels of consciousness that characterize our existences. Reproductive justice theory parallels critical race and critical feminist theories in that it challenges the liberal "colorblind" and "gender neutral" approach to US reproductive law and politics that is, in fact, neither colorblind nor gender neutral. "Critical" theories (in law, literature, ethnic studies, feminism, whiteness studies, etc.) critique the individualism and hierarchies that use purportedly neutral concepts to mask the true nature of contingent power relationships in modern societies, particularly the role of white supremacy and patriarchy in maintaining the status quo and advantaging and disadvantaging groups of people based on race and gender. Critical ways of interpreting constitutional law became urgent in an alleged postracial society in which remedies for racial injustices were defined by those in power as evidence of racism itself, or reverse discrimination, such as attacks on affirmative action and other measures for addressing racist practices. Emerging legal theory had to address the historically consistent but fluidly morphing right-wing racial ideology reinscribing white supremacy in the post–Civil Rights era.

RJT shares with CR/CFT the following characteristics:

- Relies on storytelling as primary form of communication
- Views racism and sexism as normal part of domination not aberrant
- Recognizes how elites use racism and sexism to serve them
- Views gender and race as social constructs, not immutable biological categories
- Understands how racial and gender stereotypes change over time
- Incorporates intersecting identities

While sharing these characteristics with CR/CFT, reproductive justice theory focuses on reproductive politics, intersectionality, and the human rights framework. This migrates some of the principles to new sites of struggle for reproductive control and bodily self-determination, social obligations, and entitlements. Unlike CR/CFT, our first site of struggle is not the legal system. Rather than unproductively seeking inclusion into a deeply flawed constitutional regime originated by white slaveholders, RJ works primarily in moral and political avenues in order to build a social justice movement based on international human rights standards and norms that can demand and create laws worthy of us and our dignity. Privileging legal strategies can be protractedly ineffective and limited because the law will only deliver justice when we demand it, and have the power to change it.

Women of color have long offered an intersectional framework with which to describe the structuring of gender through race and class to describe multiple forms of oppression that are simultaneous. In decrying the social and cultural construction of the concept of "woman" that only included white women, Sojourner Truth's nineteenth-century declaration of "Ain't I a Woman?" foreshadows Frances Beal's concept of multiple oppressions in her 1969 article, "Double Jeopardy: To Be Black and Female," reprinted in the 1970 anthology *Sisterhood Is Powerful*, edited by Robin Morgan. Toni Cade Bambara, who edited *The Black Woman* anthology also in 1970, greatly influenced me during my first year in college. She expressed the dilemma as beginning with an English language that has been "systematically stripped of the kinds of structures and the kinds of vocabularies that allow people to plug into their kinds of intelligences."[58] Each fought against an essentializing, overgeneralizing construction of gender that ignored the complexities of multiple identities.

Intersectional analyses were then further expanded by the Combahee River Collective Statement in 1977; by Angela Davis in *Women, Race and Class* in 1981; and by Audre Lorde, who said in *Sister Outsider* in 1984, "My fullest concentration of energy is available to me only when I integrate all the parts of who I am, openly, allowing power from particular sources of my living to flow back and forth freely through all my different selves, without the restriction of externally imposed definition." Lorde was speaking of her multiple identities as an African American, immigrant, lesbian, feminist, mother, writer, activist, cancer survivor, etc. Intersectional categories of identity are interdependent and multidimensional.

But the intersectional framework was not named until critical legal theorist Kimberlé Crenshaw coined the term in 1989 to illustrate how racial and gender oppression interact in the lives of black women. She used a traffic metaphor in which black women stand at the intersection of the race and gender streets, liable to injury from cars traveling along any axis. In the words of Crenshaw, intersectionality "mediates the tension between assertions of multiple identities and the ongoing necessity of group politics," while at the same time providing a "basis for reconceptualizing" a single identity as coalition, for example "race as a coalition between men and women of color."[59] In this sense, intersectionality does not just highlight differences. It also makes commonalities visible even as multiple identities diverge.

In her article "Demarginalizing the Intersection of Race and Sex," Crenshaw says that failing to comprehend the "complexities of compoundedness is not simply a matter of political will, but it is also due to the influence of a way of thinking about discrimination which structures politics so that struggles are categorized as singular issues. Moreover, this structure imports a descriptive and normative view of society that reinforces the status quo,"[60] i.e., white supremacy. Crenshaw introduced the word "intersectionality" in legal arguments to describe the limits of assigning mutually exclusive categories to black women in which neither race nor gender is sufficiently integrated in order to capture the particular experiences of black women. The failure to imagine the intersection of race and gender means that the needs and perspectives of African American women are unseen and neglected, and that no legal remedies for harm are available to black women because of the inability of our legal structures in the United States to incorporate multiple forms of oppression that are simultaneous. This is the basis of the aforementioned critical race theory that legal scholars such as Crenshaw, Delgado, and Matsuda have pioneered.

Critical race feminism (CRF) challenges the concept of essentialism, the idea that one "authentic" female perspective exists that can represent all women. The discipline criticizes feminist legal theory, postmodernism, poststructuralism, and liberalism for their failures to include the accounts of women of color beyond minor footnotes. Poststructuralism and postmodernism, interpreted through masculinist lenses, can be antagonistic to theories of embodiment as if lived experiences are irrelevant to developing a politics of the agency of black women and women of color. "Poststructuralism and postmodernism . . . have been often accused of an indifference to materiality. . . . To say that the body is a discursive construction is not to deny a substantial corpus, but to insist that our apprehension of it, our understanding of it, is necessarily mediated by the *con*texts in which we speak."[61]

Going further, CRF resists the essentializing of all black women as heterosexual. This type of erasure and omission silences lesbians, trans women, and gender nonconforming people, even within communities of color, begging the question of to what purpose and whose interests social constructions based on white supremacy serve. Legal scholars such as Patricia Williams, Lani Guinier, Hope Lewis, and Dorothy Roberts have pioneered critical inquiries into the teaching pedagogies of extant legal theories in the academy, calling attention to the perspectives of African American women who contest the white supremacist and patriarchal biases of the law both in theory and practice.

Crenshaw, by naming intersectionality, offered a compact and densely packed conceptual framework for moving beyond singularly ascribed identities. Intersectionality is not a new way to describe identity politics; instead it is a way to describe the interlocked nature of power relationships that advantage and disadvantage people depending on their identities. Both CR/CFT expose white male privilege and debunk the alleged neutrality and impartiality of the law, and the political, economic, and social practices arising from the prejudices of the privileged.

Human Rights Theory and Reproductive Justice

Cynicism is the universe's most supine moral position.
—*Lois McMaster Bujold*

Reproductive justice is an intentional framework to shape the competing ideals of equality and the social reality of inequality by pointing out the disparity in opportunities to determine our reproductive destinies. These are human rights standards that examine not only processes but outcomes, moving beyond American jurisprudence. The first time I heard the phrase human rights voiced through a gender lens was in Gwen Patton's essay "Black People and the Victorian Ethos" in Bambara's anthology *The Black Woman*. Patton, a legendary disabled Civil Rights activist from Alabama, was trying to reconcile her work in the anti-racist and anti-war movements with the gender oppression she witnessed in so-called revolutionary spaces. Like their white counterparts in the anti-war movement, black men believed that women in the black power movement could only be responsible for activities like "first aid, education, children, sewing" and other gender-segregated roles. This sexist diminution created a false patriarchal harmony between the hyperbinaried sexes in the belief that it aided in the "transition to the human rights struggle which will inevitably lead us to the Revolution."[62]

As a college student in 1970, I was just beginning to understand the intersectional struggle around race and gender I saw in the black power movement at Howard University. Patton's prophetic black feminist use of human rights instead of the more familiar civil rights was a powerful clue overlooked at the time. Patton's essay illustrates that black feminist theorizing using the human rights framework has a long and storied history that predates the 1994 creation of the RJ framework that also invokes the full suite of human rights.

According to historian Louise Knight, the phrase "human rights" seems to have emerged in the first decade of the nineteenth century. Thomas Jefferson used it in his address to Congress on December 2, 1806. Without an apparent sense of irony, Jefferson was referring to the foreign slave trade violating human rights because many slave owners believed that the real moral violation of slavery was capturing free people in Africa and enslaving them. In other words, those born in slavery did not have the same human right to freedom as did the captured Africans.

About a year later, a black minister, Reverend Peter Williams Jr., broadened the meaning of human rights to include all aspects of enslavement. In New York on January 1, 1808, he described the Maafa enslavement as a "flagrant violations of human rights."[63] Black abolitionist and feminist Frederick Douglass also used the phrase to protest the lynching of a black man in New York City in 1858. Douglass said:

> Human rights stand upon a common basis; and by all the reason that they are supported, maintained and defended, for one variety of the human family, they are supported, maintained and defended for *all* the human family; because all mankind have the same wants, arising out of a common nature. A diverse origin does not disprove a common nature, nor does it disprove a united destiny.[64]

In excavating this history, it is important to recognize this broadening and affirmation of the human rights paradigm a full ninety years before the ratification of the Universal Declaration of Human Rights (UDHR) by the United Nations in 1948. In 1951 African American leaders wrote a petition to the UN entitled "We Charge Genocide," calling on the United States to uphold the Convention on the Prevention and Punishment of the Crime of Genocide adopted by the UN General Assembly on December 9, 1948.

Malcolm X also spoke in 1964 about the importance of using the human rights framework in the struggle for African American liberation: "We can never get civil rights in America until our human rights are first restored. We will never be recognized as citizens there until we are first recognized as humans."[65]

Dr. Martin Luther King Jr. also called for a human rights movement focused on the US in his last Sunday Sermon on March 31, 1968, four days before he was assassinated. Disappointingly, activists in the US have just begun to build that united, indivisible human rights movement *in* the US focused *on* the US, starting in the mid-1990s. Not surprisingly, it has been women of color and African American women in particular who have led this new movement.

This work has not been without its critics and skeptics, because the United States fiercely resists having its sovereignty subordinated to the norms and standards of the international human rights regime even as it commits human rights violations like torture at Guantanamo Bay or in the Chicago Police Department. Conservatives have fought against submitting the US to international human rights standards since the 1940s, when the framework became a global standard for ending injustice and discrimination. In the 1950s US Secretary of State John Foster Dulles opposed compliance with the UDHR, mendaciously arguing that the US legal system offered more human rights protections. Apparently, he willfully ignored the existence of Jim Crow segregation for African Americans at the time that legally excluded black people from the full protection of the law or equal opportunity to enjoy the benefits of society.

In fact, many people may recognize that African Americans still do not enjoy the full and equal protection of the law with the recent continuing rash of police and white civilian killings of unarmed black men and women more than sixty years after the government signed the UDHR. Murdering people of color is baked in to the functioning of America, as the "We Charge Genocide" petition quipped, "Once the classic method of lynching was the rope. Now it is the policeman's bullet."[66] The UN has issued many scathing reports on human rights violations in the United States, particularly citing police brutality and excessive use of force against African Americans by both law enforcement and civilians. The most recent report in 2015 included 348 recommendations to address human rights violations in the US.

A number of US activists on the Left are skeptical about the usefulness of the human rights framework and practice their own particular form of American exceptionalism, believing that the way the US government has consistently undermined the UN and the human rights system makes it an unlikely source of relief for human rights violations. Some social justice activists are unfamiliar with the human rights framework and rely on myths and media accounts to assert that it offers little in terms of validation and support. Others cite the United States's failure to ratify the treaty as the reason for their reluctance, while others point out the cynical manipulation of human rights by the government in the protection of global capital rather than in the service of vulnerable people. Others question definitions of human rights that are so culturally specific and only selectively supported in democratic countries. For example, while the US claims to prioritize political and civil human rights, conservative attacks on voting rights and freedom of the press belie those claims. New biotechnologies challenge the fundamental definitions of precisely who is human by altering the genomes of future generations, demonstrating that the meanings of these rights always shift over time depending on power relationships.

Critics from the Global South who believe human rights are an imperialistic Western imposition on their societies agree with US skeptics, albeit for different reasons. Perhaps the critics are right to be alarmed because human rights claims challenge all authoritarian and theocratic regimes that deprive their citizens (especially women and LGBTQ folks) of basic human rights, including the United States. Human rights violations are a continuum with some countries performing better on certain issues and others performing worse. That the United States sometimes uses the language of human rights in diplomatic demands while violating such standards domestically is not a reason for complacency. Rather, this inconsistency is a challenge only US activists can uniquely address.

These critics make important and valid points, but despite the doubts of neoliberals, conservatives on the Right, and cynics on the Left, the global human rights framework offers—at this time—the most likely moral, political, and legal regime through which RJ goals may be accomplished. It is far more expansive and inclusive than the limited US Constitution. In terms of reproductive justice, the Constitution cannot adequately address sex discrimination against women. In fact, Sarah Weddington, the attorney who argued for abortion rights in *Roe v. Wade*, wanted the court to rule that denying women the right to an abortion was a form of sex discrimination and violated the Fourteenth Amendment of the Constitution. The court demurred, choosing not to go that far in dismantling traditional sex discrimination in the US (notably a path that Canada actually embraced when it ruled that abortion denial is a form of sex discrimination a few years later). The Supreme Court instead articulated a tenuous "right to privacy" that is not in the Constitution that allowed trimester-based government interventions in women's decision-making, with increasing state power and diminishing women's autonomy further along as the pregnancy progresses. That deeply flawed court decision permitted a patchwork of antiabortion laws across the country, with more than two thousand bills introduced in state legislatures to restrict women's human right to abortion.

Now states are interfering at conception, claiming that fetuses have rights the moment they are conceived. Antiabortion opponents misleadingly argue that certain forms of birth control are in fact abortifacients and terminate pregnancies. Lynn Paltrow of National Advocates for Pregnant Women fights in courts against the policing of pregnant women's behavior. Some have received criminal sentences for refusing doctors' orders for forced cesareans, attempting abortions, using either legal and illegal medications, or having a healthy baby who tests positive for controlled substances. These should not be criminal offenses punished with incarceration or involuntary medical interventions. A hostile Supreme Court may eventually overturn *Roe v. Wade* altogether, recriminalizing abortion in the US.

Many feminists around the world prefer to use international human rights standards to make claims for full reproductive freedom. Recognizing that women have full human rights that cannot be diminished because of a natural health condition like pregnancy, activists particularly from the Global South have urged the UN and nongovernmental organizations to affirm that women's rights are human rights, and that human rights protect abortion rights.

In addition to offering wider protection for abortion rights, human rights also offer more comprehensive protection against the denial of birthing rights. The aforementioned convention against genocide describes the prevention of births among a population as a form of genocide, or reprocide, which fundamentally contradicts reproductive justice values. Other examples include forcibly transferring children from a community, such as Native American children forcibly removed from their families to boarding schools run by white Christians. The disproportionate placement of poor and children of color in foster care throughout the US is also a human rights violation. Thus, strategies of population control and reduction violate several important human rights treaties to which the United States is obligated, having ratified the Genocide Convention in 1992.

Activists have endorsed the usefulness of the human rights framework globally for addressing public health issues like HIV/AIDS. International AIDS activist Dázon Dixon Diallo works in South Africa and the United States providing services, advocacy, and income-generating projects for women with HIV/AIDS. She points out the relationship between working to stop the spread of HIV/AIDS and community conditions: "We're not only fighting a virus; we're fighting the conditions that allow it to proliferate. We need to look at public health issues from within a human rights framework . . . the need for prevention justice," which builds upon reproductive justice theory.[67]

In terms of movement building, human rights appeal because they are a radically different way for social justice activists to examine power and inequality, and the role of state and nonstate actors, like corporations and individuals, in perpetuating violations. Human rights offer strong moral arguments for setting standards for how people should be treated and what everyone deserves as a member of human society, regardless of their identity, citizenship, abilities, etc. Human rights present strong political possibilities for bringing together various social justice movements under a unifying ideological platform not based on identity categories but our shared humanity. Although the United States has not ratified the majority of the available human rights treaties, it is possible to exert pressure on local, state, and federal governments to comply with internationally recognized human rights norms and standards, while building the political power to achieve treaty ratification by the Senate. Legal enforcement possibilities increase when backed by an educated human rights movement.

In using the human rights framework, RJT links both individual and group rights in that we all have the same human rights, but may need different things to achieve them based on our intersectional location in life. For example, if sterilizing women against their will violates the Genocide Convention, then why was California allowed to sterilize incarcerated women until very recently? In 2015 Justice Now successfully fought to pass a bill to end the coerced sterilization of incarcerated women and now works to hold institutions accountable to the new law. Should people lose their human rights because they are incarcerated? Reproductive justice emphasizes each person's individuality as indicated by intersectional markers, but without ignoring collective or group identity.

The RJ movement is a part of the effort toward building a human rights culture in the United States. Human rights must be infused into the complex and multiple beliefs, motivations, and policies of the United States. They offer a compelling counter to the culture of life rhetoric of fundamentalists, conservatives, Libertarians, and Christian nationalists. Human rights challenge those who believe our society should be stuck in the days when people had to be religiously qualified white males in order to hold power, a particularly paternalistic and authoritarian perversion of democracy inherited from US history. Offering a counternarrative, the US Human Rights Network issues annual reports on human rights violations in America and offers leadership in the human rights movement in the United States.

However, engaging with the government to fight for human rights through an RJ lens requires us to recognize the ambiguous role of the state in supporting or denying justice. For example, the government asserted that Keisha, as a pregnant twelve-year-old, was too young to make an independent decision to have an abortion, or to receive comprehensive sex education that may have prevented the pregnancy, but she is not too young to have responsibility for a baby. This is an inherently contradictory and illogical diminution of her human rights.

In addition, many human rights activists reasonably believe that the nation-state is an outmoded form for organizing human society since capital, corporations, and environmental problems, for example, are largely stateless and not confined by national boundaries. These activists compellingly argue national boundaries only serve to restrain labor forces and restrict the free movement of people, while doing little to ensure that the planet is protected from man-made or environmental catastrophes. Thus, a human rights system reliant on state actions and bound by national charters and constitutions has, by definition, a limited shelf life. However, since the nation-state is probably a feature of global politics for the foreseeable future, this concern is not an immediate challenge to exploring the present utility of the human rights regime.

It is also understandable that governments, corporations, and individuals are often reluctant to curtail their own powers by embracing human rights standards. All three entities often argue in favor of discriminatory policies to meet other objectives, such as allowing discrimination based on religion, gender, sexual preference, class, race, etc. In light of recent Supreme Court decisions like *Burwell v. Hobby Lobby Stores, Inc.*, this may extend permissible discrimination to include women who use birth control, have had abortions, or admit to having sex outside of marriage. This means the task of achieving an RJ-influenced set of policies, much less a worldview—in whatever political or social arena—is further complicated, although strides are occurring to demonstrate the national power of the RJ framework.

This is despite the sometimes-glacial reluctance of some pro-choice allies to accept the power of RJ, and the creativity and leadership of those women of color who explore and embrace it. It may not be possible to hold the United States accountable with the liberal feminist strategies and the leadership of the past. Attempting to co-opt RJT without referencing the human rights framework actually deradicalizes the theory, stripping it of its most powerful tool to challenge US imperialistic hegemony and domestic intransigence.

For example, in 2005, Planned Parenthood sponsored a conference entitled Reproductive Justice for All at Smith College, making it the one of the first mainstream organizations to attempt to incorporate the RJ framework. This conference, predominantly organized by the more progressive members of PPFA, nonetheless failed to shift the national organization into using the human rights framework or to understand the importance of the leadership of women of color organizations in its future. This failure was later illustrated in a brief controversy between PPFA and women of color organizations in 2014, when they proclaimed in the *New York Times* to be moving away from the pro-choice/pro-life dichotomy without acknowledging the pathbreaking work of women of color organizations that produced this sea change.

Claiming Our Power: Standpoint Theory

The pregnancies of women of color are a global ideological battleground on which the right to reproduce—to be mothers—is pitted against those who believe they are rescuing us from the specter of overpopulation. These ideologies and their practitioners would deny women of color not only agency and consciousness but also subjectivity or the right to narrate our own lives by lifting our voices to seek and name hidden oppressions. In response, we developed fresh concepts about workable problems to use for theoretical thinking. Women of color reclaim our subjectivity; we mine our varied heterogeneous experiences to develop comprehensive analyses and explanations of the competing and intersecting forces of power and social control in our lives.

Reproductive justice incorporates feminist standpoint theory because as black women, we occupy both an insider and outsider position within the feminist movement, the African American community, and in gender-nonconforming spaces. These intersectional positions enable us to see multiple realities in ways that are invisible to others who do not stand at our particular shifting locations. We question the indifference of those who don't believe Black Lives Matter or that Black Girls Rock! or understand the importance of the Standing Rock resistance against environmental destruction because we see patterns of injustice that are raced and gendered that others are often oblivious to.

We straddle the borderlands and choose to be bridge builders when we want to, but we fiercely reject those who involuntarily thrust us into that role for their own convenience. We can be the mules and the explainers, the dreamers and the pragmatists. Our marginality in so many locations produces a creative excitement that is transformative and enriches social discourse. By centering ourselves, we reveal, for example, the deeply disguised racist undertones of population control processes, even when camouflaged by feminist or anti-racist rhetoric. Pregnancy and coercion need a fresh examination with some men coercing women to get pregnant, and some women pressuring others not to. When black men claim our wombs as their territorial property in the struggle against white supremacy, we decry the misogyny of these claims, because we refuse to "throw away the birth control pill" to have a baby for the revolution. We refuse to accept the notion that the amazing theoretical gifts we have offered through formulating the concepts of identity politics, intersectionality, and reproductive justice make us unable to perceive misogynoir and the casual disrespect offered by those who walk on the bricks we laid that provide a pathway for others.

According to Sandra Harding, "Standpoint theory emerged in the 1970s and 1980s as feminist critical theory about relations between the production of knowledge and the practices of power."[68] Standpoint theory is part of postmodern and poststructuralist critiques from the academy that interrogate allegedly objective master narratives, much as critical race theory challenges the presumed neutrality of the law that hides its deeply rooted biases against people of color, nonwhite immigrants, queer people, and women. These dominant accounts provide inadequate space for oppositional actions by individuals and communities, replete with their tensions and contradictions. The producers of these purportedly objective accounts cannot successfully veil the material and historical conditions that create their own biases. In other words, although straight white men may claim to be able to produce a body of laws, norms, and standards that appear neutral and fair, in fact, their inherent inability to understand other standpoints results in discriminatory reasoning that almost unfailingly reinforces the status quo of their disproportionate power.

When cisgender men sue women for the right to participate in women-only spaces by claiming reverse gender discrimination, they are not dismantling the patriarchy but instead using it in stunningly unoriginal ways. They are frequently successful because our myopic legal system does not sufficiently take into account differences in power and concretized patterns of discrimination. Allan Bakke's successful 1977 claim of reverse discrimination to dismantle affirmative action is another famous example. Bakke, like many white people, claimed that any remedial actions to correct past racial and gender injustices are de facto discrimination against white people, particularly white men. This widely accepted standpoint casually disregards the centuries of continued preferences for white men in university admissions, employment, financial and credit options, politics, and police forces. Critics of reverse discrimination claims rightfully point out that equality of process often results in discrimination in outcome. If the majority of students at a university have been white for hundreds of years, using apparently neutral admissions processes will reinforce the status quo and privilege white people while not addressing the traditional patterns of discrimination that have produced such outcomes in the past and the present.

Reproductive justice is not an essentialist, reductionist framework based on the shared victimization of women of color. RJ does not insist that there is only one way to view or experience the world. All women of color are not oppressed the same way, even within ethnic groups. Instead, RJ represents the need for strategic alliances among people who experience multiple sites of domination and oppression within the social construction of gender. Societies and cultures prescribe or construct gender roles as the only appropriate behavior for a person of a specific gender. Assigning disparate values to different reproductive bodies predictably generates different reproductive experiences. All people may experience some form of reproductive oppression, but because of our individual intersectional identities, we do not experience it the same way.

This understanding of our enterprise resonates with the theory of standpoint epistemology. Standpoint epistemology foregrounds the effects of politics on knowledge production and argues that objectivity increases by input from multiple perspectives. It thus challenges accounts of reality based only on the perspective of those in power. As Harding explains, "Standpoint epistemology sets the relationship between knowledge and politics at the center of its account in the sense that it tries to provide causal accounts—to explain—the effects that different kinds of politics have on the production of knowledge."[69]

When women of color proclaim that we have a new paradigm called reproductive justice for envisioning our movement, we recognize its disturbance of the dualistic logic of the dominant social order that values sameness or commonalities over specificity and difference, as well as reason over emotion. Because we embed multiple standpoints in the injustices we experience, we embrace the ambiguities attendant to nonstatic standpoints. Both intersectionality and standpoint theory may be limited if they become reliant on fixed points of perspective in space and time. Ambiguity and temporal changes are not only necessary but desired.

Women of color are demanding "a plural consciousness" that uproots dualistic thinking that "requires understanding multiple, often opposing, ideas and knowledges, and negotiating these knowledges."[70] Gloria Anzaldúa suggests that a "*mestiza* consciousness" arising from inhabiting contradictory locations simultaneously is a valuable source of knowledge production because it "challenges dualism and is flexible and tolerant of ambiguity."[71] She writes how marginalized women engage in self-making, the creation of our own identities, that celebrates our ambiguous social locations rather than perceiving them as problematic. RJT frustrates claims of hierarchy and certitude, especially binaries. Canons from black feminists using our knowledge from sites of multiple possibilities that deconstruct the processes that devalue embodiment and brace systems of reproductive oppression may strengthen the evolution of feminist theories.

The ambiguities embedded in our paradigm threaten order, certainty, control, and power in very fundamental ways. We present a significant challenge to both the mainstream pro-choice community and our own communities that devalue women of color. Our knowledge claims contest commonly held beliefs about women of color, our sexuality, and our fertility. We rely on our own knowledge-validation processes that are outside of and often counter to the dominant theories of knowledge that deny us the power to be credible witnesses to our own experiences. As women of color acting as our own agents of knowledge, we embrace the emotions, interests, and values generated by our unique situations and standpoints. In so doing, we reject the positivist methodological approach of objectivity and distance, and do not seek to ascertain truth through adversarial debates.

We believe that Keisha's life can change. We believe that despite her significant challenges, she may overcome her childhood suffering and become self-determining and the author of her own destiny. We believe this because we have lived that reality too. As I said before, her story of childhood abuse, reproductive injustice, shame, and suffering was so much like ours before we conceptualized RJT, moving individually and collectively from the trauma of our experiences to the power of naming our own pathways of resistance.

White Allies and Reproductive Justice Theory

While reproductive justice theory challenges the pro-choice/pro-life binary and arises from the lived experiences of African American women, it is not only applicable to women of color. "Depth does not mean a chasm," to quote Luce Irigaray.[72] Every human being has an intersectional mosaic of experiences subjected to forms of bodily control by society. The creative tension between self-determination, group rights, and collective power provides an analytical foundation for unique standpoints on self, community, and society.

For white allies (and people of color, too) to successfully engage RJT with integrity, they must question neoliberal discourses about individual rights and the marketplace of choices denied to the vulnerable members of our society. In particular, white feminists must overcome their fear of challenging white supremacy by understanding that it is an ideology and not inherent in any race of people. Any devotee of human rights must contest white supremacy, and failure to do so is, by default, to be complicit in its maintenance. In the classic and often-quoted essay by Audre Lorde, "The Master's Tools Will Never Dismantle the Master's House," the line following this phrase emphasizes this point: "They may temporarily allow us to beat him at his own game, but they will never enable us to bring about genuine change. And this fact is only threatening to women who still define the master's house as their only source of support."[73]

For example, one of the frequent critiques of the pro-choice movement by radical women is how willingly they often submit to members of the Democratic Party in the hopes that it will stand up firmly for abortion rights because abortion is routine healthcare for women. The negotiations in 2009 over the Affordable Care Act (ACA) are a case in point because abortion was central to many debates about the ACA. The ACA reinforces the current Hyde Amendment restrictions, continuing to limit federal funds to pay for abortions that endanger the life of the woman or that are a result of rape or incest. The Democratic political leadership strengthened rather than weakened abortion restrictions as a concession to ACA opponents, disappointing many RJ advocates by establishing rules unique to abortion coverage, such as requiring a separate insurance premium to obtain coverage. States may ban abortion coverage in the marketplace plans available under the ACA, and twenty-five states do so.

While the political calculus of deal making to get the support of anti-choice Democratic party members is beyond the scope of this article, it is important to point out that such compromises do little to help vulnerable women obtain the full range of reproductive health services they deserve. A key question is how to hold political party leaders accountable to women's human rights when they make these rights a bargaining chip to be traded away. Attacks by conservatives on the ACA continue despite the many antiabortion concessions made, begging the question of whether proponents should have not thrown abortion rights under the bus in the first place. The ACA offered valuable insight into understanding why RJ advocates fight for undivided human rights, not trading away vulnerable people's rights for transcient political gains.

White allies must also interrogate the parallel co-optation of critiques of population control sanitized and modernized with feminist-sounding language. For example, it is fashionable in some quarters to use the term "population stabilization" as a way to describe imposing fertility control measures on communities in the Global South without addressing the root causes of underdevelopment and global exploitation that prevent these communities from controlling their own resources and destinies, violating their human right to development. Often, seemingly moderate language about environmental concerns or women's empowerment mask agendas not too far removed from earlier eugenic attempts at population control in order to contain dissent, extract natural resources from other people's land, and reduce the potential for resistance to neocolonial expropriation.

The liberal wing of the mainstream women's movement can replicate the dualisms of the patriarchy in continuing the imperialist project of colonizing our bodies and lands when this brand of feminism denies its complicity in population control rhetoric and justifications. RJT connects our local concerns to global issues. We are vigilant in challenging the vast and complex mechanisms of social control enacted to create wealth for the economically privileged through globalization. We cannot suppress the parts of ourselves—our authenticity, emotionality, and interdependence—least meaningful to the powers arrayed against us. As theorist Michel Foucault argued in *Discipline and Punish*, modern patriarchal power produces docile bodies through uninterrupted coercion of every bodily process, including reproduction. The regulation of the bodies of women of color renders us invisible through the paradox of extreme surveillance and policing, which assure the automatic functioning of power. The ultimate effect is to produce uninterrupted coercive practices and norms directed toward our every reproductive activity that, in turn, encapsulate us in an ever-changing matrix of power and domination imposed not only by the patriarchy but also by its collaborators and apologists.

The framework of RJ challenges the hegemonic discourses of abortion-focused, single-issue reproductive politics based on the priorities of liberal feminism and its opponents. Even as the bodies of women of color and trans women serve as sites of knowledge production for the mainstream women's movement, our needs and experiences are often neglected and marginalized. Feminists of color exist in an ambiguous insider/outsider status. We have options about how to amass and use our power to challenge devaluation and objectification because academics and mainstream organizations need us more than we need them to substantiate their theories and obtain funding for their operations. For example, since 1970, Title X funding for family planning providers is designed to prioritize services for low-income families, creating an economic model that depends on impoverished people accessing and using public health services. RJ advocates urge Title X–supported organizations to prioritize the needs and leadership of low-income people, particularly women of color, yet they are inexplicably slow to recognize how not doing so challenges their economic viability. The same can be said for academic institutions that incessantly study and receive funding for and about people of color but will not change their institutional biases about hiring and tenuring faculty of color.

RJT offers a powerful position reversal from which to insist on elevating the reproductive justice framework and offering a critique of the ideology of population control from the Right and the Left while challenging hegemonic practices in the academy and mainstream activism that reinforce white privilege and dominance. For women of color, RJT is at the same time about and beyond abortion.

Reproductive justice has moved into the interstices of the pro-choice movement in the United States, moving from the margins to the center. Because of RJ's challenges to institutionalized power relations, it is not a framework convenient for those who seek to maintain the status quo. The limited, dualistic, and polarizing debates based on unitary theories of gender politics mask the differences experienced by women of color. By being trapped in the dynamics of self-reflexivity as both object and subject, liberal feminists "can produce a circular, self-conforming rhetoric and a hermetic closure of thought . . . within the narcissism of the mirror image."[74] In the words of Irigaray, "They have left us only absences, defects, negatives to name ourselves."[75] Because we have to contain ourselves within language that is woefully inadequate, we have the paradoxical task of affirming our differences while working toward our unity in a foreign tongue and in a strange land.

As hooks says, women do not need to eradicate difference to feel solidarity. We do not need to share a common oppression to fight equally to end all oppressions. Lorde affirms: "It is not those differences between us that are separating us. It is rather our refusal to recognize those differences and to examine the distortions that result from our misnaming them and their effects upon human behavior and expectation."[76] It takes all of our differences to make us whole, and differences only become barriers that break us into fragments if we let them.

Conclusion

Our emancipation from this binary two-step of reproductive oppression through reproductive justice theory will present a delicate but ever-changing choreography of control and location. We are using our power—claiming our voices for ourselves—speaking for ourselves. We no longer will be a reflection of liberal feminism with a little difference. What may be most startling about RJT is our indifference as to how it is received by those who struggle to understand their own realities, much less ours, because we are refusing to dance that way anymore. No more docile bodies. Because in fact, we have been dancing with our oppressors in a circular two-step that is getting us nowhere. The music, instead of lifting our feet, is controlling our movements in that we have become its object, rather than the other way around.

Our resistance exalts the passion of Zora Neale Hurston—"I dance wildly within myself; I yell within, I whoop. My face is painted red and yellow and my body is painted blue. My pulse is throbbing like a war drum"[77]—while others only hear what we feel and can only guess what we know. Reproductive justice theorists prefer to become our own subjects, without permission and without apology. We are decentering those alienating realities and putting ourselves in the center of the lens. As well as being different, we are indifferent.

Nevertheless, our masks of conformity are never static; masks affect everything around us, mutating as survival dictates. The disguises reveal their own paradox: if they serve the needs of our oppressors, do they serve our needs as well as we think they do? The masks may alienate us from ourselves so thoroughly that we support their goals without fulfilling our own. Irigaray poetically advises:

> Let's quickly invent our own phrases, so that everywhere and always, we continue to embrace. We are so subtle that nothing can stand in our way, nothing will keep us from reaching each other, even fleetingly, as long as we find means of communication that have *our* density. We will walk through obstacles imperceptibly, without damage, to find each other. No one will see a thing. Our lack of resistance is our strength. For a long time, they have appreciated our suppleness for their embraces, their impressions. Why not use it for ourselves?[78]

Reproductive justice theory frees us from the boundaries of white supremacy to disengage from and critique an alienating worldview. As Marilyn Frye argues, oppression is the reduction of options by forces and barriers systematically related to each other in such a way as to form an enclosing structure that restricts or penalizes motion in any direction. Each option exposes one to penalty, censure, or deprivation. Because we envision infinite possibilities for RJT that will be heterogeneous and amorphous, we will not be fenced into their stifling commons, as if collectively owning the space within these cages makes us less imprisoned. There is no circumference to our circle because it widens every time we lift our voices and express our many dimensions. Our silhouettes unknown are colored in by our blood experiences. We created expansive reproductive justice language written through our ancestors exhaling in our exultations. As Tshepo Madlingozi says, "We are our makers of our history. We are our own inventors of our future."[79]

I can imagine Keisha in college attending her first feminist theory class, trying to understand what has happened in her life and to find new words to describe her path to that moment of epiphany when feminist teachings helped save our sanity and our lives. It is possible. Despite having a child at fifteen through incest, I went to college at sixteen. The path was not easy or linear, and I didn't graduate until I was fifty-five. My encounter with the antirape movement in the 1970s saved my life. I learned it could be done. I hope Keisha also learns to escape the oppressors' cages, their endless binaries, their endless oppositions. I hope she doesn't give up on herself the way society may seem to give up on her. A little hope, a little help, and all things are possible. As black feminists, we will do our best to prepare this new feminist theory and have it waiting for her when she arrives. We must always remember Keisha's story and never forget those we strive to represent with compassion and dignity.

We revel in reproductive justice theory and its world of ambiguities and find their certitude about our existences liberating. Absolutes immobilize. Mobility strengthens.

Notes

1. Brittney Cooper, "Feminism's Ugly Internal Clash: Why Its Future Is Not Up to White Women," *Salon*, September 24, 2014, http://www.salon.com/2014/09/24/feminisms_ugly_internal_clash_why_its_future_is_not_up_to_white_women/. Emphasis in original.

2. Chandra Talpade Mohanty, "'Under Western Eyes' Revisited: Feminist Solidarity through Anticapitalist Struggles," *Signs: Journal of Women in Culture and Society* 28, no. 2 (Winter 2003): 502.

3. Patricia Hill Collins, *Black Feminist Thought: Knowledge, Consciousness, and the Politics of Empowerment* (New York: Routledge, 2000), 31.

4. Nicole Hemmer, "'Scientific Racism' Is on the Rise on the Right. But It's Been Lurking There for Years," *Vox*, March 28, 2017, http://www.vox.com/the-big-idea/2017/3/28/15078400/scientific-racism-murray-alt-right-black-muslim-culture-trump.

5. Toni M. Bond Leonard, "Standing at the Intersection of Faith & Sexuality," *Ecclesio.com*, September 26, 2012, http://www.ecclesio.com/2012/09/standing-at-the-intersection-of-faith-sexuality-by-toni-m-bond-leonard/.

6. Kelly Brown Douglas, *Sexuality and the Black Church: A Womanist Perspective* (Maryknoll, NY: Orbis Books, 1999), 69.

7. Ruha Benjamin, "Catching Our Breath: Critical Race STS and the Carceral Imagination," *Engaging Science, Technology, and Society* 2 (2016): 147.

8. Quoted in María Pilar Aquino, "Latina Feminist Theology: Central Features," in *A Reader in Latina Feminist Theology: Religion and Justice* ed.

María Pilar Aquino, Daisy L. Machado, and Jeanette Rodriguez. (Austin: University of Texas Press, 2002), 150.

9. Audre Lorde, "The Uses of Anger: Women Responding to Racism," in *Sister Outsider: Essays and Speeches* (Berkeley, CA: Crossing Press, 1984), 132–33.

10. Kelly Oliver, *The Colonization of Psychic Space: A Psychoanalytic Social Theory of Oppression* (Minneapolis: University of Minnesota Press, 2004), xix.

11. Evelynn M. Hammonds, "Gendering the Epidemic: Feminism and the Epidemic of HIV/AIDS in the United States, 1981–1999," in *Feminism in Twentieth-Century Science, Technology, and Medicine*, ed. Angela N. H. Creager, Elizabeth Lunbeck, and Londa Schiebinger. (Chicago: University of Chicago Press, 2001), 241.

12. Quoted in Valerie Boyd, *Wrapped in Rainbows: The Life of Zora Neale Hurston* (New York: Scribner, 2003), 42.

13. Banu Subramaniam, *Ghost Stories for Darwin: The Science of Variation and the Politics of Diversity* (Chicago: University of Illinois Press, 2014), 245–46.

14. Audre Lorde, "Age, Race, Class, and Sex: Women Redefining Difference," in *Sister Outsider*, 114.

15. Collins, *Black Feminist Thought*, vii.

16. Banu Subramaniam, *Ghost Stories for Darwin*, 8.

17. Katherine Cross (Quinnae Moongazer), "Reproductive Justice and the Invisible Sisterhood," *Nuclear Unicorn* (blog), August 20, 2013, http://quinnae.com/2013/08/20/reproductive-justice-and-the-invisible-sisterhood/.

18. bell hooks, *Feminist Theory: From Margin to Center* (Boston: South End Press, 1984), 52.

19. Andrea Smith, *Conquest: Sexual Violence and American Indian Genocide* (Boston: South End Press, 2005), 8–9.

20. See Loretta J. Ross, "Reproductive Justice beyond Biology," Center for American Progress, https://www.americanprogress.org/issues/race/news/2017/03/15/428191/reproductive-justice-beyond-biology/.

21. Nicole Rousseau, *Black Woman's Burden: Commodifying Black Reproduction* (New York: Palgrave Macmillan, 2009), 4–5.

22. James Baldwin, "Stranger in the Village," *Collected Essays* (New York: Literary Classics of America, 1998), 119.

23. Collins, *Black Feminist Thought*, 50–51.

24. Thandisizwe Chimurenga, "On Women's Theory-Building and Transnational Feminism," *blkcowrie* (blog), November 17, 2014, http://blkcowrie.wordpress.com/2014/11/17/thandisizwe-chimurenga-on-womens-theory-building-and-transnational-feminism/.

25. Assata Shakur, "Women in Prison: How It Is with Us," *The Black Scholar* 9, no. 6 (April 1978), 8–15. http://www.historyisaweapon.com/defcon1/shakurwip.html/.

26. Mai'a Williams, "Introduction," in *Revolutionary Mothering: Love on the Front Lines*, ed. Alexis Pauline Gumbs, China Martens, and Mai'a Williams (Oakland, CA: PM Press, 2016), 1.

27. Alexis Pauline Gumbs, "m/other ourselves: a Black queer feminist genealogy for radical mothering," in *Revolutionary Mothering*, 20.

28. Laura Briggs, *Reproducing Empire: Race, Sex, Science, and US Imperialism in Puerto Rico* (Berkeley: University of California Press, 2003), 16.

29. Janet Price and Margrit Shildrick, *Feminist Theory and the Body* (New York: Routledge, 1999), 4.

30. Banu Subramaniam, *Ghost Stories for Darwin*, 120–21.

31. Ibid., 497.

32. bell hooks, "Theory as Liberatory Practice," in *Feminist Theory: A Reader*, ed. Wendy Kolmar and Frances Bartkowski (New York: McGraw-Hill, 2005), 38.

33. Ibid., 37.

34. Wendy Kolmar and Frances Bartkowski, "Introduction," in *Feminist Theory: A Reader*, 45.

35. Tshepo Madlingozi, "Taking Stock of the South African Truth and Reconciliation Commission 20 Years Later: No Truth, No Reconciliation and No Justice," Paper presented at the 3rd International Colloquium of the Instituto Humanitas at UNISINOS, September 16, 2015, 6.

36. Catharine A. MacKinnon, "From Practice to Theory, or What Is a White Woman Anyway?" in *Radically Speaking: Feminism Reclaimed*, ed. Diane Bell and Renate Klein (North Melbourne, Australia: Spinifex Press, 1996), 45.

37. Mia Bay, Farah J. Griffin, Martha S. Jones, and Barbara D. Savage, eds., *Toward an Intellectual History of Black Women*, (Chapel Hill: University of North Carolina Press, 2015), 4.

38. Collins, *Black Feminist Thought*, 22.

39. Toni Cade Bambara, "What It Means to Be a Black Woman," *The Black Collegian* (April–May 1980), 136–37.

40. Barbara Christian, "The Race for Theory," in *The Black Feminist Reader*, ed. Joy James and T. Denean Sharpley-Whiting (Boston: Blackwell, 2000), 12.

41. Pauli Murray and Genna Rae McNeil, "Interview with Pauli Murray, Interview G-0044," Southern Oral History Program Collection (#4007), February 13, 1976, http://docsouth.unc.edu/sohp/G-0044/G-0044.html.

42. Mohanty, "'Under Western Eyes,'" 501.

43. Audrey Tang, "Open Source Enlightenment 2015, Part 1," *Linkedin Pulse*, August 7, 2015, https://www.linkedin.com/pulse/open-source-enlightenment-2015-part-1-audrey-tang.

44. Michael Onyebuchi Eze, *Intellectual History in Contemporary South Africa* (New York: Palgrave Macmillan, 2010), 190–91.

45. Desmond Tutu, *No Future without Forgiveness* (New York: Doubleday, 1999).

46. Kameelah Janan Rasheed, "Stakes Is High—and Black Lives Are Worthy of Elaboration: A True Stories Conversation between Kameelah Janan Rasheed and Rachel Kaadzi Ghansah," *Gawker*, June 7, 2014, http://gawker.com/stakes-is-high-and-black-lives-are-worthy-of-elaboratio-1587471910.

47. bell hooks, *Talking Back: Thinking Feminist, Thinking Black* (Boston: South End Press, 1989), 12.

48. Rickie Solinger, "Offending Women," *Women's Review of Books* 32, no. 3 (May/June 2015): 10–11.

49. bell hooks, *Teaching to Transgress: Education as the Practice of Freedom* (New York: Routledge, 1994), 63.

50. Lisa Diane White, personal communication with Loretta Ross, September 5, 2017.

51. bell hooks, *Ain't I A Woman: Black Women and Feminism* (Boston: South End Press, 1981), 86.

52. Washington Coalition of Sexual Assault Programs, "African American Community," December 22, 2015, http://www.wcsap.org/african-american-community.

53. Women of Color Network, "Women of Color Network Facts & Stats: Sexual Violence in Communities of Color," June 2006, http://www.doj.state.or.us/victims/pdf/women_of_color_network_facts_sexual_violence_2006.pdf.

54. Barbara Smith, ed., *Home Girls: A Black Feminist Anthology* (New York: Kitchen Table: Women of Color Press, 1983), xxxiii.

55. White, "Women of Color Helping Ourselves."

56. hooks, *Feminist Theory*, 63.

57. Collins, *Black Feminist Thought*, 3.

58. Kalamu ya Salaam, "Searching for the Mother Tongue: An Interview with Toni Cade Bambara," *First World* 2, no. 4 (1980).

59. Kimberlé Crenshaw, "Intersectionality and Identity Politics: Learning from Violence against Women of Color" in *Feminist Theory: A Reader*, 50.

60. Kimberlé Crenshaw, "Demarginalizing the Intersection of Race and Sex: A Black Feminist Critique of Antidiscrimination Doctrine, Feminist Theory and Antiracist Politics," *University of Chicago Legal Forum* 1, article 8 (1989): 166–67.

61. Janet Price and Margrit Shildrick, *Feminist Theory and the Body*, 7. Emphasis in original.

62. Gwen Patton, "Black People and the Victorian Ethos," in *The Black Woman: An Anthology*, ed. Toni Cade Bambara (New York: Washington Square Press, 1970), 182.

63. Manisha Sinha, *The Slave's Cause: A History of Abolition* (New Haven, CT: Yale University Press, 2016), 152.

64. Frederick Douglass, "The Claims of the Negro Ethnologically Considered" (address, Literary Societies of Western Reserve College, Rochester, NY, July 12, 1854). Reprinted in *African-American Social and*

Political Thought: 1850–1920, ed. Howard Brotz (New York: Transaction Publishers, 1995), 243. Emphasis in original.

65. Malcolm X, "Letter to the Egyptian Gazette (August 25, 1964)," *Malcom X* (blog), July 2013, http://malcolmxfiles.blogspot.com/2013/07/letter-to-egyptian-gazette-august-25.html.

66. "We Charge Genocide (1951)," *BlackPast.org*, accessed January 2017, http://www.blackpast.org/we-charge-genocide-historic-petition-united-nations-relief-crime-united-states-government-against.

67. Dázon Dixon Diallo, "HIV/AIDS and the Women's Health Movement," *HIV Risk Reduction* 8, no. 1, accessed December 17, 2014, http://www.hiveis.com/documents/WomensHealthMovement_Dazon.pdf.

68. Sandra Harding, "Introduction: Standpoint Theory as a Site of Political, Philosophic, and Scientific Debate," in *The Feminist Standpoint Theory Reader: Intellectual and Political Controversies*, ed. Sandra Harding (New York: Routledge, 2004), 1.

69. Sandra Harding, "Rethinking Standpoint Epistemology," in *Feminist Epistemologies*, ed. Linda Alcoff and Elizabeth Potter (New York: Routledge, 1993), 55–56.

70. Gloria Anzaldúa, "La Consciencia de la mestiza: Towards a New Consciousness" in *Feminist Theory*, 60.

71. Ibid., 46.

72. Luce Irigaray, "When Our Lips Speak Together," trans. Carolyn Burke, *Signs: Journal of Women in Culture and Society* 6, no. 1 (Autumn 1980): 75.

73. Audre Lorde, "The Master's Tools Will Never Dismantle the Master's House," in *Sister Outsider*, 112.

74. Rosalind Delmar, "What Is Feminism?" in *Feminist Theory*, 34.

75. Irigaray, "When Our Lips Speak Together," 71.

76. Audre Lorde, "Age, Race, Class and Sex: Women Redefining Difference," in *Sister Outsider*, 115.

77. Quoted in Valerie Boyd, *Wrapped in Rainbows*, 126.

78. Irigaray, "When Our Lips Speak Together," 77. Emphasis in original.

79. Madlingozi, "Taking Stock," 2.

Transforming Silence: The Personal, Political, and Pedagogical Prism of the Abortion Narrative

PAMELA BRIDGEWATER TOURE

It is necessary to teach by living and speaking those truths which we believe and know.

—Audre Lorde

I am an activist, lawyer, and law professor. Among other things, I teach a seminar on reproduction and the law. In this seminar, I help students understand that reproductive rights are an important part of the larger, more comprehensive pursuit of justice and freedom. Thus, I connect reproduction to slavery, war, eugenics, Civil Rights, and sexual liberation movements. I also introduce them to reproductive exploitation in various forms, such as forced C-sections, coerced sterilization and contraception policies, and the ever-evolving issues created by advanced reproductive technologies.

I intend that my students will understand that despite the popular, political, and legal discourse of the day, abortion is a relatively small segment of the broader pursuit of reproductive freedom. Notwithstanding, students are most engaged during the section on abortion. Cloning is a distant second. Perhaps it is because most of my students are women of reproductive age, most self-identify as feminist, and although it is not a prerequisite, they identify as pro-choice. While these identity points have never hindered our ability to look at the issues from both sides of the debate, they do shape how abortion is connected to other issues in the course. My students consistently explore reproduction through the lens of the current abortion debate.

Over the years, my students have incorporated their personal experiences, political stances, and morals about abortion into their analyses of the issue. The discussions have been rich and informative. Students respect each other's life stories, and seem eager for those stories to inform their understanding of very difficult issues. Conversely, I have not shared my story in class. In fact, I felt uncomfortable when asked for my personal or political feelings on abortion. I purposefully avoided taking a position or revealing personal information because I believed that would hinder the students' learning environment. Although I had long suspected and challenged the utility of the objectivity myth law schools purportedly have, I thought it best to leave myself at the door when teaching the subject that has most defined who I am as a lawyer, activist, and ultimately as a law professor.

My students must have been aware of my efforts to avoid personalizing or politicizing my lectures because over the years they have developed sophisticated ways of getting me to reveal where I stand and how I came to stand there. One year, my students asked me how I came to be interested in practicing in this area of law. I saw this as simply another opportunity to talk to students about my career path and practice experience. When I started to talk about clients, cases, and litigation strategies, they made it clear that what they wanted was more personal information. Another student said, "Tell us *why* you practice in this area, not *how*." I identified myself as a pro-choice feminist. I described my work in abortion clinic legal defense, and finally, I told them about how my work on other issues within the women's health and anti-violence movements led me to work on reproductive justice.

But I stopped there. I did not tell them about my work as an escort for women trying to navigate the maze of anti-choice protesters on any given Saturday in front of reproductive service clinics. Although I am an out lesbian, I did not describe the ambivalence I sometimes experience in dealing with legal issues related to reproductive sex while knowing that my nonreproductive sexual activities are marginalized within the RJ movement. Most significantly, I did not explain how I became personally aware of the importance of the right to choose to terminate conception.

My lack of full disclosure was not due to an ideological opposition to including personal narrative in my scholarship or in my life as a lawyer. In fact, I employ narrative methodologies in my legal scholarship as well as my activist work. I especially recognize and value personal narrative in critical race, feminist, and queer legal theories. The law school classroom, however, was different. I, like many law professors, tend to provide less personal information rather than more. Regardless of our scholarship or politics, our classrooms tend to illustrate our adherence to the myth of objectivity. We rarely, if ever, ask our students to bring what they know about the world into the classroom. The legal system asks them to internalize and accept what judges accept about reasonableness and this is the training we provide.

We, in turn, rarely bring our personal experiences to the subjects we teach. Perhaps it makes us less vulnerable. Maybe it allows us some distance from the subject and our students. It could be that students with dissenting views will feel safer if we do not express ours. Perhaps it lets us get on with the business of teaching the law, undisturbed by the realities of life. We might merely be modeling our professors, who made similar pedagogical decisions. For better or worse, the net result is that we keep important parts of ourselves out of the classroom.

For me, this situation changed rather dramatically during a 2001 reproductive rights conference at Hampshire College in Amherst, Massachusetts. The first session I attended was an abortion speak-out—a forum for women to share their personal abortion stories. I learned a great deal about how women view abortion and experience reproductive decision-making. First, we heard from women who had illegal abortions pre-*Roe*. Women in this group spoke of hushed inquiries, clandestine meetings, desperation, and long drives to unknown places. They shared their stories of dark rooms, masked doctors, and pain.

The next group consisted primarily of young women who had had abortions in the last ten years. From them I learned that abortion equals shame. With their voices low and their heads lower, these women spoke of shame for being sexual and shame for deciding to terminate the pregnancy. Some, depending on other aspects of their lives and identities, expressed shame about how having an abortion would be seen in light of their racial, religious, and class identities. Others spoke of the shame they felt while asking the judge to permit them to terminate the pregnancy their father/uncle/brother caused, shame for not having enough money, shame for having to go to a public clinic, shame for taking too long to decide, shame for saying no, shame for saying yes, shame for not insisting on contraception, and on and on.

When the last of the scheduled speakers took her seat, the moderator invited members of the audience to come up and share their abortion stories. Without a plan, I approached the microphone and told my story. Due in large part to the privileges of my background, mine was a story of empowerment, self-discovery, and courage. I did not struggle to raise the money to pay for the procedure or overcome a language barrier in obtaining services. In sharing my abortion experience with the audience of students, lawyers, activists—women and men—committed to reproductive freedom, I experienced the value of my personal narrative, free of shame or guilt, in the pursuit of reproductive freedom. After the speak-out, several people asked if my story had been published or if I used it in my class. I said, "Of course not." I did not see how my story would fit into my vision of legal pedagogy.

My response sparked a conversation about the utility of personal narrative in the movement and in the classroom. One pro-choice feminist activist asked, "If abortion stories are relegated to closets, how will we know if what we are protecting actually exists?" From this, I was convinced that abortion experiences should be a part of my syllabus: not the truncated doctrinal stories but real, full, rich stories of women and their abortion experiences. I still did not think using my own story was appropriate. I could not imagine how I could stand in front of my class and tell the story. *Perhaps I could add it anonymously*, I thought. I did not see the utility of telling my story until a young woman volunteered hers. She said that if telling her story in person would help a lawyer understand why it is important to keep abortion legal, she would gladly come to my class. I said, "No, I will tell my own story." Courage can be contagious.

It is because of that courageous young woman, my colleagues, activists, and the other women whose lives we dissect in our classes that I now use my personal abortion story as the framework for teaching the post-*Roe* evolution of the reproductive rights doctrine. Doing so has added incredible depth to my understanding of the issues facing pro-choice advocates and activists, and has also served to help me and my students better understand the ways in which the legal landscape regarding abortion relates to women's lives, including and beyond their need for reproductive autonomy. What follows is the previously omitted chapter from the story of how I came to my work as a reproductive justice advocate, activist, and teacher of a seminar on reproduction and the law.

I was sixteen, a junior in high school, and I was pregnant. I knew I did not want to be pregnant. I knew that neither my boyfriend nor my parents wanted me to be pregnant. I recall hearing my parents talk about sex: "You will not be another girl who has to drop out of school to have a baby. The Reverend Dr. Martin Luther King would not approve of it, neither will we." In other words, my reproductive choices were my key to realizing Dr. King's dream. My reproductive practices were integrally connected to racial uplift.

Interestingly, they did not tell me not to have sex, nor did they tell me how to protect against unwanted conception. For a black, Southern, middle-class high school girl from an educated, politically liberal family, pregnancy was the problem. So I set out to resolve the problem. I got the yellow pages, turned to abortion, closed my eyes, picked three doctors, and chose the one with the friendliest sounding name. I chose Dr. R.[1] I called his office and got the price for the procedure. He had a sliding scale, $150–$210, based on how much I could afford and how far along

I was. I made the appointment for the next week. When the time came, my boyfriend and I went together. In the waiting room there were barely, slightly, and really pregnant women. Everyone seemed so friendly. The women talked about their jobs, churches, children, and travel plans. One woman who was about eight months pregnant smiled at me. It was the most comforting smile I had ever received. I was convinced that she knew I was there for reasons very different from hers, and yet she smiled to comfort me. I smiled back.

When my name was called, I went into a small room with the nurse practitioner, who explained the procedure in detail. She told me about the risks. She answered my questions and told me that she needed to take a blood sample to confirm that I was pregnant. After the confirmation, she asked me about my family and my medical history. Finally, she asked me whether I was sure I did not want to have a baby. I said, "Yes, I'm positive." After signing the consent forms and paying the bill, she took me to meet the doctor. He told me his name and asked me about school and sports. After a short chat about the procedure, he said that he would leave the room and the nurse would help me prepare. He later gave me a shot in my arm and I went to sleep. After the procedure, a nurse led me to another room with a big comfortable chair in which I reclined and went back to sleep, covered by a blanket. When I woke up again, the nurse told me that everything went well and I would be fine. She said the anesthesia might make me nauseous and weepy, and I might have cramps and bleeding. She gave me some orange juice, a cookie, an over-the-counter pain reliever, a "What to Expect" fact sheet with a number to call if I had any problems, and an extra-long sanitary pad. I dressed myself and went home.

I use this story to introduce the abortion rights doctrine and to show how current laws combine to create a very different experience for young women today. As we trek through the doctrine and survey the political discourse around abortion, we note how the parental or judicial consent requirements, waiting periods, and restricted funding for entities providing abortion information restrict access to abortion procedures for the clear majority of women in the United States. We also discuss how clinic violence, public shaming, and intramovement tensions further threaten the participation of doctors, lawyers, and advocates.

In comparing my story to the doctrinal landscape of abortion today, students are quick to point out that I could find a doctor to do the procedure by just looking in the phone book. Today, a woman would have to decipher the coded language that masks anti-choice organizations. Also, the number of doctors willing to advertise in the phone book has decreased dramatically because of violence and harassment. Similarly, many medical schools no longer offer the procedure as a part of their core curriculum. Some schools and residency programs do not offer training in abortion at all.

Another difference my students find striking is the fact that I was able, at sixteen, to decide, arrange, and undergo the procedure with the consultation of people of my choosing, not my parents. Unlike many young women today who cannot obtain an abortion without parental permission or the consent of the court, I could look at my life, look at my body, look at my dreams and goals, and make an informed decision in my own best interest. My students have asked me whether I would have made the same choices if there had been parental notification or judicial consent laws in effect when I was sixteen. There is no way for me to know for sure. I can, however, say with certainty that I would not have been able to arrange and undergo the procedure within a week of finding out I was pregnant. Time was of the essence, and if I had been required to process with my parents or appeal to a court, I would have required a costlier and more complicated procedure.

My experience in the doctor's office was also different from what women today face because the information regarding my options flowed freely. The woman who answered my call told me about abortion as well as other options. When I told her that I knew I wanted an abortion, she told me about the procedure and the cost over the phone. Clinics do not give information so readily over the phone today. Whether it is because of the gag rule or the threat of clinic violence, doctors who perform abortions and their staff are forced to give as little information as possible about their services over the phone.[2] Most clinics with sufficient resources have two phone lines: one for the public and general inquiries, and a private number for their patients after their initial visit.

Today many young women report that they are delayed in having an abortion because of an imposed waiting period. In many states, women must make two appointments: the first for counseling and the second for the actual procedure. As with the parental notification laws, waiting periods can also make the procedure more costly and complicated. This is a frequent experience of women who must travel from another state because there is no abortion provider in their area. The costs mount as these women must factor in missed work or school and hotel and travel expenses, along with the price of the procedure. Often, for a variety of reasons, women must lie to protect their privacy when they miss work or school or when they must leave the state. For these women, the waiting periods further complicate their lives because detection could mean violence, homelessness, or public humiliation.

Waiting periods, limited access to doctors, and increased expenses also combine to make women more vulnerable to clinic violence. Women who must choose clinics rather than private doctors must navigate the anti-choice protestor—sometimes twice. If so, the protesters have two opportunities to condemn the woman and try to show her the "error of her ways." While in no other medical context are patients subjected to this type of treatment, women choosing abortions often remember the violence or harassment they endured as causing increased anxiety before, during, and after their procedures. When students hear my story, someone always asks about the protestors. They are shocked to hear that there were no protestors or escorts. There was only one security guard there to make sure no one parked in the doctors' spaces. Once, a student who is an escort at an abortion clinic added, "Those were the good old days."

As one might expect, there are times when students go further in exploring aspects of my personal story. One such moment occurred when a student asked whether my abortion experience resolved any tension I might feel as a lesbian involved in abortion clinic defense, "because abortion is not really a lesbian issue." Questions regarding aspects of my identity as a black woman and a lesbian often come up with people I work with in the movement. While I had not prepared to discuss this in my lecture, I saw the question as creating the coveted "teachable moment" and embraced it as such. I informed the student that there are so many lesbians who work as frontline abortion clinic defenders that Saturday mornings can easily be mistaken for a mini-lesbian Pride rally. Also, while straight women tend to question lesbians' presence in the reproductive justice movement, I have never heard a woman being escorted into the clinic complain about who is making sure she arrives safely inside. Finally, I explain that lesbians who support and defend reproductive freedom recognize that it is not only straight women who have abortions. Lesbians who engage exclusively in nonreproductive sex, like all women and girls, are vulnerable to rape, molestation, incest, and other forms of sexual violence that may result in conception. Abortion is a lesbian issue because abortion is a women's issue.

The student's question about my abortion story and my lesbian identity also provided an excellent segue into a discussion on abortion clinic violence. Lesbians are particularly vulnerable to clinic violence, yet they make up most escorts for clinics—something anti-choice activists appear to be acutely aware of. Anti-choice terrorists have no difficulty in making the connection between lesbians and reproductive choice. The more fanatic elements of the anti-choice movement have targeted their violence and harassment at lesbians for decades. One of the most public and violent episodes happened in 1996 in Atlanta when two bombs were detonated: one outside an abortion clinic and one inside a lesbian bar. Police investigators discovered that the bombings were carried out by the same person, Eric Rudolph.[3]

I take my students on a post-*Roe* journey via my personal experience. I do not doubt the pedagogical value of this journey. Students not only learn the material better, they also learn how personal experiences can shape and enrich their lives as lawyers. However, I have benefited most from this pedagogical evolution. I no longer leave myself at the classroom door, and this undoubtedly makes me a better teacher. My students were being deprived of a deeper conceptualization of lawyering generally and of this area of law in particular. The fact that I feel more integrated, less evasive, and more present creates an atmosphere of collegiality. Also, students who often criticize their infantilization in law school appreciate me trusting them with my opinions and experiences.

Obviously, there are limits to the type and extent of personal information I share with my students. In this regard, however, sharing personal experiences while also teaching has helped me and my students understand how pervasive the law is. By comparing the ways law shapes our lives with the way we, as lawyers, can shape the law, students learn to see themselves as active participants with valuable opinions, positions, and experiences, and not just objective bystanders. We all learn that speaking one's truth—whether attorneys, clients, students, or teachers—creates the potential for empowerment and understanding.

Notes

1. I do not use his full name because of the threat of targeted harassment and clinic violations. This threat is especially real in Florida, where two doctors have been murdered by abortion clinic terrorists.

2. Gag rules are constitutionally permissible restrictions on the amount and type of information clinics that receive public funds can give to women in need of reproductive services.

3. Eric Robert Rudolph, also known as the Olympic Park Bomber, is an American domestic terrorist convicted for this crime and for a series of antiabortion and antigay bombings across the South between 1996 and 1998, which killed two people and injured over 120 others.

Reproductively Privileged: Critical White Feminism and Reproductive Justice Theory

CAROLINE R. McFADDEN

The 2016 election of President Donald J. Trump energized a new wave of feminist activism in the United States as the fear of rollbacks to reproductive freedom became increasingly concrete and dire. The widely publicized and heavily attended 2017 Women's March in Washington, DC, illuminated this powerful display of dissent. However, the march was sharply criticized for being dominated by white women and its omission of women of color, indicating that despite the explosion of nonwhite feminist theories and critiques of mainstream white liberal feminism, the long-standing problems within feminist organizing across difference continue.

The Women's March is just one of many examples of white women's failure to recognize white supremacy and privilege—including reproductive privilege. Reproductive justice theory (RJT) is a necessary framework for understanding what the Women's March missed. Born out of the intersectional lived experiences of women of color, RJT offers a more comprehensive and powerful vision for the future. RJT is grounded in an understanding of realities that white women simply do not and cannot live. White women are unable to fully understand the multifaceted and intersectional racialized marginalization experienced by women of color because we do not embody it. If RJT is the lens, privilege is the fog.

Because I am a white feminist myself, I am attempting to fully understand the implications of my own whiteness and my own reproductive privilege. White women have reproductive privilege in relationship to women of color, and despite myths to the contrary, privileges are not something to be dismissed or ignored, but used to ensure that everyone enjoys them. For example, as a sexually active cisgender white woman, I am unlikely to be racially profiled when using birth control, nor am I viewed as a racial stereotype if I seek social services or go to a public health facility. Nor do I especially risk deportation or incarceration, or a coerced sterilization. If I have a problem with illicit drugs, it will be viewed as a public health rather than a criminal justice matter.

While these are just a few examples of reproductive privilege, I also recognize that white women are cast in the role of breeders for white supremacy, and I'm likely to be severely criticized if I remain childless by choice, seek a voluntary sterilization, or if I'm a lesbian or a trans man. White children are commodified in the global marketplace, so my presumed fertility may be especially vulnerable to egg harvesting, adoption exploitation, or medical coercion during childbirth. Any gender nonconformity will be criticized and punished by a white supremacist society, yet those oppressions do not erase the unearned advantages of my whiteness. Sexuality, pregnancy, and motherhood are deeply racialized experiences understated by many white feminist activists and theorists. The reproductive privilege of white women depends on the disenfranchisement of others.

Yet, what was once seemingly invisible to women of privilege is made visible by the voices of reproductive justice activists. That production of knowledge—their political and emotional labor—laid down the road that the Women's March attendees and every feminist activist walks upon. Because of this human-rights-based theory, white women can study and learn these realities and interrogate the ways they interlock with our own lives.

White people are racially challenged through contrived ignorance about white supremacy. We don't notice whiteness because we don't have to, except in encounters with the racialized "other." Along with the benefits it affords to those in power, the structural, cultural, and economic impacts of whiteness are intentionally euphemistic and engineered to be disguised. It may seem as though whites are disadvantaged due to racism and white supremacy, psychological dysfunction, and moral distortion; but on the contrary, whites receive immeasurable benefits simply because of our whiteness regardless whether we are aware of it.

Black women used their hearts and minds and bodies and histories to create an RJ theoretical lens that helps us understand reproductive injustices. White women, too, can use our own hearts and minds and bodies and histories to theorize—but carefully. White women can analyze the particular reproductive challenges we face, but we must not generalize our experiences as the norm. We must grapple seriously with the ways that our stories intertwine with women of color, including how we are situated within a global framework. Those interconnections are not always pretty or palatable, but often laden with racism, colonialism, imperialism, and privilege, which is why we must be vigilant in our examination of ourselves and our communities. We must truly care, even when our experiences aren't at the center of a theory or a praxis. Otherwise, our scholarship isn't comprehensive, our activism isn't inclusive, and our feminism is violent.

RJ theory has much to offer white feminism because anyone can use it to examine various social locations. Every human being has identical human rights, but an array of intersectional positionalities determine whether these rights are protected or violated. RJT provides an unparalleled approach to the full achievement of universal reproductive justice for all.

However, I fear the historical trend of white feminists co-opting the work of feminists of color. Our past behavior indicates a pattern of using nonwhite feminist frameworks and language to replicate oppressive behaviors in new ways. For instance, the original Million Woman March in Philadelphia led by black women in 1997 focused on rebuilding and uniting black communities. Twenty years later, white organizers of the Women's March on Washington first chose the title "Million Women March" without researching this history. Initially, they failed to incorporate the same anti-sexist and anti-racist frameworks of the black women's march in 1997.

RJT offers invaluable insight into the fight for social justice that white feminists *must* seek out, listen to, and learn from, but I do not believe that RJT is all white women need because of our particular privileges and social locations. Instead, I suggest we use a similar but different lens to magnify, deconstruct, and dismantle white supremacy. In doing so, we can theorize about reproductive justice from a place that recognizes our racial and imperial privilege, and focuses on the ways white organizations, individuals, and communities are entangled in and buttressed by the racial, social, and economic oppression of women of color. This might better provide a more effective role for white allies and, not so incidentally, save the soul of the feminist movement that is mired in stagnation and innumerable policy losses.

I propose that white allies adopt the lens of critical white feminism (CWF). CWF can be generally defined by its name, that is, feminism that is critical of whiteness, emanating from previous critical race and critical feminist theories developed by people of color. While the term "critical white feminism" is my own, the ideas that I present are neither new nor original. In reality, feminists of color have been making these arguments for decades without recognition from white feminists. CWF is an approach that I believe is necessary for an anti-racist transformation of white feminist theory to expand the scope of feminist thought to critically consider whiteness and its privileges by blending aspects of critical white studies and feminist theory to examine power relationships through an intersectional lens.

Both critical white studies and feminist studies are often limited in their ability to adequately address the complex interconnectivity of racial and gender privilege and oppression. Feminist theorists strive to provide a framework for understanding oppression, imagining liberation, inciting societal change, and achieving social justice. However, most feminist theory written by white middle-class women is unsuccessful in this mission of understanding the oppression of all women and conceptualizing comprehensive solutions. In general, feminist scholarship produced by white feminists largely neglects the impact of white supremacy on reproductive politics and is therefore inadequate, while assuming a white norm that is a false narrative. Two major flaws of mainstream feminist theory are its assumption that whiteness has minimal significance in delineating gender oppression, and the reluctance to critically interrogate whiteness.

White identities allow white feminists to have a sense of ownership, legitimacy, and belonging to the feminist movement. I refer to this problem as "white feminist racism" and argue that white feminists understate the ways in which whiteness and privilege facilitate problematic theorizing that assumes a hubristic universality, while at the same time criticizing cisgender white men for doing the same. While several white feminists do prioritize interrogating whiteness—such as theorists Ruth Frankenberg, Martha Mahoney, Peggy McIntosh, Rickie Solinger, Ann Russo, and Chris Cuomo, and artists Lucy Lippard and Arlene Raven—I argue that more white feminists should follow their lead.

Although the feminist movement loudly rejects instances of overt racism, the movement reflects the dominance of whiteness by normalizing it. That is, whites regard themselves and their experiences as common, standard, and conventional. All things related to whiteness, including culture, experiences, and beliefs are considered by white people to be normal. They believe that their race and its implications need not be investigated because there is nothing about whiteness to investigate.

Unlike white feminist theories, the field of critical white studies provides a foundation for exploring whiteness in a racist society to address conceptions and implications of whiteness. Critical white studies are a result of critical race theory, which was formulated by the contributions of people of color such as Mari Matsuda and Kimberlé Crenshaw. Crenshaw coined the term "intersectionality" to analyze disparities in power, not differences in identity. Critical race theory was developed to convey how the legal system supports inequalities of all kinds.

Critical white scholars define whiteness in a variety of ways and continue to contest its meaning. Whiteness should be understood here as an invisible and influential racial category, with implications for power, dominance, and normativity. It is important to use the term "white supremacy" to signify the system that enforces and maintains the racial hierarchy. Black philosopher Charles W. Mills defines white supremacy in *The Racial Contract* as the system of domination by which white people of Anglo descent have historically ruled over and, in certain important ways, continue to oppress people of color.[1] The system of white supremacy upholds the superiority of whiteness in several ways, including white normativity and invisibility, which facilitate racism. Constructed as universal truths through perspectivism, white norms are imposed on society in general. The standards for all people, then, are determined by whiteness. Whereas whites are regarded in this paradigm, nonwhites are disregarded, and, as we know, disregard is an implicit form of racism. As an implicit process, all of this happens as though whiteness were not involved. So, similar to the invisibility of whiteness, the racialized structure of society goes unrecognized and white supremacy operates covertly, allowing whites to act in racist ways unknowingly and knowingly.

Because the causes and effects of whiteness are rarely explored, the works of critical white theorists are necessary for understanding the hidden mechanisms and dynamics of our racialized society. However, critical white theories often examine racism and whiteness without attention to gender, and are therefore inadequate, as well. As I envision it, CWF has the potential to breathe new life into the movement by encouraging white allies to express the best of their humanity. The purpose of CWF is to conceptualize an inclusive and transformative anti-racist feminist framework and agenda; challenge white feminist racism and white feminist hegemony; encourage open and honest communication between feminists across differences; and facilitate feminist solidarity and mobilization. Specifically, CWF has several objectives: to establish racism as a priority feminist issue; to expose whiteness as an invisible, normalized, hegemonic, and privileged racial identity; to explore the interconnectivity of white supremacy, patriarchy, capitalism, and other systems; to address hierarchical power structures that exist within feminism; and to decenter white women and demarginalize women of color.

A main pillar of CWF is the intentional exploration of the experiences of women of color along with the intensive examination of the white feminist racism that may exist in daily interactions, unconscious perceptions, and theoretical discourse. CWF examines how engagement with other people upholds or interrupts oppression, and if the manner of the interaction becomes oppressive itself.

A mirror is a useful metaphor. Noted anti-racist trainer Shakti Butler says, "People are either mirrors or windows. If you're a mirror, you're saying 'there's only one of us here.'"[2] That is one use of a mirror, only to see oneself when looking at another person, while remaining oblivious to their humanity. Seeing others as a utilitarian way of reflecting only on oneself is objectifying and dehumanizing. This erasure of others does not produce qualitative self-reflection, but instead is a narcissist and unfortunately frequent feature of white supremacy. For example, exaggerated white fears of African Americans walking, jogging, driving, or merely existing in situations that trigger white fragility can lead to deadly consequences for black people. Whites perpetuate racism and maintain the system of white supremacy through ignorance, along with moral and cognitive dysfunctions, which allow white people to think and act in oppressive ways while they believe that they are, in fact, thinking and acting in fair and reasonable ways. Through the veil of white supremacy, whites people's perceptions of others and themselves are not always consistent with reality.

In contrast, María Lugones uses Elizabeth Spelman's phrase "boomerang perception" to illustrate how white women should interactively recognize women's differences and plurality.[3] According to Spelman boomerang perception happens when "I look at you and come right back to myself." Boomerang perception is a self-reflective process that happens when one thinks about oneself after perceiving the difference between oneself and another. This approach can counteract and reverse the problematic tendency of inactively acknowledging women's differences: to consider another without reflecting on ourselves. In this way, white women and women of color are "faithful mirrors" who are able to reveal their true selves to each other.[4] A true self is not an isolated self that engages in self-reflection without cognition of others; instead, a true self interprets itself in relation to others by comparing and contrasting similarities and differences, not as a stimulant for fear and uncertainty, but as an act of human solidarity. Thus, between white and women of color feminists, reciprocal reflection and genuine critical regard for each other provides the opportunity for a clearer image of self, much like faithful mirrors can reveal painful realities.

Therefore, as Lugones argues, many white feminists avoid perceiving women of color as "faithful mirrors" because they wish to "block identification with that self" they see reflected back at them. According to Lugones, this blockage occurs because the reality of the white self enmeshed in white supremacy is inconsistent with the white perception of self as a postracial being. In order to truly understand whiteness and truly understand their own racism, white feminists must actively and reflexively regard all people as situated in a white supremacist construct. Critical white feminist anti-racist transformation, then, requires critical self-interaction and critical interaction with feminist women of color to collaborate to deconstruct white supremacy, much of which is missing thus far in most white feminist theory and action.

Critical white feminism allows white women to perceive how white normativity invisibly shapes their lives, leads them to assume that their experiences as women are universal as opposed to race-specific, and blinds them to the realities of people of color. Furthermore, white feminists can better recognize that whiteness facilitates racist and exclusionary tendencies because CWF provides the foundations for an interrogation of racial privilege. When white feminists subscribe to white normativity and universalize womanhood, they fail to take into account the power differences between women, even when women of color are included in feminist discourse.

RJT inspires us to blast open the hegemonic discourse of reproductive rights and excavate white supremacy's role in reproductive injustices locally and globally to create a transformation of white feminist theory. As an example, integrating RJT and CWF enables a critique of population bomb theories that demonize the fertility of populations in the Global South while underexamining imbalances in global resource distribution. White feminists are part of the chorus of voices seeking to impose fertility-directed population controls on vulnerable women around the world, masking these goals with problematic feminist rhetoric. A CWF/RJT approach would counter these assumptions by interrogating why half of the world's wealth is controlled by 1 percent of the population, creating systematic and intentional underdevelopment, and how Western policies, militaries, and corporations reproduce such inequitable relationships.

In the US, critical white feminist theory demands more from white communities than individual disavowing of racial privilege and overt racism. White women generally do not speak about racism because they do not consider it to be their problem, while women of color are expected to bear the burden of educating white women about white supremacy, but please do so without getting too angry! Without an interrogation of their own racial identities as white women, there will be no substantial change within feminist theory and practice.

It is important, also, for feminists to seriously consider the emotional responses to the realization of critical white feminism. As Audre Lorde reminds us, any discussion among women about racism must include the recognition and use of anger. Feminists must regard the emotions within themselves and each other. According to Lorde, we cannot allow our fear of anger to deflect us nor seduce us into settling for anything less than the hard work of honestly excavating unjust power relationships.[5] Furthermore, white feminists must recognize the fear, denial, guilt, blame, and shame associated with the process of exploring whiteness and privilege.[6] Because emotions are a part of the human condition, it is impossible to separate them from feminist theorizing and organizing. Instead, feminists must be aware of them and prepare for the painful process of responding to their own and others' emotions.

Of course, white supremacy harms marginalized communities, but it also degrades the integrity and dignity of white folks by persuading many white people to act and vote against their own interests. Rather than allowing white nationalists to speak for all white people, critical white feminism requests that white allies speak against injustices on behalf of our communities and in support all of humanity.

For example, rather than dismissing the Confederate flag as synonymous with white heritage and identity, it should be recognized as a gateway drug into the netherworld of fascism, as illustrated by Dylann Roof's 2015 murder of nine black people in Charleston, South Carolina. CWF encourages white feminists to grapple with their own positionality within a problematic web of power by emphasizing human interdependence rather than social hierarchies by promoting principles of human dignity and human rights to become dominant values in the white community.

This includes not only the theoretical ponderings of academics but practical applications for all social justice activists. For feminist activists operating at the legislative level, in education, social work, healthcare, business, or at home, I ask: How does whiteness and white supremacy proliferate in your field? In what ways does your privilege fog your reproductive justice lens?

Critical white feminism might also help with feminist collaboration. White feminist racism thwarts cross-racial feminist relationships and organizing. Successful feminist organizing requires open and honest dialogue across all identities, a conversation that should not be distorted by unacknowledged power dynamics between members. White feminists continuously meet women of color unequally in their attempts to organize and dialogue, by oppressing women of color through disregard, disrespect, and ignorance, and an insistence on invading boundaries. While feminists of color have demanded that an anti-racist feminist agenda is needed for solidarity and community, most white feminists fail to implement anti-racism in theory and practice. An interrogation of whiteness unearths the racialized power structures and hierarchies that white feminists do not readily perceive. It is through this process that white women can resist their authoritative inclinations and dialogue with women of color in an egalitarian discourse that analyzes power structures. CWF is a beneficial approach to understanding and resisting obstructions to feminist solidarity and action.

One common tactic used by anti-racist white women who wish to be allies is to attempt to affect change in communities of color, both at home and abroad, instead of focusing on white communities. This tendency is problematic because members of our privileged communities are more likely to hold positions of power in government and business. I encourage white feminists to ask themselves: How are your families and communities contributing to oppressive structures? Do the men, women, LGBTQ people, and children you love think and act like oppressors, allies, or false allies? How does your community influence those surrounding you? What about you? What leaders are you following? Who are you volunteering with? Who are you donating money to? Where do you live? What schools do your children attend and why? What businesses and financial institutions do you use, and what projects do they fund? Ultimately, all people participate in the social and economic forces that affect reproductive politics. We must ask ourselves if our participation protects our privileges as white women in the US. We must ask ourselves whether we deploy our unearned resources—such as media attention, leadership opportunities, and funding—to support women of color and challenge white supremacy.

In an era when our political leaders make it easy for us to turn on and fight each other for the dwindling resources available to us, it is all the more important that we no longer construct, participate in, or comply with white supremacy. White feminists must take responsibility for ourselves and our mistakes, demolish and rebuild our current conceptualization of reproductive oppression, and use our shared power to move forward toward a world of infinite possibilities achieved through reproductive justice.

Notes

1. Charles W. Mills, *The Racial Contract* (Ithaca, NY: Cornell University Press, 1997), 1–2.

2. *Mirrors of Privilege: Making Whiteness Visible*, directed by Shakti Butler (Oakland, CA: World Trust), streaming online, https://world-trust.org/mirrors-of-privilege-making-whiteness-visible/.

3. María Lugones, "On the Logic of Pluralist Feminism," in *Feminist Ethics*, ed. Claudia Card (Lawrence: University Press of Kansas, 1991), 41.

4. Ibid., 42.

5. Audre Lorde, "The Uses of Anger," in *Sister Outsider: Essay and Speeches* (Berkeley, CA: Crossing Press, 1984), 128.

6. For more on the emotional responses to whiteness, see Allison Brimmer, "Investigating Affective Dimensions of Whiteness in the Cultural Studies Writing Classroom: Toward a Critical, Feminist, Anti-Racist Pedagogy" (PhD diss., University of South Florida, 2005); and Diane Gillespie, Leslie Ashbaugh, and JoAnn DeFiore, "White Women Teaching White Women about White Privilege, Race Cognizance and Social Action: Toward a Pedagogical Pragmatics," *Race Ethnicity and Education* 5, no. 3 (2002): 237–53.

Centering Reproductive Justice: Transitioning from Abortion Rights to Social Justice

BEVERLY YUEN THOMPSON

Introduction

In Miami, young women travel from the Caribbean Islands, Central American countries, and the greater southern-Florida area to access abortion services at A Choice for Women clinic. For some, this is an international journey because abortion is illegal in their home countries. For others, they are lucky enough to live in a country with safe and legal abortions available in urban centers if not in rural ones. On Saturday mornings pro-life protesters surround A Choice for Women. They have a sign that threatens the life of the doctor as he enters the clinic—he responds with a one-finger salute. Other signs condemn the patients, and the targeted women scrunch down in their seats. One sign in particular reads, "This is a site of genocide." Teenagers from the local Catholic high school stand on the grass, holding a banner decorated with a bloodied fetus between them. The pro-lifers have been standing outside of this clinic for three years now, counterprotested by Miami Clinic Access Project (MCAP), a network of pro-choice activists. However, each week they are outnumbered, although most clinics in Miami are free of protesters.

Nationally, abortion remains legal but heavily restricted. The procedure is rarely taught in OB/GYN residency programs. Most providers are facing retirement and fewer than 15,800 doctors do 1.3 million abortions. While pro-choicers have the backing of the law—as pro-lifers once did—the government presents a "negative liberty" argument for abortion rights (free from legal restrictions) rather than a positive liberty argument (making abortion accessible for all). Because of this entrenched framework of legality and "choice," the feminist movement has emphasized electing pro-choice candidates and participating in electoral politics as its primary strategy. This legalistic and grassroots framework has designated the legal right to abortion the central issue for a reproductive rights agenda.

This emphasis on choice implies that as long as abortion remains legal, it can be chosen by any woman. While this may be true for women with resources, for others with limited resources, many barriers precede abortion, including financial, geographical, social, or religious obstacles. Because abortion is not covered by Medicaid, it is difficult for poor women dependent on the government to afford. With nine out of ten abortion providers located in urban areas, rural women may spend hours driving to the closest clinic. If a mandatory-waiting-period law exists in the state, the patient will have to take additional time off of work and purchase a hotel room in addition to the expenses of the procedure. With such barriers to abortion access, many women may have little choice over their reproductive options. This narrow focus on choice has consistently overlooked the reality of access barriers that many women face: poverty, lack of education, lack of healthcare, racial discrimination, parental consent, imprisonment, immigration status, military enlistment, or welfare restrictions.

For over two decades, women of color have organized around a broad-based political platform addressing the intersections of their oppression. Out of these women of color organizing efforts, SisterSong emerged to address issues of reproductive justice. This framework is based upon three human rights: to be able to have a child, to be able to not have a child, and to parent the children one has. The reproductive justice framework emphasizes a different history than that of legal abortion restrictions; rather, it examines deep-rooted historical systems of oppression that provide insight into today's continuing social injustices. This history is one of slavery, war, colonialism, and genocide—products of an overwhelming apparatus of organized state violence. This history is international in scope; it is a story of migration, corporate globalization, and solidarities of people across borders.

In this paper, the abortion rights and reproductive justice frameworks will be examined, seeking out common interests and intersecting issues. The history of reproduction for women of color will be reviewed briefly to contextualize the contemporary social issues surrounding their reproductive experiences. Out of these histories, women of color began organizing around their particular issues that were overlooked by a predominantly white, middle-class, pro-choice movement, as well as other race-focused activist organizations, which did not mention sex and gender. Women of color conducted health disparities studies within their own communities when they realized that their experiences were rarely researched by professionals. With their findings, they were able to create a social justice agenda that addressed their communities' issues. While the pro-choice and women of color organizations often worked on separate but parallel issues, they occasionally came together with successful stories of collaboration.

Legality and Grassroots Activism: The Framework of Abortion Rights Discourse

Abortion existed long before the rise of the medical industry in a realm of midwives and healers knowledgeable about abortifacients and naturopathic cures. With the creation of the American Medical Association in the mid-1880s, male doctors sought legitimization for their profession, and therefore worked to delegitimize and criminalize female midwives and healers. Under the banner of public health (and morality), abortion was soon relegated to the realm of institutionalized medicine and soon after, criminalized completely. Connecticut was the first state to pass legislation on abortion in 1821. Other states followed suit, and within decades, abortion was outlawed nationwide. By 1873 Congress passed "the Comstock Law," making it a crime to mail obscene publications including information on birth control and abortion, against which Margaret Sanger fought so vigorously.

It wasn't until 1960 that the FDA approved "the pill," thus beginning the repression against reproductive control. However, it was not until 1965, with *Griswold v. Connecticut*, that married couples were legally able to access contraception. Only later did this right extend to single individuals. "Therapeutic abortions" were only available in hospitals for cases of rape, incest, and to save the mother's life. Additionally, these therapeutic abortions were primarily performed on middle-class white women who could afford the procedure. They were rarely ever offered to women of color and low-income women. In order to obtain the procedure women would plead their cases before a panel of doctors, and many presented suicidal narratives in order to meet stringent requirements for the procedure.

It was not until the late 1960s that "fourteen states liberalized their laws to permit access to therapeutic abortions in cases of fetal deformity, rape, incest, or more broadly defined threats to a woman's mental health than suicide."[1] New York legalized abortion in 1970, "making its policy the most liberal in the country."[2]

Roe v. Wade legalized abortion nationally in 1973, and with this great victory, the abortion rights movement that had been advocating for legality largely dismantled. The legal framework of *Roe* was rooted in privacy rights, the creation of the trimester concept, and recognizing fetal viability in the third trimester—all of which provide openings for subsequent legal attacks. Additionally, while Roe made abortion legal, it did not guarantee accessibility. Within months of *Roe,* "hundreds of bills to restrict abortion, most written in consultation with church leadership, were introduced into municipal councils and state legislatures across the country."[3] Pro-life forces construed a multifaceted assault on the newly protected right, blindsiding the weakened pro-choice movement. The Hyde Amendment passed in 1976—restricting government funds from abortion provisions—disproportionately affecting poor women and women of color.

Approximately fourteen states continued to pay for abortion voluntarily. Previously, the government paid for nearly one-third of all abortions between 1973 and 1977 (294,600), but that number dropped to fewer than 2,500 after the Hyde Amendment. Stephanie Poggi reminds us of Justice Thurgood Marshall's dissenting words, "For women eligible for Medicaid—poor women—denial of a Medicaid-funded abortion is equivalent to denial of legal abortion altogether. By definition, these women do not have the money to pay for an abortion themselves."[4]

In 1984 President Ronald Reagan cut off funding for the International Planned Parenthood Federation and the United Nations Fund for Population Activities. By 1989 another substantial blow was struck with the Supreme Court case *Webster v. Reproductive Health Services,* imposing restrictions on the use of public facilities for abortion. By 1990 restrictive abortion bills were pending in state legislatures across the nation.

The religious Right had the abortion rights movement on the defensive. They pushed forward an entire platform of religiously tainted laws that enforced "traditional" gender roles. Restrictions on abortion was part of their legal assault that also included mandatory antiabortion counseling, twenty-four-hour waiting periods, parental notification, and reduced medical training for doctors. In the forty-three years since *Roe,* states have enacted 1,074 abortion restrictions as of 2016. Of these, 288, or 27 percent, were passed between 2010 and 2016. Even amidst all these restrictions, the national pro-choice organizations have been reluctant to counter pro-life activity. Rather, their efforts continue to revolve largely around lobbying and electoral politics. The religious Right has also fought against the Equal Rights Amendment, gay marriage, and programs supporting women and children.

Another of their achievements includes abstinence-only education, which outlaws any information on contraception and abortion. "Nearly $1 billion in federal and state matching funds has been spent since 1996 on programs that promote chastity until marriage."[5] Empirical studies have found no basis for the effectiveness of abstinence-only programs, yet "the Bush administration requested $206 million in funding for abstinence-until-marriage programs just for 2006, more than double what was spent in fiscal year 2002."[6] During Bush's term as governor of Texas in 2000, "Texas ranked dead last in the nation, fiftieth out of fifty, in the decline of teen birth rates among fifteen-to-seventeen-year-old females."[7] The United States is the only industrialized nation that ranks among developing countries for teen births, just behind Thailand and directly before Rwanda. Teen birth rates are highly malleable through policy. For example, the Netherlands has reduced its teenage birth rate by a staggering 72 percent in thirty years while also having the lowest teenage abortion rate in the industrialized world.

Grassroots Frameworks

Pro-Life Grassroots

Pro-life proponents not only made overwhelming strides in legislation; they were also active in the streets. The pro-life movement was born directly following *Roe v. Wade*. Before *Roe v. Wade*, the pro-choice movement had largely been an underground abortion referral movement, and legalization rendered that unnecessary. For the pro-life movement, "the Church provided an infrastructure, communications network, material backing, ideology, and people—in short, the resources and organizational facility that helped mobilize the movement in its early stages into a national presence."[8] Several organizations existed before 1973: "Pro-lifers for Survival, an anti-nuclear pacifist group, was founded in 1971 and Feminists for Life organized soon after."[9] Pro-life picketing at clinics began as soon as they opened in 1973. Between 1977 and 1979, clinic violence erupted as eight abortion clinics (seven in the Midwest) were hit with fires. Joseph Scheidler had publicly emerged by 1980, launching Pro-Life Action League in Chicago. He would later author *Closed: 99 Ways to Stop Abortion*, a manifesto for clinic protests, blockades, and the violent fringe.

In the 1980s, violence at clinics escalated. The pro-life movement was flourishing in the grassroots, among churches and extended social networks. The movement was emboldened and energized from their success in increasing abortion restrictions. They continued their offensive momentum by establishing new strategies, including the co-optation of direct action tactics and civil rights language from the Left. One campaign launched in 1983 revolved around the movie "*The Silent Scream*, a film that depicted the abortion of a twelve-week fetus in wrenching detail."[10] This movie became the galvanizing force for recruiting foot soldiers.

On March 14, 1985, Pensacola, Florida, was flooded with activists who marched from Pensacola Junior College to the Ladies Center, making it one of the largest demonstrations in antiabortion history. Operation Rescue (OR) conducted a mass siege during the Democratic National Convention in Atlanta, capitalizing on the media saturation. Randall Terry also coordinated nationwide days of action in 1988. On the first day of OR's coordinated Day of Rescue, there were some "2,644 arrests in thirty-two cities across the United States."[11] After the arrests, they practiced jail solidarity, calling themselves Baby John and Baby Jane Doe to withhold their real names. They flooded the jails and refused to post bail. Some hardcore followers devoted their lives completely to this tactic, traveling around to different protest events. Offshoot organizations developed, including the Lambs of Christ, Christians in Action, Army of God, Defensive Action, Pro-Life Direct Action League, Missionaries to the Pre-Born, Advocates for Life Ministries, and Officers for Life. "According to Operation Rescue's figures, by 1990 over 35,000 people had been jailed and 16,000 risked arrest in 'rescues.'"[12] By the end of the decade, Operation Rescue was in retreat from numerous pro-choice lawsuits, government fines, and federal RICO charges.

By 1990 the pro-life mass movement had subsided, but the violent fringe increased their activities. On March 10, 1993, forty-seven-year-old physician David Gunn was shot in the back with a .38 caliber revolver during an antiabortion demonstration outside the clinic where he practiced in Pensacola.[13] Dr. Gunn was the first abortion provider to be killed. The violent vigilante wing of the pro-life movement believes that murdering abortion providers is the best way to stop abortion. Author Cristina Page presented these numbers in 2006:

> Over the past twenty-five years there have been no fewer than 140,000 incidents of violence and disruption under the banner of the pro-life cause, including 7 murders, 17 attempted murders, 41 bombings, 172 arsons, 373 invasions, 3 kidnappings, 1,141 vandalisms, 100 butric-acid attacks, 655 anthrax threats, 139 assaults, 365 death threats, 474 stalkings, 605 bomb threats, and 10,666 hate mails and harassing calls.[14]

According to researchers, by the end of 1985, 92 percent of abortion clinics reported harassment, ranging from picketing of clinics to vandalism, an increase of approximately 60 percent from 1984.[15] Other tactics included "sidewalk counseling," "crisis pregnancy centers," and "pharmacist refusals." Sidewalk counselors target women "at risk for abortion" and attempt to intervene at the last second in front of the clinic. The same people targeted women through crisis pregnancy centers (CPC), a more institutionalized form of sidewalk counseling. CPC's routinely offer free pregnancy tests and use that time to promote a pro-life message through their films, literature, and/or verbal harassment. Since the 1990s, Pharmacists for Life have organized pharmacists to refuse to dispense emergency contraceptives (EC), and sometimes even the pill, based upon their religious opposition.[16] Such refusals have been reported in nineteen states, but the extent of the problem is unknown.

Pro-Choice Grassroots

The pro-choice grassroots movement gained a great deal of momentum leading up to the historic *Roe v. Wade* decision. Organizations began to appear as early 1961. Patricia Maginnis, a medical technologist who had herself undergone an illegal abortion, founded the California-based Society for Humane Abortion. Within a year of its development, the National Organization for Women (NOW) endorsed repealing abortion bans. By 1969 the National Association to Repeal Abortion Laws (NARAL) was established at the First National Conference on Abortion Laws, held in Chicago in February 1969. The Boston Women's Health Collective educated women about their biology, contraceptives, and abortion starting in 1969. Feminist groups began abortion referral services. In Chicago, when the Abortion Counseling Service of Women's Liberation, a network often simply called "Jane," found out that one of their referral doctors was not a doctor at all, they decided that they could learn to perform abortions. This would stop their reliance on men, as well as reduce the price for their female clients. "Jane identified the basic problem for women as a lack of control" over their own bodies and reproductive destines.[17]

With the passage of *Roe v. Wade*, many feminist organizations continued with other campaigns; few organizations remained to maintain abortion rights and monitor the legislative process. The ones that did remain included the ACLU Reproductive Freedom Project (formed in 1974), the Reproductive Rights National Network (R2N2) (dissolved in 1984), and the Religious Coalition for Abortion Rights (RCAR) (formed in 1973). In 1993 the National Network of Abortion Funds was created to help fund abortions for impoverished women.

These organizations were ill-prepared to counter the tactics of the pro-life movement. NARAL responded to *The Silent Scream* with a "Silent No More" campaign. In 1988 this forum allowed women to share stories of abortion, both illegal and legal. Implicit in these stories was the underlying theme that abortion had been a positive, if not perhaps difficult, choice. However, this campaign was nearly eclipsed with the pro-life movement's own version of a "Silent No More" campaign promoting women's stories of abortion tragedy. "Defending the basic right to choose on so many fronts—in Congress, state legislatures, and the courts as well as on clinic sidewalks—left little time."[18] With the rise of Operation Rescue and other militant organizations, feminists organized clinic defenses and counterprotests in front of women's clinics—the final frontier of access. As escorts, pro-choicers would physically shield the patients from the pro-life demonstrators as they walked to the entrance. Again, the pro-choice movement was forced into a defensive posture, counteracting with lawsuits and injunctions against protesters, security guards, and security equipment.

Reproductive Justice: Toward a Holistic Vision of Women's Health and Rights

After examining the legal cases surrounding abortion rights, Ruth Colker remarked, "The abortion debate has not represented a reproductive health perspective. In the cases and literature, it often sounds as though women find themselves pregnant without ever engaging in sexual behavior or using contraceptives."[19] By placing women within their sociohistorical context of reproductive decision-making, women were confronted with striking differences along racial lines. White, middle-class women were pressured to have children and historically were unable to limit their fertility, and this became a central demand for feminism. However, women of color were discouraged from reproducing, and often lacked control over their reproductive conditions. For women of color, an emphasis on the right to abortion did not specifically address their needs; rather, they wanted to address "adequate prenatal care and freedom from forced sterilization."[20] "The terrain of reproductive and sexual rights [can be examined] in terms of power and resources: power to make informed decisions about one's own fertility, childbearing, child rearing, gynecologic health, and sexual activity; and resources to carry out such decisions safely and effectively."[21] Sonia Correa and Rosalind Petchesky define the ethical principles underlying this reproductive justice framework as: "bodily integrity, personhood, equality, and diversity."[22]

The Reproductive History of Women of Color

In her monumental historical narrative *Killing the Black Body*, Dorothy Roberts implores us:

> Considering this history—from slave masters' economic stake in bonded women's fertility to the racist strains of early birth control policy to sterilization abuse of Black women during the 1960s and 1970s to the current campaign to inject Norplant and Depo-Provera in the arms of Black teenagers and welfare mothers—paints a powerful picture of the link between race and reproductive freedom in America.[23]

Under slavery, black women's bodies were the property of white men, and they faced rape, abuse, forced marriages, forced births, an inability to properly raise their children, and of course, the rights to her children were not her own. While lynching kept black men away from white women, white men owned both their white wives and their black slaves. The crime of rape did not apply to white men (unless he violated another white man's property).

For Native American women, the US government waged a genocidal war against their people—seizing the land, destroying the culture, breaking familial ties with boarding schools, and sterilizing up to one-fourth of all the women. While Chinese men were used as labor for the railroads and in the South, their legal status remained insecure. By 1882 the Chinese Exclusion Act was passed, no further laborers could immigrate, and wives in China were barred from joining their husbands. Chinese men could not marry white women because of discrimination and antimiscegenation laws, and therefore, they either married black women or remained bachelors in male-dominated Chinatown areas. In 1850 California passed an antimiscegenation statute "that forbade unions between whites and 'negroes and mulattoes,' adding 'Mongolians' to the list in 1880."[24] No restrictions were placed on people of color marrying each other because by definition, they were already "racially impure."

Eugenics-based laws became popular: limiting immigration, interracial marriage, and promoting targeted sterilization. In 1909 involuntary sterilization for eugenics purposes passed in California, making it the third state with such practices, following Indiana and Washington. Interestingly, New Jersey and Iowa declared sterilization laws unconstitutional as well as cruel and unusual punishment.[25]

Additionally, "people considered genetically defective, including epileptics, imbeciles, paupers, drunkards, criminals, and the feebleminded" were banned from getting married in twenty-four states by 1913.[26] The Supreme Court upheld the use of involuntary sterilization based upon eugenics reasoning in the 1927 decision *Buck v. Bell*. With this judicial approval, more states enacted laws for compulsory sterilization, bringing the total number to thirty.

The United States became the first nation in the world to permit mass sterilization as part of an effort to "purify the race." By the mid-1930s, nearly twenty thousand Americans had been sterilized against their will.[27] And by 1940, thirty states banned interracial marriage. Involuntary sterilization peaked during the years of WWII; and after its association with Nazi Germany, the practice was stigmatized. An estimated sixty to seventy thousand women were sterilized, with twenty thousand of those taking place in California. Puerto Rican women faced involuntary sterilization by the United States government, extending to one-third of all reproductive-age women, the highest rate in the world by 1968.[28]

Puerto Rican women also faced high-risk testing of birth control products, including the pill in the 1950s, by several "American contraceptive researchers, including Dr. Gregory Pincus, Hale H. Cook, Dr. Clarence J. Gamble, and Adaline P. Satterthwaite, under the aegis of Margaret Sanger's Planned Parenthood Federation of America. . . . As of November 1958, 850 Puerto Rican women had participated in the birth control trials in San Juan, Humacao, Puerto Rico and also Port-Au-Prince, Haiti."[29] By the 1970s, well over 25 percent of Native American women had been sterilized, and a study conducted by Princeton found that "20 percent of all married African-American women had been sterilized by 1970."[30] Depo-Provera and Norplant were tested on some fourteen thousand low-income women in the United States without their consent, including African American and Native American women. Therefore, poor women of color often faced the dangerous task of testing contraceptive products in order to make them safer for more privileged women.

By the 1960s, some things were changing. The United States moved from a more discriminatory immigration policy based upon quotas to "the family reunification model until the Hart-Celler Act of 1965."[31] The Supreme Court case *Loving v. Virginia* ruled that antimiscegenation laws were unconstitutional in 1967. It was not until 1979 that California did finally rescind its law allowing involuntary sterilizations.

Women of Color Organize

The Committee for Abortion Rights and Against Sterilization Abuse (CARASA) provides us with the best example of a wide-ranging forerunner to current reproductive justice organizations that centered both abortion rights and sterilization abuse, in addition to a comprehensive platform on reproductive issues. CARASA was formed in 1976 and struggled to unite across racial, class, and sexual divisions by supporting an "inclusive feminism." Jennifer Nelson states that

> CARASA activists believed that by ending federal support for abortion, and by continuing funding for sterilization, the U.S. Government promoted permanent methods of population control for poor women and women of color, while making nonpermanent methods of fertility such as abortion less available.[32]

With a small core of dedicated women, they were able to take on several campaigns: CARASA cofounded R2N2, an umbrella organization for national and grassroots groups that situated abortion rights within a broader social justice and anti-racist context. Workplace safety, "particularly around the mandatory sterilization of working women of reproductive age exposed to hazardous materials on the job," became another strong campaign. Battery maker Johnson Controls was sued for requiring women to show proof of sterilization for employment.[33] CARASA also developed a Child-Care Committee because they "understood that poor women, working class women, and women of color all needed child-care as much as they needed access to abortion."[34] Comprised of a small group of women, CARASA struggled under overextended campaigns, differential prioritization, and continued divisions along race, class, and sexual identity lines. The group disbanded after several years of vigorous activism.

In 1968 "Cha Cha Jimenez, a young Puerto Rican activist, and a group of Puerto Ricans allied in the Young Patriots Organization, a politicized street gang, founded the Young Lords Organization (YLO) in Chicago. The YLO drafted a 13-point platform at the founding that echoed the Black Panther Party's 10-point platform."[35] The organization had a core group of Puerto Rican feminists who ensured that women's rights were included, unusual for a nationalist organization. The YLO principles were a precursor to the reproductive justice tenets created decades later, and YLO protested the high rates of sterilizations of women in New York City by organizing working class and low-income Puerto Ricans in the South Bronx, Harlem, and on the Lower East Side.

Since then, there have been numerous organizations working on reproductive health issues for Latinas, particularly against sterilization abuse. In 1979 the Hispanic Health Council of Hartford, Connecticut, conducted a random sample of 153 Puerto Rican households and discovered a sterilization rate of 50 percent, the highest rate in the world.[36] This research produced a project called Mujeres en Acción por Salud Reproductiva: Northeastern Project on Women and Reproductive Health.[37]

Many other Latina health organizations have sprouted, including the Latina Roundtable on Health and Reproductive Rights, founded in October 1989; the National Latina Institute for Reproductive Health, founded in 1994; the National Latina Health Organization; and finally, Colorado Organization for Latina Opportunity and Reproductive Rights, founded in 1998 by seven committed sexual and reproductive health practitioners and activists troubled by the high teenage birth rate and high HIV rate among Latinas.

In 1983 more than fifteen hundred African American women gathered at Spelman College in Atlanta for the first National Conference on Black Women's Health Issues. Emerging from this conference was the National Black Women's Health Project (NBWHP), the first-ever women of color reproductive justice organization and the foremother of other organizations. Byllye Avery, the founder of NBWHP, articulated a vision "beyond the reproductive health emphasis prevalent in the larger movement to include work on chronic disease, pioneering innovative health prevention programs, and other self-help and educational activities."[38]

Another organization, African American Women Evolving (AAWE; later renamed Black Women for Reproductive Justice), was established in Chicago in 1996. The women that founded the organization had previously been involved with the Chicago Abortion Fund, which had provided thousands of low-income women in Illinois and surrounding states with the information, referrals, and direct financial assistance they needed to have safe, affordable abortions since 1985. AAWE set out to address health concerns in their particular community by conducting research and providing health education and preventative care. The group's first public event was a conference entitled Black Women: Loving the Mind, Body, and Spirit. In 2000 AAWE spent a year administering a reproductive health survey to three hundred African American women in Illinois in order to discover the dominant health concerns of the community. Furthermore, they conducted a survey of pharmacies in the Chicago area to assess the availability of EC and to raise awareness within the black community.

In 1997 the SisterSong Women of Color Reproductive Health Collective was organized to bring together the voices of women of color working on reproductive health and rights issues, and propelled a movement using reproductive justice as its central organizing framework—and changed history.

Charon Asetoyer founded the organization Native American Women's Health Education Resource Center (NAWHERC) in 1988, due to the high rate of fetal alcohol syndrome (FAS) among babies on the Yankton Sioux reservation and among children born to Native American women in general. The first women's health organization located on a reservation in the United States, FAS was the first issue that NAWHERC tackled. The organization conducted its own studies of FAS from 1986 to the present, in addition to studying the impact of Norplant and Depo-Provera in the Native American community. In 1990 NAWHERC was able to present its material in a public forum, a conference entitled Empowerment through Dialogue. A historic three-day gathering, the conference brought more than thirty Native women, representing over ten nations from the Northern Plains to Pierre, South Dakota.

Asian/Pacific Islanders (API) have most recently entered the arena of reproductive justice. The first organization, Asians and Pacific Islanders for Reproductive Choice, opened in 1989. It was later named Asians and Pacific Islanders for Reproductive Health (APIRH), then Asian Communities for Reproductive Justice, and is now Forward Together. Like the other organizations, APIRH conducted its own community health research, with approximately twenty volunteer female researchers that interviewed 1,215 adults in Los Angeles, Sacramento, and San Francisco.[39] In Sacramento, APIRH was able to hold a conference entitled Opening Doors to Health and Well-Being in 1995, attended by over 150 API women. Spanning the years 1999 to 2003, APIRH took a leading role in an environmental justice campaign focused on the largest medical waste incinerator located in Oakland. Another powerful organization was founded in 1993 by a twenty-six-year-old Korean immigrant named Mary Chung, the National Asian Women's Health Organization (NAWHO). The organization heavily emphasized community health research and has presented several conferences, including the 1995 Coming Together, Moving Strong: Mobilizing an Asian Women's Health Movement and two in 1997, the Quality of Our Lives: Empowering Asian American Women for the Twenty-First Century and Silent Epidemics: A National Policy Summit on Depression and Asian American Women. NAWHO has published over twenty research reports that they make available to the community. The most recent API organization is the National Asian Pacific American Women's Forum, founded in 1996, which leads a campaign to challenge restrictions on abortion based on the allegation that API in the United States are pressured to have abortions based on the gender of the fetus.

Social Inequalities and Reproductive Justice Issues

When women of color began organizing around reproductive justice in their own communities, and researching issues particular to them, they could not limit their efforts to an abortion-rights framework. While women of color did suffer disproportionately when abortion was illegal, when legal, there continued to be numerous obstacles that effectively made choice very difficult to obtain. Furthermore, the right to abortion wasn't the overall concern for many; other issues were equally significant: ending sterilization abuse, the right to raise healthy children with adequate resources, and the right to parent their own children. Therefore, issues of healthcare access and freedom from poverty were central concerns. For poor women who rely on government subsidies, it is imperative that the government offer a balanced array of options so that women can exercise a real choice.

Women living within the confines of state control are the most vulnerable to suffering restrictions on reproductive healthcare and abortion. For example, in 1960 in New Orleans, local officials "criminalize[ed] the second pregnancies of women on public assistance; after they were threatened with imprisonment and welfare fraud, many of these African American women and children disappeared from the welfare rolls."[40] Sterilization and long-term contraceptives such as Norplant and Depo-Provera are still provided and encouraged by the state, thus promoting such permanent solutions for low-income women.

States violate the privacy of pregnant women by secretly searching them for evidence of drug use and turning that information over to the police. In 1989 Charleston, South Carolina, initiated a policy of arresting pregnant women whose prenatal tests indicated drug usage. If these same women had had abortions, they would have escaped punishment, in effect criminalizing their choice to give birth. Courts ruled that this practice did not violate the Fourth Amendment's prohibition on unreasonable searches because the search qualified as as fetal protection, upheld in 2001 by *Ferguson v. City of Charleston*. While states may use fetal protection arguments, most do not provide drug rehabilitation programs or sufficient prenatal care. Additionally, long-term contraceptives have been used as court-ordered punishment for charges of child abuse and neglect. A court demanded Norplant implantation for a woman convicted of child abuse shortly after it was approved by the FDA in 1990.

Other women have been imprisoned until childbirth to allegedly prevent drug abuse during pregnancy where prenatal care is usually substandard, miscarriages are not considered emergencies, and women are commonly shackled during labor and childbirth. The vast majority of the more than two-hundred thousand women incarcerated are mothers. Maintaining relationships with their chidren becomes far more challenging with limited visiting hours, the high cost of collect phone calls, and distance.

Incarcerated women have difficulties reuniting with and caring for their children once released. They are ineligible for public housing, food stamps, public assistance, student loans, or many jobs because of their felony convictions. Many have lost custody of their children in a system that also promotes familial separation over family unification. According to Dorothy Roberts, foster care policies reflect race, class, and gender hierarchies. While children of color comprise only about 30 percent of the general population, they are about 60 percent of children in foster care.[41]

For Latina and Asian American women, immigrant stereotypes affect access to healthcare. Xenophobia is used to pass legislation limiting the access of immigrants to the healthcare system, thus intimidating immigrants who may be eligible. Xenophobes falsely accuse women of birthing "anchor babies" simply to enable a familial migration. The pregnant immigrant woman becomes another policed, suspect category linking racial and reproductive oppression. Immigration laws also interfere with women's ability to parent their children as families are often separated. Many women of color, particularly API women, face numerous barriers to healthcare including lack of health insurance, weak enforcement of regulations mandating interpretation and translation services, and health professionals who are untrained to serve diverse communities. Culturally competent medical providers are important for Latina and API women, who may face various cultural obstacles in obtaining the reproductive healthcare necessary for cancer prevention and often experience disproportionate rates of cervical cancer because of barriers for regular preventative Pap tests.

Global Women

A reproductive justice philosophy recognizes that we live in a global community where women are disproportionately affected by poverty, childrearing responsibilities, and serious health hazards related to reproduction. US women of color have connected with other women at international forums for human and women's rights. While corporate processes of globalization are disproportionately empowered, globalization also provides opportunities for social justice resistance and alliance building. The global reproductive justice movement holds the potential to facilitate these connections.

While population explosion theorists demonize poor women's reproduction, they underexamine the imbalances in global resource distribution. "The reality is that 20% of the world's population controls 80% of the global wealth. In other words, it is not the population growth of the developing world that is depleting the world's resources, but the overconsumption of these resources by the richest countries of the world.[42] Globally, women in so-called "developing nations" face many obstacles: lower rates of primary and secondary education, early marriage and childbirth, lack of control over their own bodies and reproductive options, education on contraception and HIV/AIDS, lack of prenatal care and healthcare, home births without emergency care, lack of employment options, depleted nutrition, environmental pollutants, and lack of access to clean water.

Globally, pregnancy can be the most dangerous condition women face. Over three hundred million women in the developing world suffer from short- or long-term illness brought about by pregnancy and childbirth; 529,000 die each year, making it the leading cause of death, disease, and disability among reproductive-age women.The disparities between industrialized and developing countries are enormous. Maternal mortality is highest in Africa, where the lifetime risk of maternal death is one in sixteen, compared with one in twenty-eight hundred in industrialized countries. Of all maternal deaths, less than 1 percent occur in high-income countries, and of all child deaths, over 50 percent occur in only six countries: China, the Democratic Republic of the Congo, Ethiopia, India, Nigeria, and Pakistan.[43] Because these issues of maternal and infant mortality can be solved through funding healthcare infrastructures, these issues must be centrally placed on a global agenda. However, the exact opposite is implemented. Women's access to reproductive and healthcare options are political, biased, and limited. Developing countries receiving IMF/World Bank funding are forced to privatize healthcare infrastructure as a condition of their loan, negatively impacting the most impoverished.

Many countries have liberalized their abortion laws so that the procedure is permitted; yet the most impoverished women still suffer from outlawed abortion, the "global gag rule," and lack of healthcare, especially prenatal care. While the dividing line between legal and illegal abortions has serious health implications, there also exists a wide disparity in deaths from illegal abortion. While both Latin America and the Caribbean and Africa have similar percentages of illegal abortion, 94 and 98 percent respectively, the number of deaths from unsafe abortions is strikingly different: two thousand in Latin America and the Caribbean and thirty-six thousand in Africa. In Asia, there is a 38 percent rate of unsafe abortions, and 28,400 deaths annually.

In developed nations it is a different picture altogether. North America has an unsafe abortion rate of 0.05 percent, or less than one death, while Europe has a 9 percent unsafe abortion rate with less than sixty deaths annually. Abortion is further restricted by the "global gag rule," which has been reinstated by every Republican president since Reagan. Officially titled the Mexico City Policy, and initiated in 1984, it mandates that no US family planning assistance can be provided to foreign NGOs that use funding from any other source to perform abortions in cases other than a threat to the woman's life, rape, or incest; provide counseling and referral for abortion; or lobby to make abortion legal or more available in their country.[44]

Indeed, the pro-life movement has pushed for a global agenda: several organizations have been granted consultative status at the United Nations including NGOs such as Concerned Women for America, Focus on the Family, and the Right to Life Committee. Wreaking further havoc, the Abstinence Clearinghouse website boasts of 350 affiliates operating to discourage condom use in African countries with the world's highest rates of HIV.

US women of color learned to frame women's rights within a human rights framework from the global women's health movement. By utilizing this framework, women can make connections across national boundaries, and create a stronger foundation for rights, beyond a privacy discourse. There are many examples of incorporating women within human rights work and extending demands to include reproductive health and gender equality. At the 1994 International Conference on Population and Development Programme of Action, access to accurate health information, including comprehensive sex education, was defined as a basic human right. Women asserting rights over their bodies and reproduction should be incorporated within international declarations as well as the United States legal system.

Conclusion: Building Agendas and Alliances

The radical Right has been instrumental in presenting a comprehensive political platform that connects discourses of family values, gender roles, marriage, abortion, and school prayer; yet the pro-choice movement has been afraid to develop such multi-issue alliances for fear they would weaken the singular focus on abortion. However, backpedaling and compromising has not contributed to a strengthened pro-choice movement or the security of abortion rights. The reproductive justice framework uses human rights to remind us to equally emphasize the right to have a child; the right to *not* have a child; and the right to parent one's own children. In January 2017, Democratic Congresswomen Barbara Lee of California and Jan Schakowsky of Illinois, alongside Pro-Choice Caucus cochairs Diana DeGette of Colorado and Louise Slaughter from New York and one hundred other members of Congress, reintroduced the EACH Woman Act with the support of eighty-two women's health, rights, and justice advocacy organizations. This bill ensures coverage for abortion for every woman, regardless of the amount she earns or how she is insured.

It is time for the women's movement to seriously defend the human rights of *all* women and to center their analysis on women of color, in particular. By defending the human rights of those in the most vulnerable position, the movement will ensure the widest possible social benefit, rather than emphasizing the needs of those with the most resources.

Notes

1. Sharon Gold-Steinberg and Abigail J. Stewart, "Psychologies of Abortion: Implications of a Changing Context," in *Abortion Wars: A Half Century of Struggle, 1950–2000*, ed. Rickie Solinger (Berkeley: University of California Press, 1998), 357.

2. Patricia Baird-Windle and Eleanor J. Bader, *Targets of Hatred: Anti-Abortion Terrorism* (New York: Palgrave, 2001), 35.

3. Ibid., 40

4. Stephanie Poggi, "The Hyde Amendment Violates Reproductive Justice and Discriminate against Poor Women and Women of Color, in *Reproductive Justice Briefing Book: A Primer on Reproductive Justice and Social Change*, ed. Rickie Solinger and Loretta J. Ross, Pro-Choice Education Project/SisterSong Women of Color Reproductive Health Collective, last updated 2007, http://protectchoice.org/downloads/Reproductive%20Justice%20Briefing%20Book.pdf.

5. Christina Page, *How the Pro-Choice Movement Saved America: Freedom, Politics, and the War on Sex* (New York: Basic Books, 2006), 65.

6. Ibid., 73.

7. Ibid., 70.

8. Faye Ginsburg, *Contested Lives: The Abortion Debate in an American Community* (Berkeley: University of California Press, 1989), 43.

9. Ibid., 45.

10. William Saletan, *Bearing Right: How Conservatives Won the Abortion War* (Berkeley: University of California Press, 2003), 37.

11. Baird-Windle and Bader, *Targets of Hatred*, 114.

12. Faye Ginsburg, "Rescuing the Nation: Operation Rescue and the Rise of Anti-Abortion Militance," in *Abortion Wars*, 228.

13. Marcy J. Wilder, "The Rule of Law, the Rise of Violence, and the Role of Morality: Reframing America's Abortion Debate," in *Abortion Wars*, 81

14. Page, *How the Pro-Choice Movement*, 102.

15. Ginsburg, *Contested Lives*, 50; Patricia Donovan, "The Holy War," *Family Planning Perspectives* 17, no. 1 (1985): 6.

16. Carole Joffe, "Pharmacists' Refusals and Reproductive Justice," in *Reproductive Justice Briefing Book*, 11.

17. Laura Kaplan, "Beyond Safe and Legal: The Lessons of Jane," in *Abortion Wars*, 34

18. Wilder, "The Rule of Law," 74

19. Ruth Colker, "An Equal Protection Analysis of United States Reproductive Health Policy: Gender, Race, Age, and Class," *Duke Law Journal* (1991): 328.

20. Elizabeth Martínez, "In Pursuit of Latina Liberation," *Signs: Journal of Women in Culture and Society* 20, no. 4 (1995): 1027.

21. Sonia Corrêa and Rosalind Petchesky, "Reproductive and Sexual Rights: A Feminist Perspective," in *Culture, Society, and Sexuality: A Reader* ed. Richard Parker and Peter Aggleton (New York: Routledge, 2007), 298.

22. Ibid., 304.

23. Dorothy Roberts, *Killing the Black Body: Race, Reproduction, and the Meaning of Liberty* (New York: Vintage Books, 1997), 4.

24. Alexandra Minna Stern, *Eugenic Nation: Faults and Frontiers of Better Breeding in Modern America* (Berkeley: University of California Press, 2005), 87.

25. Ibid., 100.

26. Roberts, *Killing the Black Body*, 65.

27. Loretta J. Ross, "African American Women and Abortion," in *Abortion Wars*, 170.

28. Roberts, *Killing the Black Body*, 43; Angela Davis, "Racism, Birth Control, and Reproductive Rights," in *From Abortion to Reproductive Freedom: Transforming a Movement*, ed. Marlene Gerber Fried (Boston: South End Press, 1990), 24.

29. Jennifer Nelson, *Women of Color and the Reproductive Rights Movement* (New York: NYU Press, 2003), 124.

30. Dorothy E. Roberts, "Punishing Drug Addicts Who Have Babies: Women of Color, Equality, and the Right of Privacy," in *Abortion Wars*, 133.

31. Stern, *Eugenic Nation*, 154

32. Nelson, *Women of Color*, 6

33. Deborah Stone, "Fetal Risks, Women's Rights: Showdown at Johnson Controls," *American Prospect*, Fall 1990, http://prospect.org/article/fetal-risks-womens-rights-showdown-johnson-controls.

34. Nelson, *Women of Color*, 163.

35. Sandi Morgen, "Movement-Grounded Theory: Intersectional Analysis of Health Inequities in the United States," in *Gender, Race, Class, and Health*, ed. Amy J. Schulz and Leith Mullings (San Francisco: Wiley, 2005), 401.

36. Nelson, *Women of Color*, 126.

37. Candida Flores et al., "La Mujer Puertorriquena, Su Cuerpo, y Su Lucha por la Vida: Experiences with Empowerment in Hartford, Connecticut," in *From Abortion to Reproductive Freedom*, 224.

38. Morgen, "Movement-Grounded Theory," 402.

39. Jael Silliman, Marlene Gerber Fried, Loretta J. Ross, and Elena Gutiérrez, *Undivided Rights: Women of Color Organize for Reproductive Justice* (Boston: South End Press, 2004), 177.

40. Loretta J. Ross, "The Color of Choice: White Supremacy and Reproductive Justice," in *The Color of Violence: The INCITE! Anthology* (Boston: South End Press, 2006), 62.

41. Dorothy Roberts, "Foster Care and Reproductive Justice," in *Reproductive Justice Briefing Book*, 29.

42. Ross, "The Color of Choice," 58.

43. World Health Organization, "Facts and Figures from the World Health Report 2005," The World Health Report, http://www.who.int/whr/2005/media_centre/facts_en.pdf.,1

44. Jacqui Alexander, "Mobilizing Against the State and International 'Aid' Agencies: 'Third World' Women Define Reproductive Freedom," in *From Abortion to Reproductive Freedom*, 54.

Retrofitting Choice: White Feminism and the Politics of Reproductive Justice

ERIKA DERKAS

The eve and early moments of the new millennium represented sobering times globally as we bore witness to systematic rapes as part of the genocide against Bosnia and Herzegovina, settler colonialism in Palestine, mass migration from civil unrest, and the mass incarceration and slayings of black and brown bodies. While many liberals and progressives are stunned by the rise in brutality and racism sweeping through Europe and the US, many others recognized fascism, imperialism, and other "-isms" as integral to our inglorious history. As postcolonial studies scholar Homi Bhabha argues, these -isms are the benchmarks through which the story of Western colonization is told.

This essay is directed toward white people coming from a critical white feminist standpoint who stand with multiple generations of social justice activists and scholars. It is a particularly pertinent time for white feminists to make real progress in the fight against imperialist white supremacy. This essay offers guidance, not directives, to white feminists working in or considering the value of reproductive justice theory and organizing, and suggests we take careful stock of our whiteness and our position within the RJ movement.

Calling White People in for Reproductive Justice

Where might we commence? The work begins by calling other white folks in, not out (unless appropriate), and by working within our communities and white mainstream organizations. For RJ to succeed as a critical movement struggling for radical social transformation, it is necessary for white feminists to contest white supremacy within our own spaces and organizations in consultation with people of color before we can productively build alliances. RJ evolved from the ideas, lived experiences, and sisterhood of black women, women of color, and queer people of color who understand how white supremacy gains meaning from the pernicious representations of their allegedly defective, undeserving, and disposable bodies. But RJ is not only relevant for women of color, gender nonconforming people of color, and queer people of color. As Justina Trim of SisterSong says,

> Reproductive oppression is permeated all throughout society. It's the way you are treated when you walk down the street at night. It's the way that children who are born in low-income communities are more likely to develop asthma, because power plants are strategically placed in nearby areas, making the air toxic to surrounding households. It's when it takes longer for you to buy Plan B at the drugstore. It's that feeling in your chest that you had when Tamir Rice was shot and killed at twelve years old.[1]

White anti-racist, anti-imperialist feminist allyship is necessary to the RJ movement, as systems of oppression are mutually interdependent. This is a passionate appeal to do better than simply recognizing sexism, homophobia, racism, and Islamophobia, and move into active contention. It means being proactively resolute in reversing centuries of genocide and structural violence in favor of community well-being. It requires resisting false narratives, committing to critical self-examination, and standing with people of color. However, *standing with* means resisting the temptation to *occupy* people of color (POC) space. Others more experienced in countering white supremacy will lead. In the most basic way, feminist allyship means refuting white privilege and color blindness, i.e., making the deconstruction of the uninterrogated power of whiteness within the feminist movement one cornerstone of any genuine challenge to multiple overlapping oppressive systems.

I came to this movement the same way as most: a personal experience recognized, understood, and attended to through politics. In this case, my direct experience and those of family and friends with abortion amid a swell of evangelical pro-life aggressiveness in the late 1980s and early 1990s brought me face-to-face with the issue of reproductive rights. The structural and the personal always operate in dialectic with one another. My subsequent engagement with the pro-choice movement took a critical turn when I began to understand, as Marlene Gerber Fried has challenged for decades, that liberal notions of choice and equity translated into a movement dominated by white middle-class cisgender women—a movement that has failed to understand how abortion is linked to other structural forces.

Working in women's centers in California helped me connect the notions of choice, race, class, and heterosexism, and see the complexity of our experiences as contextual, historic, eclectic, and involving deep-rooted structural forces rather than individual beliefs, decisions, and outcomes. Later my decision to undergo voluntary sterilization and choose intentional childlessness clarified the relationship between my potential to reproduce white supremacy and national and international population control policies directed at communities of color. I was pressured to not sterilize myself, and I understood that my situation was totally dissimilar to the types of pressures women of color often experience.

My work evolved into campaigns to contest Project Prevention (formerly known as Children Requiring a Caring Kommunity). Barbara Harris launched this infamous program to sterilize poor women and women of color (WOC) around the country who are assumed to be struggling with addiction by offering them two hundred dollars. After Project Prevention began targeting prisons, I repositioned my activism to contest its exploitation of incarcerated women in the Bernalillo Detention Center of New Mexico. My activism continued with WOC- and QPOC-led organizations (e.g., the Committee on Women, Population and the Environment, Young Women United, and INCITE!*)* and white allies (e.g., Lynn Paltrow of the National Advocates for Pregnant Women). I engaged in campaigns and strategy meetings across the country, from New Mexico, Seattle, Los Angeles to New York City, where various activists came together under the organizing efforts of, for example, Theryn Kigvamasud'vashti of Communities against Rape and Abuse. I worked with radical feminists to counter privatized eugenics in the United States and internationally.

One problem with allyship in the RJ movement is that some white feminists only address white supremacy at a cursory level. Since becoming an allied member at the first SisterSong conference in 2003, I have watched white feminists drop in while neglecting to understand the complex, duplicitous, and nuanced interplay of racism and other phobias and hatreds. For many white feminists, RJ is just the flavor of the month, a merit badge worn to avoid reflection on one's own and/or organizational racism, ahistorical naïveté, and offensive appropriation (e.g., institutional tokenism and co-optation to gain funding and credibility).

This cursory dismissal has a long history with white feminists using WOC for their own agenda through racially privileged institutions. They not only are complicit in perpetuating white supremacy but also further entrenching unequal relationships and positions. The ethical obligation in identifying, deconstructing, and transforming one's standpoint as white feminists within the RJ movement means being aware of our relationships and responsibilities to marginalized communities. White activists and scholars who utilize RJ cannot advocate for human rights, racial justice, and reproductive well-being without holding ourselves and our organizations accountable to marginalized communities and individuals. The epistemologies and ontologies which form the principles guiding relationships, responsibilities, and behaviors among and between anti-racist, anti-imperialist, antipatriarchal, antiheterosexist, and anti-ableist communities and activists are necessarily subject to ongoing critical evaluation, dismantling, and transformation for the engagement with RJ to be genuine, deep, and effective.

Dismantling White Supremacy and White Privilege

Such internal critique involves reckoning with whiteness. A white identity is far more complex than just genetics. Embedded are expectations about what and to whom one is obligated. A very different composition and responsibility exists for white feminists using RJ. It means contesting unearned, stolen, socially constructed, and assumed privileges built off the lives of others, despite our own possible and marginalized struggles. Therefore, part of the challenge to white supremacy entails working for ourselves and our communities. This requires accountability for and to white communities in challenging fascistic tendencies within them, such as rigid kinship systems; calling out cultures criticizing people who don't meet "normal" (read: white, middle-class) standards of behavior and comportment; excessive policing both by the state and within communities; and alienating and isolating patterns of social and familial relationships.

We cannot only resist overt forms of racism. These represent the most obvious hateful attacks, but they are the easiest to identify and we hope all folks would stand against this. But we must also oppose white privilege used by those who do not consciously support the ideas of white supremacists. Radical white feminists are accountable by vigilantly contesting all overt and subtle forms of white supremacy.

For example, it is possible for a white rape survivor in the anti-violence movement to exhibit white privilege and be oblivious to white supremacy on the Left. Women of color leaders in the anti-violence movement experience this frequently, as the critical INCITE! conferences can attest.

White survivors may press for more police sensitivity training regarding gender-related violence without considering that many women of color are reluctant to call the police, given the historical and contemporary role police have in brutalizing people within the community.

We recognize race is entangled with all other positionalities creating a multitude of experiences, conditions, and treatments. These forces of white supremacy (racism, classism, nationalism, homophobia, transphobia, ableism, ageism) give life to each other through the juxtaposition of deserving, usually white, cisgender women against disposable bodies (WOC, LGBTQ folks, immigrants, women of the Global South, low-income women, able-varied women, and incarcerated women). It is how whiteness gains its discursive normativity for which the "other" is created. Paradoxically, this notion of whiteness also caused many white people to experience sexist, heterosexist, transphobic, classist, and ableist oppression because they too may not fit the ideal of whiteness.

Under white supremacist ideology, the rubric of white femininity coincides with the ability to reproduce. Therefore, a commitment to RJ could have very real consequences to white people's bodily integrity as embracing RJ threatens the empire of white supremacy. The normalization of white femininity is built on the depiction of the allegedly failed femininity of others through oppression configured by race, age, class, heterosexuality, gender normativity, nationality, and economic productivity. Undoubtedly those fitting squarely in privileged positions benefit most from and support this idealized white femininity more readily. However, white anti-racists, feminists, queer activists, and anti-imperialist abolitionists are constructed as troubling bodies. White allies contesting white supremacy may face a loss of prestige, preferential treatment in housing, jobs, and advancement; difficult relationships with family and friends; Internet trolling; and violence. But we are not constructed as essentialized others. We are not exploited, objectified, and rendered invisible in the same way that WOC and QPOC are and have been.

For white feminists to meaningfully engage with RJ as scholars, activists, and organizations, we must risk moving beyond sympathy or intellectual understanding and support anti-oppression organizing, especially in the white community. We must be committed to reflexivity, sincere listening, and empathy. This requires giving up privilege and space, avoiding micro-aggressions, and growing both as an individual and a community, all of which must be anchored in love, not anger. In the words of Maurice Mitchell, any anxieties we may feel about getting it wrong or making mistakes has nothing to do with ending white supremacy except as part of the predictable process of divesting ourselves from noxious ideas and practices. Calling on POC to dismantle white supremacy or to help navigate white pain is a manifestation of white privilege and misuses the transformative power of RJ. White supremacy is constructed, maintained, and enforced by white people and white privilege, and we are the people who must deconstruct it as part of our obligation and specific role in the human rights movement.

Reproductive Justice Organizing through a White Lens

White feminists should resist false narratives of our racialized reproductive history. Such narratives continue to legitimize white-led organizations with myopic visions. For instance, the notion of a universal sisterhood put forth by many white-led feminist organizations denies the complicit dynamic white women had under the institution of US slavery, where the rape and brutalization of black women was tolerated, or the ongoing reluctance to recognize that US imperialism claims the bodies of black and brown individuals of the Global South as domestic servants, victims of trafficking, and criminalized migrants. White opposition to immigrants' human rights support the white supremacist project of white people's domination of this country, while ignoring the a priori claims of Indigenous people.

White organizations and organizing efforts that have continuously been challenged for their exclusionary practices have falsely assumed that inclusion is the yardstick by which progress is measured. Thus, attempts to incorporate WOC and QPOC into many organizations have largely failed. Assimilation into existing organizations often does not equate with progress or freedom. These organizations do not operate in a vacuum, and without challenging internal structures and politics, they often replicate the systems of oppression they claim to contest, silencing marginalized voices. Moreover, often integration is a one-way street on which people of color are asked to abandon their cultural identities and political views to fully assimilate into the organization or movement. Such notions of progress reinforce racist institutions and practices and ultimately distract from the deep structural forces of oppression. For example, as Angela Davis argues, the 1967 referendum to make Australian Aborigines citizens represents a push not for true justice but rather assimilation and, by default, legitimization of racist institutions (e.g., constitutions, laws, criminal justice systems, and notions of individual freedom): "What does it mean to have formal rights when the conditions of life render these rights relatively meaningless?"[2] Instead, many social justice advocates and Indigenous leaders fight for agency and autonomy, not inclusion.

There is a great deal of risk-taking for many WOC and QPOC in building alliances with white feminists, and, on the most basic level, our commitment to RJ means being aware of power differentials. Black feminist theorists have argued that black women, queer, and able-varied individuals of color generally are positioned within structures of power in fundamentally different ways from white individuals. While some white feminists gravitate to POC-led organizations, the presence of whiteness in POC spaces can be unhelpful if done in problematic ways. The words of Frantz Fanon from neocolonial times are relevant:

> And then the occasion arose I had to meet the white man's eyes. An unfamiliar weight burdened me. A real world challenged me. In the white world the [person] of color encounters difficulties in the development of [their] bodily schema. Consciousness of the body is solely a negating activity. It is a third-person consciousness. The body is surrounded by an atmosphere of certain uncertainty . . . And I was battered down by tom-toms, cannibalism, intellectual deficiency, fetishism, and racial defects . . . I took myself far off from my own presence...What else could it be for me but an amputation, an excision, a hemorrhage that spattered my whole body with Black blood.[3]

This extensively cited quote bears witness to what the colonial embodied black person experiences when the dominated encounters the colonizer. Fanon's palpable narrative of dehumanization urges us to explore the historic and contemporary experiences with oppression that mark the persistent relations among the dominant and other. Given that these relations are historically produced and ever-changing, white people and particularly white feminists working in the RJ movement must pay heed to this potential dynamic. Such encounters between white people and POC often highlight deep-rooted psychological structures that are gendered and sexualized (through fetishism or exotification) and must be destabilized. It is only a part of the obligation that white feminists owe WOC and QPOC.

White allyship is all too often prematurely sought. The work within white communities must continuously occur before such collaborations are pursued if we want to engage productively to unify anti-racists' challenges through global resistance to Islamophobia, to the occupation of Palestine, to homophobic and transphobic violence, to mass incarceration, to the institutions of authority that brutalize marginalized communities, and their struggles railing against aggressive capitalism that damages the earth and defames those who sacredly guard her. We must back each other up, hold each other up, and actively fight to protect one another. It is time to complicate the politics of white communities and make more capacious the political consciousness of our movements.

Uma Narayan, Chandra Talpade Mohanty, and Jacqui Alexander, among others, have unsettled familiar mainstream feminist theorizing and activism regarding experience, human rights, white anti-racism, and progress that are built on false universal claims. The multiple forces of oppression that configure the lives of different groups in various ways are not accurately reflected, analyzed, or attended to within mainstream Western white feminism. Often lacking is the full commitment to decenter the center, neglect to develop self-reflexive critiques, and deconstruct white privilege. Such half-hearted commitments are prone to reinscribe the cultural values of the dominant white feminist establishment. Therefore, as Ofelia Schutte has argued, white feminists must enlist practices which derail our habitual perspectives and foregrounded frameworks and practices, and challenge accepted ways of thinking. For instance, the pro-choice movement is only now shifting (albeit glacially) the universal liberal framework of "choice." Anaynna Bhattacharjee's work on law enforcement agencies demonstrates how the US prison system, police, the former Immigration and Naturalization Service, and border patrol systematically undermine women's caretaking or caregiving and reproductive capabilities. It is precisely these narrowly defined renditions of reproductive rights and single-issue movements that fail to capture the frequency of these abuses and how they threaten the bodily integrity of those targeted.

A problem may be how white people organize Black Lives Matter rallies. The problem is not that white people working in predominantly or exclusively white regions can't assert that "black lives matter" but rather how they do it. White people must stand up for racial justice and contest white supremacy; however, well-intentioned folks may be unaware of how whiteness operates in such contexts. Consciously or not, "standing with" often translates into POC being "spoken for" or using language that fails to accurately account for power differentials created by white experiences. Given that Black Lives Matter is an organization created by black women and led by POC, whites organizing Black Lives Matter rallies could rightly be construed as appropriation and a space invasion. Rather, white-led organizations can organize supportive rallies using their own culturally and historically relevant language. For instance, Showing Up for Racial Justice (SURJ), a white-led racial justice allyship network, organizes white allies using a historical civil rights model where black-led movements asked whites to organize themselves. Organizers of the Black Lives Matter movement requested that SURJ rally themselves; as the cofounder of Black Lives Matter Alicia Garza stated, "We are grateful to our allies who have stepped up to the call that Black lives matter, and taken it as an opportunity to not just stand in solidarity with us, but to investigate the ways in which anti-Black racism is perpetuated in their own communities."[4]

Race shifting refers to gains obtained by exploiting the fluidity of the social meaning of race through *sliding in and out* of a racial identity not of one's own, such as black people passing for white for obvious power and assimilation advantage. Cultural appropriation, however, always involves exploitation of marginalized communities by those from dominant groups. What compels people to adopt a contrived racial identity to either gain legitimacy for social justice work, display some form of self-enlightenment, deflect racism, or to ridicule others (as in minstrel shows or blackface performers of early twentieth century) is directly related to the legacy of white supremacy. Land grabbing, exotification of otherness, white guilt, and the search among whites for purpose are some of the explanations. Non-Indigenous claims were and remain central to state-sanctioned appropriation of Indigenous lands to undermine treaties and access resources, from mineral rights to casino revenues.

On a positive note, we witness the commitments of white feminists who participate in the RJ movement with integrity and respect. The primary attendants at the contesting CRACK summit in NYC in spring 2005 were WOC and QPOC organizations with a few white feminists also present. However, all those in attendance offered perspectives, insights, and genuine listening. We learned from one another and strategized against the encroachment of privatized eugenics and specifically how it looked in our respective communities. We sought connections between our specific strategies, not so much in their similarities, but rather discovered relationships through their radical differences.

In other moments, such as the first Color of Violence conference in 2000 in Santa Cruz, some white activists learned not to let white guilt cause paralysis or to succumb to self-deprecation and off-handed remarks to assuage guilt. When both the WOC and white women were asked to break into discussion groups, an uncomfortable moment arose but it was also an opportunity to pause, to be accountable, and not rely on WOC to educate white people about violence and intersectionality. The challenge was to step aside, give up space, and grapple with questions of *where do I fit* and *what obligations do I have to white communities, communities of color, women, and queer people of color*?

We will make mistakes but commit to learning from them and to always coming back. Such considerations do not render white feminists' work in the movement and passion for overall reproductive well-being inconsequential and superfluous; rather they are essential to the dismantling of white supremacy, its impacts on all people's bodies and lives.

Benefits of Joining the Reproductive Justice Movement

What we will gain as white people fighting white supremacy through reproductive justice is infinitely more precious than all our perceived disadvantages: we live up to our human rights values and do our social justice work with integrity. We prepare a better future for ourselves, families, and communities by learning to be appropriately white in partnership, not domination, with the rest of humanity. We can gain an internationalist multiracial framework so our struggles can become more enduring and meaningful. Our success in dismantling structures of oppression depends on it!

Getting there entails real and tangible work by and among white feminists committed to RJ. It means that white people need to recognize that unlearning white supremacist thinking is an ongoing process and it will never magically dissolve the advantages afforded whiteness. To be out in our communities, using our privilege and platforms to push for the active dismantling of all forms of oppression is key to creating fundamental change. This includes more tangible efforts like truth-telling sessions among whites, deep dialogue, and actions to transform systematic and continued injustice in our communities, workplaces, relationships, and cultural institutions, and deepening anti-racist commitment *in* white communities.

Organizations like Training for Change adopt this type of strategy while also devoting space to POC-only workshops. The controversial Macklemore and Ryan Lewis song "White Privilege II," an ironic use of rap by white rappers to talk about white privilege, brought forward critical engagement through art about whiteness and the use of privilege, influence, and wealth to talk about white supremacy and state violence against black people. White anti-racist and social justice activists have created spaces for white activists, while continually dialoguing with POC-led organizations, designed to collectively develop deeper political analysis, vision, strategy, and organizing skills, in turn leading to public actions and community struggles which expose and combat systemic oppression. Anti-racist training workshops designed by white anti-racist organizers in our communities help engender this deeper commitment, will nurture the next generation of social justice activists, and build a legacy of accountable white people to the mosaic of movements fighting for reproductive justice.

Furthermore, to make anti-racist discourse normative, a broad base of white support must be created. Organizers who understand their contextual and historical positions of race and privilege recognize that white feminists can access white allies unavailable to POC and use them to support the capacity of organizations beyond our own. Bringing folks even at the risk of it being messy and draining means making anti-oppression work routine. Whites sincerely engaged in social justice activism generally and RJ specifically cannot construe themselves as special people in the fight for justice and human dignity. To frame oneself as exceptional from the rest of white people based on a sense of moral righteousness alleges one's individual uniqueness, while not necessarily offering quality work in the struggle against globalized forms of oppression.

Reproductive justice is evocative of the ongoing yearning for freedom. This is not about the quality of any individual's life but rather the constant collective yearning for new worlds, "habitable futures,"[5] collective agency and autonomy, and achieving all of this for those who most embody the struggle: people who have been enslaved, oppressed, incarcerated. As Angela Davis says, "There is no such thing as the freedom of a single individual—that is limited freedom—if freedom at all. 'Making America Great' means constructing the kind of society that should have been created after slavery (after the colonization period) by retooling the whole society, creating institutions that would allow for the inclusion of the previously enslaved."[6]

Notes

1. Loretta J. Ross, email message to author, April 21, 2017.

2. Angela Davis, Lannan Talks (speech delivered in Santa Fe, New Mexico, November 2, 2016).

3. Frantz Fanon, *Black Skin, White Masks* (New York: Grove Press, 2008), 112.

4. Alicia Garza, "A Herstory of the #BlackLivesMatter Movement," *Feminist Wire*, October 14, 2014. www.thefeministwire.com/2014/10/blacklivesmatter-21.

5. June Jordan, *Some of Us Did NOT Die: New and Selected Essays*, (New York: Basic Books, 2002), 280.

6. Davis, Lannan Talks.

POLICY, PRACTICE, AND ACTIVISM

"She Doesn't Deserve to Be Treated Like This": Prisons as Sites of Reproductive Injustice

RACHEL ROTH

I knew when you went to jail you gave up some rights, but the rights over your own body?

—Pamela Forney, imprisoned in Pasco County, Florida

During the past forty years, prisons have become increasingly significant arenas of conflict over women's bodies and women's rights. As a strict system of physical confinement and punishment, imprisonment has unique institutional characteristics, and yet it also provides a microcosm of reproductive politics. Nowhere is race and class stratification more evident than in the criminal justice and prison systems, where poor women and men of color are dramatically overrepresented relative to their numbers in society. And prisons are one place where the metaphor of "choice" is sorely inadequate to describe what is at stake in political struggles over reproduction. A pregnant woman in prison cannot choose between a midwife and a doctor; she cannot even choose who will be in the room with her when she gives birth.

Every dimension of reproductive justice is negatively affected by imprisonment—from access to abortion and basic medical care to maintain one's health and fertility to the ability to form and maintain relationships with one's children. Medical neglect in prisons and the erosion of parental rights both fit into a long history of reproductive oppression suffered by poor women and women of color, including the sale of children under slavery, the forced removal of Native children to government boarding schools, restrictive immigration policies, sterilization abuse, bans on public funding for abortion, and punitive welfare policies.

This essay explores prisons as sites of reproductive injustice by focusing on barriers to abortion and safe childbirth. After defining the concept of reproductive justice, the essay reviews the limits of the constitutional right to medical care in prison and the racial and class biases that characterize the criminal justice and prison systems. It then examines barriers to abortion care and pregnancy care to show that institutional resistance to abortion is not the result of a commitment to healthy pregnancy and childbirth. Rather, the failure to provide both forms of vital medical care is part of a widespread pattern of institutional neglect.

Research on reproductive abuses in prison presents a "tip of the iceberg" problem—we only know those instances that have come to light through the court system, the press, or primary research. Other instances have doubtless occurred because of the structural problems that limit access to healthcare in prison settings. Literally closed to the public, with no obligation to report on the outcomes of pregnant women in their custody, most jails and prisons operate without any meaningful oversight. This "fiefdom" scenario underscores both the constraints on documenting the full scope of abuse behind prison walls and also the need to do so.[1]

Reproductive Justice

> *Reproductive justice exists when all people have the social, political, and economic power and resources to make healthy decisions about our gender, bodies, sexuality, and families for ourselves and our communities. Reproductive justice aims to transform power inequities and create long-term systemic change, and therefore relies on the leadership of communities most impacted by reproductive oppression.—Forward Together*

The term "reproductive justice" encompasses the full scope of women's reproductive lives, from decisions about whether and when to have children to the ability to raise children with dignity. These priorities reflect women's need for reproductive self-determination in a country where poor women and women of color have been subjected to coercive sterilization or other practices designed to destroy their right to motherhood.

Feminists of color and socialist feminists have worked for years to broaden our understanding of the political terrain of reproduction. A group of African American women originally coined the term "reproductive justice" in 1994 after meeting with activists from around the world at the International Conference on Population and Development in Cairo. As long-time activist Loretta J. Ross explains, "Not wanting to use the language of 'choice' because they represented communities with few real choices, they integrated the concepts of reproductive rights, social justice, and human rights to launch the term 'reproductive justice.'"[2]

By infusing reproductive rights with a social justice orientation, reproductive justice goes beyond abstract rights and individual privacy, emphasizing women's ability to truly exercise their rights. This framework also emphasizes women's agency to make decisions while at the same time recognizing that individual women live their lives as members of communities that have distinct histories of oppression, including population control. These insights help us to understand the meaning of reproductive rights in the prison context, where official declarations of rights by the courts in no way guarantee women's ability to access healthcare or to carry out their own decisions.

The Constitutional Right to Medical Care

> *You're helpless. It's not like you can get in your car and leave looking for competent medical care.—Bernadette Fogell, imprisoned in Delaware*

People in prison are the only group in the United States with a constitutional right to medical care. The right to medical care has its roots in the Eighth Amendment's prohibition of cruel and unusual punishment. In 1976 the Supreme Court recognized that when the government punishes someone by incarceration, it is obligated to meet that person's basic needs. In *Estelle v. Gamble*, the Supreme Court explained that an incarcerated individual "must rely on prison authorities to treat his [or her] medical needs; if the authorities fail to do so, those needs will not be met." The Supreme Court further explained that "deliberate indifference to serious medical needs" constitutes the "unnecessary and wanton infliction of pain," whether by medical personnel or by corrections officers who intentionally deny or delay access to care.[3]

In practice, securing needed medical care can be daunting, as numerous lawsuits and investigations attest. Women encounter multiple barriers to care—from copayments they cannot afford to having to convince a guard that they need to see a doctor. Since its landmark 1976 ruling in *Estelle*, the Supreme Court has retreated on prisoners' rights, making it more difficult for people in prison to enforce their right to medical care or to seek redress for violations. Court decisions draw a sharp distinction between the everyday concept of medical malpractice and the higher standard of "deliberate indifference," which is very difficult to prove because it turns on the subjective state of mind of the person being sued as opposed to the objective injuries suffered by the person deprived of medical care. In 1996 Congress further eroded the rights of people in prison by passing the Prison Litigation Reform Act, which limits people's access to the courts and also limits judicial monitoring of prison conditions after winning a case.

Despite the vulnerability and serious needs of incarcerated people, the United States has no national standards to implement the constitutional right to medical care in prison. Typically, each system—the federal Bureau of Prisons, the federal Bureau of Immigration and Customs Enforcement, state Departments of Corrections, and thousands of local jails—establishes its own policies and procedures, with little oversight. Although there are organizations that accredit institutions of confinement, a minority of institutions have gone through the process. The National Commission on Correctional Health Care, considered the leading organization on medical accreditation, reports in 2011 that it has accredited nearly five hundred prisons and jails, which account for nearly four hundred thousand people—or, less than 20 percent of the total population of people in prison.[4] Moreover, accreditation is no guarantee of consistent access to appropriate medical care. There are no surprise inspections to ensure that institutions adhere to policies. And policies, especially those pertaining to reproductive healthcare, may be inadequate in the first place.

Privatization is another powerful barrier to medical care. Although public agencies run most prisons and jails, private, for-profit companies operate some of them, and private companies win contracts to provide medical services in many more. The profit motive inevitably creates disincentives to providing the best care because every dollar spent on medical care lowers the company's earnings. Equally troubling is the way these companies shield themselves from public scrutiny and accountability by claiming that their policies and actions are private, despite the fact that they are providing public services. Sometimes, governments collude in this attempt to shield themselves from scrutiny. In Delaware, for instance, the Department of Corrections refused to answer a Freedom of Information Act request from the ACLU by insisting that the medical policies used in the state's prisons belonged to the private company Correctional Medical Services.[5]

Prisons and Social Injustice

> *[Prisons] function as the default solution for a vast range of social problems that need to be addressed by other institutions.—Angela Davis and Cassandra Shaylor*

Prisons both reflect and reinforce social disadvantage: prisons confine primarily poor women and men, and when those women and men get out of prison, they find that having a criminal conviction makes it that much harder to get a job, housing, or education. Fully half the women awaiting trial in the Massachusetts Correctional Institution Framingham, for example, are stuck behind bars because they cannot afford to pay their fifty-dollar bail.[6] In addition to economic insecurity, women who wind up in prison have usually suffered physical and sexual abuse and struggled with substance use or mental health problems. Many experience new traumas inside the system, and few get the individualized treatment they need.

More than two hundred thousand women are imprisoned in the United States, representing about 10 percent of all people imprisoned in this country and an astonishing 30 percent of women imprisoned worldwide.[7] These statistics reflect the number of women locked up on a given day; many more spend time in jails, prisons, and immigration lock-ups over the course of a year. Although women have always been a minority of those imprisoned, they have been entering prison at a faster rate than men for some time, with numbers increasing more than eightfold since 1980. When probation and parole are included, over 1.3 million women are under the authority of the criminal justice system.[8] The adoption of harsh mandatory sentences has driven these numbers and created a system that locks up people who pose little threat to public safety, taking the greatest toll on those who have the fewest advantages to begin with.

Policing and criminal courts are arenas of considerable racial discrimination. In January 2006, for example, more than 82 percent of women serving time in New York state prisons for drug offenses were women of color.[9] These statistics might create the impression that white women don't use drugs, but we know this isn't true. What the statistics really show is different rates of surveillance, arrest, prosecution, and conviction, as well as unequal access to drug treatment and other resources that might keep women with drug problems out of the criminal justice system in the first place.

On the national level, the racial dynamics of women's incarceration changed during the first decade of the twenty-first century. The number of African American women in state and federal prison dropped, while the number of white and Latina women rose. In 2000 African American women were incarcerated at six times the rate of white women; by 2009 they were incarcerated at about three times the rate.[10] While the smaller black-white disparity among women sentenced to prison is an important development, racial disparities remain substantial, and the total number of women in prison remains basically steady.

Most women in jail and prison are mothers, and more than half have children under age eighteen, almost two-thirds of those in state prison.[11] In addition, 4 to 5 percent of women are pregnant when booked into prison or jail.[12] Women in prison are often considered unworthy of motherhood, as prison policy, public discourse, and public policy demonstrate. Prison policies undermine parent-child relationships by limiting visiting hours or eliminating in-person visits altogether, charging exorbitant rates for collect phone calls or video visits, and imprisoning people far from home. In many states, the one prison for women is in a rural area, even though most of the women come from cities. Some Departments of Correction send women to serve their time in other states. As one example, Hawaii sends women all the way to a prison in Kentucky.

Public discourse tends to be simplistic and punitive. In response to a news story on *MedPage Today* about the shackling of pregnant women in labor, for example, one reader commented: "It's 'dehumanizing'??? WHO CARES? These women are in prison for crimes that THEY DID. Why treat them like real people?"

After a twenty-one-year-old woman died in a jail cell of internal bleeding caused by a ruptured ectopic pregnancy, several people commenting on the *Post-Standard* website essentially blamed her for her own death: "If this individual did not do anything wrong, she would have not been in jail"; "She put herself in that situation"; "She should've made better choices in her life." One reader went so far as to speculate, "In and out of jail? What kind of mother is that? Maybe this was gods [*sic*] way of saying it wasn't meant to be." These comments reflect widespread animosity toward women in prison, as well as a simplistic focus on individual "choices" that ignores any structural conditions that might contribute to a woman's imprisonment.

Finally, public policies take their toll. Going to prison for even a short time can mean losing custody of children, forever. Federal and state laws mandate the termination of parental rights if a child has been in foster care for fifteen months in a twenty-two-month period, and only a few states make any exceptions for parents who are in prison.[13] Women who make it out of prison with their legal relationship to their children intact may still find that they cannot be reunited with them. If they have a felony drug conviction, as so many do, they may well find that they are no longer eligible for public housing, food stamps, driver's licenses, or loans to go back to school—resources that would help them land on their feet and build a better future for themselves and their families. Finding a job with a criminal record is challenging even in a good economy, let alone when times are tough. Given the racial distribution of poverty and the racial biases of criminal justice administration, these policies fall especially heavily on women of color, permanently undermining their right to be mothers.

Reproductive Injustice: Barriers to Abortion Care

> *I was completely helpless and felt that I had no control. I was truly afraid that I was going to be forced to have the baby.—Jane Doe, who had to sue a sheriff in order to obtain an abortion*

> *It's been a hard personal journey. I'm really hoping that nobody else has to go through what I've gone through.—Yuriko Kawaguchi, who was prevented by a municipal judge from having an abortion when she was in jail*

Time and time again, in at least twenty states and the District of Columbia, women have had to fight for the right to abortion—and in some cases, have lost and been forced to continue pregnancies against their will. Many prisons and jails have no official written policy to tell women how to go about requesting an abortion, and staff members how to go about meeting a woman's request, since obtaining an abortion will always entail a trip to an outside medical provider. Agencies within the US government provide examples from both ends of the transparency spectrum. The federal Bureau of Prisons (BOP) published its policy in the *Federal Register* decades ago, and later made it available on the Bureau's website. In contrast, the Bureau of Immigration and Customs Enforcement (ICE) had no publicly available information about abortion access for detained women until 2011. Because of the Hyde Amendment, neither agency pays for abortion unless the pregnancy endangers a woman's life or resulted from rape or incest. Both agencies are responsible for arranging for abortion appointments and transportation.

At the state level, only California has a statute affirming the rights of women in jail and prison to access abortion care. Legislatures almost always delegate the issue to Departments of Correction, which often delegate it further to individual prisons that use decision-making processes that are closed to the public. About one-quarter of state prison systems have no official written policy on abortion. Others do not release their policies to the public or have ambiguous policies that require interpretation and therefore invite discretion on the part of prison personnel. Little information exists about the nation's three-thousand-plus jails. In New York, a systematic review of county jail policies found that almost half of the fifty-two counties with female prisoners had an abortion policy, but only thirteen of these unambiguously guaranteed women's rights—even though public policy in New York supports women's access to abortion.[14]

Federal courts and state courts of appeal have been very clear that women in prison do not lose the basic right to make decisions about pregnancy and abortion. The constitutional right to an abortion has been recognized since the 1973 decision *Roe v. Wade*. It is grounded in the Fourteenth Amendment's guarantee of privacy and personal liberty, and applies to women inside prison as much as to women outside of prison. Some judges and legal scholars believe that the Eighth Amendment right to medical care also protects women's right to an abortion. The one case to address the question of public funding found that women who cannot afford an abortion must be provided one at the jail's expense.[15] And yet the well-established nature of women's rights has not stopped prison and jail personnel from trying to deny women abortion care, or at least obstruct women's access to abortion.

A case from Phoenix in Maricopa County, Arizona, conveys the difficulties that women endure when they try to assert their right to an abortion. A woman identified as "Jane Doe" learned the day before her sentencing hearing that she was pregnant. Nineteen years old, with four months in jail and two years of probation ahead of her, Doe decided she did not want to have a baby. Her attorney asked the prosecutor if she could stay out of jail just long enough to get an abortion, but the prosecutor said no, assuring her that she would be able to do so when she was in the jail's work furlough program.

The prosecutor's assurances took on a hollow ring once Doe was in jail. She was cleared for furlough, but never given an assignment. For the first week, she tried to no avail to find out how to obtain an abortion, and then she was moved to a part of the jail where her access to the telephone was restricted. A jail physician suggested that adoption was the better course. Eventually, she learned that she could have an abortion if she could meet, without regular use of a telephone, the following requirements: she needed to have someone outside the jail schedule an abortion and pay for it, hire an attorney to obtain a court order authorizing transportation outside the jail, and pay for jail personnel to take her to a clinic—all to conform with an unwritten policy decreed by Sheriff Joe Arpaio, who ran the jail.

This obstacle course was in marked contrast to the sheriff's other policies, which included taking prisoners outside the jail for medical care and also for nonmedical purposes, such as visiting sick relatives or attending a funeral, all without the involvement of the courts. Doe's parents were willing and able to pay for her to have an abortion, and yet the obstacles were almost insurmountable. Doe's criminal defense attorney declined to assist with this matter, so her parents found a public defender to seek the required court order. When the public defender was pulled off the case, he suggested they call the ACLU, and only then did things finally start to go right. The ACLU attorneys, who had worked on similar cases in other states, were able to get a court to order the sheriff to take Doe to a clinic. By this time, eight weeks had passed since she was taken into custody.[16]

Throughout his twenty-three-year tenure, Sheriff Arpaio liked to call himself the "toughest sheriff in America," and he garnered national attention for his punitive practices, such as making people work on chain gangs in the hot desert sun. But his resistance to providing access to abortion care is not unusual. Indeed, Jane Doe's case illustrates several common problems experienced by women seeking abortions from within the confines of prisons and jails: long delays, unwritten policies, difficulty gaining information, and restricted communication with the outside world. Across the country, women have been told they must get a judge's permission and must come up with the money for an abortion and for the cost of transportation and staff time as well. Given the tendency to site prisons in rural areas, and the concentration of abortion services in urban areas, these requirements can put abortion out of reach without ever explicitly denying women's rights. In other instances, women *are* denied; someone simply says, "No, you cannot have an abortion." In one such case, a Missouri prison reversed a long-standing policy to take women who could afford an abortion to a clinic, via an internal memo, with no notice to the public.

Restrictions on abortion fall especially heavily on poor women and women of color, for two reasons: These groups of women are overrepresented in jail and prison and more likely to experience unintended pregnancies, reflecting racial disparities in access to healthcare. Women of color, most notably African American women, are also more likely than white women to terminate a pregnancy. These factors mean that women of color are disproportionately burdened by barriers to abortion.

Although news stories and court documents about conflicts over abortion access rarely identify a woman's racial or ethnic background, sometimes this information is available. In one case, a sentencing judge in Somerville, New Jersey, appointed a guardian for the fetus of Sonya Jackson, a thirty-one-year-old African American mother of two, who had asked to leave the county jail for an abortion appointment. The move was widely reported by the press, and a minister who runs a pregnancy center visited Jackson in jail with promises of child support and bail money. She had the baby. In another case, a sentencing judge in Cleveland, Ohio, gave jail time instead of probation to Yuriko Kawaguchi, a twenty-one-year-old student from Japan, specifically to prevent her from obtaining an abortion. A state court of appeals ordered her released on bail, but by that time it was too late to terminate the pregnancy in the state of Ohio. Kawaguchi had the baby.

Decisions about pregnancy and abortion are deeply personal, and yet they are also shaped by the larger political, economic, and social context of women's lives. Some women have already decided to have an abortion before they get arrested or sentenced; others learn afterward that they are pregnant, or become pregnant while imprisoned. Among the top reasons that women generally give for deciding to have an abortion are their caregiving responsibilities and their inability to afford a baby. While some women say they are not ready to be mothers, a majority already have at least one child. Landing behind bars intensifies these concerns, and may prompt even women who intended to have a baby to reassess their plans. Women in jail or prison have to figure out who can take care of any children they already have, as well as make plans for a new baby. Their families tend to have few resources, and taking "kin care" foster care payments sets the clock ticking to terminate the mother's parental rights. Fears about medical neglect in prison and the prospect of being immediately separated from their newborn may be too much to bear.

Reproductive Injustice: Barriers to Safe Childbirth

I feel if she did wrong, she should be punished for it. If you did wrong, you should have to pay for it, but she doesn't deserve to be treated like this.—Loannza Staten, whose granddaughter was left to give birth all alone in a prison cell

In virtually every case that I have handled involving healthcare claims of women, I have found women who lost pregnancies or newborns due to the prison's atrocious neglect.—Elizabeth Alexander, Director of the ACLU National Prison Project

Women in prison and jail have long reported problems with pregnancy care. A study in the King County Jail in Seattle, Washington, found that the pregnant women "all complained of being uncomfortable, lacking pillows and chairs, having to sit on cold cement, being exposed to toxic cleaning materials, and feeling constantly hungry."[17] A report about Massachusetts found that pregnant women went hungry or ate "empty calories" and were given extra-large sizes of standard clothing instead of maternity clothes, including pants that were too long and created the risk of tripping and falling. While virtually every state prison system has an official policy to provide prenatal care to pregnant women, jails are less likely to have such policies. In New York, for example, 43 percent of county jails have no policy on prenatal care, and women nationwide report being less likely to receive obstetric exams or pregnancy diets in jail than in prison.

Pregnant women in custody encounter too many problems to enumerate here. Among the most serious are the prison staff's refusal to take bleeding seriously, a problem associated with miscarriage and stillbirth, and their failure to recognize when women are in labor, a problem associated with women giving birth inside their cells, as well as the routine practice of shackling pregnant women and the failure to provide postpartum care.

A woman serving time in a California state prison describes her experience several months into her pregnancy:

> I went for my monthly checkup. They couldn't find my baby's heartbeat. . . . [Five days later] I was in a lot of pain and was spotting a lot. I told my housing staff and he called the [Medical Technical Assistant]. She told him I didn't have proof, that she wouldn't see me. At that time the bleeding slow[ed] down so I put a pad on. It was blood on it but not good enough for her. She told me that *all pregnant women bleed*. I told her that I was a high risk and when I seen the doctor last week he couldn't find a heartbeat. So she called the doctor and he told her to send me back to my unit. . . . [Three days later at 3:00 a.m.] I lost my baby in my bathroom.[18]

This story is not uncommon. Court records and other documents show that corrections officers and medical personnel ignore, disregard, and discount women's own knowledge that something is happening and that they need medical attention. One woman, six-and-a-half months pregnant, was locked bleeding overnight in the cell of a small Minnesota jail because she could not make bail and the jail did not want to pay to take her to the hospital; another, four or five months pregnant, was locked in an "observation cell" in an Arkansas jail for three days, after she had already been bleeding for three days in a group cell. Both women lost their pregnancies. In some cases, to be sure, nothing can be done to prevent a miscarriage or stillbirth. However, in these cases, no one even tried to intervene or to provide a safe and humane setting for what is a physically and emotionally traumatic event. Women who experience pregnancy loss need medical attention to ensure that the miscarriage is complete and to monitor the possibility of infection or hemorrhage.

In the summer of 2007, a young African American woman named

Shakira Staten gave birth alone in the Lackawanna County Prison in Pennsylvania. Staten was brought from her cell to the medical ward around midnight, and when a nurse decided that her contractions weren't "consistent enough," she was placed in an individual locked cell. The cell had a closed-circuit camera, but the only way to get anyone's attention was to yell, pound on the door, or lob wet toilet paper at the camera. Guards, not nurses, monitored the cell. Whenever she could get anyone to listen to her, Staten said that she needed to go to the hospital. At one point, she got down on her hands and knees to try to keep the baby from coming out, but the guards just told her to stay in her cell, which is where she wound up giving birth, all alone.

Staten's family broke the story to the local media, where it received extensive coverage. In the controversy that ensued, prison officials first denied any wrongdoing, and then suggested that Staten had planned to give birth in the prison so that she could sue the government and get the charges against her dropped. According to internal prison records, prison personnel said that Staten was dancing and singing, "I got it! I got it! I'm in the money," after seeing her story in the paper.[19] This far-fetched accusation relied on insidious stereotypes of African American women as welfare cheats, out to fleece the system. Since the time of Ronald Reagan, conservatives have used the idea of welfare fraud and the image of the "welfare queen" "to portray an image of widespread depravity and criminality among low-income women of color."[20] Here was a young woman of color, a young mother, locked up for criminal charges, a perfect screen for such projections, especially if they could deflect attention from the prison's own failures. After weeks of negative publicity, the county prison board apologized to Ms. Staten.

Unfortunately for Staten, her lawsuit against the prison for violating her right to medical care was dismissed in 2010 because her lawyer missed filing deadlines. After the dismissal, she said, "I just can't believe I had to bring a child into the world like I did."

While most women who have babies in a prison cell are not subject to the kind of pillorying that Staten was, their stories do share certain elements in common: No one believes women when they say they are in labor, and no one conducts a proper exam to check for signs of labor. Sometimes, it becomes clear after the fact that the prison staff had no way to monitor contractions or no skill in this area. All too often, corrections officers who have no medical training make judgment calls about complicated medical issues.

Pregnancy care policies are notably silent on when to take a woman in labor to the hospital. In New York, for example, not a single county jail has a written policy explaining when to take a woman in labor to the hospital. And yet the details of such policies, where they do exist, can be problematic. When writing a policy in the aftermath of Staten's prison cell birth, for example, the co-owner of the private medical company proposed taking women to the hospital if they are at least twenty-four weeks pregnant and have been having contractions for at least an hour, or if the contractions are five minutes or less apart. His reasons for setting the threshold at twenty-four weeks are deeply troubling. First, he said that a fetus of less than twenty-four-weeks gestation probably wouldn't survive anyway, implying that a woman experiencing pregnancy loss at twenty-three weeks would not require medical attention outside the prison; and second, he said that pregnant women might "abuse" the system by insisting on going to the hospital each time they had a contraction.

Women who do make it to a hospital are often taken there in shackles, labor in shackles, and may even give birth chained to the hospital bed. Casandra Brawley had a baby while she was serving time at the Washington Corrections Center for Women. When the prison nurse decided to send Brawley to the hospital, corrections officers first strip-searched her and then placed her in full restraints, including a metal chain around her full-term belly and handcuffs that bound her hands to the waist chain. The officers kept one of her ankles shackled to the bed at the hospital, even after an epidural, removing the leg iron only during her cesarean surgery. After the ordeal, Brawley, said, "I am still a person and I didn't feel like I should be treated like a caged animal."

International human rights organizations and national medical, public health, and legal associations oppose the shackling of laboring women as demeaning, dangerous, and unnecessary. An emerging consensus in the federal courts agrees with this view, holding that such shackling amounts to cruel and unusual punishment. Until 2008 only three states had statutes limiting the use of restraints on women in labor. Since then, thanks in large part to coalitions spearheaded by reproductive justice, civil rights, and medical advocates, nineteen additional states and the District of Columbia have passed laws to restrict this practice.[21] The laws vary in scope, from those that limit the use of restraints throughout pregnancy to those that set limits only when women are in "active" labor and giving birth. While these laws represent important progress in recognizing the problem, they have not solved the problem, because they lack meaningful enforcement provisions and consequences for violating the law. Without constant monitoring and advocacy from groups in the community, these laws may be no more than symbolic victories.

Finally, prisons and jails neglect the needs of women separated from their newborn babies. They fail to provide appropriate postpartum care, counseling, or any physical comfort. Some prisons give women less than twenty-four hours in the hospital before bringing them back to prison, and women report that they go without six-week checkups or the care needed to heal properly from a cesarean delivery. After giving birth in the secure ward of the Denver Health Medical Center, twenty-two-year-old Maria Casillas was returned to jail, where she was subjected to the typical strip-search routine, ordered to bend over, expose herself, and cough repeatedly: "I had six stitches and it hurt. I told them, 'I just had a baby. It hurts.' They said they didn't care and told me to cough harder.'"[22]

Mass Imprisonment as a Barrier to Reproductive Justice

> *I think these kinds of stories get people to realize that the people we put in prison are still human beings and they are our neighbors and friends and, if not, they will be when they get out.—Catherine Wise, Pennsylvania Prison Society.*

As the stories above show, problems with pregnancy-related medical care behind prison walls are widespread. In some ways, helping women to obtain abortion care is more clear-cut. Abortion is an either-or situation—either a woman will be able to terminate her pregnancy or not—while prenatal care can be a more ambiguous matter of whether the quality of care is so bad as to be unconstitutional. Because women have a well-established right to terminate a pregnancy, petitioning federal judges to order a jail or prison to take a woman for an abortion has worked very well. Local judges have been less receptive, and have even been the ones to block access, as the case from Cleveland demonstrates. The key is for women to be able to connect with organizations such as the ACLU Reproductive Freedom Project and the National Network of Abortion Funds that can get their case before a federal judge and provide the financial assistance they need to carry out their decisions. Lawyers have also engaged in administrative advocacy short of going to court, and this has improved women's access to abortion, but is also subject to backsliding when prison and jail administrators change.

There is no reason to believe that the US system of imprisonment will ever be able to consistently deliver constitutional standards of confinement or medical care. The sheer size of the US prison system, the decentralized and increasingly privatized nature of the system, and the general disregard for the humanity of people in prison are formidable barriers to positive change. A class action lawsuit against the state of California lays bare the problem: the federal judge presiding over the lawsuit was moved to place the entire system into receivership by the "uncontested" finding of a court-appointed expert "that a prisoner needlessly dies an average of roughly once a week" from neglect or incompetence.[23]

While it is crucial to stand up for better treatment of people inside prison, it is not enough. It is also essential to work on several other fronts. First, we must reduce the number of people who wind up in prison to begin with. This is a multifaceted challenge in itself that includes working to change the goals of policing; eliminate the use of cash bail systems that keep so many lower-income people in jail before trial, something that increases their chances of being convicted and sentenced to time behind bars; repeal mandatory sentencing laws; and change the parole and probation practices that send so many people back to prison for technical violations such as missing an appointment with their parole officer. Second, we must improve the prospects for people who are released so that they can have a realistic chance of staying out of prison. This means dismantling barriers to public assistance, employment, and other resources that people need to build a secure life. And, third, we must limit the harms inflicted on children whose parents go to prison. This means adopting policy changes that respect parent-child bonds and support other vital family relationships to ensure children's emotional and physical security during periods of separation, including alternative sentences for people who have primary caregiving responsibilities for children.

Analyzing imprisonment through the lens of reproductive justice has the potential to alter the way people think about prisons and enlarge the circle of those who care about what goes on inside prisons. First, including imprisonment on the reproductive justice agenda brings it to the attention of reproductive health and rights organizations. Second, the reproductive justice framework recognizes both the individual harms suffered by people inside prison and the impact of imprisonment on communities. While this chapter has focused on direct harms to women, the imprisonment of men certainly affects women, families, and neighborhoods. Racial patterns of incarceration are similar for women and men, but the incarceration rates of men are much higher; in 2005, for instance, more than half a million African American men ages twenty to thirty nine served time behind bars. Across the country, in the poorest neighborhoods, political geographers have identified "million dollar blocks"—city blocks where so many residents have been sent to prison that the cost of their incarceration will exceed one million dollars.

Today, the United States leads the world in incarceration, but not in public education, health status, or life expectancy. This dubious distinction costs taxpayers about eighty billion dollars a year. The decision to invest so heavily in prisons drains money away from such critical needs as good schools, healthcare, and environmental protection. Without a shift in political priorities, we will not achieve a society that embodies principles of reproductive justice. At the same time, the very idea of reproductive justice may provide a new way to understand the problems of people in prison and the ways that the overarching problem of mass imprisonment affects us all.[24]

Postscript: This anthology went to press in the wake of the 2016 presidential election. As a result, many more people are living in fear and vulnerable to arrest and imprisonment. The new administration promises to deport undocumented immigrants by the millions and revive the War on Drugs even as some states are moving to decriminalize marijuana and find better ways to treat people who use heroin and prescription pain medication than criminalization. This shift in power makes reproductive justice all the more important as an organizing tool and vision for the future.

Notes

1. A note on terminology: While prisons, jails, and immigration "detention centers" are distinct types of institutions administered by different government agencies, I sometimes use the term "prison" generically to encompass all forms of involuntary confinement by the state.
2. Asian Communities for Reproductive Justice, "What is Reproductive Justice?" Forward Together, accessed 2016, http://strongfamiliesmovement.org/what-is-reproductive-justice.
3. Estelle v. Gamble, 429 US 97 (1976), 103.
4. NCCHC (National Commission on Correctional Health Care), *NCCHC Annual Report* (Chicago, 2011).
5. ACLU v. Danberg, C.A. No. 06C-08-067-JRS (Delaware Super. Ct. 2006)
6. Erika Kates, "Gender and Justice Project on Female Offenders, 2009–2012," Wellesley Centers for Women (2012), 1.
7. Aleks Kajstura and Russ Immarigeon, "States of Women's Incarceration: The Global Context" (Prison Policy Initiative, 2015).
8. Danielle Kaeble and Thomas P. Bonczar, *Probation and Parole in the United States, 2015* (Washington, DC: United States Bureau of Justice Statistics, 2016).

9. Women in Prison Project, "Women in Prison Fact Sheet," Correctional Association of New York, March 2006, http://www.correctionalassociation.org/wp-content/uploads/2012/05/Women_in_Prison_Fact_Sheet_2006.pdf.

10. Marc Mauer, "The Changing Racial Dynamics of Women's Incarceration" (Washington, DC: The Sentencing Project, 2013), 10.

11. Lauren E. Glaze and Laura M. Maruschack, *Parents in Prison and Their Minor Children*, (Washington, DC: United States Bureau of Justice Statistics, 2008, revised 2010).

12. Carolyn Sufrin, Alexa Kolbi-Molinas, and Rachel Roth "Reproductive Justice, Health Care Disparities, and Incarcerated Women in the United States," *Perspectives on Sexual and Reproductive Health* 47, no. 4 (2015).

13. These states are California, Colorado, Nebraska, New Mexico, New York, and Washington. The New York and Washington laws afford families the most flexibility to protect parent-child relationships.

14. Reproductive Rights Project, "Access to Reproductive Health Care in New York State Jails," New York Civil Liberties Union, last updated 2008, https://www.nyclu.org/sites/default/files/publications/nyclu_pub_healthcare_jails.pdf.

15. Monmouth County Correctional Institute Inmates v. Lanzaro, 34 F.2d 326 (3rd Cir. 1987).

16. Doe v. Arpaio, 1 CA-CV 05-0835, (January 23, 2007).

17. Carole Schroeder and Janice Bell, "Doula Birth Support for Incarcerated Pregnant Women," *Public Health Nursing* 22, no. 1 (2005), 55.

18. Letter to Legal Services for Prisoners with Children, quoted with permission.

19. Borys Krawczeniuk, "Inmate Accused of Planning Birth," *Times-Tribune*, August 22, 2007.

20. Kaaryn Gustafson, "To Punish the Poor: Criminalizing Trends in the Welfare State," (working paper, Women of Color Resource Center, Oakland, CA, 2003), 5.

21. As of December 2016, the twenty-two states with laws against shackling are: AZ, CA, CO, DE, FL, HI, ID, IL, LA, ME, MD, MA, MN, NV, NM, NY, PA, RI, TX, VT, WA, WV, and also DC. Federal agencies including BOP, ICE, and the Marshals Service have their own policies, but Congress has not passed a law on shackling.

22. Tina Griego, "In the Name of National Security: DIA Anti-Terror Raid, Mom's Deportation Shatter Family," *Rocky Mountain News*, December 7, 2002.

23. Jennifer Warren, "U.S. to Seize State Prison Health System; A Federal Judge, Citing Experts' Reports of Fatal Incompetence and Neglect, Will Name A Receiver for the $1.1-Billion Program," *Los Angeles Times*, July 1, 2005.

24. For complete endnotes and references, see the version of this essay posted at the Prison Policy Initiative Research Clearinghouse: https://www.prisonpolicy.org/research.html.

We Need to Talk about Disability as a Reproductive Justice Issue

KATIE O'CONNELL

At first blush, I don't appear to be disabled. Unless you notice subtle symptoms—like when I press on my sinuses, hold a hot mug or cold glass to my eyes, or am unable to find words when speaking—you might never know. But like 25.3 million other Americans, I suffer from a chronic pain condition. Between three and seven times a week, I endure migraines. Every day my neck and shoulders twinge with pain. Some weeks my nausea is so bad that I'm lucky to keep a glass of water down. When a migraine strikes, I often lose vision in one or both eyes. I'm fortunate enough now to work from home, but when I was in an office with fluorescent lights bearing down on me, bouncing off the bright white walls, I would have to leave work a few times a month with a blinding migraine. I would take the metro home, usually getting off a few stops early because the swaying of the train made me so nauseous I was going to vomit.

Every morning I take four pills, and every night I take an additional three. If it's a migraine day, and at least fifteen days of the month are, I drink a licorice-flavored powder or take the only pill that has ever worked to stop the migraine. Without insurance, some of these pills cost thousands of dollars. Every three months I go to my neurologist's office and get prescription Botox injections in my shoulders, neck, head, and face to alleviate the migraines. The next day my eyebrows make me look like Spock, and I have bloody pin pricks all over my forehead. My disability is not always visible, but it is debilitating, and it controls so much of my life.

Folks in the mainstream reproductive rights movement do not talk about disability enough. Some of this is because they do not know how to talk about it—the pro-life movement has successfully seized control of this conversation, a conversation where pro-choice activists *should* excel. The reproductive rights framework centers autonomy and self-determination, concepts that are very familiar to those in disability rights activism. Instead, a pro-life movement of misogynists, racists, and sometimes violent terrorists have historically made more concerted efforts to include people who are disabled, as well as their communities and concerns, in their public messaging. Fetal disability narratives are central to pro-life rhetoric, where they decry the abortion of fetuses with disabilities as a form of eugenics. Reproductive *justice* advocates have done a far better job than others in the reproductive health and rights movements in including a disability rights framework into the broader movement, but all approaches are still lacking. People with disabilities are routinely excluded from activist spaces whether that's because locations are inaccessible, actions lack online components, or hashtags like #StandwithPP are used (after all, not everyone who supports Planned Parenthood can stand).

I think there is a certain discomfort with engaging the pro-life movement on their appropriation of a disability rights framework. No one in reproductive justice wants to advocate for a position that has been accused of being eugenicist, an untrue label the pro-life movement loves to slap on people who advocate for abortion rights. They trot out the numbers of women who abort fetuses diagnosed with Down syndrome. They frame these statistics as proof of eugenics and proof that the abortion rights movement is immoral and harmful. They manipulate the numbers to claim that pro-choice activists don't care about people with disabilities. They frequently frame disability in terms of children and fetuses to avoid drawing attention to their lack of support for adults with disabilities. All in the name of winning their single-minded battle to make abortion inaccessible.

But what pro-life activists don't talk about is the infrastructure, largely of their own creation, that contributes to people aborting fetuses with disabilities. Like many women who have abortions, women who choose to abort fetuses with Down syndrome and other abnormalities often do so because they already have children they're providing for, they live in poverty, or they experience other structural oppressions that prevent them from carrying to term. (Just a quick note that I'm saying women here, because the statistics I refer to only studied cisgender women having abortions. Otherwise, I have intentionally used gender-neutral language, as I am committed to lifting the experiences of all people who have abortions, not just cisgender women.)

Studies show that between 70 and 85 percent of women with a prenatal diagnosis of Down syndrome choose abortion. It is important to recognize that some of these women may consider carrying their pregnancies to term, but in addition to other reasons they chose abortion, and are often swayed by class or another marginalized status. Children with disabilities may require costly additional care such as specialized healthcare, education, diet, therapy, and more. Parents who work outside the home already must pay exorbitantly for childcare, so parents who work outside the home and have children with disabilities must pay even more or stay home. Either way, there is a devastating loss of income. Institutions are not set up to help parents raise high-needs children, particularly when those parents face other barriers like racism, immigration status, queerphobia, and socioeconomic oppression.

Reflecting on my own experience with disability, if I were to get pregnant right now I would have no choice but to have an abortion. I cannot survive without taking my medications, and they would cause severe fetal abnormalities. Pregnancy would cause hormonal shifts that could drastically worsen my chronic migraines. Beyond that, I know motherhood would be incredibly difficult for me. This is *not* to say that people with disabilities are not fit to be parents, or cannot be good parents, but I feel that the chronic pain I experience daily precludes me from raising children. Any noise during a migraine can instantly take me from a five to a ten on the pain scale. Holding something heavy for too long can trigger a cervical spasm (in my neck) and prevent me from moving my head for a week.

I worry constantly that I will miss incredible moments in the lives of the children I don't even have. Some nights I've wept for hours just because I missed dinner with a friend. I simply can't imagine what it would be like if I had a migraine when my child had a piano recital or a big game or graduation. And most importantly, I can't fathom the regret and pain I would feel if I passed migraines on to my biological child. My grandmother, father, mother, and both sisters experience migraines to varying degrees, and the fear that any child of mine would have them is enough to make me not want to have children. Controlling my own reproductive future is absolutely vital to me as a disabled woman. It ensures I can stay on my medication guilt-free. It means I don't have to worry about passing a genetic disability onto future children. It means I can continue to afford my medications and not worry about how that money impacts my family.

Choosing not to have children due to my disability does *not* mean that I think other people with disabilities should not have children. Disability has long been an excuse for the medical establishment to forcibly sterilize women. Parents with disabilities are stigmatized as being unable to appropriately care for their children. People with disabilities are also sterilized due to the rationalization that they would birth children with disabilities, in other words, children who are considered to be undesirable and a drain on resources in the eyes of a capitalist society. Furthermore, the US Court system has repeatedly affirmed the rights of guardians of people with disabilities to request sterilizations for the people who depend on them. As Human Rights Watch has reported, some people with disabilities who are sterilized are unable to comprehend or consent to the procedure, and are particularly vulnerable.

This reprehensible practice is a damaging symptom of the larger societal narrative about people with disabilities. The narrative, as I mentioned before, is that people with disabilities are a drain on resources. We are undeserving of public funding for our care, which is why it is so expensive for families to raise children with disabilities. We are incapable of making our own decisions. We are burdens. I have heard that I am lucky to have a partner who is so understanding of my migraines, anxiety, and depression. My sister (who is on disability due to the severity of her migraines) has heard that her former partner was "brave" to be with her. We are told we are defective, defunct, and pitiable. We are told we are not worthy or capable of making our own reproductive choices, and we are not fit to be parents.

The need for reproductive justice activists to talk about disability is clear. People with disabilities and parents of children with disabilities are disadvantaged by the healthcare, childcare, education, and economic systems. In addition, it is appalling that pro-life leaders include folks with disabilities in the narratives of their movement, especially because ultimately, they do not practice what they preach. Like they do with other marginalized groups, such as women and people of color, they care about a fetus with a disability when it is in utero and then do absolutely nothing to support a child with disabilities when they are born.

We reproductive justice advocates are better than this. We want to upend these systems and make them work for marginalized people. We want all people to be in control of their reproductive futures. So, we need to talk about disability, what reproductive freedom looks like for those of us with disabilities, and what it looks like to radically change culture and institutions to better support folks with disabilities.

Reproductive Justice and Resistance at the US-Mexico Borderlands

ANNA OCHOA O'LEARY and WILLIAM PAUL SIMMONS

Introduction

Undocumented migrant women and children entering the United States through the Sonoran Corridor in Arizona encounter a series of states of exception that exacerbate their preexisting vulnerabilities. Maria Cristina Morales and Cynthia Bejarano have recently labeled this interlocking web of oppressions a form of border sexual conquest, and in this context, migrant and immigrant women are disproportionately impacted. Not only are they excluded from claiming basic rights, they are also subject to greater governmental scrutiny, and their attempts to access healthcare programs and services for monitoring their reproductive and sexual health have been increasingly obstructed. Though women's agency is severely constricted in this context, it is still present, and often manifests in unexpected ways. Drawing on research of the reproductive strategies of immigrant women, this chapter uses a reproductive justice framework to explore the creative and multiple forms of resistance employed by immigrant women to retain control of their sexual health and reproductive choices in the border region.

We begin by identifying the reproductive justice framework, which helps us to better understand the structural determinants impacting agency and resistance. We then examine a selection of Arizona laws to illustrate how they pose a threat to women's reproductive choices. Finally, we turn to two border-region studies to further explore women's agency and resistance in this context and conclude by highlighting some of the previous findings and positing questions for advancing future research.

Introducing Reproductive Justice

Attempts to understand the experiences of these women should be undertaken from a reproductive justice framework. RJ has been succinctly described by SisterSong as:

> The right to have children, not have children, and to parent the children we have in safe and healthy environments—is based on the human right to make personal decisions about one's life, and the obligation of government and society to ensure that the conditions are suitable for implementing one's decisions.[1]

The RJ movement arose out of frustration by women of color and women with limited economic means with the priorities of mainstream, mostly white women's movements. Mainstream movements have focused heavily on legal battles to ensure women the right to choose their reproductive health strategies, especially abortion. However, the reproductive justice movement problematizes the notion of choice, and focuses on social and economic obstacles to women exercising their right to choose. The RJ movement also tends to look at reproductive health in a more holistic manner, looking at issues such as miscarriage, infant mortality, maternal mortality, and pre- and postnatal care. Reproductive justice also looks at women's health within a broad range of factors that affect women's health and agency, such as women's right to work, marry whom they please, and build the type of family they want. We contend that immigration status is among the factors that must also be considered.

Reproductive justice stresses group rights and community conditions in addition to individual rights. A woman's ability to determine her reproductive destiny is based on the economic conditions and her values, and those in her community, allowing, for example, the ability of couples to limit family size if they desire. The RJ framework thus requires a more sustained engagement with structural factors and their intersections—such as the interlocking webs of immigration-control-related oppression—and more emphasis on the ways already marginalized women are further marginalized through limited reproductive choices. Nonetheless, an RJ framework argues that marginalized populations exercise agency—although constrained and socially contingent—so that phrases like unwanted or unintentional pregnancy need to be deconstructed as do the many empirical studies that seek to measure women's reproductive "choices."

Arizona's Twin Assaults on Immigrants and Reproductive Health

For nearly a decade, the border state of Arizona has sustained attacks on both migrant and reproductive rights. These attacks gained momentum in 2004 with nativist legislation coming from the Republican-controlled legislature (fig. 1). The trend culminated when the state's infamous SB 1070 was signed into law by Governor Jan Brewer in 2010. Passed because the Arizona legislature felt the federal government was not doing enough to combat illegal immigration, this "show your papers" law was widely characterized as the most extreme anti-immigrant measure of its time. It was challenged as unconstitutional and on June 25, 2012, the US Supreme Court struck down three of the contested provisions but kept in place the controversial Section 2(B), which requires law enforcement officials to check the immigration status of anyone detained for violation of any other law, including traffic violations, if they have "reasonable suspicion" that the person is in the country illegally.

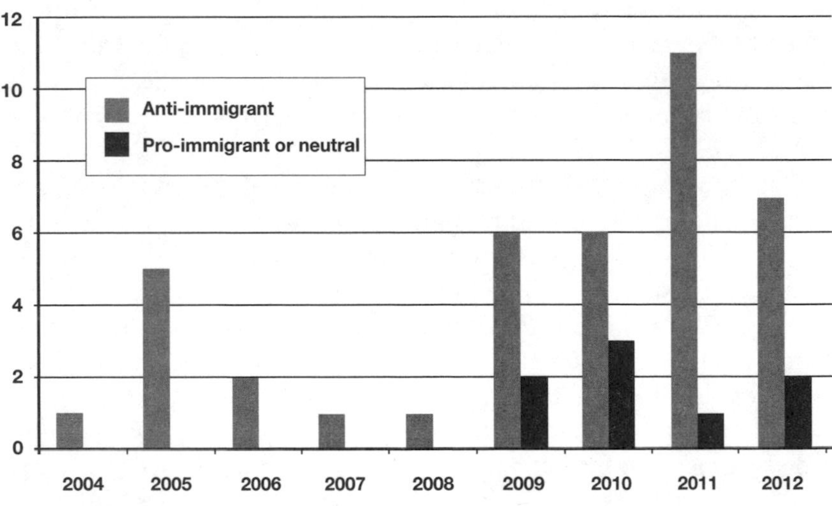

Fig. 1. Numbers of Immigration Control Laws Enacted in Arizona. Data from the National Conference of State Legislatures's Immigration Policy Project and the Arizona State Legislature website.

After SB 1070 was passed in Arizona, other state governments were emboldened to emulate the extreme effort, with many of their provisions partially blocked by the courts. However, Arizona's SB 1070 and its progeny were just the tip of the iceberg, with hundreds of laws being enacted throughout the nation. In 2006 more than five hundred anti-immigrant state bills were introduced across the United States, a trend that peaked in 2007 when the number of bills reached 1,562 as most every state in the union considered some form of immigration regulation.[2]

Laws which restrict immigrants' ability to integrate into the nation's socioeconomic fabric follow a doctrine called "attrition through enforcement" or "policies of attrition."[3] This doctrine is premised on the existence of numerous agencies imbued with inherent authority and already performing the work of immigration enforcement in one capacity or another—such as E-Verify and workplace investigations—that could, or should, be further empowered to enforce restrictions on undocumented—particularly Mexican—immigrants accessing public resources (fig. 2). The result of its application would be laws so utterly hostile to immigrants as to encourage them to "self-deport." However, the problem with this approach is the ahistorical nature of the concept, which fails to consider the long-standing geographical and international con-

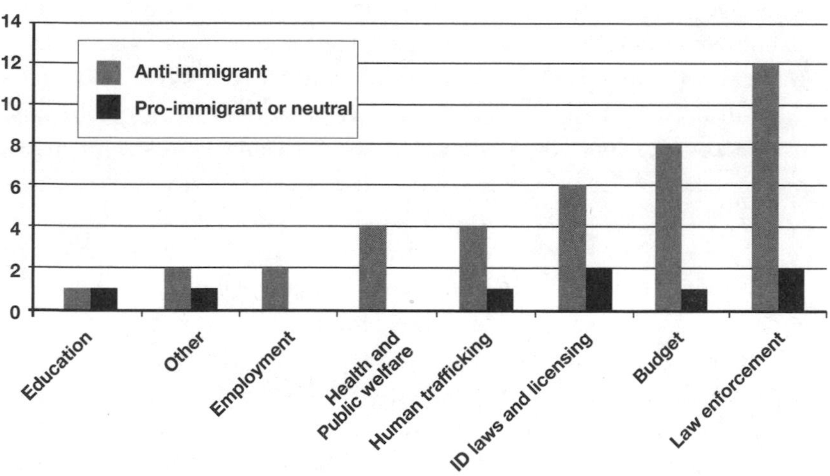

Fig. 2. Immigration Laws Enacted in Arizona by Category of Law, 2004–2012. Data from the National Conference of State Legislatures's Immigration Policy Project and the Arizona State Legislature website.

nections between the United States and Mexico forged over generations of cross-border households and other socioeconomic relationships.

In addition, immigrants have had to contend with repressive local law enforcement measures restricting their mobility. Arizona is home to the Maricopa County Sheriff's Office's notorious "crime suppression sweeps" that started in 2006. Targeting largely Latino neighborhoods, the Sheriff's Office would flood these areas with officers, but these sweeps resulted in very few arrests, mostly for petty crimes.

Anti-immigrant rhetoric together with anti-immigrant policies and media images of immigrants as criminals have pushed undocumented populations further underground. Not only are hate crimes against immigrants increasing, the upsurges nationally in anti-immigrant laws increase migrants' mistrust of law enforcement personnel and social service providers. Indeed, a recent study in Maricopa County, where Phoenix is located, showed that more than 50 percent of Latinos said "they do not feel safe when local law enforcement is involved in immigration enforcement," and close to half said they were "more afraid to leave their house because local law enforcement is involved in immigration enforcement" and thus, were "less likely to contact the police if they have been a victim of a crime because they fear they (or others around them) will be asked about their immigration status."[4] Not surprisingly, policies that repress individuals by making them afraid to leave their home have a generalized chilling effect on healthcare-seeking behaviors.

The state of Arizona passed some of "the nation's most extreme laws that limit women's right to abortion and contraceptive care," with Governor Jan Brewer being labeled one of five governors with the absolute worst records on abortion.[5] A litany of legislative measures were enacted, with many of them now tied up in the courts. For example, Arizona HB 2036, signed into law in 2012, banned almost all abortions after twenty weeks of pregnancy, with a drafting quirk that defined weeks of gestation from the last menstrual period, effectively banning all abortions after eighteen weeks, except those required by a medical emergency. The law was upheld by the federal district court, but struck down by the Ninth Circuit Court of Appeals on May 21, 2013.

HB 2800 signed into law by Arizona Governor Jan Brewer in May 2012 prohibits funding for organizations that perform or provide abortion services, essentially defunding Planned Parenthood clinics in Arizona. A federal district judge issued a temporary injunction in February 2013. However, a similar provision was added to the Medicaid expansion bill passed in 2013. Other restrictive laws remain in effect. One

2009 law requires a physician to perform all surgical and medical abortions. HB 2564, also signed into law in 2009, makes the previously mandated twenty-four-hour waiting period more draconian by requiring physicians to provide the necessary information to women in person at least twenty-four hours before the procedure, thus requiring two office visits with physicians present. The law also requires notarized parental consent to the abortion and allows providers to refuse to make available emergency contraception on "moral or religious grounds." As a consequence, Planned Parenthood was forced to stop abortions at seven of its ten Arizona offices.

In 2013 a law sponsored by Arizona state representative Steve Montenegro amended Arizona Revised Statute 13-3603.02, a class-three felony for anyone to seek an abortion based on the sex or race of the child, or the race of a parent. The law now requires that prior to an abortion, providers must obtain a signed affidavit from the mother stating that her decision is not based on the child's sex or race. Furthermore, the father or maternal grandparents are allowed to bring a civil action on behalf of the unborn child if abortion is based on sex or race selection. Medical personnel who do not report violations of this law may be charged with a felony. The law was immediately challenged by the American Civil Liberties Union, the National Association for the Advancement of Colored People, and other groups; however, the challenge was rejected by a federal district court judge in October 2013. Although the ruling will likely be appealed to the Ninth Circuit Court, the law potentially makes it more difficult for women of color to obtain an abortion and opens up women's reasons for obtaining an abortion to greater legal scrutiny.

Montenegro tried to argue that higher abortion rates among minority women were due to race-selection of fetuses, but disregarded the underlying structural factors, such as poverty and limited access to medical care, that most likely account for the higher abortion rates among resource-poor women of color.

With these laws, two seemingly contradictory trends emerge. On the one hand, health services for immigrant women to help monitor their reproductive and sexual health are being increasingly restricted or denied based on immigration status. On the other hand, there is a growing trend to limit abortion services for all women. The distinctions drawn between immigrant and nonimmigrant women resonate with arguments made by other scholars writing about the use of women's bodies to define nationhood. Referred to as "stratified reproduction," these scholars have pointed out that political power, based on the structurally unequal distribution of resources determined by existing social divisions, consequently results in the validation of the reproductive future of those with status (e.g., white women), while diminishing those of others, such as Latinas, who do not possess the same status. In Gálvez's words:

> [D]eclining birth rates are viewed as a sign of progress and civilization, enabling the fetishization of the child in elite sectors and the marginalization or even the attribution of abject status to the children of the poor. No matter how few children immigrant mothers have, their children are always excessive.[6]

Not surprisingly, the Arizona legislators who support anti-immigrant bills have often been the same ones advocating for antiabortion regulations. For instance, six of the seven legislators who cosponsored HB 2443, the law that bans abortion based upon race or gender, also cosponsored the notorious anti-immigration measure SB 1070 during the previous legislative session.

The Reproductive Justice Framework and the Borderlands

The increase of women immigrating in search of better opportunities (feminization of migration) is related to numerous factors, but can be understood within the broader context of neoliberalism and globalization. With options for entering the United States legally being increasingly restricted, many resort to living and working in the US without legal authority, and this puts women's reproductive health at greater risk.

From the start, migrant women often must navigate states of exception on their journey to the US, and because of their marginal status they are more vulnerable to sexual assault and other attacks. After reaching their destinations these women face an atmosphere where their civil and reproductive rights seem to be systematically stripped away. We can picture these women as victims of the numerous structural and political factors that cause them to migrate and affect them on the journey, and after they reach their destination, prompt questions about how they navigate these interlocking webs of oppression.

Nevertheless, very few studies have looked at reproductive health at the US-Mexico borderlands for migrant women and adolescents. Here we will focus on two major issues and how they might intersect at the borderlands: first, the effects of the violence women endure on the migrant journey itself, including the effects of polyvictimization and its sequelae on these women; and second, the ever-changing larger structural factors faced by female migrants including changing attitudes in Mexico and the acculturation process after their arrival to the United States.

Violence and the Migrant Journey

The corridors of migration are marked by both the vulnerability and agency migrants experience. These experiences themselves are couched within a series of states of exception—where a certain group becomes excluded from rights and government protection. Migration further exacerbates states of exception by the proliferation of ideas premised on binary distinctions between those with legal citizenship and those without, and in turn legitimizes the exclusion and/or demonization of groups considered to have no status. States of exception serve further to normalize a logic and the practice of mistreatment of abject groups.

Migrants, especially women and children, face harrowing paths trying to enter the US. Their journeys have become more dangerous as the border has been militarized and as migration has become a big business increasingly dominated by organized syndicates or cartels. Each year, hundreds of migrants die and countless thousands of others become lost, disoriented, dehydrated, or suffer other traumas in the deserts and mountains of the Southwest. Recent studies have documented particular risks for migrant women, especially sexual violence.

The issue of sexual assault bears weight in our discussion of reproductive justice for several reasons, not the least of which is that many (if not most) of the women migrating are of reproductive age and thus at risk for unwanted pregnancies. In one sample of sixty-six migrant women interviewed in Altar, Sonora, forty-six were of child-bearing age.[7] In spite of this, forty-nine reported that they did not have access to a medical service program, and the birth control methods used by the majority of the women interviewed were limited to condoms and oral contraceptives. Nineteen women in this study reported having had to change contraceptive methods due to their scarcity.

William Paul Simmons and Michelle Téllez found that many women experienced multiple forms of violence in their home villages, along the journey, and once they arrived in the United States. They reported a number of traumatic examples of sexual violence.[8] Marla Ann Conrad also found that many migrant women who were repatriated to Mexico reported being the victims of a number of different types of violence, including sexual violence.[9] During their migration, the women reported psychological abuse, sexual abuse, and economic abuse. It is clear the immigrant women who cross the border are already experiencing multiple vulnerabilities due to poverty, racism, discrimination, and legal status, and often feel that they are to blame for their sexual assaults. In many ways, the violence against women at the border has become normalized. A Catholic nun who works at the border noted that when she asked migrant women if they had suffered any sexual violations, the women often respond by saying "*lo normal*" (the usual). Simmons and Téllez conclude that "victimization is more of a 'condition' than an 'event.'"[10] Or, as Olivia T. Ruiz Marrujo writes, "Along the U.S.-Mexico and Mexico-Guatemala borders, sexual violence has become [a] fact of life for migrant women."[11] To illustrate, a recent report by Human Rights Watch, *Cultivating Fear: The Vulnerability of Immigrant Farmworkers in the US to Sexual Violence and Sexual Harassment*, shared the story of Patricia M., a migrant farmworker raped by the foreman. With no family in the United States, she did not tell a soul, saying, "I felt very sad and very alone." There was no other work available, so her only option was to continue working at the farm. "He kept raping me and I let him because I didn't want him to hit me. I didn't want to feel pain." Patricia eventually found out she was pregnant.[12]

The physical, psychological, and social effects of the abuses women endure are complex, iterative, and long-lasting. Recent research has shown that this form of multiple victimization, or polyvictimization, is especially pernicious, with each instance of abuse having a cumulative effect on the victim's physical and mental health. Unfortunately, social services set up to protect and aid these victims in Mexico's northern border regions (such as in the state of Sonora) are overwhelmed by the sheer number of cases, and they are mostly ill-prepared to deal with multiple victimizations. Migrant women and children, facing the plethora of anti-immigrant laws in Arizona and beyond, must navigate an increasingly byzantine process just to receive the most basic of physical care. Such laws lay siege to almost every aspect of immigrant's livelihood from employment to education to health.

Indeed, we would expect that anti-immigrant and anti-reproductive-choice laws create a culture of fear and confusion for many migrant women and serve as yet another form of violence they are subject to. Immigrant women who are already marginalized by their status and the various structural, physical, and daily violence they already face, are not met with humane policies once they arrive in the US, but with more violence. The polyvictimization and its sequelae are undoubtedly exacerbated by federal and state policies.

Changing Attitudes about Reproduction and Acculturation

We would expect dramatic disparities in accessing reproductive health services for populations of immigrant women, as studies in many countries have documented much poorer health outcomes for immigrants. In addition, many studies document the distinctions between US-born and migrant women's reproductive health. Immigrant women have been found to be very concerned about their reproductive health but possess limited knowledge about choices and limited access to health programs. In general, "immigrant women are less likely to receive adequate reproductive healthcare, including cervical and breast cancer screening and treatment, family planning services, HIV/AIDS testing and treatment, accurate sex education and culturally and linguistically competent services."[13] A study of Mexican-immigrant women in New York City found that women had little knowledge about contraception and did not often see healthcare providers until they were pregnant.[14] Further, according to a policy analysis by the National Latina Institute for Reproductive Health (NLIRH), "The majority of undocumented immigrant women do not have access to affordable health insurance."[15]

It is also necessary to include an understanding of preexisting attitudes toward fertility and knowledge about contraception carried by migrant women as they move to new destinations. Often ignored are the perceptions migrant women retain from the social policies and attitudes toward family size in their sending countries. Francine D. Blau has argued that immigrant women mimic the fertility in their countries of origin and therefore it is important to acknowledge the changes we see in immigrant fertility of Mexican immigrant women in the United States as strongly related to changes in Mexico.[16] Mexico has undertaken significant and successful measures to curb population grown over the years, and a review of the scholarly literature indicates that shifts in attitudes about fertility and corresponding behaviors have been developing for over twenty years. Mexico has undertaken several initiatives to improve reproductive health including the establishment of a Directorate of Reproductive Health in 1995 and providing free treatment for HIV/

AIDS. Mexico has also established a series of policies to benefit the most vulnerable parts of the population. In 2007 Mexico passed a national law decriminalizing abortion during the first twelve weeks of pregnancy. Though many Mexican states have not yet allowed access to abortion, Mexico City provides both public-sector and private abortions, and as of 2012, more than eighty-nine thousand abortions have been performed. Further, the use of contraceptives has increased significantly in the past twenty years as has the "unmet need for contraception."[17] In this way, Mexico's role in forging pathways by which reproductive justice is articulated, understood, and respected must be considered in the attitudinal shifts among immigrant and migrant women.

Once in the United States, research shows that choices about family size and the spacing of children are also commonly influenced by acculturation and desires to provide them a higher quality of life. Moreover, the longer women remain in the United States, the more empowered they are likely to feel to take increased agency over their reproductive heath. The ability to control the number and spacing of children also enhances employment possibilities and economic earnings, which when considered with the importance of financial remittances to communities back home, provides a pathway toward greater social status.

Acculturation, the adaptation to different cultural values and behaviors of the United States that comes through the inherently strong connections with other Latinas in the United States and over generations, is also important to consider in this discussion. In her 2009 study, "Differences in Contraceptive Use across Generations of Migration among Women of Mexican Origin," Ellen K. Wilson finds very little change in contraceptive use between first-generation and 1.5-generation—migrants brought to the US as young children—Mexican immigrant women, but the acculturative change is markedly more dramatic between generation 1.5 and US-born women of Mexican origin.[18] In this regard, it is necessary to consider emerging thoughts among more contemporary Latinas as important conduits for acculturation and change. Although other factors have been systematically explored to gauge the impact of acculturation—such as sexual activity, health insurance coverage, education, marital status, income, work, and religiosity—here we will focus on the use and attitudes toward abortion and sterilization.

Christine Dehlendorf and Tracy Weitz report that Latinas have abortions at more than twice the rate of non-Hispanic white women, though less than African Americans.[19] However, another study by the NLIRH reports that much of this disparity can be traced to higher numbers of unintended pregnancies. Wilson finds that Mexican American women are more like to have unintended pregnancies, compared to immigrant women.[20] The NLIRH reports that when Latinas become pregnant, they are only somewhat more likely to have an abortion compared to white women. In 2004, 22 percent of Latinas' pregnancies ended in abortion, compared to 15 percent of pregnancies among white women."[21] Despite these higher percentages, Dehlendorf and Weitz convincingly argue that women of color and lower-income women suffer from a lack of access to abortion services, which can be largely traced to costs and difficulties in finding abortion providers.[22] Consistent with this contention are findings from Wilson showing that among Latina women in their twenties and those thirty or older, the only mediating variable that had a statistically significant association with contraceptive use among different generations of Latina women was poverty.[23]

These reports and research studies call into question those cultural theories around unintended births in the Latina community that claim that Latinas/os are more "pro-life." For instance, a survey by NLIRH found that Latina women show strong support for access to legalized abortion. For example, 74 percent of Latino/a registered voters agree that a woman has a right to make her own personal, private decisions about abortion without politicians interfering, and 67 percent of Latino/a voters say they would give support to a close friend or family member who had an abortion. The survey also found that Latina women strongly opposed government policies that create obstacles to obtaining an abortion. They also indicated that they were willing to disagree with church leaders on abortion issues; 68 percent agreed with the statement, "Even though church leaders take a position against abortion, when it comes to the law, I believe it should remain legal."

Many RJ advocates worry that sterilization is overrecommended to Latinas and other communities of color. Sterilization is one of the most effective but more expensive of contraceptive options and must be considered in light of larger constraints to accessing healthcare programs. Anna Ochoa O'Leary et al. contend that it may be that increased restrictions to accessing these programs in the United States force immigrant women to consider sterilization as a viable option.[24] The use of surgical sterilization was the most common method of birth control by the eighty women surveyed in research by O'Leary and Azucena Sanchez.[25] Most notable was that this was the most common method of contraception in participants from a subsample of women who belonged to households where they or a member of the family were undocumented. Indeed, Joseph E. Potter et al. found that among Latinas in El Paso, Texas, there was a large unmet need for sterilization "at nine months [from the baseline survey], 65% wanted no more children, and of these, 72% wanted sterilization. Only five of the women interviewed at 18 months had undergone sterilization." Reasons for not getting sterilization included "not having signed the Medicaid consent form in time and having been told that they were too young or there was no funding for the procedure."[26]

In sum, despite the numerous structural obstacles to immigrant women's reproductive health, there is some evidence of women's agency in these studies—much of which can be traced to both the early formation in attitudes about family size—institutionalized through various national-level family planning programs in Mexico, and their settlement among previous generations of Latinas in the United States whose notions about reproductive self-determination shows a growing alignment with the principles of reproductive justice.

Empirical Studies of Reproductive Justice at the Borderlands

In the most thorough studies of women's reproductive health at the borderlands, the "Border Contraceptive Access Studies," immigration and documentation were not explicitly considered in the analysis as the researchers were focused on influencing the availability of over-the-counter (OTC) birth control. These well-designed surveys included over one thousand women in the El Paso area, approximately half of whom used birth control pills obtained as OTC medication in a pharmacy in Ciudad Juárez, across the border from El Paso, and half got theirs from a clinic in the United States. Interestingly, the border had little direct relevance in this study, besides allowing the researchers to conduct a natural experiment on OTC versus prescription medication. According to Kimberly Inez McGuire, Associate Director of Government Relations and Public Affairs at NLIRH, "Immigrant women in Texas tell us that accessing birth control, cervical cancer screening, and other reproductive care is so difficult here in the United States, they're forced to cross into Mexico in order to get the care they need."[27]

In a second study, the reproductive healthcare strategies of a small sample of immigrant women and their access to these services subsequent to greater anti-immigrant laws in Arizona were studied in 2008–2009 in Tucson, Arizona. For the research, eighty immigrant women were interviewed using a short demographic and health indicators survey with both open- and closed-ended questions. Researchers partnered with the Mexican Consulate's health referral program, *Ventanilla de Salud*, and El Rio Community Health Center to help recruit research participants. From the data, two subsamples (C and D) were constructed. Using proxy variables extracted from the open-ended questions, the researchers determined those participants in whose households all members were regularized family members or US citizens (for subsample C), or if an undocumented member was present (subsample D). In some cases, the interviewed women were undocumented.

Figure 3 shows the distribution of the sample of women by their period of entry into the United States. To determine the relation between women's reproductive life cycles and the timing of migration, the period of entry into the United States was contextualized within recent major economic developments. The time periods were divided in three major categories: pre-NAFTA, post-NAFTA, and pre-Recession. The pre-NAFTA category includes the women who had been living in the United States fifteen to thirty years or more before NAFTA went into effect in January of 1994. NAFTA undermined many subsistence economies in Mexico, forcing many women to migrate.[28] Not surprisingly, the ma-

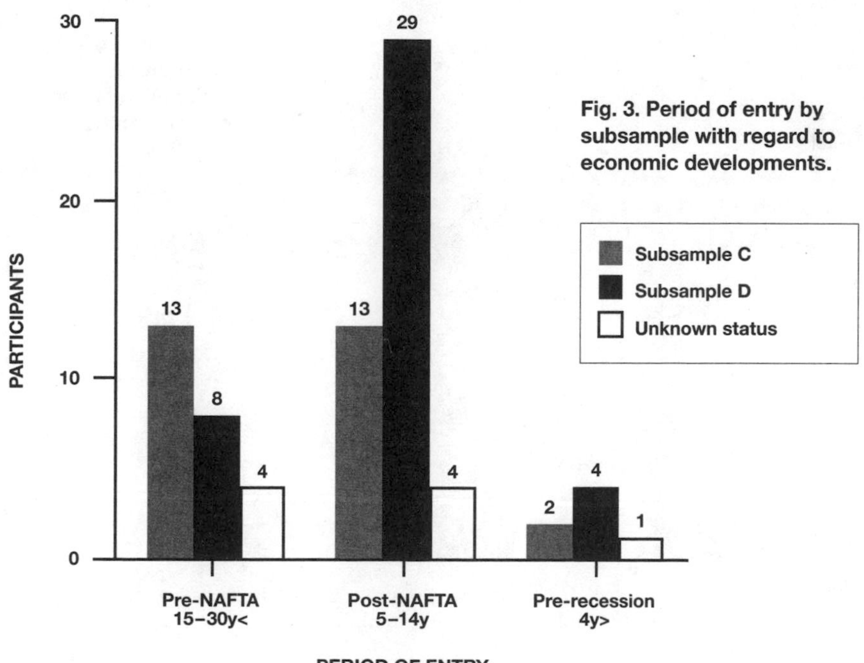

Fig. 3. Period of entry by subsample with regard to economic developments.

jority of the women who are part of the subsample D (n=29) entered into the US after NAFTA came into force. Moreover, with more women entering the United States during prime reproductive age, the probability that they would give birth to children in the United States was also affirmed. Moreover, and as figure 4 illustrates, most of the participants entered the US after NAFTA: twenty-one of them entered with their Mexican children and twenty-three later gave birth in the United States. In this way, the consequences of women's migration at peak productive and reproductive age may be one of the least understood consequences of NAFTA.

The results of this study show that even before the proliferation of state immigration control laws from 2004 to 2008, the rate of birth among immigrant women had been steadily declining and is consistent with a 2012 Pew Research analysis that shows that the plunge in births by immigrant women started with the 2007 to 2008 Great Recession. The Tucson research reveals another important point: immigrant women from subsample D (n= 39) were using the most effective contraceptive methods (hormonal and surgical). This preference could be a strategy to adapt to the restrictive policies regarding immigration and access to public healthcare services. The narratives indicated an under-

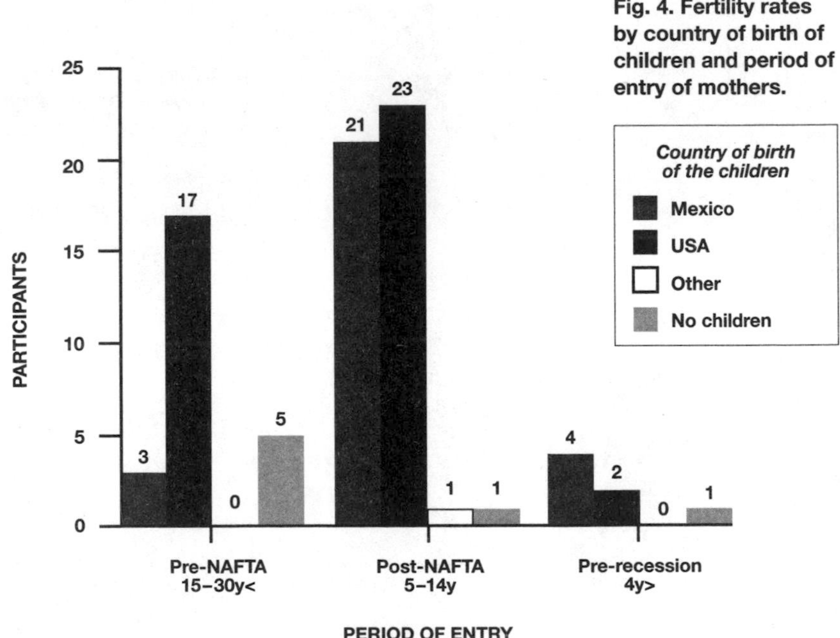

Fig. 4. Fertility rates by country of birth of children and period of entry of mothers.

standing that by having fewer children, the women could better provide for them. However, it cannot be ignored that the two dominant birth control methods used are also the most cost effective.

A content analysis of the open-ended responses by the women from subsample D indicates it is very stressful for them to apply for healthcare services because they fear being humiliated or being further scrutinized. Arizona law requires the agencies administrating healthcare applications to report those that they suspect as being in the United States unlawfully, potentially resulting in their deportation.

Conclusion: Toward Reproductive Self-Determination

Despite unprecedented recessionary budget crises across the nation, state legislatures have paid inordinate attention to stripping away the rights of migrants and women. Alyshia Gálvez has argued that the fertility of immigrant women, and in particular Mexican immigrant women, has drawn tremendous but unwarranted scrutiny from lawmakers who see them as a drain on public coffers.[29] The idea that their supposed excessive fertility amidst poverty is irresponsible and an affront to progress has been used to garner support for more laws restricting their access to public services. As Jonathan Xavier Inda has pointed out, in the mid-1990s, policymakers became increasingly focused on cost studies that calculated the "price tag" of providing public services to undocumented women and their children.[30] Such studies not only estimated the public costs incurred for Medicaid financed births (including prenatal care), but also the costs of the postnatal care of immigrant women and their children (including supplemental nutritional programs). Immigrant women were largely scapegoated in the 1994 campaign for California's failed Proposition 187.[31] Not surprisingly, with marginalized sectors of society becoming more visible, and more children in schools and health facilities by 1995, US lawmakers legislated the Personal Responsibility and Work Opportunity Reconciliation Act of 1996 which brought greater restrictions on women's access to healthcare services and social safety net programs at a critical time when migration from NAFTA-affected areas would surge.

But herein lies an important contradiction. On the one hand, access to health services that so-called hyperfertile immigrant women might use to control the number and spacing of children is increasingly denied them, and on the other, the right to access abortion and family-planning services such as Planned Parenthood is also being challenged.

However, it is our contention that though women's agency is severely constricted in the context of migration, it is still present and manifests in many, often unexpected ways. Based on the empirical studies, women use various strategies to circumvent restrictions on their ability to make decisions about their reproductive and sexual health. If the woman is ineligible for services in the United States, she may opt for surgical sterilization or buy OTC contraceptives or abortifacients in Mexico, where they are more accessible and less expensive. If women cannot cross into Mexico due to their immigration status, others buy the medications for them. Many immigrant women are teaching their children about abstinence and birth control and encouraging sex education. However, often these familes must pay full price for their medical services, potentially incurring long-term debt.

An understanding of the economic imperatives of how women are strategizing their reproductive choices highlights their agency against great odds. Unfortunately, the academic literature has failed to keep pace with the lived experiences of these women. This neglect is in part because of the twin attacks on immigrant women that make it very difficult to conduct interviews with this marginalized group, especially if they are undocumented. However, applying the reproductive justice framework to the reproductive health of migrants in Arizona raises some fundamental questions that should be addressed in a more sustained fashion. These include:

1. How do abortion restriction laws differentially impact women at different places in their reproductive life cycle?
2. Even if the laws do not directly target Latina women in general, how does the acrimonious atmosphere created around immigrant women impact them?
3. How are the sensibilities of immigrant women impacted by the harsh political rhetoric characterizing them as public welfare burdens and their infants as "anchor babies"?
4. How are reproductive rights experienced by immigrant women, and how do these experiences compare to their expectations?
5. How do the multiple forms of violence these women face affect their reproductive health?

To be sure, overall immigration from Mexico and Latin America has been decreasing sharply since the 2008 US economic recession—also often attributed to increased border enforcement—but foreign-born women still represent a significant portion of all mothers giving birth in the United States. There is strong historical evidence that anti-immigrant sentiment may be weighing heavily on immigrant women as their reproductive choices increasingly become the objects of greater governmental scrutiny. In this context, immigrant women are doubly impacted as their attempts to access healthcare programs and services for family planning information, professional advice, and for monitoring contraceptive use are becoming increasingly restricted. As of this writing, little empirical work has been done on the reproductive choices of immigrant women in the borderlands, where they may suffer greater repression, as a way to understand the reproductive health strategies of immigrant women throughout the United States.

Acknowledgments

The authors would like to thank students Laura Abril Rios-Rivera from the Universidad Autónoma de México and Aungelique Rodriguez from the University of Arizona Summer Research Institute Program for their assistance.

Notes

1. "Why Is Reproductive Justice Important for Women of Color?" SisterSong, last accessed 2012, http://www.sistersong.net/index.php?option=com%5Fcontent&view=article&id=141<emid=81.

2. Helen M. Harnett, "State and Local Anti-Immigrant Initiatives: Can They Withstand Legal Scrutiny?" *Widener Law Journal* 17 (2008): 365–82.

3. Jessica Vaughan, "Attrition through Enforcement: A Cost-Effective Strategy to Shrink the Illegal Population," April 2006, Center for Immigration Studies, http://cis.org/node/645.

4. Cecilia Menjívar and William Paul Simmons, "Insecure Communities in Maricopa County: Latino Perceptions of Police Involvement in Immigration Enforcement," (report presented at the Insecure Communities and Community Mistrust forum, Phoenix, AZ, December 11, 2013), 2.

5. Alison Tanner, "5 Governors with the Absolute Worst Records on Abortion," *Mic*, December 19, 2012, https://mic.com/articles/21122/5-governors-with-the-absolute-worst-records-on-abortion#.yoPTldDbM.

6. Alyshia Gálvez, *Patient Citizens, Immigrant Mothers: Mexican Women, Public Prenatal Care, and the Birth Weight Paradox* (New Brunswick, NJ: Rutgers University Press, 2011), 31.

7. Anna Ochoa O'Leary and Gloria Ciria Valdéz-Gardea, "Neoliberalizing (Re)production: Women, Migration, and Family Planning in the Peripheries of the State," in *Feminist (Im)Mobilities in Fortress(ing) North America: Rights, Citizenships, and Identities in Transnational Perpective*, ed. Anne Sisson Runyan, Amy Lind, Patricia McDermott, and Marianne H. Marchand (Farnham, UK: Ashgate), 75–94.

8. William Paul Simmons and Michelle Téllez, "Sexual Violence against Migrant Women and Children in Arizona," in *Binational Human Rights: The U.S.-Mexico Experience*, ed. William Paul Simmons and Carol Mueller (Philadelphia: University of Pennsylvania Press, 2014), 55–86.

9. Marla Ann Conrad, "Women's Testimonios of Life and Migration in el Cruce" (master's thesis, Arizona State University, 2013).

10. Simmons and Téllez, "Sexual Violence."

11. Olivia T. Ruiz Marrujo, "Women, Migration, and Sexual Violence: Lessons from Mexico's Borders" in *Human Rights along the U.S.-Mexico Border*, ed. Kathleen Staudt, Tony Payan, and Z. Anthony Kruszewski (Tucson: University of Arizona Press, 2009), 31.

12. Human Rights Watch, *Cultivating Fear: The Vulnerability of Immigrant Farmworkers in the US to Sexual Violence and Sexual Harassment*, May 15, 2012, http://www.hrw.org/sites/default/files/reports/us0512ForUpload_1.pdf.

13. National Latina Institute for Reproductive Health, "What We Do: Immigrant Rights," Last updated 2014, http://www.latinainstitute.org/en/what-we-do/immigrant-women.

14. Gabriela S. Betancourt, Lisa Colarossi, and Amanda Perez. "Factors Associated with Sexual and Reproductive Health Care by Mexican Immigrant Women in New York City: A Mixed Method Study," *Journal of Immigrant and Minority Health* 15, no. 2 (2013): 326–33.

15. National Latina Institute, "What We Do."

16. Francine D. Blau, "The Fertility of Immigrant Women: Evidence from the High-Fertility Source Countries," in *Immigration and the Workforce: Economic Consequences for the United States and Source Areas*, ed. George J. Borjas and Richard B. Freeman (Chicago: University of Chicago Press, 1993).

17. Davida Becker and Claudia Díaz Olavarrieta, "Decriminalization of Abortion in Mexico City: The Effects on Women's Reproductive Rights," *American Journal of Public Health* 103, no. 4 (2013): 590–93.

18. Ellen K. Wilson, "Differences in Contraceptive Use across Generations of Migration among Women of Mexican Origin," *Maternal and Child Health Journal* 13, no. 5 (2009): 641–51.

19. Christine Dehlendorf and Tracy Weitz, "Access to Abortion Services: A Neglected Heath Disparity," *Journal of Health Care for the Poor and Underserved* 22, no. 2 (2011): 415–21.

20. Wilson, "Differences in Contraceptive Use."

21. National Latina Institute, "What We Do."

22. Dehlendorf and Weitz, "Access to Abortion."

23. Wilson, "Differences in Contraceptive Use."

24. Anna Ochoa O'Leary, Marianne Marchand, Edmundo Meza Rodriguez, Salena Meyer Loredo, and Laura Abril Rios-Rivera, "Mexican Women and Family Planning Trends: A Cross Border Synthesis" (paper selected by the Puentes Consortium, 2103).

25. Anna Ocha O'Leary and Azucena Sanchez, "Anti-immigrant Arizona: Ripple Effects and Mixed Immigration Status Households under 'Policies of Attrition' Considered," *Journal of Borderlands Studies* 26, no. 1 (2011): 115–33.

26. Joseph E. Potter, Kari White, Kristine Hopkins, Jon Amastae, and Daniel Grossman, "Clinic Versus Over-the-Counter Access to Oral Contraception: Choices Women Make along the US-Mexico Border," *American Journal of Public Health* 100, no. 6 (2010): 228.

27. Michelle Chen, "Invisible Immigrants: What Will Immigration Reform Mean for Migrant Women?" *Dissent*, April 24, 2013, https://www.dissentmagazine.org/online_articles/immigration-without-women.

28. Anna Ochoa O'Leary and Azucena Sanchez, "Mixed-Immigration-Status Households in the Context of Arizona's Anti-immigrant Policies," in *Anti-immigrant Sentiments, Actions and Policies in North America and the European Union*, ed. Maonica Verea. (Mexico City: Centro de Investigación sobre América del Norte de la Universidad Autónoma de Mexico, 2012).

29. Gálvez, *Patient Citizens*.

30. Jonathan Xavier Inda, *Targeting Immigrants: Government, Technology, and Ethics* (Malden, MA: Blackwell Publishing, 2006).

31. Ibid., 104–5.

Black Women and Civic Engagement

LA'TASHA D. MAYES

"Black women were the only ones who tried to save the world Tuesday," read an article by Charles D. Ellison posted on *The Root* on November 9, 2016. This headline is the best way to describe the outcome of the 2016 presidential election and the collective feeling of the 94 percent of black women who voted for reproductive justice. In any conversation about that election—undoubtedly a watershed moment for the RJ movement—all anyone could ever say is black women showed up and showed out. Black women vote, exercise our civic duty, and lead the new American majority because of our understanding of liberty *and* liberation.

When black women vote, lead in any capacity, or run for elected office, we do it with the past, the present, and the future in mind. Deep in our ancestry, and through a time-honored tradition of participating in the civic life of our neighborhoods and our nation, exists a ferocious resistance to reproductive oppression. Through multiple presidents, voting rights laws and restrictions, limited elected representation, a divided pro-choice/pro-life electorate, and without an influential black women's policy organization at the state and federal level, black women have boldly organized for RJ. From the West Coast to the Rust Belt to the South, black women have valued civic engagement as an essential part of growing and evolving our movement.

While black women are the literal and figurative backbone of our US democracy, white supremacy, gender discrimination, and class oppression consistently undermine our potential power. Black women breathe life into the concept of intersectionality, and our civic life intersects with our human right to control our bodies, sexuality, gender, work, reproduction, and ability to form families. Our political power at the local, state, and national levels intersects with our ability to achieve reproductive justice.

New Voices for Reproductive Justice was founded in Pittsburgh in 2004 with a commitment to civic engagement and a mission to cultivate the leadership of young women of color. Our very first campaign was to register young black women ages eighteen to thirty to vote in the 2004 presidential election. Not only did we understand the importance of winning organizing and policy victories on issues important to our constituency, but also our ability to influence the decision-making process and the civic life of our Pittsburgh community.

During those early days, we faced the reelection of President George W. Bush, and that made it imperative to build our voting power. Inspired by the leadership of black women and women of color, the March for Women's Lives in 2004 was the catalyst for the creation of not only New Voices but countless RJ organizations, and the emergence of the most brilliant minds in our movement and beyond. During the Bush era, we endured the global gag rule, inaction to approve Plan B over-the-counter, and federal abortion bans. Yet, black women still voted in every election as our basic civic duty and organized for RJ as our higher calling.

New Voices asserted our right to exist in civic spaces created to exclude us. We normalized the leadership ability of young black women while navigating a terrain dominated by middle-aged conservative white men and well-meaning second wave white feminists. Conventional wisdom was always offered as the reason why young black women had to wait "our turn" for leadership, why an RJ movement would not be successful in places like Pittsburgh, or why a black person would never be president. We knew then that this conventional wisdom was proxy for institutional racism and systemic oppression in civic and political life. This wisdom lacked imagination.

New Voices created the Voice Your Vote! Project in 2008, a pilot program to build upon our voter engagement efforts in 2004 and to turn out young black women to vote. We kept unapologetically talking about RJ. We kept showing up and demanding our seat at the table and quickly learned we had to create our own tables. New Voices kept confronting leadership that did not represent the reproductive justice interests of black women. It was almost as if our leadership, especially of young black lesbian women, was a novel trend always doubted and underestimated. We proved otherwise with the historic election of President Barack Obama in 2008.

Our RJ movement could not have foreseen the rise of Barack Obama as the leader of the United States. Both his campaign and presidency encouraged black women to experience hope, anticipate change, and celebrate black joy. President Obama's leadership meant a promise fulfilled by and for our ancestors, and a belief that RJ was possible in our lifetime. President Obama repealed the global gag rule just three days into his presidency—a powerful assertion of his commitment to RJ. In 2009 he formed the White House Council on Women and Girls that created the It's On Us culture-change campaign to end sexual assault on college campuses. That same year, he signed the Lilly Ledbetter Fair Pay Act into law to protect against pay discrimination and to advance equal pay. He also signed the Ryan White Treatment Extension Act reauthorizing the Ryan White HIV/AIDS Program that today serves over five-hundred thousand people, or approximately half of all Americans living with HIV.

President Obama appointed to the US Supreme Court Sonia Sotomayor—the first Latina and woman of color—and Elena Kagan. Our nation witnessed sweeping changes to our healthcare system through the Patient Protection and Affordable Care Act (ACA) that gave millions of Americans healthcare access in 2010. The ACA increased access to contraception despite staunch religious opposition. This legislation, also known as "Obamacare," is the hallmark of the Obama administration. President Obama directed the US Department of Justice not to defend the Defense of Marriage Act in 2011, and marriage equality became the law of the land in 2015. He signed the Violence Against Women Act that was reauthorized in 2013 and 2016, and expanded protections for Native, immigrant, and LGBTQ people.

Most recently, President Obama applauded the five-to-three Supreme Court decision in *Whole Woman's Health v. Hellerstedt* to end Targeted Regulation of Abortion Providers (TRAP) laws in 2016. In his last act for RJ, the US Department of Health and Human Services finalized regulations on Title X, prohibiting states from denying a healthcare provider funds "for reasons other than its ability to provide Title X services." These services include contraception, pregnancy testing, prenatal care, breast cancer screenings, and sexually transmitted infection testing and treatment. Many black women strongly supported the presidency of Barack Obama, his actions to advance RJ, and his legacy to codify human rights as law at the vast intersection of race and gender.

However, the Obama administration did not escape vocal criticism from black women and the RJ movement. There were significant opportunities missed to advance RJ during the Obama era. The concessions made in the ACA, beginning with the Stupak-Pitts Amendment, devastated access to abortion in health insurance plans and isolated abortion care from basic healthcare, creating a long rippling effect. That very night in 2009, black women from New Voices and across Pennsylvania were on Capitol Hill among the four hundred women of color lobbying to defeat this amendment during the SisterSong Membership meeting. When President Obama created the My Brother's Keeper Community Challenge, a noble call to action to address persistent opportunity gaps faced by boys and young men of color, black women like Kimberlé Crenshaw and her organization, the African American Policy Forum, expressed grave concern for the exclusion of girls and young women of color. One thousand women of color and two hundred black men signed open letters to President Obama to ensure gender equity. At the end of 2015, Prosperity Together, a collaboration of foundations, announced a one-hundred-million-dollar funding initiative committed to economic security focused on women and girls of color.

There were also missed opportunities during the Obama administration to dismantle the pernicious Hyde Amendment that prohibits low-income women from using Medicaid for abortion care with exceptions determined by each state. Black women like US Representative Barbara Lee lead the legislative, policy, and organizing charge to pass the Equal Access to Abortion Coverage (EACH) Woman Act in partnership with statewide policy advocacy organizations like New Voices and national policy coalitions such as In Our Own Voice: National Black Women's Reproductive Justice Agenda and All Above All.

In Our Own Voice is a pioneering national policy initiative that serves as the unified voice of black women on Capitol Hill and in the states served by its organizational partners: New Voices for Reproductive Justice in Pennsylvania and Ohio, Black Women's Health Imperative in Washington, DC, SisterLove in Georgia, Black Women for Wellness in California, SPARK Reproductive Justice NOW in Georgia, Women With a Vision in Louisiana, and SisterReach in Tennessee. In Our Own Voice launched in 2014 and focused on abortion rights and access, contraceptive equity, and comprehensive sex education. Our legislative advocacy, opinion polls, and strategic communications have benefited the entire RJ movement while centering racial justice and exposing anti-black racism among our opponents and allies. In Our Own Voice bolsters the RJ work of black women to organize locally and leverage our political power as a collective.

Black women elected President Obama with 96 percent of our vote in

2008 and 2012, making black women a powerful voting bloc in national politics. The "rising American electorate" is a term coined in 2008 by the Voter Participation Center to describe unmarried women, people of color, and young people. Another term to describe the rapidly changing demographics in our country and political landscape is the "new American majority." The latter captures more fully and accurately the power that young, unmarried people of color wield in our democracy.

According to the Higher Heights Leadership Fund and the Rutgers Center for American Women and Politics report "Voices. Votes. Leadership. The Status of Black Women in American Politics, 2015," black women surpassed all other race and gender subgroups in voter turnout in both the 2008 and 2012 presidential elections. Knowing that voting alone will not achieve liberation for black people, the question becomes how does our movement for RJ build political power through a form of civic engagement that also builds a powerful organizing base for political resistance?

New Voices for Reproductive Justice is dedicated to the health and well-being of the black women, femmes, and girls we serve in Pennsylvania and Ohio. We measure health through eight dimensions: physical, emotional, spiritual, cultural, political, economic, environmental, and social well-being. Political health and well-being means grassroots community organizing, policy advocacy, and civic engagement. Working closely with the Groundswell Fund, the largest RJ funder in the country, New Voices developed our nonpartisan Integrated Voter Engagement (IVE) program to further refine our Voice Your Vote! Project.

The IVE model is relational and not transactional, defying all ideas about how you engage marginalized voters and constituents in a process that builds voting power, cultivates an informed electorate, and alters power relationships in communities and institutions. When done well, IVE transforms the people it serves into dynamic, politically savvy leaders, organizers, advocates, and culture-change agents for radical social change. After three election cycles of implementing our IVE program, New Voices has achieved over 250,000 contacts to black women voters ages eighteen to forty-nine, black LGBTQ voters, formerly incarcerated black voters, and black youth voters. Our Voice Your Vote! Project has accelerated our organizing for RJ in Pittsburgh, where our work began, and expanded our footprint across Pennsylvania and Ohio, with offices in Philadelphia and Cleveland. Many of the black women and femmes we serve are often shocked by our knocks on their doors or phone calls to talk about reproductive justice. Moreover, they are astounded that there is an organization led by, for, and about black women, femmes, and girls that centers their lived experience.

It is imperative to develop black women and femmes as RJ champions within our families and communities, our social change movements, and the institutions that mete out oppression. Black women and femmes as candidates, elected and appointed officials, and policymakers are our reality and our future. The work of black women like Jessica Byrd, who helps black women run for political office, challenges the political machine to unhitch itself from white supremacy or implode from the inside out, given the incredible lack of representation of black women in Congress, state legislatures, and local government.

Reproductive justice activists are the best candidates for elected office because we understand the meaning of liberty and liberation is based in the power of intersectional praxis. Whether it is a city council election in Pittsburgh, a state house race in Georgia, Michigan, or Wisconsin, or women of color making herstory in the US Senate, black women are changing the political game with our movement for reproductive justice.

Black women, femmes, and girls will not try to save this world any longer. We will create our own new worlds where RJ is a human right and civic engagement is the highest standard. Intersectional liberation will be both the means and the end to race and gender oppression.

Wise Women Gathering Place: An Indigenous Community-Based Culture Project

ALICE SKENANDORE and ERIKA DERKAS

Introduction

Programs that address pregnancy, sexually transmitted infections, and sexuality for teens are tricky to administer in general, but those which simultaneously respect Native culture and language may seem more daunting. Yet more and more programs have proven possible and effective. Turning to culture, research, and proven methods to dialogue with Native youth has advanced the programs developed by Indigenous cultural projects like Wise Women Gathering Place (WWGP). WWGP ensures that young people understand in a holistic and respectful way to consider STIs, HIV, unintended pregnancies, and the risks they may run. They also learn about healthy relationships and effective communications during their stages of change. Many assume these considerations start at home or that youth get information at school, but, in reality, that may not be the case. WWGP provides resources, education, and knowledge to students, thus empowering them with accurate information on sexual health. Wise Women Gathering Place uses a midwifery-centered approach that links reproductive and birth justice to issues like violence against women, multigenerational trauma, and sexual and reproductive health.

Improving sexual health for Indigenous youth through comprehensive sexual health education is challenging in Indian country, partially because sexual and reproductive decisions are shaped by traditional and contemporary social norms, and partly due to the complex legacy of colonization. The amassed and incessant disruption of culture, family, and community regarding the health and well-being of Indigenous communities demonstrates this. Specifically, the interruption and oppression of family values and Indigenous cultural strengths created a rift in teen value systems. The forced loss of cultural resources such as land, language, and traditions affected the health and knowledge of Indigenous youth. Issues related to multigenerational cycles of single-parent families, alcoholism, and other stressed conditions limited their knowledge about relationships, sex, and sexuality.

Moreover, the historical relationship between Indian Health Services (IHS) and Native communities is fraught with exploitation and abuse. Not surprisingly, confidentiality concerns arise when seeking services from IHS. Furthermore, Native communities have a culture of acceptance regarding adolescent pregnancy and childbearing. Therefore, the need to increase self-sufficiency that ensures health and well-being for children is urgent in Indian country.

Incorporating Native American culture and language has proven effective for several programs in cutting the high rates of STIs and unplanned pregnancies in their communities. Programs including Wisconsin's WWGP, Oregon's Native STAND (Students Together Against Negative Decisions), We R Native, and *Native VOICES* are among several efforts that understand the need for a culturally sensitive curriculum to support Native youth learning the basics of sex, sexuality, and healthy lifestyles. In many ways, such programs celebrate localism, as culturally relevant information is delivered by tribal members to tribal communities who have not been afforded any other medium.

This, however, begs the question: How do tribal communities get to the point where sex education is embedded within Native teaching and understanding of sex, sexuality, and healthy lifestyles within a historical and contemporary context of dominant Western thought? Western education doesn't offer much, if anything, that is accurate about Indigenous ceremonies and teachings. Indigenous people are rallying to use cultural teachings, traditions, and the educational settings of tribal youth to develop a more respectful and mature approach to learning about these topics. Some organizations are also designing health resources to meet young people where they are: on the Internet. We R Native is a multimedia health resource for teens and young adults that includes a great deal of information about sexual health. It includes videos that approach sexual health and STI prevention with a little bit of humor and cultural relevance. *Native VOICES* is a series of twenty-three-minute educational videos that have proven to reduce STIs and increase STI testing among teens and young adults.[1] This essay focuses on the energies of Wise Women Gathering Place as one of the many successful programs enhancing resiliency among tribal youth.

History of Wise Women Gathering Place

Wise Women Gathering Place originated in 1992 with Alice Skenandore, an Indigenous community midwife. It began as a grassroots circle of Native American women holding weekly meetings around the kitchen table, with children in tow, learning about midwifery, and later including apprenticeships. The term "midwife" means attending births at home; it is a tradition among Native people throughout the world. Women gave birth to their babies assisted by caring women from their community. There is little written history from which to gain reference for this information, but according to Alice, it does stand to reason that babies were born in safe places fostered and supported by their communities.

The exact time of birth is the moment of primary imprint for both infant and mother. This is a moment of irrecoverable importance in terms of cultural, emotional, physical, and spiritual union. All cultures have a long tradition of birthing practices which support the safe birthing of infants and sustain the union of the mother-infant pair. In many Indigenous cultures, there were women who helped mothers to give birth to their babies using herbs, music, rattles, massage, oils, hot stones, water, corn, and many other articles, recipes, and rituals to assist in the process. These helping women, or midwives, learned to assist through the time-honored apprenticeship method. Through apprenticeships, the learning came directly from the specific community in which the woman served.

This is a very critical point. It is important to the culture of the birthing family because a person with no knowledge of their birthing traditions could unintentionally insult or harm the family because of ignorance. The birthing family deserves to have confidence in their relative, friend, or neighbor who serves as their midwife. It is a matter of self-determination and self-sustainability of the community. Women give birth in the security, warmth, and comfort of home and family.

WWGP, organizing around belief that midwifery has always been a "cradle to grave" role for the wise women of all communities, was officially founded in 1998, building on the legacy Alice started. The importance of WWGP cannot be overstated. Racist misogynists, often seeking profits for the medical industry, routinely excluded midwifery traditions through laws governing accepted legal medical practices. The men saw the great power of women as threatening and wanted to seize that power through calculated attacks and bureaucratic control. Today many once well-established midwifery communities are disjointed and segmented through various licensures and certifications that have pitted one against another. However, WWGP encourages their community of over one hundred members to embrace a culture of peace, respect, and belonging.

Local tribal communities have relied on WWGP for help with teen pregnancy prevention, domestic violence prevention, cultural healing from historic trauma, and support groups for people harmed by sexual assault. The group develops and implements programs derived from the needs and desires of community members by recognizing that local cultures are a rich resource for enhancing the welfare of Indigenous youth and all tribal members. As midwives embedded in the community, women of this collective hear what is needed from community members. This point must be emphasized because Indigenous midwives see their role as an integral part of the community. They recognize the importance of honoring the decisions and desires of the community, and providing caring support to meet those needs.

With each request, WWGP responds by raising funds, seeking training, creating programs, and engaging the community. WWGP is so much more than any one component; rather, it is a much larger holistic program. The women developed community-based cultural programs to address sex, gender, and sexuality. One component was dedicated to abstinence education, which originated from tribal teachers' requests for help with reducing teen pregnancies.

How Native young people learn about sex and sexuality is complicated in contemporary times. There is a great deal of exploration and some confusion for youth, especially considering the conflicting messages adolescents receive. Dr. Stephanie Craig Rushing, the project director at the Northwest Portland Area Indian Health Board, reports there is a prevailing assumption that students get information at school, within their spiritual or religious circles, or at home. In fact, many Native youth are vulnerable to misinformation about adolescent sexual health. The media is still the most ubiquitous and influential sex educator for young people, and it is saturated with sex negativity and intolerance for dissident bodies that do not conform to dominant notions of desirability. Movies, television, and music may be the real extent of their sex education.

Dr. Craig Rushing surveys teens and young adults on their media use, asking where they go to get health information, specifically when they have questions about sensitive topics like sex or accessing birth control. Not surprisingly many of them are turning to the Internet to find answers to their questions about what is happening to their bodies during adolescence and puberty.[2] This information may not be factual, especially concerning topics such as risky behaviors and exploring sex. Understanding this dynamic, WWGP helps build education tools that teachers and educators can use in their classrooms. Talking about these topics with young people in ways that do not instill fear or judgment opens conversations and destigmatizes these topics. Moreover, using traditional teachings and stories within educational settings enhances confidence among participants to engage in such conversations.

WWGP developed the Community-Based Abstinence Culture project (C-BAC) in 2002. The goal of C-BAC was to reduce the incidence of premarital sex among teens while promoting a supporting culture of abstinence through traditional tribal teachings, not religious dicta. They created a dynamic space where teens could individually and collectively transform their lives into a culture of meaningful, productive behaviors with healthy, positive beliefs and attitudes about themselves and their sexuality. Enhancing pride in their identities encourages the confidence building necessary for teens to understand their value and be their own agents in sexual situations.

The C-BAC program provides services to eighth grade students at the Oneida Nation Turtle School and Menominee Tribal School. The WWGP programs enable youth to foster healthy relationships which build personal self-esteem, enrich their circle of friends, and expand their worldview; and in turn helps them avoid STIs and unintended pregnancy. By not only working with youth but also with their families, WWGP creates a community of individuals and families who possess the motivation, knowledge, resources, and skills to peacefully coinhabit their environment. Each person has an individual sense of safety, opportunity, fulfillment, and belonging, and each one is encouraged to sustain these values for every person, for all time.

Often young people and adults shy away from frank conversations about sex and sexuality. This is why it is so important to put such issues front and center in culturally relevant ways that relate to Native preteens and teenagers. Although people are often shy when they come into a setting to talk about what is happening with sex, their bodies changing, or their relationships, they appreciate the opportunity to explore these issues. The shyness expressed at the beginning usually ends with very engaging, intimate, mature conversations.

C-BAC's strategy features a long-term approach that incorporates methods appropriate to the culture of the students. C-BAC facilitators are Native people familiar with each community and the meshing and interweaving of culture in their particular communities. They are committed to their community and this program. Further, community support extends to the schools in working with teachers who believe in the program. Each school devotes several hours a week to C-BAC for a full academic year.

Traditional Teachings

Much of ceremonial and traditional teachings have implied learnings around gender, identity, and sexuality that can be utilized within an instructive setting for sex education. A complete understanding of the lessons embedded within certain rituals is often gained when connecting them to concrete experience or hearing histories of why such ceremonies are practiced. Some stories that youth perhaps never heard, or maybe were taken for granted when their grandma, auntie, mom, or dad talked about them, can be utilized in sex education settings. In turn, hearing teachings about respecting each other and honoring diversity take deeper root. Looking at traditional stories, with figures in nature whose role helps to communicate a particular life lesson to listeners, is helpful. The behavior of such figures also offers lessons on how to lead a life of balance and happiness by asking what happens when the figure does these things and takes risks. Students really look at it with a different lens when using traditional teachings and stories. For instance, in considering to move slowly rather than making decisions abruptly, or the need for patience when it comes to certain relationships, or how being in the context of alcohol or drugs could lead to other risky behaviors stand as a few examples.

Moreover, the importance of seeing a bit of themselves in these conversations and stories that reflect themselves culturally cannot be overstated. People generally gravitate to information that speaks to their everyday lives and experiences, and therefore, when sex education campaigns or promotional materials do not reflect the lived experiences of

Native youth, then it is easy to dismiss that information. For this reason, facilitators involved in WWGP programs are Native people familiar with each community. Students look at them as an elder or respected person and as someone who is an authority and with whom they can build trust. The model is based on an inner-tribal curriculum, and their lessons and tools resonate not only with the students but also with the educators, community, and tribal leaders alike.

Many within the pro-choice movement shudder at any mention of abstinence-based sex education. They are correctly suspicious of an imperfectly disguised antisex bias that avoids offering evidence-based sex education. However, Wise Women Gathering Place refutes that narrative. The tradition-based, nonreligious abstinence-education component to reduce teen pregnancy on the reservation counters the perception that these programs need to be anchored in narrow religious doctrine bereft of scientific evidence and cultural relevancy.

We have seen that peer education, combined with a Native education model, is moving toward eliminating health disparities in sex understanding among tribal youth.

The students who participated in WWGP were above the national averages and above nonparticipants in many respects. Seventy-five percent of the WWGP students surveyed reported they were now wearing condoms, compared to the national average of 70 percent at the time and compared to the 60 percent of tribal students not participating in WWGP. The program reported that of the 157 youths who had participated in WWGP, five pregnancies were reported compared to the thirty-two reported for the 136 who were not in the program.[3]

Sex education programs that do not consider cultural context are often not relevant to Native youth. The issues of consensual sex, cultural expectations, body acceptance, and historical context are often missed in universal state-mandated programs. In many ways WWGP is an ideal organization for sex education for several reasons. The organization focuses on the community as well as the individual, and is located within a community viewed as in need of cultural strengthening. Programs such as WWGP allow for access to information, control, and ownership.

This is empowerment in its true form. If you only have access to programs created and distributed by someone else, it is hard to tell your own story, to own your voice, or your image. The WWGP program is housed on tribal land, run by tribal members who are a known part of the community, and thus sustains tribal voices on culture, history, daily goings-on that include healthy outcomes for tribal youth. Having, not just access, but combined control and ownership over sex education is powerful, and that power belongs to the people. At the end of the day, Indigenous communities need more from sex education programs than what presently exists. Wise Woman Gathering Place represents an example of Native women taking the initiative on how Indigenous people claim space in the sex education field.

Notes

1. *Native America Calling*, "Native HIV/AIDS Awareness," KUNM Public Radio, March 18, 2016, http://www.nativeamericacalling.com/friday-march-18-2016-native-hivaids-awareness/.

2. Ibid.

3. Alice Skenandore and Janet Hagen, "Key Findings of the C-BAC Program," Wise Woman Gathering Place C-BAC Program, 2007, https://www.wisewomengp.org/discovery-dating/the-c-bac-project/c-bac-key-findings/.

HIV Prevention and Reproductive Justice: A Framework for Saving Women's Lives

DÁZON DIXON DIALLO

Change women's lives, change the epidemic. The face of HIV/AIDS in the United States has gotten browner, younger, and more female. Rates of infection have diminished among some populations of those at greatest risk—such as men who have sex with men—but for others, particularly for young black men who have sex with men, and black women who have sex with men, HIV/AIDS rates continue to climb. In 2007 the US observed an *increase* in the number of new HIV infections—by as much as 50 percent—for the first time in over ten years; this increase was centered largely among people of color.[1] The Centers for Disease Control and Prevention's (CDC) latest epidemiology on women and HIV suggests that, while infections appear to be slowing in the general population throughout the country, HIV transmission through high-risk heterosexual behavior is still on the rise among women, African Americans, and Latinas and Hispanics. Southern women experience the brunt of this reality.

HIV/AIDS is a problem that, while ever-present, is invisible to the naked eye. Most Americans are fortunate enough to go through life with the HIV/AIDS epidemic as a background issue, but, for the 1.2 million Americans living with HIV/AIDS, it is at the forefront of every decision, relationship, and sexual encounter. More than three hundred thousand of those living with the disease in the US are women and girls. Women and girls are increasingly at the center of the global pandemic and represent nearly half of the world's AIDS cases.[2] The vast majority of these women become infected through sex with HIV-positive men.

We now know that, among the populations at greatest risk for sexual transmission of HIV, there are no indications that individual sexual behaviors are different or unique to the most-affected populations. Black and Latina women do not engage in risky sexual behaviors at different rates from their white counterparts. Yet, because of the high HIV prevalence in their communities, these women are more likely to become infected, with less exposure than white women.

Several key factors drive the women's HIV/AIDS crisis, factors that are both elusive and difficult to tackle. They include women's increased biological vulnerability to HIV transmission and lack of control over use of barrier methods of HIV prevention, and the political, cultural, and economic conditions that impede women's access to reproductive health education, treatment, and care. These structural impediments must be addressed systemically by reducing violence against women and girls; ensuring universal access to quality education and healthcare; guaranteeing inclusive research and clinical trials; and alleviating the effects of poverty on women and children.

Almost three decades into the global AIDS epidemic, gender inequality and women's low socioeconomic status remain two principal drivers of infection. Yet, current HIV/AIDS responses fail to tackle the social, cultural, and economic factors that not only increase women's risk for HIV but also unduly burden them with the epidemic's consequences.[3] Reproductive justice and prevention justice (PJ) offer a different, and potentially more successful, way to approach the issue.

Reproductive Justice, Prevention Justice, and HIV/AIDS Prevention

Reproductive justice is defined as the complete physical, mental, spiritual, political, social, and economic well-being of women and girls, based on the full achievement and protection of women's human rights. Reproductive justice maintains that, for Indigenous women and women of color, it is important to fight equally for the right to have a child; not to have a child; to parent one's children; and to control birthing options, such as midwifery.[4] The RJ analysis offers a compelling framework for empowering women and girls that is relevant to every American family because it focuses on the ends—better lives for women, healthier families, and sustainable communities—rather than engaging in a divisive debate on abortion and birth control that neglects the real-life experiences of women and girls.

The RJ framework analyzes how a woman's ability to determine her own reproductive destiny is directly linked to her community's conditions—conditions that are not merely a matter of individual choice and access. Reproductive justice addresses the social reality of inequality, specifically inequalities in opportunities to control our reproductive destinies. Reproductive justice moves beyond a demand for privacy and respect for individual decision-making to include the social supports necessary for one's individual decisions to be optimally realized, and the government's obligations to protect women's human rights. Our options for making choices must be safe, affordable, and accessible; three minimal cornerstones of government support for all individual life decisions.

The HIV Prevention Justice Alliance is an emerging coalition of HIV/AIDS prevention advocates and activists who believe the best way to prevent HIV/AIDS is to ensure that *all* of us have the economic, social, and political power and resources to make healthy decisions about our bodies, sexuality, and reproduction for ourselves, our families, and our communities. The PJ framework acknowledges that HIV prevention cannot be separated from human rights, thereby changing both the way we look at HIV prevention and how we advocate for it. Prevention justice places the people and communities that are *most* affected by the epidemic at the forefront of policy efforts.

To date, US HIV prevention efforts have focused on identifying and changing individual behaviors that can contribute to the virus's spread, such as unprotected sex and unsafe drug injection. Traditional prevention efforts also involve exploring "risk factors," the behaviors and/or traits that increase the odds of an individual engaging in risky behaviors such as drug addiction or commercial sex work, as well as assessing the specific populations most likely to engage in high-risk behaviors. This focus has, however, failed to accomplish the CDC's goal of halving HIV transmission rates. In fact, as noted, in some communities HIV/AIDS rates are rising once again.

Addressing HIV/AIDS from a PJ standpoint involves examining both community and structural conditions that increase infection risks for individuals and groups. The US prevention field has been relatively slow to create and implement strategies that specifically address the structural, social, and systemic problems that may increase an individual's infection risks more than another's. For example, PJ explores whether a resource-poor black mother is more susceptible to HIV because she prefers intercourse without a condom or because she "chooses" unprotected sex in order to keep the man who pays her bills, feeds her kids, and secures their housing in her life.

Reproductive and prevention justice acknowledge the key issues that increase women and girls' vulnerability to HIV/AIDS, including violence against women, poverty and economic dependence, lack of prevention technology, and the marginalization of HIV-positive women in leadership. A reproductive and prevention justice approach necessitates addressing these factors and changing our current approaches to reducing the incidence of HIV/AIDS among us women and girls.

Dangerous Intersections: Violence against Women and Gender-Based Violence

Violence against women plays a crucial and devastating role in increasing women's risk of contracting HIV. It is a key reason why women are more vulnerable to HIV infection than men. It is both a cause and a consequence of infection and, as such, is a driving force behind the epidemic.

Fear of violence prevents women from accessing HIV/AIDS information, being tested for the virus, disclosing their HIV status, accessing services to prevent HIV transmission from mother to child, and receiving treatment and counseling even when they know they have been infected. Women who are victims of gender violence have an increased risk of contracting HIV/AIDS because they experience diminished capacity to negotiate risk reduction with abusive partners. Women who are living with HIV/AIDS are at increased risk for being the victims of gender-based violence because of their status.[5]

Reproductive and prevention justice calls for, at a minimum, the following mechanisms to address the intersection of HIV risk and violence: collection and analysis of data on the relationship among sexually transmitted infections (including HIV/AIDS) and gender violence; the integration of HIV/AIDS prevention and/or treatment into care networks for victims of domestic and sexual violence; and education of staff in government- and community-based service delivery and of the general public.

In Women's Hands: Prevention Research and Technology

Women and girls must have prevention tools they can either independently control or administer for themselves. The future of prevention is showing us that behavioral research must be coupled with biomedical and social science research as a means of identifying multisectoral approaches to HIV prevention. Behavior interventions, along with vaccines, microbicides, and other medicinal compounds, will have the best chance of causing a positive reduction in the HIV epidemic, especially among women and girls who have almost no female-controlled options for safer sex practices.

The quest for a "magic bullet" solution, whether a single behavioral or biomedical intervention, is not likely to end the AIDS crisis. We urgently need theories, assessment tools, and hybrid prevention strategies that address risk in the context of vulnerability and directly address the root causes of vulnerability.

HIV and Women's Development: Sustain Families, Reduce Risks

Poverty and economic desperation are significant underlying causes of the HIV/AIDS pandemic. Women are particularly vulnerable to the disease for economic reasons: a woman's lack of livelihood increases her incidence of transactional sex (in exchange for food or basic life essentials), coerced sex, multiple partners, early sexual debut, untreated sexually transmitted infections, and early or unplanned pregnancy. The use of microcredit programs in the developing world offers a clear example. Microcredit programs provide savings, credit, and insurance services to owners of tiny businesses in impoverished communities—many specifically target women for involvement. Microfinance services have significantly increased women's economic independence and decreased their vulnerability to disease and violence; the availability of microcredit is shown to lead to significant and rapid improvement of household income.

Targeting women with microfinance services is an effective and sustainable way to make a real impact on HIV/AIDS, because women are most at-risk of contracting HIV/AIDS for economic reasons and tend to be the primary caregivers of AIDS orphans and other vulnerable children. Women in the developing world tend to be self-employed and are already poised to utilize a loan to expand their small enterprises. Likewise, women tend to invest their increased income to improve their children's lives, including proper nutrition, healthcare, education and shelter, thereby reducing poverty levels for subsequent generations.

Where poverty, inequality, and AIDS are combined, they do disproportionate harm to women and girls. Research suggests that women who have access to, ownership of, and control over income, property, and other assets are better able to avoid relationships that threaten them with HIV, and to manage the impact of HIV/AIDS. In the United States, increasing self-sufficiency and reducing economic dependency (especially among women in "developing communities") has also been proven effective.[6]

I Am Not the Enemy, I Am the Answer: HIV-Positive Women's Leadership

In its *Agenda for Action on Women and AIDS*, the Global Coalition on Women and AIDS (GCWA) states that experience has shown HIV/AIDS policies and programs will not work for women until women's organizations—especially those of, for, and by *HIV-positive* women—help shape their content and direction.[7]

Local and national networks of women living with HIV are being established in more and more countries. But, much more must be done to strengthen women's participation in the meetings, forums, and programs that influence and shape their lives. The GCWA calls on national governments to support efforts that promote equitable representation of women at the highest levels in national political, executive, legislative, and judicial structures; ensure that organizations led by and serving women are more widely and meaningfully active in the forums where AIDS programs are designed, funded, and managed; provide more funds to build the advocacy and leadership skills of women living with HIV, so they can participate effectively in the processes that affect their lives; and build partnerships between women's rights organizations and groups working on HIV/AIDS to more effectively lobby for change.

SisterSong is a membership organization that uses reproductive justice as an organizing framework to challenge inequalities, empower women and girls, and help them to transform both themselves and their communities. Juanita Williams, a South Carolina–based HIV-positive activist who was on the management circle of SisterSong, when asked what she thinks the key roles are for HIV-positive women in the struggle for effective HIV/AIDS prevention strategies said,

> Give [us] a voice and a platform for that voice. . . . Give [us] a safe place to let [our] voices be heard and validate them. Positive people are not taken

seriously, and positive women are taken even less seriously. People think positive people are way down on the totem pole. We need positive women's voices to continue to fight the stigma. How do we do that? We tell our stories and reflect each other. I am not the enemy, I am the answer. If you silence my voice, then what happens to my behavior?[8]

Notes

1. David Brown, "Estimate of AIDS Cases in U.S. Rises," *Washington Post*, December 1, 2007, http://www.washingtonpost.com/wp-dyn/content/article/2007/11/30/AR2007113002535.html.

2. Centers for Disease Control and Prevention, "HIV Surveillance in Women," June 2007, 4. http://www.cdc.gov/hiv/topics/surveillance/resources/slides/women/index.htm.

3. UNAIDS, UNFPA, and UNIFEM, "Women and HIV/AIDS: Confronting the Crisis," 1. http://www.unfpa.org/sites/default/files/pub-pdf/women_aids.pdf.

4. Rickie Solinger and Loretta J. Ross, eds., *Reproductive Justice Briefing Book: A Primer on Reproductive Justice and Social Change*, last updated 2007, Pro-Choice Education Project/SisterSong Women of Color Reproductive Health Collective, http://protectchoice.org/downloads/Reproductive%20Justice%20Briefing%20Book.pdf.

5. Ibid.

6. Pan-American Health Organization (PAHO), "*Propuesta de Proyecto sobre Las Redes de Atención a la Violencia Doméstica y Sexual como Punto de Entrada para el Tratamiento y Prevención del VIH/SIDA (Project proposal on the networks of attention to domestic and sexual violence as point of entry for the treatment and prevention of HIV/AIDS)*" (Washington, DC: PAHO, June 2005), 2.

7. International Center for Research on Women, "Property Ownership for Women Enriches, Empowers and Protects," 2005, https://www.icrw.org/wp-content/uploads/2016/10/Property-Ownership-for-Women-Enriches-Empowers-and-Protects-Toward-Achieving-the-Third-Millennium-Development-Goal-to-Promote-Gender-Equality-and-Empower-Women.pdf.

8. Juanita Williams, in *Speak Up! Newsletter of the Positive Women's Network*, Spring/Summer (2011), 1.

The Reluctant Reproductive Justice Organizer and Birthworker

LUCIA LEANDRO GIMENO

The need for change bulldozed a road down the center of my mind.
—Maya Angelou

Lump in My Throat

I have started this essay several different times. Hands shaky. Fire in my belly. Racing thoughts. How do you start talking about something that feels so intensely loaded and personal? Talking about the complicated connection between reproductive justice and trans justice feels urgent and timely. Saying things that need to be said is a risky endeavor. Losing respect for people or people losing respect for you has real personal and movement-building consequences. What calms me is knowing that staying silent is no longer serving anyone. I don't want to stay silent when I see trans people, and trans women specifically, being excluded. I don't want to stay silent when trans people erase the contributions of people of color, especially black women and other women of color. These are the symptoms of how white supremacy and colonization are played out. As activists and organizers, we often shallowly lure each other into allyship when we name who's not present but don't do anything about it. We haven't taken the time to build authentically, to hold space, to name the ways white supremacy and patriarchy have impacted us differently. Not expansively building around liberation work means we let the systems that impact us further divide us, silence us, and withhold access to the tools we need to have hard and messy conversations about how to build connection and solidarity.

As a mixed race, Afro-Latinx, transmasculine femme with light skin, I've been asked too many times who my people are, which is actually a question of which side I feel more aligned with. What I realize is that choosing a side is a false dichotomy. I'm not choosing which oppression to lead with. I'm leading with all of me and that means that, as a bridge person, my work is to create space that organizers and activists can come to and talk about building a new way forward. I want to be bold and get into the discomfort around how we build toward our collective healing. I offer these words as a call to put down the "I'm more oppressed than you" mask and show up vulnerable, to create opportunities, to struggle with love. This is the long-term strategy. While urgent, we can't rush through it and not do it with deep intention to our triggers, harms, and experiences of violence. This is the work. Essex Hemphill was bold in his visions of how as a black, gay man he needed to learn to show up for black women and to not let the experience of racism erase the privilege around being a cisgender man. "But we so-called men, / we so-called brothers / wonder why it's so hard to love *our* women / when we're about loving them / the way America / loves us."

I blame racism and misogyny for the ways we turn on each other sometimes. I also blame capitalism. Not just for competing for foundation dollars and government grants; it also impacts how we think of each other as not being connected or important to each other's survival. If we are constantly underresourced and erased from our contributions and political frameworks—and the very traditions that make midwifery, nursing, and birthwork possible—then being asked to stretch and think about issues that don't seem obviously connected to us is virtually impossible. Capitalism breeds fear that we are not enough or don't have enough and limits what is possible. We are afraid to think big and wild because it's "too hard," we may not win, or we may be left behind.

One of the few places we can't be colonized is in our dreams. Our dreams hold powerful messages from our ancestors, and are where we get inspired to act when waking life seems filled with grief and mourning. The call around RJ has always been expansion, which is about women of color being seen as whole people and not just women or whether they can access abortion services. My interest in getting to the hard shit is because our lives depend on it. And I don't just mean literal death, but the death of imagination as well. When our imaginations die we don't live full lives and don't dare to live in our full power. We all come from powerful ancestors who dreamed a better world, and it's up to us to build off of what our elders left behind.

Showing Up with Some Reluctance

I came to RJ and birthwork very reluctantly. It felt like I had to choose between aligning with trans folks or cisgender women of color and I wasn't interested in playing into that dynamic. Also, it meant confronting the deep loss of not being able to carry a child due to endometrial cancer; that to save my life meant removing my uterus. It felt very selfish to enter birthwork because I knew it would heal the parts of me that needed to be healed. I was hesitant because I never thought family and reproductive health would ever be my political focus and birthwork seemed to be increasingly popular and I thought to myself, "Who needs another doula?" It felt too personal and where I'd have to show up fully and also have difficult conversations. As a transmasculine femme cancer survivor with future parental dreams, I often encounter people's surprise that, as a masculine person, I wanted to carry a child. Even with more spaces dedicated to trans parents who birth, it is still something people feel confused by, why a seemingly "woman's" experience would be something that I desired. I let go of the guilt of feeling like I was entering birthwork for personal gains (i.e., healing) and wanting to learn about creating a family. I also wanted to help shift the ideas around who gives birth and why. My question shifted to: Could there be more doulas who are trans people of color?

I began to see my role as a bridge builder but also as a holder of contradictions. In my experience, birthwork, originating in black and Indigenous traditions in the US, has been dominated by white people. Specifically white, straight, cis women. When I enter spaces that reflect more queerness and gender expression, I'm confronted with a sea of white, transmasculine people. Common theme: whiteness. When connecting with RJ organizers, I mostly see cisgender women of color. In these spaces I get to breathe a lot easier because I feel at home and grounded in where I come from. There is never a question of the need to center people of color in the conversation around reproductive health. The values that get upheld are around collective liberation and access while oftentimes in birthwork it is more about the individual person or family.

Yet still, my heart secretly yearns to get to the conversation I've been wanting to have: How do we include trans people, especially trans femmes of color and trans women of color, and uplift the legacy and work of cisgender women of color? Being raised in a radical, lesbian, feminist of color family and community in the colonial city of Boston, I am familiar with the love and struggle around how cis women and trans people build together. Without the labor, love, and genius of women of color (cis and trans), I could not be here and have the political and social space to be in my truth as a transmasculine femme.

I've always wondered if there is a different way we can honor that legacy. Part of that is recognizing why there is this distance between RJ and trans justice. The disconnect and some outright hostility (in both directions) is a product of how we are impacted by the colonial project, capitalism, and white supremacy. The same system we are fighting against is one that has us fighting each other because we have forgotten (or intentionally don't want to remember) how our issues are connected.

What will it take to mend the disconnect? More accurately, what will it take to remember that once upon a time, before Christopher Columbus, communities on every black and brown continent held hands, shared meals, raised children, kept each other safe, led rituals, and gifted each other with magic? I was raised with the understanding that women of all gender expressions experience violence because their lives are undervalued and only needed as a prop to literally and figuratively uphold patriarchy, misogyny, and capitalism. As a young woman and survivor of child sexual abuse, I am all too familiar with gender-based violence. In 2005 I began to identify as trans and the conversations I had with myself were: What kind of transmasculine person do I want to be that doesn't go against the values and experiences of the women who raised me and who were in my life? How do I not betray where I come from and the source of power that has nurtured my growth while also coming into my own power and destiny and not playing into the hands of sexism to uphold my masculinity?

My first conversation with myself wasn't about physical or medical changes. It feels deeply ironic that part of my metamorphosis had anything to do with masculinity, given my experience of sexual violence. It felt like a loss from a space that shaped my feminist politics while owning my privilege as a masculine person. One of the things that also resonated was still wanting to be a parent someday. I pushed that conversation to the back of my mind because I really had to think a lot about how I would relate differently or similarly to women and femmes. When I think about the tension and disconnect between RJ and trans justice, I often think about my own journey around gender, family, and home. It's not just about nonprofits or political campaigns but also about people and how we deal or don't deal with the contradictions and big questions around honoring where we come from in order to figure out where the hell we're going.

Presently, as a transmasculine femme, the work that feels the most scary and exciting is going back to our roots. The places that created such spaces for affirmation but also places of pain. Someone told me once that wanting to talk about trans liberation and reproductive justice feels like going into the lion's den. My immediate response was, "Well, into the lion's den I go." Being a mixed, Afro-Latinx, transmasculine femme, raised working class and educationally privileged and newly chronically fatigued, I occupy that gray space filled with the thickest tension. I see this work as part of a larger call from our ancestors to remember where we come from, that cis and trans and queer and straight folks have always been part of each others lives. If we look at our traditions around birth and community and family, they have always included us. Part of what colonization and white supremacy have done is erase the fact that we need each other and that we are being attacked by the same systems. We've lost so many of our archives and artifacts and stories. While this is a loss, our strategies must include dreams, intuitions, and political analyses to imagine differently. I believe our ancestors speak through us. The more we connect and rebuild with one another, the more the messages and ways forward will become clearer.

White Trans People Don't Speak for Me

When I think about RJ, I think about the amazing black and brown women who fought hard to create a new framework that speaks the realities of race, class, and gender in ways that white, feminist women largely have a hard time grasping. I think the hard part to name is the transphobia that has existed. Oppression is in reaction to oppression. A lot of the trans institution-building has been led by white trans people, which is inherently anti-black, pro-respectability, and using "cis" as a dirty word. There have been decades of trans-people-of-color-led resistance and organizations, but those spaces are few and far between and vastly underfunded. If the people who are challenging you resemble the white supremacist, colonizing bodies that have erased, murdered, and enslaved your people, how could you listen? The very lives of women of color (cis and trans) are being mercilessly attacked and used to uphold power structures. Women are often jailed, or even killed, for defending themselves against violence, shamed for being single parents, and are grossly underpaid for their labor. How do we enter a conversation that acknowledges the misogyny and erasure of women *and* the transphobia that also erases women (cis and trans)?

What if we started from a place of forgiveness and grew to a place of mutual learning about the deep history that actually embraces all of our family members? I've become accustomed to sitting in that gray area where I talk with other femmes of color about being tired of masculine people playing out their misogyny. I also hear how harmful it has been for transmasculine and gender nonconforming folks to access reproductive healthcare from places that say they understand and see us. As my neck pivots back and forth, what seems so clear is that part of what white supremacy does is decontextualizes and dehistoricizes how these tensions have come to be.

What is my responsibility as a transmasculine femme who has easier access to RJ spaces because my body theoretically can reproduce a child? More specifically, what is my role, if at all, in helping support the mending between trans women and cis women, especially in communities of color, not because we're more transphobic but because that is the community I come from and am invested in. Often transmasculine people occupy so much space when it comes to reproductive issues that we end up playing out misogyny toward all women in the name of trans inclusion. How do we, as trans people, not employ the slash-and-burn strategy created by white supremacy when cis women make mistakes and even get angry and act out their transphobia on us? Do we ever take a step back and wonder: Are they responding to misogyny and erasure as black and brown women? Are they responding from that ancestor place of having survived slavery and colonization because to be female is always to be less than human?

My freedom will not come at the expense and erasure of femmes and women. That is not my movement. How do we build intentional spaces where we can make space for the ways we've not had each others' backs, and how to make a new way so that we can really challenge each other with love, to not operate from our trauma and fear but from love? If we operate from love it means that we give ourselves and each other the opportunity to demonstrate how we want to be respected and how to be in solidarity with us. We can share stories, traditions, rituals, and healing practices and create the access we so rightly deserve. Through love we can connect our struggles and transform our trauma into strategies for the most epically gorgeous family reunion.

No More Allies: Entering the Conversation Differently

The key to our survival lies in our abilities to create whole selves and whole communities and to undo the divisions that have been drawn across our lands and bodies. However, before we can achieve this kind of solidarity, it's important to highlight the kinds of bridges that need to be built and the binary busting that needs to be done before we can forge the kinds of alliances that deepen our understanding and practice of identity politics.

—Lisa Weiner-Mahfuz and Ana-Maurine Lara

In my lifetime I've had the privilege of working at places like the Audre Lorde Project, serving on the founding board of FIERCE, and helping raise money for the Sylvia Rivera Law Project where that tension and conversation was always being had. While it wasn't always easy, it was about respecting where people are and creating containers for connection and education. Conversations led by or that center queer and trans people of color reflect the nuances and possibilities of how to better struggle toward solidarity. I don't want any more allies. Allies, in my experience, don't show up when you need them most but use their status to avoid dealing with their privilege. Solidarity is a call and response strategy that asks people to do work on the personal, political, and spiritual level around showing up, witnessing, and taking action in big and small ways. I come to this conversation born female-identified and having survived sexual abuse and endometrial cancer. This is my entry point into the conversation.

Our bodies and minds have been targets. Especially by the medical establishment and the police. What pieces of history do trans women and cis women share? The pieces of history about the body and how they have been controlled, criminalized, and commodified. From 1929 to 1974 women in North Carolina were sterilized without their consent, many of whom were black women, some as young as ten years old. They were categorized as mentally unfit because they were considered "promiscuous" and/or poor. Sex work in the US is an industry that includes both trans and cisgender women who are criminalized for engaging in sex work. A large number of sex workers are trans women of color because often that is the only means of economic survival.

How are we to move forward? We have our stories, histories, and dreams to pull from. Cisgender and trans women share stories of grief around being talked out of having agency over their own bodies.They also have a rich history and present-day genius that we can't afford to keep separated. Let's be bridge people to help redefine our future. There are so many ways to shift the culture of disconnection. Do community research and learn about when our bodies have been used to keep us silent and ashamed, and where we have been in solidarity with each other. Talk to your elders, ask them how they struggled and what they learned. Make meals and talk about what you value and how to build with each other and learn how you can show up. Leave your egos at the door. There should only be room to make mistakes, hold each other, and learn. Organize and strategize from a place of love and abundance and know the history that connects us all.

Mothering While Poor: Utilizing the Reproductive Justice Framework to Build the Capacities of Young Mothers

BENITA MILLER

Back in the Day: An Introduction

My mother was sixteen in 1969 when she gave birth to my brother, and thirteen months later I followed. My father was seventeen when he first became a father and eighteen when he became my mother's husband. I was raised in a working-class community on Detroit's east side. My parents are far removed from the day they were pushed out of high school and into adulthood. Their marriage has resulted in four children and nine grandchildren. Nowadays, my mother's a registered nurse and my father has been building cars at Chrysler's Jefferson North Assembly Plant since 1971. My parents have owned two homes, the one I grew up in with my siblings and the one I now visit with my own children in tow. My siblings and I have all been exposed to postsecondary education, an expectation that is now the norm among the network of my parents' grandchildren.

I know that my parents' success is exceptional. Family life and especially parenthood is complex; both my sisters were teen parents and never married and my brother and I are divorced. I raise my children full-time, and my brother has weekend visits with his children. In the months following my husband's departure from the home, my once stable finances were strained, causing me to pay bills, max out credit cards, and finally seek financial help from my parents. I watched both my sisters struggle with missed child-support payments and conversely watched my brother struggle to make support payments. Being a family is hard, and it is even harder without a safety net. For poor women of color without a viable social network of family and friends doing a little bit better than they are, the only thing they can rely on is public entitlements. Yet consistently policymakers have made it increasingly difficult for these women to secure basic resources to support themselves and their children.

I share my story because I identify with the teenage mother, not only because of my mother's life, but as a middle-class black woman who recently experienced financial insecurity. I appreciate the personal safety net available to me and know that I am fortunate. But in my daily work, I witness the impact of how decades of restructuring and reducing public assistance to young mothers has compromised their ability to raise healthy families with all the necessary resources and social supports.

I look at the young mothers I work with wrapping their arms around young men on the brink of fatherhood and know that their lives will not be like my father's as there are no auto factories brimming with jobs paying a wage high enough to sustain a household. These families cannot live on love alone, and free trade agreements and deindustrialization have created an economic opportunity gap for young families desiring to build a future. Their children will not be able to grow up and call home for help when their financial resources become strained because antipoor public policies erode public supports.

Welfare Reform

More than two decades ago, spurred by the momentum of a conservative movement and centrist Democratic policies, President Bill Clinton honored his presidential campaign promise and put an "end to welfare as we know it" when he signed the Personal Responsibility and Work Opportunity Reconciliation Act in 1996. The sweeping welfare legislation halted sixty-one years of aid to poor women and children. Indeed, the reforms resulted in a steep decline in the welfare rolls, but the mostly women leaving the rolls entered the workforce at the low end of the labor market. And consequently, along with low-paying work, many women, mostly single mothers, were forced to cobble together an assortment of government programs, such as WIC, housing subsidies, and supplemental security income, just to survive.

Just to demonstrate the monumental task of pulling it all together, my staff and I recently spent two days scouring the Internet and working the phones assisting a young mother of two in her search for an apartment. This young woman receives cash assistance, childcare subsidies, rent payments, food stamps, and WIC. Each month her income from all these sources falls below one thousand dollars. Not much to live off of in New York City for a single person, let alone a family of three. Before anyone has grandiose fantasies of a welfare queen, here's her backstory: she graduated high school, attends college, and works. Despite her efforts to improve her economic conditions, without stable housing she, like anyone made to live in her situation, falls short. She and her children have cycled in and out of the city's shelter system for more than a year because few landlords accept rent subsidy programs. Apparently, public assistance is slow to pay its bills, and New York City can only afford to provide her with temporary shelter but not the safe, permanent housing her and her children need.

Given that she's holding up her end of the bargain in pursuing life, liberty, and happiness—and I add for the conservatives among us, self-sufficiency—it is not only immoral but violates the US Declaration of Independence and the Universal Declaration of Human Rights that she and her children lack safe and stable housing. But instead of addressing the very real needs of young women like her, on the heels of welfare reform, middle-class fantasies kicked in and our government developed and funded fatherhood initiatives and marriage promotion programs.

Fatherhood Initiatives and Marriage Promotion

George W. Bush's administration, with Democratic support, provided funding up to fifty million dollars a year in 2005 for activities promoting fatherhood, such as counseling, mentoring, marriage education, enhancing relationship skills, parenting, and *activities*—not *jobs*—to foster economic stability. Moreover, the federal Deficit Reduction Act of 2005 provided funding of $150 million a year for healthy marriage promotion and fatherhood.

Both these initiatives have roots in welfare reform. In late 1997, the federal Office of Child Support Enforcement funded Responsible Fatherhood Demonstration Projects in eight states. These programs attempted to improve the employment and earnings of under- and unemployed noncustodial parents, and to motivate them to become more financially and emotionally involved in the lives of their children. But improving the outcomes of these poor and uneducated fathers proved to be a far greater challenge than pushing poor women into low-wage work so that they could feed and clothe their children.

Approximately one hundred billion dollars in child support is owed to America's children. However, the reality is that the bulk of fathers who owe child support payments are often poor themselves. According to the General Accounting Office, these fathers' average earnings are less than seven thousand dollars per year. They are technically eligible for food stamps. Most children these fathers are responsible for supporting are in extreme poverty. More than four in ten poor men (disproportionately men of color) who father children out of wedlock have already been to jail or prison by the time the baby is born and about half have not graduated high school. So, in many instances the measures taken to enforce these fathers' financial obligation to their children are ineffective because oftentimes child support orders are set too high and little value is placed on the material goods fathers attempt to provide their children. Also, in many cases few resources are available to improve fathers' employability, and with the exportation of manufacturing jobs there is not much work to go around given the employment and education histories of these fathers. At the end of the day, when a poor father has no potential to provide even minimal support for his children, he substantially reduces any engagement with them.

Often, young mothers tell me that they don't want to "get child support" from the fathers because he does what he can and they don't want "child support in their business." It took me years and a divorce to understand how vulnerable low-income women of color must feel when their parenting is put under a spotlight. While I have a private support agreement with my children's father, I could not imagine being compelled by the government to provide such information to secure entitlements. I realize now the women were not protecting the fathers but attempting to keep their lives private, especially since payments remain with the government for women receiving certain entitlements. In short, fatherhood initiatives do little to eliminate poverty for poor women and in some instances compromise informal support agreements between private parties.

Marriage Promotion: Governmental Matchmaking

For a brief period, in poor urban areas throughout the country, churches and community groups held "marry your baby's daddy" weddings, unwittingly promoting a socially conservative agenda which continues in its failure to advance the economic outcomes of these now "intact" families under the guise that black families were embracing long-lost values. But because Americans love romantic endings where the boy wins the girl's heart, it isn't far-flung that the promotion of these marriage and fatherhood initiatives by philanthropic and community-based groups continues to surge. The support for these initiatives seems to be rooted in our cultural obsession to have every family reflect the Ozzie and Harriet model (or in the case of poor black families, James and Florida Evans from *Good Times*), raising their children and striving for the white-picket-fence life conjured up as part of the American dream. But without adequate income and the continual dismantling of social welfare programs and safety nets, policymakers are asserting that poor and low-income families would move out of poverty if the adults were legally married. Or at the very least, marriage would curb the multiple children poor men produce with different women. Instead, marriage promotion policies burden poor women who are made to think marriage is a more viable path out of poverty than meaningful government support to obtain education and training.

Oddly, the fact that the government has entered the matchmaking business on behalf of poor women has not caused great alarm. Marriage promotion has essentially linked marriage as a social policy to entitlement services. So, instead of guaranteed economic support, poor women and children must wait for a Prince Charming to emerge from the hordes of poor men being trained in responsibility as part of the fatherhood initiatives. This is not sound social policy and hampers the ability of poor women to choose how they wish to partner.

But on the other side of the economic divide, a growing number of older, unmarried, and mostly white women have become single mothers by choice. These women are potential allies of the poor mothers subject to policies imposing father involvement and marriage, but instead distinguish themselves from these women based on their education and economic status, often making it plain that they don't have to rely on public funds to raise their children. These women rightfully assert control over their family structure, in a way suggesting they are entitled to do so because they and their children won't be a public burden and they exercised good judgment in deciding to become a single parent. Arguably, these women's posture is consistent with the notion that welfare is poor judgment and poor education leads to an impoverished life requiring government intervention rather than meaningful support.

Conclusion

I am not antifather or antimarriage. I am altogether pro-family, believing the government must improve its commitment to poor and low-income families and not through initiatives that fail to lift people out of poverty. Public safety nets are critical to ensuring that all women who choose motherhood benefit from adequate supports as part of their human rights entitlements, and are enabled to produce good, productive citizens. As a start, policymakers should consider the following:

- Increase cash benefits under TANF so that the basic needs of poor women and children are adequately met.
- Make TANF time limits more flexible so that poor women needing additional supports and resources are not penalized. It is unrealistic to assume that the five-year timeframe works for all women.
- Create diverse training and vocational options pursuant to TANF to allow poor women to explore new and different skills that might prove transferable in the ever-expanding global job market.
- Incentivize secondary education so poor women can pursue secondary education beyond community college.
- Develop GI Bill–type incentives for poor families who choose to wed or live in the same household by establishing programs that specifically assist with home ownership through lending and financial literacy—a cornerstone in transferring wealth across generations.

Beyond the Trees: Stories and Strategies of Environmental and Reproductive Justice

LAURA JIMÉNEZ, KIERRA JOHNSON, and CARA PAGE

As women of color and Indigenous women, we find ourselves at the particular intersection of multiple issues, ideologies, and identities. As we live out the legacy of colonization upon which the United States was founded, we are not unaware of the efforts to control and contain our communities through the creation and expansion of institutions like the prison- and medical-industrial complexes. Our existence in these political/social/cultural locations, within our respective regions and geographies, calls us to be active in the struggles for justice—racial, environmental, economic, reproductive, gender, and sexual—as strategies of resistance and sustainability for ourselves, our families, and our communities.

This piece is to begin weaving the collective stories of our struggles and resiliency, to create a political and historical context of the environmental justice and reproductive justice movements, and to highlight intersections between our movements and strategies. We are also seeking to engage political discourse and critical response to the implications of population control ideology. This ideology reinforces the continued blaming of social burdens and environmental degradation on the fertility of women of color and Indigenous women, and has been used to fuel classist, ableist, homophobic, and racist practices under the guise of environmental and reproductive rights. Recently population control strategies have reemerged and are gaining popularity as the most optimal approaches to ensure environmental safety and sustainability which will subjugate and target our bodies and communities. While we agree that we must address the impact of climate change, environmental toxins, and overconsumption, we seek to pull the blame off of women of color and poor communities and target the true root causes—war, rapid urban planning, industrialization, and the lack of governmental and corporate accountability—that has contributed to the state of our bodies' and earth's lack of well-being and safety. We have concerns that using population control ideology as a response to our environmental conditions will only regenerate particular policies and practices used to coerce, and control women of color and Indigenous women, incarcerated people, people with disabilities, the LGBTQ community, and other disenfranchised communities.

In writing this, our hope was to share with the broader progressive movement a dialogue between Indigenous and women of color reproductive and environmental justice organizers across the United States, who are on the ground mobilizing creative strategies to ensure the safety and sustainability of our communities. From our networks, we called on several individuals to join the conversation: Bianca Encinias of the Southwest Network for Environmental and Economic Justice (New Mexico); Vanessa Huang of Justice Now (California); Shawna Larson of Alaska Community Action on Toxics; and Cara Page of the Committee on Women, Population, and the Environment (Georgia).

We also want to recognize the many voices not included in this conversation. Certainly, in the aftermath of Hurricane Katrina, we would need to go deeper into the Southern regions to gather their particular experiences based on historical and contemporary practices of coercion and control in the Southeast. As well, the Northeast has had an important role and impact on organizing strategies against environmental and reproductive injustices. We know we have barely touched the surface, especially with the current food, climate, and water crises across the nation and the globe. There will be many more critical conversations to have in our movements toward building strategies of our resistance, sustainability, and survival. That said, we hope you will find the following experiences and stories as told by the very women who live and work at these intersections informative and inspirational for fueling cross-movement action and strategies.

In our process, we held one round-table discussion, with four environmental and reproductive justice organizers, and asked a few individuals to tell stories of their organizing to understand the traditions and intersections of our movements. The questions we used to generate stories and conversation included:

— What is the historical moment of population control?
— What is the impact of the medical and prison industrial complexes on our bodies and communities?

— What are the intersections of the reproductive justice and environmental justice movements?
— What do our strategies look like on the ground?

The following is a culmination of those voices and stories.

Shawna Larson: I'm Shawna Larson. I'm Ahtna Athabaskan and I am Sugpiaq on my mom's side. I'm from two different tribes here in Alaska. There are 231 federally recognized tribes here in the state of Alaska, so we have 40 percent of the nation's tribes here. I live close to my community and I've worked with Alaska Community Action on Toxics [ACAT] for the last eight years as the environmental justice program director.

Bianca Encinias: My name is Bianca Encinias and I'm with the Southwest Network for Environmental and Economic Justice [SNEEJ]. We're located in Albuquerque, New Mexico, and are a network of sixty grassroots community-based organizations located in Texas, New Mexico, Colorado, Arizona, and California and the northern border states of Mexico. I've got two and a half projects: I work on state projects with the New Mexico environmental justice working group, as well as kicking off a new campaign called the LUCHA campaign, which stands for the Land Use Community Health Action campaign, which is where we will be targeting the practices of the Department of Health and Human Services toward environmental justice. And, when I have the time, I want to do a Women's Commission. I was born and raised in New Mexico and my family has been here for many generations, prior to it being part of the United States.

Vanessa Huang: This is Vanessa Huang. I work with Justice Now and we are a human rights organization based in Oakland, California, that partners with people in women's prisons, and with communities outside of prisons to end the prison industrial complex. And I also organize with a new coalition, Transforming Justice, which is national, and we work to support local organizing to end the criminalization and imprisonment of trans- and gender nonconforming communities. I was born and raised mostly here in California; I spent some time living in Taipei as a toddler, and in Providence, Rhode Island, in New England in my early twenties. My title is campaign director for Justice Now.

Cara Page: I am Cara Page and I'm based in Atlanta, Georgia, and I am the former director of the Committee on Women, Population, and the Environment [CWPE]. CWPE is an international alliance of feminist health practitioners, organizers, and scholars who challenge the mythology and ideology of population control still used to target and blame women of color and our communities as the root cause of environmental degradation. I am building a collective of healers and organizers called Kindred. It will be based in the South to build, honor, and support regenerating traditions of healing and wellness as part of our organizing strategies to sustain our organizers and the communities that we work with. We will also be working on community-based and holistic models of healing as a response to the trauma and conditions of the medical industrial complex.

Laura Jiménez: How would you define environmental and reproductive justice differently than environmental and reproductive rights, and where are the intersections between the two?

VH: I enter the work and relate to those movements and have become part of those movements by way of my work in the prison industrial complex abolition movement. The environmental justice, reproductive justice, and other justice movements are, for me, about collective liberation and are about centering the margins, and ensuring that our self-determination and community autonomy are first and foremost, and that we're prioritizing the work that has historically been mar-

> *And when I think about the earth, like here in New Mexico, I'm first generation urban, or semi-urban I'd say, because we grew up in a rural community, but on the outskirts of the city. So, what happened in my generation is that we got disconnected from the land. I was fortunate to grow up with my grandparents living next door, so we still had the connection to that, like, land-based way of living. But, as my grandparents have died off, or my grandmother has gotten too old, we've become dependent on going to the grocery stores for food, right, so putting all these chemicals into our bodies, and seeing how that's impacted the health of our bodies and the health of our children, right. So, when I look at the reproductive justice and the environmental justice movements and where they intersect, whether its forced through the government or through the contamination of industry, we're seeing the impacts on our reproductive system.*
>
> *—Bianca Encinias*

ginalized by systems of oppression. So, the anti-prison-industrial-complex movement recognizes the ways that surveillance, policing, confinement, and deportation collaborate to control our populations—folks from communities of color, working-class communities, the trans- and gender nonconforming communities, the disability communities, poor communities, migrant communities—and recognizes all the ways that our communities overlap. Specifically, this movement understands how these tools of the prison industrial complex are continuing legacies and tools of imperialism, and how the legacies related to forced migration into this land and internal displacement within this land connect to colonialism and slavery.

It's really hard to ignore, for instance, how controlling the population of people of African descent in the time of slavery continues to happen through the Thirteenth Amendment with the rise of mass imprisonment in the US context. And that control has been magnified and expanded to more communities now in the current prison industrial complex by moving people out of our communities, tampering with folks' abilities to birth within the prison system, and through the dealing out of premature deaths.

I see the intersection playing out, between reproductive justice and anti-population-control and environmental justice and economic justice work, through the way that the political economy uses institutions of confinement, and the industry of confinement in particular, to target and harm the environments where our communities have less access to institutional power to say, "We don't want a prison here." We see that happening all over Central California and that having clear, devastating impacts on air quality and fresh water supply and levels of toxicity and obviously control and use of land that takes away folks' self-determination and our political and economic social power to control our own resources.

BE: I agree with what Vanessa said. I think that a key component of the environmental justice movement is self-determination and this idea that we speak for ourselves. So, I think that's one of the key components that came out of the First People of Color Summit that was held in 1991 in Washington, DC. That we speak for ourselves, and that we're the experts of our communities, right?

And so with self-determination being key to it, I think it's also how we expanded the definition of environmentalism—looking at it as where we live, work, play, pray, and go to school. I mean typically mainstream environmentalism has been about conservation, preservation, protecting the trees, protecting the animals, or a lot of times, privatizing or federalizing the land. Looking at a place like New Mexico, there has been a history of land struggle and environmental mainstream groups that have come here, using our language in their literature, and wanting to federalize land while they were actually taking lands away from native, Indigenous, and Chicano people.

The environmental justice movement started more formally in the 1970s, when the first Earth Day was called, but the term was coined in the early 1990s. But if you look in a lot of the different movements that were going on in the community, it could go back as far as even the Civil Rights Movement, the American Indian movement, the Chicano movement, and others. A lot of those folks who were involved in those particular movements were talking about their communities being contaminated. In my community, we found out in 1980 that the government and corporations were contaminating our land, so we were already organizing protests or actions.

While mainstream environmental groups were fighting for preservation and conservation, we grew up fighting the city's only sewer-treatment plant for contaminating our community. We were out there fighting for a healthy environment to live for many of our children; fighting for clean water, for clean air, affordable housing, and access to affordable healthcare, issues like that. So, for me, where I think there are intersections is the right to control our bodies and how to make decisions. Historically, our bodies as women of color have been controlled by the government, right? If our people were on welfare or WIC or Medicaid or whatever, it was always like they were trying to control our bodies, whether it was through sterilization, forced birth control, or contaminating our bodies, in some ways that's being forced onto us.

The first environmental justice People of Color Summit, was held in 1991 in Washington, DC, and this was where some of the leadership came together and started to define environmental justice as a movement. They laid out the seventeen principles that were supposed to guide our work, that were called the Principles for Environmental Justice. A second summit was held in 2002.

SL: It's helpful for me to listen to this discussion because I definitely agree with everything that has been said, and it has always been that way, but we just haven't articulated it in the ways that we are today.

I think it's really important to look back through a broad-based historical overview, and especially to look at the governing laws of the United States Constitution, to understand our movements—where they were and where they've gone. I think it's interesting just to compare the idea of rights versus justice because if you think about the US Constitution, "justice" only appears once and it's in the preamble—"We the people of the United States, in order to form a more perfect union, establish justice, ensure domestic tranquility"—that's the only time that justice is mentioned in the Constitution. And the Constitution is about defining what people's rights are, but it's all being defined by a very specific population, at a time when all the killing and segregation, wars and slavery, and all these things had gone on. So it's these mostly white male slave- and property-owners that are writing this document, and I think everything we see today really is a spin-off of that problem.

In the governmental structure that was created such a long time ago, I don't even think they could fathom the way that things are today. I mean, I don't think they thought of GMOs [genetically modified organisms] at that time. I don't think they thought about genetically engineered corn, you know? They were happy just to grow corn and live—even though they stole the land and got the seeds from other people. And I've heard Tom Linzey say, "There's never been an environmental movement in the history of the United States, because historically movements have driven rights into the Constitution." So, for example, compare the abolitionists with the environmental movement, the abolitionists were not asking for a slavery protection agency like we got the Environmental Protection Agency [EPA], and that's a great way to sort of think about what are these movements doing and how do they intersect?

Kierra Johnson: What has been the impact of population control ideology on our movements?

BE: I think the difference between the environmental justice movement and the environmental movement is the same kind of thought process as population control. They think they have all of this kind of expertise and knowledge. All of a sudden, it's trendy to be "green" and organic. In New Mexico we have a flood of hippie earth folks who have come here all of a sudden because "they've discovered it"; they are the experts on this stuff. Well, our people have been living like this for hundreds of years and this is nothing new to us, but unfortunately whether you're a Native person, or you're a Chicano person, when you've become urban, you've lost a lot of that connection to the land. So a lot of our young people, including my generation, have lost a lot of that knowledge and so we are having to reclaim it.

I think another thing that happens within the environmental movement is the blaming of our communities. A few years ago, the Sierra Club had an article on climate change, and basically what the article concluded was that because Latinos had so many babies it was basically our fault for climate issues here in the United States. So that's just been a big battle for us with mainstream environmental groups advocating for population control and claiming that we're having too many children, we're contributing to this contamination, and that we are the reason for all these negative environmental factors.

SL: I'll just build off some of the things that Bianca was saying. I know I've heard people talking about it and a lot of times the people who have the idea of population control are led by white people, and usually white males. I think it ties back into the government structures put in place and how that was also led by white male slave- and property-owners.

I think the best way that I can identify with this as an Indigenous person is the way the government system came into Alaska. Alaska is an extremely large state and we don't actually have that many people here; we're under a million people here. In the lower forty-eight states, they created reservations for the tribes, but in Alaska they chose to create corporations. We now have thirteen regional corporations. The way that the Bureau of Indian Affairs [BIA] plays into it is actually the perfect way to think about it, because in order to be seen at the Native hospital here, you have to have your BIA card, which shows your blood quantum. There's been lots of talk about how even-

When you promote alternative energy and fuel we have to ask how the production is impacting our communities. For example, ethanol and the production of corn: Corn is a main staple for a lot of stuff not just fuel. How is this really impacting countries like Mexico, where corn is a primary staple for food especially for poor Indigenous communities? I was out in Mexico for a meeting in Puerto Pinasco and they were talking about how corn prices are skyrocketing and are becoming unaffordable for them. And then we destroy more land to produce more corn and in reality, who is really using those cars? I understand the concepts but I don't think we are thinking about how these things are impacting communities of color and Indigenous communities around the world.

—Bianca Encinias

tually you're going to have to be a specific amount of blood quantum before you can be seen at the hospital, and the same for these corporations. In 1971 all Alaskan Native people were enrolled on the registers of these corporations and made to be shareholders, and so instead of living on reservations, we're shareholders. The interesting thing about this is that they'll slowly bleed us out of these two things, for a blood quantum. Obviously, unless you are able to continue being with people of your own heritage, and that can change drastically over even five generations, you have to think about whether your kids and their children will still be able to go and get medical care.

A lot of people talk about it, and they say, "Oh those Natives, they get free medical care, they get it so easy," but it's not free. A lot of our ancestors died and a lot of our land was taken away before we were given this so-called "free medical care." It's through this medical care that they have done things like test hepatitis B vaccines on us without us knowing or even doing forced sterilization.

One of the things that happened when I delivered my baby was I had a fourth-degree tear and they didn't check me properly before they let me go, so I had to go back and be completely reconstructed a week later. The hospital staff told me how happy I should be because this happens a lot, but for those women [who] have to fly on planes and go to villages that are so remote in Alaska they never find out. It means that these women heal open with no distinction between the vagina and anus—it makes intercourse, conception, and hygiene a major problem and makes the women prone to infections. Culturally we don't talk about these things, especially with white male doctors who live in the city, and so [these women] never come forward and they heal that way; they heal totally open.

It's a lot similar to government and industrial complexes coming together to control us and our bodies through the medicine they give us. One of the chemicals that we are working on is Lindane, the chemical that is primarily used to treat head lice and scabies. When there's an outbreak in Alaska, in a community, in a school, in a village, they want to treat all the kids. They send notes home and they want all the parents to get this medicine and all the kids to be treated at once, so that it doesn't "spread"—not that it's going to kill you if you ever have head lice. Lindane is a pesticide that has been banned in more than fifty countries, including most recently Chile and Mexico. It is also one of the chemicals that is being added to the Stockholm Convention on Persistent Organic Pollutants [POPs]. The European Union has already phased this chemical out and also the state of California has already banned this chemical. Exposure to this neurotoxic organochlorine has been linked to seizures, developmental disabilities, and hormone disruption. It is known to be particularly hazardous to children. But nationwide in the US, although they've banned it for agricultural uses, the Food and Drug Administration is still allowing it to be used for head lice and scabies.

CP: I just want to add to what everyone has been talking about, in terms of really looking at how population control has been generated as an actual theory and practice of genocide. This has been used to promote the fear of consumption and social dependency by blaming poor communities, communities of color, people with disabilities, women, and incarcerated and queer communities as people who will consume and burden our social systems and natural resources. This of course denies the conditions of what's truly happening, in terms of looking at one-fifth of the world's white and wealthiest populations consuming almost three-fourths of the world's resources. The mythology of population control allows for racist, classist, heterosexist, ableist, and homophobic assumptions and justifies violence against our communities under the guise of national security and state control.

I'd even like to take it one step further and look at the marriage between an old theory of population control and the new practices of privatizing community crops, seeds, and the genetic makeup of our bodies. With the new field of genetic technologies merged with the field of contraceptive technologies, what has been the impact for our communities' well-being, medicinal practices, and food supplies? Population control is not just blaming and targeting our communities but actually working through science and contraceptive technologies to control our bodies, our traditions, our crops. We need to take scientific research into our own hands, within our RJ and EJ movements to understand the cumulative effect of what these practices mean for our communities. We need to look at the contemporary ways population control looks in terms of altering our DNA, our crops, and seeds that are completely changing our cellular memory.

VH: For me, I think about the impact of population control ideology both on a personal level and also in relation to the movement work that I am doing as a female-bodied person of Chinese descent. Just really being present with the ways that China's population control methods collaborate with heteropatriarchy has impacted my own and my peers' experiences diasporically based on which bodies are valued over other bodies and whose bodies are thrown away if you're only allowed to have one kid.

And then the particular impact that has had on women-identified and/or female-bodied folks, including trans and gender nonconforming folks and those of us who feel a little more fluid. So that even when I go to a Chinese herbalist to get a reading; my yin/yang imbalance of the female deficiency is not seen as only female or male but rather gender identity is seen as something that's fluid, evolving, and changing. The idea of disposability is really present in how the prison industrial complex is able to thrive, grow, and to maintain itself because certain people's bodies from certain communities are still seen by the white owning class and nontrans folks as disposable. We also see that playing out in public space sites, gentrification locally in our neighborhoods in Oakland, and everywhere else that I've seen it. Also transnationally, how that plays out in a neoliberal context, and whose land is taken away, and compromised and the process of corporate globalization.

I think that particularly, as climate change intensifies, we see a particular impact on what folks have already talked about, the blaming of our populations for that, when what we're really talking about is control over space and environment by people in power. What we are really talking about is the blaming of people of color and Chinese and people with disabilities and queer folks for being unsustainable when the root of it is that capitalism and imperialism are unsustainable.

So in terms of the work we do to challenge imprisonment and confinement and surveillance, we see how this disposability plays out in the different strategies we use based on the kinds of medical abuse and neglect that happen in a prison setting. And we see patterns of sterilization abuse happening within a prison setting and how that's normalized because people who are placed in prison are disposable and aren't seen as really human.

LJ: What are the potential strategies and intersecting opportunities for assuring safety, resiliency, and sustainability for our environments and bodies?

CP: For me, there's an obvious intersection in terms of really looking deeply at what it means to fight for sovereignty of land and body. I'm excited to look at how we think about our bodies as environments, and really expand this idea that environment is not just something that is external to our actual physical bodies—it is all of our political, physical, spiritual, and emotional environments. And my hope is that in terms of thinking about safety, we are imagining what it means to not only ask for safety from state violence and communal abuse, not only safety from environmental toxins, but actually to expand the question to include the safety of what we're actually putting into our bodies. How can we imagine pushing back on who has the knowledge of "what is best for us"? How do we not continue to depend on the medical industrial complex, the food industrial complex as systems that know better than what we know? I think that Bianca said it in terms of how Indigenous nations have been raised living on the land, how in all of our regions—myself being a descendant of African American Georgia sharecroppers—how have we been removed from our natural resources and ways of knowing how to survive and sustain our well-being.

How are we thinking about safety being something multiplicitous to our bodies and our environments? For the communities I am working with on coercion and reproductive control, I want the safety of food connected to the medical treatment of our bodies as one [and] the same. I'm interested in thinking broadly about how we think about all of our environments. Who controls it, how do we intuitively know it for ourselves?

BE: In terms of potential strategies, I think Cara already hit it, right? For me I'm thinking about how do we come together as Indigenous people from around the world, as people of color here in the US? How do we start to reclaim that which has been stolen or taken from us, right? So how do we bring women of color together to even talk about these issues and make it an even broader conversation with more people at the table? How do we share the different kind of projects that we're working on?

We're doing an apprenticeship program where this organization called Kalpulli Izkalli partnered with Young Women United, and what we're doing is working with some of the elder women from Kalpulli Izkalli to learn—we're called *promotoras tradicionales* [promoters of traditional health knowledge]. We're learning how to plant and how to identify herbs, and then from there, we'll learn how to make tinctures and teas. We participate in these clinics where they're mentoring us to learn how to do *limpias* [spiritual cleansings]; we have talking circles where we just talk as women about different things, about our body, the environment, and food. A discussion we were having a few weeks ago was about that birth control that's out and their big thing they brag about on the commercials is having your period for only one or two days, and it'll be great because you'll only have your period so many times a year. And it's just like, wow, maybe we should be having conversations about how it seems like knowledge has been passed down about our bodies and how they cleanse themselves for a reason naturally. So, what are going to be the long-term effects of a birth control that only lets you have a period one or two times or three times a year, right? So, just creating those kinds of spaces and it being intergenerational.

And then I think of how, in terms of sustainability, how do we create opportunities in our communities? We're working on a community garden so that later on we can give the food out, but also sell it. So how do we create economic sustainability and jobs, and how do we promote and give out healthy food within our community, and also bring back traditional medicine, right?

VH: Right now we're seeing a trend of doulas and midwives really prioritizing reproductive justice, and focusing on communities that are targeted for imprisonment and deportation and confinement and surveillance. We are seeing doulas reaching out to those in the prison industrial complex movements to partner with us and in that conversation negotiating some of the tensions. The reason why they're reaching out to us is because they want to promote health for folks who are in a situation where their health is being severely compromised and deteriorated and we're seeing premature deaths. They are recognizing [that] they don't want to strengthen the prison system, and to potentially position themselves in alignment with a movement to abolish the whole system. So, I would just hone in, again, on a potential strategy and intersecting opportunity to focus back on the framing of the question. To challenge how the prison industrial complex normalizes how the state surveils, polices, confines, and deports; to shift ways of thinking that dehumanize and essentialize and demonize our populations and that render us disposable; to shift ways of thinking that insist upon only two genders; and to shift ways of thinking that insist that the lives of people with disabilities aren't worth living.

As Shawna was saying earlier, it is important to make the links between slavery abolitionists who weren't pushing for a slavery protection agency, so we shouldn't be pushing for a prison protection agency. We should really know that we need to do work that reduces imprisonment and the way to keep our communities whole and thriving is to really support the building of accountable communities and to challenge prison expansion when the state presents it to us. Not settling for less than resources going into our own programs and our food security and our healthcare, rather than the state pushing so-called "state-provided services" in a prison setting for those things.

SL: It's interesting as I think back on it and just listen to the conversation and try to think of how to articulate these things and frame them. It's funny, it's humorous to me to think about it. From my Indigenous perspective, these people came on a boat from Europe, they came here, they came into our area, and they took our land and they claimed our knowledge and they took over and then we tried to explain sustainability to them and they refused to listen and then they raped and pillaged the land and blamed us for overpopulation. And when I think about what happened as they came over on the boats, I understand how I'm colonized as an Indigenous woman. You know?

About six years ago I was invited to testify in front of a UN rapporteur, Ms. Fatma Zohra Ouhachi-Vesely of Algeria about toxic waste issues. There were three of us that were able to make it: myself, a person from Sonora, Mexico, and Francisco Calí, who is from Chimaltenango, Guatemala. So we realized after we testified that we were all talking about the same issues—low-birthweight babies, birth defects, learning disabilities, and cancer. And the three of us realized that it didn't matter if it was North or South or East or West, that these issues are pervasive all around the world. So we started looking at these issues and understanding it's just a big cycle: from the communities in Mexico and Guatemala, where they are putting the [pesticide] tanks on their backs and spraying these horrible chemicals; then they volatilize and migrate to the North where our communities are finding them in our traditional foods, our polar bears, our seals, and in our breast milk. So we thought it would be a great opportunity to create what we called the North–South Indigenous Pesticide Network. A victory that the network gained two years ago in 2006 was when we hosted a conference at the request of the community in Río Yaqui (Sonora, México) and the traditional leaders, after hearing the full explanation about the chemicals, they put a ban on pesticides being sprayed on their traditional lands and they were supported by the Mexican government in doing that.

—Shawna Larson

A health aide named Annie Alowa lived out on St. Lawrence Island which is occupied by two communities: they're called Siberian Yupik people. The elders there talk about how the military came and brought enough supplies to last them for fifteen years. When they left, all they took with them were their rifles and backpacks, and left thousands of barrels with different types of waste in them, solvents and fuels which they brought when they came. Annie noticed a lot of low birthweight babies, trouble conceiving, cancers in the reproductive areas, inability to carry babies to term, and a lot of learning disabilities that they never saw before, as well as high rates of asthma and diabetes. So she went to the military to get all this waste cleaned up, and they basically sent her all the way around in a giant circle. Then she met my boss, Pam Miller, who had just started ACAT, and the first case ACAT took on was Annie's, and since then we have secured millions of dollars to help the community to clean up. But still, the community is fighting because we would tell the military to test in one area, and the Army Corps of Engineers would test in other areas, where they didn't think they would find anything. The elders would tell us, "No, no, no, that's not where they were, test under the school. That's where they were." So we would test in the places the elders found and then we would find all these high rates of PCBs. And so, we still see these contaminants not only in their blood, but also in the traditional foods that they eat, as well as the water.

—Shawna Larson

I can understand how my people have been colonized and the ways that has been adapted into my life and what I pass on to my kids.

I have this quote that I carry everywhere, "Environmentalism is just a symptom of colonization." The whole "green," greenie movement idea, "organics," I think that they are just really a form of colonization and how it plays out. For us, the work that we do in rural communities is to try to pry apart traditional thinking from Western thinking and colonization because they start getting melded together in communities. In our villages and rural areas, we still practice traditions such as hunting whale, seals, and birds, and gathering eggs, greens, and berries. But we do that to supplement our income because a gallon of gas in rural communities is now seven dollars a gallon. So, economic oppression plays a huge part into this, in understanding that as the prices rise, people are starting to really think about their choices at the store. A gallon of milk is also seven dollars!

But it's interesting to think about potential strategies, because we're trying to think outside the box and how do we do that when we're thinking about abolishing these systems? What is outside of the box? My mother-in-law always says, "Oftentimes, people say they're thinking outside the box, but they're just decorating the inside of the box with a nice Navajo rug on the wall, or changing the color, versus actually thinking outside of the box." So, how can we really potentially strategize about intersecting opportunities? When I started this work, there were days when I thought, those people need to just get back on the boat and go back to where they came from. But our Chief here, he's so good, he said, "We need to welcome them here, they're not going to go away, they're here, and with a good heart, in a good way, we welcome them here and we figure out ways to work with them to improve." And I think in terms of colonization, it's interesting to look at nonminority populations and to see how they really don't understand they're even colonized. How do you do that outreach and education to them to help them understand that they're in the same system that we are in, and that they're dying, too?

KJ: We know there are people working at a community grassroots level with efforts that have organically been a part of these communities. Within our environmental justice and reproductive justice movements, who is actually doing this intersectional work on the ground?

BE: The Southwest Network has started the LUCHA campaign, where we've decided to target the Department of Health and Human Services [DHHS] on a national level, and we're actually starting to begin discussions with the Asian Pacific Environmental Network, the Indigenous Environmental Network, and Citizens for Environmental Justice to build a national campaign. Because the public health officials at DHHS go out and say, "The reason why Native Americans have the highest diabetes rates in the world is because of poor diets and they don't exercise." And we need to change that racist paradigm and stop blaming individual behavior.

I'm sure for all people, there are some things that as individuals we could all be changing, but the reality is, should we be looking at uranium mining and how is that linked to rare cases of cancer and diabetes? So that's kind of a big deal, we're challenging the very basis of public health ideology. So that's something we're starting to work on a national level, but it's rooted in our local work.

That's an example of how we're lifting up some other issues, how we impact and change state policy, by building a statewide coalition, and a movement within the state on environmental justice, through bringing Native, Chicano, and African American communities here together with our white allies to address environmental justice. It also shows how on a federal level we start to challenge some of these very racist, sexist, etc., ideologies that are being deeply entrenched within our agencies.

SL: Within our organization we've just been hosting women's reproductive justice and environmental health round tables so that women have a voice in the community to talk, and it's a great way to cross over environmental justice and reproductive justice issues. We are doing that in the cities and out in some of the rural communities. Recently we went into the community of Bethel, which is a Yupik community; it's a city actually, and there are fifty-two villages up and down the river that all intersect in this larger hub community. By doing this, we are also getting on the agendas of some of the meetings that are happening—they're fighting a gold mine proposing to come into their area. We're also talking about the fact that when the EPA or the state environmental agency come in, they are primarily white people coming into rural, Indigenous, traditional communities and they are saying, "You know how the system works." They are telling these communities how they have to participate in the regulatory system and how they have to do health impact assessments. And so we bring forward the fact that if you continue to participate in this capitalistic government system, you'll continue to get the same results. The mines will come in and you will continue to not have a sovereign relationship with this government of the United States. Tribes are sovereign; we have self-determination, and we talk about how the federal government doesn't really recognize our sovereignty. We're not sovereign because the feds tell us we're sovereign, we're sovereign because we've always been sovereign, and we define that for ourselves, what our sovereignty looks like.

We also share stories about how communities around the lower forty-eight are starting to pass ordinances. For villages, it doesn't apply so much, but in cities, like the city of Bethel, since it's a "federally recognized" city, they have the right to pass ordinances within their own town. One of the things that they've been talking about in Bethel is passing an ordinance to ban cyanide, which states that these corporations aren't allowed to bring cyanide through the city of Bethel. If the corporations are not able to do that, they're not able to get it upriver to the mine where it would be used, and so people are thinking about actually starting to change the structure of law and challenging the government structure. So we're not just looking to the same health impact assessment and the same systems under the EPA and under the US Constitution that are going to continue to yield us the same results really.

VH: I'll speak to two things: One, we've been over the years working with people in California's women's prisons to self-organize and to develop an astounding peer health education and survival network inside. Which involves building multiracial alliances, and alliances across gender identities, gender presentations, and across health and across abilities and sexualities. I think that opportunity for alliance building is because the prison industrial complex is so crosscutting and that its targets have increased over time and it shows us so manifestly the ways that our populations are controlled by the confluence of all these systems. That's one way that we see folks organizing to survive and doing it in intersectional ways.

Another struggle that has really been a focus over the last few years is supporting the organizing of people in women's prisons, and trans women who've recently been locked in men's prisons. We've done this nationally in conversation with the reproductive justice, gender self-determination, and queer liberation movements to amplify our collective opposition to the construction of so-called "gender responsive" prisons, which is a new policy trend being pushed at the national level, and at different local regions around the country. Part of this process has been challenging proposals to build them at the state as well as local levels. Locally, we did effectively strip the prison construction from its legislative vehicle, bringing the opposition of people in women's prisons into conversation with local EJ activists in the Central Valley.

CP: I would love to add two examples in the Southeast. One is the New Orleans Women's Health Justice Initiative, which is a clinic that really transpired as a communal response to how New Orleans and the Gulf Coast were ignored after Katrina. This is a women of color–led clinic, doing healing-based response practices for both the lesbian, gay, bisexual, and trans community as well as for heterosexual women, predominantly low-income and women of color and women with disabilities. They are also doing major mobilization around the intersections of EJ and RJ, by organizing for public housing, providing free health clinics, and doing organizing institutes across communities on issues of population control, state violence, environmental

[and] reproductive justice, safety, and responding to police brutality and heightened violence that's happened since Katrina. In relationship to the well-being of the community and the environments that they are trying to live in and regenerate in particular, they are looking at ways to transform thinking about health and healthcare through a justice lens. And it's a powerful example of resiliency and sustainability and ways that people are really seeing the intersections.

The second example is from the work that I've been doing on the ground in the South in partnership with the Committee on Women, Population, and the Environment to work with health practitioners, health advocates, and community organizers on how are we going to transform the language of health and transform practices of healthcare. These practices are oftentimes based on a public health ideology that comes out of a history of actually looking at people as disease. Public healthcare really came out of a rooted idea that if we can "fix" these people, then we won't have as much burden on our healthcare system. So, transforming this idea that health is not a pathology, that health is not about fear of sex, fear of sexuality, fear of gender, fear of bodies, but actually how can we think about health, well-being, healing, as ways to respond to the conditions of our social/political/cultural oppression? And how to not only transform this healthcare system that is only identifying us as disease, or with disease, but think about sustainability and systems of wellness that go beyond the body. We've been using storytelling as a tool to talk about how healthcare has controlled many of our communities and thinking about ways to transform the language and the practices. Some of these stories have also led to women talking about the right to a safe environment and we are trying to build these links by beginning to tell our collective stories.

Conclusion

As the conveners of this conversation, we were honored to hold such an expansive dialogue that built an even deeper analysis of the environmental and reproductive justice movements by using our movements' principles to critique the legacies of slavery, colonialism, and continued state and communal practices of coercion and control. In the privatization and corporatization of healthcare, prisons, water, and other systems or natural resources, time and time again we see the burden of proof

> *I live in my community; I know the place on the river where my grandma was born and I know who I am and that I have the responsibility to my people and my children to do this work. It's very clear to me, and so, even though the work is very hard, because you do see a lot of people dying of cancer, and you do see all the hardships that we all see in our communities, I just know that I have this responsibility. And I think, one day, I'll see my ancestors when I cross over, and I want to know that when I go there, when they see me, they'll be able to know that I did the best I could while I was here.*
>
> *—Shawna Larson*

shifting to the victimized individuals to prove their injustices as if environmental toxins or sterilization abuse was an isolated incident and not a broader practice of genocide against our communities. Placing the burden of reducing the earth's carbon footprint on individual women or communities will not achieve the reduction of environmental contamination nor will it eradicate the oppressive and abusive circumstances which have created these crises if it is not within a context of ending oppression and state violence.

The environmental degradation and reproductive oppression that we are experiencing necessitates that our strategies for healing, self-determination, and communal autonomy be used to build the intersections between our movements. This conversation pushes us to imagine what sustainability can look like for our physical, emotional, and spiritual environments that transcend the idea that some bodies and some environments are expendable. We want to appreciate the interviewees for their tremendous courage and commitment to their transformative work and vision. We invite you to continue this dialogue across our movements to weave our stories of resistance and begin building our strategies wider and farther.

The Welfare Family Cap: Reproductive Rights, Control, and Poverty Prevention

DIANA ROMERO and MADINA AGÉNOR

Introduction

In the mid-1990s the Personal Responsibility and Work Opportunity Reconciliation Act, or welfare reform, permitted states to impose policies pertaining to the sexual and reproductive-related behaviors of poor women. One such policy involved a "fertility prevention as poverty prevention" strategy, meaning the adoption of the family cap or child-exclusion policy by several states. Specifically, the family cap denies additional income support to poor women who have a baby while enrolled in Temporary Assistance to Needy Families (TANF), the federal cash assistance program. Policymakers saw fertility prevention via the family cap as a mechanism for poverty prevention, and an opportunity to penalize poor women who were "irresponsible" for having children.

A total of twenty-four states implemented the family cap. Such a "welfare policy" suggests that policymakers believe poor women decide whether to have children on the expectation of additional income support from the state; and therefore it is assumed that the absence of additional cash assistance will result in poor women giving birth to fewer children. Implicit in these policies is the belief that there is a causal association between individual sexual and fertility-related behaviors and poverty. While some have pointed to cross-sectional studies documenting associations between the two, very little research has examined the role played by important preexisting structural and sociodemographic factors (e.g., the availability of community-level resources). As such, the conclusion, for example, that childbearing among certain groups of women leads to poverty ignores the preexisting circumstances of women's lives that may already predispose them to economic and other social disadvantage.

We examine this specific poverty-prevention policy in three distinct ways. First, we place it in the broader historical context of reproductive control of marginalized women (i.e., poor women and women of color). Second, we consider this policy within a human and reproductive rights framework. And third, we review the available empirical analyses that have attempted to determine whether poverty-prevention policy has been effective.

Reproductive Regulation of Poor Women of Color: An Extensive History

Consideration of a social policy such as the family cap must be placed in a broader historical context related to past efforts to regulate the reproduction of poor or otherwise marginalized women in the United States. Currently, black and Latina women are disproportionately represented among women enrolled in TANF. Thus, policies that seek to restrict the sexual and reproductive rights and freedom of welfare recipients, such as the family cap, can have a greater impact on them and their families compared to other women. In addition, an analysis of various welfare policies indicated that the *racial* makeup of a state played a role in the implementation of the family cap in that state. Specifically, the researchers found that family caps and stringent time limits were significantly more likely in states with higher percentages of African Americans and Latinos in their welfare caseloads. The evidence of a racial factor in state adoption of such a policy, as well as the disproportionate representation of women of color in current TANF caseloads, adds to the social importance of assessing its effect on both fertility *and* poverty.

Attempts to control the reproduction of women of color in the US are not new. In the early twentieth century, the rise of the eugenics movement extended reproductive control to all of society's "unfit" and "feebleminded" members, such as the mentally and physically disabled, immigrants, and the poor. As a result, birth control became a means of limiting the growth of "undesirable" populations, including African Americans, Native Americans, and Latinos.

In order to understand the social significance of reproductive choice for black women, one needs to examine their sexual and reproductive experiences throughout history. During slavery, black women were not only valuable for their labor but also for their reproductive capacity. As a result, the oppression of female slaves illustrates the intimate relationship between productivity and reproduction, which in turn served to subjugate black women's reproductive autonomy in the name of producing economic goods and children to fuel the system of slavery. While black women were forced or coerced to reproduce during slavery (e.g., by being punished for not bearing children or being rewarded for becoming pregnant), they were *discouraged* from bearing children during the twentieth century.

Today, black women's reproductive options and decisions continue to be constrained by a range of social, economic, and political factors including poverty and economic insecurity; racism and classism; lack of access to healthcare and accurate health information; dependence on government funding to access sexual and reproductive health services; lack of access to lawyers and advocacy organizations to defend their reproductive rights; and social expectations about motherhood that rely on middle-class ideals. As a result, many contemporary black women, as well as other women of color and poor women, are denied true reproductive choice, which refers to the decision of whether, when, how, and with whom to give birth to a child.

Moreover, the US government has set forth and upheld a number of legal decisions that undermine women's reproductive choice, namely restricting their access to safe, publicly funded abortions and supporting forced medical procedures that place the fetus above a woman's reproductive health and rights. These court decisions have a disproportionate impact on women of color and poor women, as they are more likely to rely on government-subsidized sexual and reproductive health services. In addition to compromised access to safe abortions and increased exposure to coercive childbirth practices, women of color and poor women have been subject to a number of other government-sponsored initiatives jeopardizing their reproductive choice, including sterilization abuse and the coercive use of contraceptive methods such as the birth control pill, Depo-Provera, Norplant, and the IUD as a requirement for public assistance or fulfillment of court-ordered alternatives to incarceration.

Sterilization

Both blatant and subtle forms of sterilization abuse have been used by the state to undermine reproductive choice among women of color and poor women. Some of the most blatant coercive uses of sterilization occurred during the 1970s, and relied on the eugenics-rooted idea that certain groups of individuals, namely women of color and poor women, should not bear children because "socially undesirable traits" such as poverty and "welfare dependence" are hereditary.[1] These violations of women's reproductive autonomy and choice included the Indian Health Service–sponsored hysterectomies performed on Native American women under twenty-one years of age without informed consent. In a 1976 report, the Government Accountability Office (GAO) found that the consent forms provided to Native American women undergoing sterilization failed to inform them about the nature, purpose, risks, and consequences of the procedure, as well as their right to withdraw their consent at any time without being penalized by the loss of benefits. Other IHS infractions included not presenting women with alternative procedures; failing to uphold the seventy-two-hour waiting period mandated by the government prior to performing a sterilization; soliciting consent from women directly after they have given birth; and obtaining consent *after* performing the procedure. In total, various studies have found that, during the 1970s, the IHS sterilized at least 25 percent of all Native American women between fifteen and forty-four years of age.[2]

In other forms of sterilization abuse against women of color and poor women, physicians agreed to deliver the babies of black women enrolled in Medicaid or perform abortions for low income black women only if they "agreed" to being sterilized. Some service providers threatened to rescind poor and low-income women's public benefits if they did not "consent" to being sterilized. Furthermore, in 1974, a federal district judge in Alabama found that 100,000 to 150,000 poor women were sterilized every year under the auspices of government programs. The court also noted that government representatives had threatened to deprive some of these women of their welfare benefits unless they underwent sterilization.

The Latino experience has been similar. During the 1950s and 1960s, sterilization increased sharply among Puerto Rican women both on the island and mainland. In Puerto Rico, the prevalence of sterilization reached its peak in 1965, with one-third of ever-married women between the ages of twenty and forty-nine having been sterilized. Researchers have linked the high proportion of sterilized Puerto Rican women to the lack of other available forms of contraception and a relatively favorable government attitude toward the utilization of the procedure within this population. Furthermore, the birth control pill, which was developed during the late 1950s and early 1960s, was primarily tested on Puerto Rican and Mexican women under troubling conditions regarding informed consent and the protection of human subjects.

The factors that rendered—and *continue* to render—poor women and women of color particularly vulnerable to coercive, government-sponsored sterilizations include some physicians' belief that poor women and women of color are unable to use nonpermanent methods of contraception effectively; the lack of access to accurate, factual information about contraceptive options and the resources necessary to enact it; and the prioritization of sterilization over other sexual and reproductive health services in government funding schemes.

Sterilization abuse is not a new phenomenon. At the beginning of the twentieth century, a number of states throughout the country passed "involuntary sterilization laws" aimed at preventing reproduction among people deemed "socially inadequate" and likely to produce "defective offspring," including the mentally ill, alcoholics, epileptics, criminals, and the poor. These laws were rooted in eugenic theory, which sets forth the idea that intelligence and other individual characteristics are determined by one's genetic makeup and therefore passed down from generation to generation. Involuntary or eugenic sterilization laws were widely supported by government officials. For example, in *Buck v. Bell*, a landmark case in 1927, the US Supreme Court upheld the constitutionality of an involuntary sterilization law in Virginia. During the trial, Justice Oliver Wendell Holmes noted that sterilization was necessary "in order to prevent our being swamped by incompetence" and to "prevent those who are manifestly unfit from continuing their kind."[3]

Similarly, in the 1950s, policymakers in a number of states, including Maryland, Delaware, Virginia, Iowa, Mississippi, and North Carolina, introduced legislation promoting the control of poor women's fertility as a way of decreasing welfare expenditures. Although none of these bills were passed into law, they sought to tackle poverty and decrease public spending by controlling poor and low-income women's fertility through the coercive use of sterilization. Moreover, while sterilization was being promoted among poor women regardless of race, it was simultaneously being discouraged among white women of higher socioeconomic status.

Today, the more blatant forms of sterilization abuse that occurred prior to and during the 1970s have been replaced by more subtle forms of abuse. For example, coercion occurs when physicians are more likely to "encourage" women of color and poor women to undergo sterilization, as well as when government policies (such as the family cap) punish women receiving cash assistance for having an additional child by depriving them of benefits. Other subtle forms of sterilization abuse include obtaining "consent" from a woman to perform a sterilization procedure without providing her with all of the necessary information—for example, that sterilization is permanent and cannot be reversed—at the time the decision is made.

Even though these contemporary forms of sterilization abuse are more subtle than the involuntary sterilization laws of the past, they also represent a significant violation of women's fundamental reproductive autonomy and choice. In recent years, Children Requiring a Caring Kommunity (CRACK)—now known as Project Prevention—was implemented in California by a private resident in order to decrease the number of births among women who use drugs. In order to achieve this goal, CRACK provides previous and current drug users two hundred dollars to undergo sterilization or use another long-acting birth control method. This initiative is a particularly coercive program that now operates in thirty-nine states and the District of Columbia.

Norplant

In the 1990s, government legislation and funding schemes were used to *both* overtly and covertly coerce poor women and women of color to use Norplant, a long-term method of contraception, the use of which required a procedure by a health professional to discontinue. Similar to sterilization, the government-sponsored promotion of Norplant among poor women and women of color was also rooted in eugenic theory—namely the idea that certain groups of individuals are socially unfit to reproduce—as well as the premise that poor women are incapable of making sound reproductive health decisions on their own.

Two forms of legislative initiatives that promoted the coercive utilization of Norplant were proposed in the past: first, "encouraging" women enrolled in the federal cash assistance program to have Norplant implanted in their arm with financial incentives, and second, punishing women who have been convicted of using drugs while pregnant by forcing them to get implanted with the contraceptive device. These proposed government initiatives violated these women's human right to procreate; reproductive and decisional autonomy; right to self-determination and informed consent, including the right to refuse a medical procedure; and bodily integrity. Moreover, by specifically targeting women, women of color, and poor women, these various interferences with women's reproductive choice undermine gender, racial/ethnic, and class equality.

A number of scholars have argued that, in order to justify policies such as involuntary sterilization laws and the coercive use of Norplant among welfare recipients, policymakers and the media utilized rhetoric and images depicting black and poor women as morally inferior, their behavior as irresponsible, and their sexuality as "out of control." These problematic popular representations of poor women and women of color are deployed to portray these groups of women as responsible for their own poverty and thus undeserving of public assistance. As a result, political leaders have essentially convinced the general public that poverty and economic insecurity among women enrolled in the cash assistance program are products of their immorality, lack of personal responsibility, and uninhibited sexuality as opposed to macro social and economic processes, including unemployment, the lack of affordable housing, and a failing public education system that does not provide quality, evidence-based sex education.

Thus, public-policy discourse has often pinpointed promoting "moral values" (e.g., heterosexual marriage, patriarchy, the nuclear family model) and controlling—or even eradicating—sexual activity among poor and low-income women as the solution to ending poverty in the United States. Indeed, a number of politicians have argued that decreasing, or even eliminating, childbearing among poor and low-income women will prevent the birth of additional members of the "social underclass," and thus reduce social ills such as crime, unemployment, and poverty. In addition, women enrolled in the TANF program have often been accused of giving birth to additional children in order to receive increased cash assistance. These accusations perpetuate the idea that poor women and women of color are morally bankrupt, greedy, and more interested in "playing the system" or "living off of the government" than "getting out of poverty."

Research has shown that the attitudes white people hold toward people of color—whom they believe to be the main recipients of cash assistance—influence their support for the program. In addition, a number of scholars have suggested that public opinion affects the level of benefits allocated to TANF participants by influencing politicians' policy decisions about the program. Indeed, in 2003, Martin Johnson found that, although policy choices around welfare are not only shaped by racial issues, the racial composition of a state's TANF caseload and a state's racial attitudes affect the decisions policymakers make about the welfare program, that is, the amount of the cash benefit and the treatment of program participants. Specifically, he found that states with a greater proportion of people of color on its welfare rolls and negative racial attitudes toward individuals of color tend to provide smaller benefits and treat program participants more insensitively than those with a smaller proportion of participants of color and more positive racial attitudes.[4]

Human and Reproductive Rights within the Family Cap Context

The family cap policy raises a human rights issue concerning its appropriateness; mainly how does the existence of the family cap policy align with covenants pertaining to human and reproductive rights? Although various scholars have highlighted the importance of considering the family cap within a human rights framework, there is no evidence that policymakers or state welfare administrators have done so. Since the passage of welfare reform, very few presentations at major national welfare and public policy conferences have addressed the family cap. Furthermore, we have not come across any documentation of discourse among policymakers or welfare agency personnel charged with implementing the policy concerning the appropriateness of a reproductive-related policy applicable only to women receiving economic assistance from the state.

The 1948 United Nations Universal Declaration of Human Rights (UDHR) was among the first of several contemporary international human rights documents. There are four articles pertaining to the imposition of the family cap: that all are born free and equal in dignity and rights (Article 1), deserve protection from interference with privacy, family, and home (Article 12), and have the right to marry and found a family, entered into with free and full consent (Article 16); that motherhood and childhood are entitled to special care and assistance; and that all children, whether born in or out of wedlock, shall enjoy the same social protection (Article 25).[5]

Other human rights covenants and conventions relevant to the family cap and that have either been endorsed or ratified by the United States include the 1965 International Convention on the Elimination of All Forms of Racial Discrimination (ICERD) and the 1966 International Covenant on Civil and Political Rights (ICCPR). At least one legal scholar has clearly documented the specific components of these covenants that make the family cap a direct violation of reproductive rights and welfare reform a violation of monitoring requirements, the prohibition of retrogression, and gender discrimination.

There are several other human rights documents, however, that have not been endorsed or ratified by the United States, despite strong support from countries around the world. These include the 1966 International Covenant on Economic, Social, and Cultural Rights (ICESCR), the 1989 Convention on the Rights of the Child (CRC), and the 1979 Convention on the Elimination of All Forms of Discrimination Against Women (CEDAW). These three documents clearly attest to the rights violations presented by the family cap policy by virtue of its differential treatment of women based on their economic and social standing (ICESCR), discrimination against poor women who have children (CEDAW), and differential treatment of children born to poor mothers (CRC).

CEDAW is especially relevant to the family cap policy given that Article 16(1)(e) states that women be given the "same rights to decide freely and responsibly on the number and spacing of their children and to have access to the information, education, and means to enable them to exercise these rights." The premise of the Convention is that "discrimination against women in marriage and family life is not only a human rights violation in itself but often the basis for discrimination in other areas of their lives."[6] Thus, various forms of discrimination are addressed, with the intent of abolishing social attitudes and cultural practices based on the belief in the inferiority of women. As a result, Article 13, which addresses areas of economic and social life, and Article 16, addressing discrimination in marriage and family relations, both strongly pertain to the family cap. Of 192 UN member states, the US is the only industrialized nation that has not ratified CEDAW; the other states that have not ratified the Convention as of this writing include Iran, Palau, Somolia, Sudan, and Tonga. Despite lack of federal ratification of CEDAW, over 190 organizations in the US have supported its ratification.

One legal scholar has shown how states and municipalities in the United States have successfully adopted components of these human rights documents despite lack of federal ratification. Another legal approach taken has been the use of state equal rights amendments (ERAs) to argue against the discrimination inherent in the family cap. Ironically, in some cases, the devolution of welfare programs from the federal to the state level means that state law may be the best approach to protecting poor women's equality rights, particularly in the context "of reproductive-based discrimination inherent in the child exclusion provision." It is argued that in light of federal devolution and in deference to state autonomy, courts may determine that the policy is "repugnant to the principles guaranteed by the state's own constitution."[7]

There is yet another body of relevant international documents that provides a basis for considering the appropriateness of policies such as the family cap. Population issues and the status of women were specifically addressed at two conferences in the mid-1990s where it was affirmed that universal human rights include reproductive rights. The 1994 action plan of the World Conference on Population and Development in Cairo, Egypt, introduced a new paradigm for population issues, which shifted from a demographic focus to a rights-based framework. It defined the basis for population and development programs as the promotion of equality between the sexes, promotion of women's rights, and elimination of violence against women to ensure that they could control their fertility *without coercion.*

Similarly, the 1995 action platform of the Fourth World Conference on Women in Beijing featured a chapter on sexual and reproductive rights, including the need to review country-level legislation concerning the criminalization of abortion (considered a serious public health problem). In addition, it emphasized the need to guarantee self-determination, equality, and sexual and reproductive security to all women. The United States signed both of these documents. Yet, the welfare family cap policy is an explicit government action that differentially treats poor and nonpoor women; presents an economically coercive environment for women's reproductive decision-making, which has been shown in some circumstances to be associated with increased abortion; and jeopardizes women's self-determination in the process.

As the foregoing section points out, an argument can and has been made for considering reproductive rights as part of human rights. Moreover, we have situated the family cap—a distinctly welfare policy—within the reproductive and human rights framework given its clear reproductive focus. Nonetheless, it must be acknowledged that in this country, these arguments have fallen short of the ultimate goal to ensure women's reproductive autonomy and equity. Thus, with regard to the family cap, which is both poverty- and reproduction-specific, it may be worthwhile to advance the notion of welfare rights, or "social citizenship." As Hartley Dean points out, however, the challenge remains in framing such an approach that serves both the Global South *and* developed capitalist nations, such as the US, given the ideological aversion to and perceived threat of "social programs" to economic and social stability.[8]

Has the Family-Cap Policy Been Effective?

The main empirical question regarding the family cap is whether it has had any impact on the sexual and reproductive health behaviors of poor women leading them to have fewer births. There have been limited empirical evaluations of the policy's impact in states that implemented the family cap, as well as studies examining the effect of welfare policies on fertility at the national level. One attempt to determine the policy's effectiveness by reviewing the few family cap evaluations conducted to date proved difficult due to the nature of the data and lack of comparability across evaluations.[9]

Findings from evaluations accompanying the family cap waivers in New Jersey and Arkansas—the first states to implement the policy—were mixed. In Arkansas, there was no difference in birth rates between those welfare recipients subject to the family cap and recipients *not* subject to it. In New Jersey, the family cap was associated with increased contraception and a decrease in pregnancies and births; however, the number of abortions increased.

With one exception, results from other quantitative studies have not demonstrated an effect on reduced childbearing of the family cap specifically or of restrictive welfare policies more generally. Ann Horvath-Rose and Elizabeth Peters examined the impact of welfare policies on nonmarital birth rates for all women with vital statistics, birth data, and state-level panel data from 1984 to 1996. They found a negative correlation between state welfare waivers, such that more restrictive states had lower nonmarital birth ratios.[10] Melissa Kearney, however, used vital statistics data from 1989 to 1998 for women fifteen to thirty-four years of age and at risk of being on welfare to examine if denial of incremental benefits upon the birth of a child had an impact on birth rates in states with and without the family cap, and did not find evidence of an effect.[11] Phillip Levine introduced the concept of the "fertility decision tree," stating that a woman's fertility behavior and final birth outcome depend upon several preceding stages: sexual activity, contraception, pregnancy, abortion, and birth. His method examined the impact of abortion and welfare policies, along with economic conditions from 1985 to1996, on all of these stages simultaneously and did not find a systematic effect of welfare waivers on fertility-related behavior.[12]

One analysis that used the Panel Study of Income Dynamics to examine the association between welfare policies implemented before the PRWORA (pre-1996) on the risk of a subsequent nonmarital birth among low-income mothers found that they did not have the desired influence on women's childbearing behaviors, and that the family cap policy had no significant effect on subsequent nonmarital childbearing. Parity, gender of other children, and marital and cohabiting status were more likely to influence women's childbearing decisions.[13] Another study used the 1989 to 1999 Current Population Survey to compare trends in out-of-wedlock birth rates among unmarried and less-educated women with at least one child in the first five states to implement the family cap with similar women in states that did not implement the family cap, as well as a within-state comparison examining trends in birth rates for single mothers compared to married mothers in family cap states. When they compared changes over time in the birth rates of single and married women in the five family-cap states to changes over time in the birth rates of single and married women from non-family-cap states, there was no evidence that family cap policies reduce out-of-wedlock births.[14]

Another study examined the effect of the family cap on birth and abortion rates among women at risk for welfare using birth and abortion records from twenty-four states and New York City between 1992 and 1999. Using parity, the researchers created two groups of women—at risk of being on welfare versus not at risk—and compared within- and across-state differences in births and abortions between the two groups. They found that trends in birth and abortion rate differentials between the two groups in family cap states were similar to trends in non-family-cap states, concluding that the family cap had no effect on birth and abortion rates.[15] In an effort to investigate the impact of welfare-reform policies (including the family cap) on nonmarital childbearing among adolescents, Kathleen Harris et al. used the National Longitudinal Study of Adolescent Health from 1994 to 2002. From their analysis, they concluded that "consistent with other research, the effects of welfare policies on family formation behaviors are weak or non-existent."[16]

A more recent analysis conducted by Diana Romero sought to directly examine poor women's fertility within the context of the family cap policy using the 1995 (pre–welfare reform) and 2002 (post–welfare reform) National Survey of Family Growth (NSFG). Individual- and state-level differences in fertility-related behaviors of welfare recipients and nonrecipients were compared. Specifically, the individual-level analysis compared poor and nonpoor women with regard to contraceptive use, pregnancy, abortion, sterilization, and births, and found there were *no* differences except for abortion. In 1995 poor women were more than twice as likely to have had an abortion than were nonpoor women (2.8 *vs.* 1.3; $p<.05$). In 2002 the difference in rate of abortion between poor and nonpoor women increased (4.3 *vs.* 1.2; $p<.001$). The state-level analysis compared the reproductive behaviors of welfare recipients residing in family cap states with those in non-family-cap states. Prior to the implementation of the policy, there were no significant differences between poor women in family cap and non-family-cap states and these findings persisted in 2002, suggesting a lack of effect of the policy.[17]

Finally, Romero et al. conducted a qualitative investigation of the factors poor women in family cap states base their reproductive decisions on. This study is, to our knowledge, the first examination of this policy from the perspective of women subject to it. They interviewed thirty-two current or former welfare recipients at community-based health clinics and welfare offices in northern New Jersey to learn about their knowledge of the policy and their attitudes regarding contraceptive use and fertility-related decision-making. Contraceptive use did not differ between current and former welfare recipients, suggesting that the family cap policy may not have influenced poor women's reproductive behaviors. Only two of the thirty-two women had heard of the family cap policy, yet their knowledge of it was incorrect. After being informed of the policy, over half reported that it would not influence their decision to use contraception, and three-quarters of the women said the policy would have no influence on their decision to have a child while receiving TANF. Instead, they indicated that their fertility-related decisions were more likely to be based on their personal and relationship circumstances rather than on government policies, thus, questioning the assumed connection between knowledge, behavior change, and poor women's childbearing decisions.[18]

The results of these quantitative studies, utilizing various relatively large data sources, have mostly contradicted family cap policy expectations. Although the specific relationship between income support and childbearing behavior remains unclear, there is very little evidence that women subject to the family cap have fewer children. Given the findings from the qualitative study with poor women in New Jersey regarding their knowledge of the policy and factors that influence their reproductive decision-making, the lack of an effect is not surprising.

Discussion

There are unfortunately many examples of policies and programs in this country that were designed to discourage, coerce, or compel marginalized women to behave in specific ways with regard to sexual activity and childbearing. There is clear evidence of overt racism and classism in the history of family planning programs and social services for the poor. The public health literature has consistently shown that reproductive decision-making is a process influenced by myriad social and cultural factors. Notions about the importance and timing of motherhood relative to individual economic circumstances vary. Moreover, the strong positive association between women's educational attainment, economic development, and reduced fertility would suggest that approaches other than the family cap—advanced education, childcare that enables women to maintain employment, and family-friendly work-based policies—might be more in line with factors that affect both fertility and the potential need for governmental cash assistance.

A social policy such as the family cap can make a powerful statement about the beliefs and principles of a society. In addition, social policies have the power, and indeed are designed, to effect changes in the day-to-day lives of members of society. As US welfare policy currently stands, policymakers in almost half of the country have deemed childbearing unacceptable among poor women. In effect, they have taken the approach of fertility prevention as poverty prevention. Yet, fertility among poor women has not decreased and poverty rates have increased in the past several years. One can also envision the slippery slope of possibilities extending from reproductive regulation of poor women to low-income people who, for example, do not own a home, cannot provide academic enrichment programs to their children, have not accrued adequate savings, do not have advanced education themselves, do not have health insurance, and/or are employed in industries not deemed able to provide an adequate income for families with children.

To date, most official reports concerning welfare reform state that it has been a successful policy on the basis of a greater than 50 percent reduction in caseloads and increased work activity since its inception. The absence of comprehensive, state-based evaluations of other policies, such as the family cap, make it very uncertain what individuals' experiences have been. Our review of analyses conducted by researchers mostly outside of administrative or state agency environments indicates that the policy has not influenced poor women's fertility in the desired direction. What we do not know is how the thousands of women and children subjected to the family cap over the past decade have fared with regard to their overall health and well-being. This seems like a concern policymakers and social program administrators would share and insist on exploring. However, to paraphrase a recent comment by a state welfare director explaining the lack of past or planned evaluations of their family cap policy, it is an old policy that is just not on the radar anymore.

As public health professionals, we would suggest that the family cap policy make it back onto the "radar" of state policymakers and welfare agency administrators—both in light of research findings regarding its lack of effectiveness and the human rights violations inherent in it. It is time for the government to undertake a critical analysis of the assumptions under which the policy was passed, as well as assess its effects on relevant reproductive health outcomes, maternal and child health and well-being, racial/ethnic health disparities, and poverty.

Notes

1. Susan L. Thomas, "Race, Gender, and Welfare Reform: The Antinatalist Response," *Journal of Black Studies* 28, no. 4 (1998): 422.

2. Maria Brave Heart-Jordan, "The Return to the Sacred Path: Healing from Historical Trauma and Historical Unresolved Grief Among the Lakota" (PhD diss., Smith College for Social Work, 1995); Jane Lawrence, "The Indian Health Service and the Sterilization of Native American Women," *American Indian Quarterly* 24, no. 3 (2000): 400–19; Amnesty International, *Maze of Injustice: The Failure to Protect Indigenous Women from Sexual Violence in the USA* (New York: Amnesty International USA, 2007).

3. Charlotte Rutherford, "Reproductive Freedoms and African American Women." *Yale Journal of Law and Feminism* 4 , no. 2 (1991): 225–90; Andrea Tone, ed., *Controlling Reproduction: An American History* (Lanham, MD: SR Books, 1997).

4. Martin Johnson, "Racial Context, Public Attitudes, and Welfare Effort in the American States," in *Race and the Politics of Welfare Reform*, ed. Sanford F. Schram, Joe Soss, and Richard C. Fording (Ann Arbor: University of Michigan Press, 2003).

5. UN General Assembly, Resolution 217 A, "Universal Declaration of Human Rights," accessed on August, 8, 2016, http://www.un.org/en/universal-declaration-human-rights/.

6. Hanna Schöpp-Schilling, "The Nature and Scope of the Convention," in *The Circle of Empowerment: Twenty-Five Years of the UN Committee on the Elimination of Discrimination Against Women,* ed. Hanna Schöpp-Schilling and Cees Flinterman (New York: The Feminist Press, 2007), 10–29.

7. Risa Kaufman, "State ERAs in the New Era: Securing Poor Women's Equality by Eliminating Reproductive-Based Discrimination," *Harvard Women's Law Journal* 24 (2001): 219.

8. Hartley Dean, "Social Policy and Human Rights: Re-thinking the

Engagement," *Social Policy and Society* 7, no. 1 (2007): 1–12.

9. US Government Accountability Office, *Welfare Reform: More Research Needed on TANF Family Caps and Other Policies for Reducing Out-of-Wedlock Births* (Washington, DC: US GAO, 2001).

10. Ann Horvath-Rose and H. Elizabeth Peters, "Welfare Waivers and Nonmarital Childbearing," in *For Better and for Worse: Welfare Reform and the Well-Being of Children and Families*, ed. Greg J. Duncan and P. Lindsay Chase-Lansdale (New York: Russell Sage Foundation, 2004).

11. Melissa Schettini Kearney, "Is There an Effect of Incremental Welfare Benefits on Fertility Behavior? A Look at the Family Cap" (working paper, National Bureau of Economic Research, Cambridge, MA, 2002).

12. Phillip B. Levine, "The Impact of Social Policy and Economic Activity Throughout the Fertility Decision Tree" (working paper, National Bureau of Economic Research, Cambridge, MA, 2002).

13. Suzanne Ryan, Jennifer Manlove, and Sandra L. Hofferth, "State-Level Welfare Policies and Nonmarital Subsequent Childbearing," *Population Research and Policy Review* 25, no. 1 (2006): 103–26.

14. Wendy Tanisha Dyer and Robert W. Fairlie, "Do Family Caps Reduce Out-of-Wedlock Births? Evidence from Arkansas, Georgia, Indiana, New Jersey and Virginia," *Population Research and Policy Review* 23, no. 5/6 (2004): 441–73.

15. Ted Joyce, Robert Kaestner, Sanders Korenman, and Stanley Henshaw, "Family Cap Provisions and Changes in Births and Abortions" (working paper, National Bureau of Economic Research, Cambridge, MA, 2004).

16. Kathleen Harris, David Guilkey, and Eve Veliz, "Welfare Reform and Non-Marital Childbearing in the Transition to Adulthood" (paper presented at the Association of Public Policy Analysis and Management Annual Fall Research Conference, Washington, DC, 2003).

17. Diana Romero, unpublished analysis of the 1995 and 2002 National Survey of Family Growth.

18. Diana Romero, Hannah Fortune-Greeley, Jorge Luis Verea, and Debbie Salas-Lopez, "Meaning of the Family-Cap Policy for Poor Women: Contraceptive and Fertility Decision-Making," *Social Work in Public Health* 23, no. 1 (2007): 165–82.

Making Art for Reproductive Justice

RICKIE SOLINGER

The call for reproductive justice is now at the heart of reproductive politics. But getting there hasn't been a piece of cake. After all, since the 1960s, the shorthand language of "choice" has stood for what every "modern woman" needs and for what defines a modern woman—as a shopper, a job seeker, an Internet browser, a consumer of health insurance, and as a person managing her fertility.

Choice (responsible choice!), a bedrock concept justifying and characterizing neoliberal individualism, is widely imagined as the key source of personal dignity, and includes, for many Americans, the choice not to have a child when one is or might unwillingly be pregnant. RJ proclaims the limits of choice. It points out the hostile or friendly social and political contexts in which choices are made. RJ points out the obvious: that deciding *not* to reproduce is only part of what people do reproductively, and emphatically defines the right to *have* children as a fundamental human right, not a class or a racialized privilege. RJ foregrounds the right to be a mother and the right to raise one's children in dignity and safety. RJ asks, what does it take to achieve these human rights? And having gathered information, RJ activists make demands on the polity.

It's all so fundamental and logical and humane—and speaks so clearly to the lived reproductive experiences of individuals. But still it's a hard sell in a culture drunk on choice. So you've got to use every tool you can put your hands on. Including art.

Art, after all, invites people to see. It has the potential to invite people to see things they otherwise might (passively) not see or (actively) render invisible. For example, an RJ art-maker might ask: How is it possible to lock up more than two million men and women in the United States, but have only scant public attention to this feature of our society and almost no high-level, high-profile attention by public officials? How is it possible for our systems of incarceration to operate on such a thoroughly racialized basis, and to have this aspect of our society so thoroughly eclipsed? What does white supremacy and racialized poverty have to do with media boredom and public deafness and public blindness—and ultimately public acquiescence, or acceptance of the prison industrial complex? The RJ artist is interested in how looking at the prison system—really seeing it, in some sense—helps us resist the politics of public invisibility and public inaudibility regarding the impact of the criminal justice system on the reproductive lives and chances for parenthood of millions of people in the United States, and the consequences of these impacts on families and communities and on the integrity of the nation as a whole.

Strictly speaking, neither art nor the subject of incarceration has been at the center of my life's work as a scholar and activist, even while I have focused on questions of what racism looks like, how it functions, how it has been institutionalized today and in the past. Specifically, as a historian, I keep focusing on this RJ-inflected question, "Who gets to be a 'legitimate' mother in the United States and who does not?" I am interested in how the answers to this question have been decided and enforced over time. What has the state had to do with it? What have individual women making choices had to do with it? And most fundamentally, what have white supremacy and class had to do with who is allowed to be a so-called legitimate mother in this country and who has been excluded from that category—and at what cost to persons, communities, and society as a whole?

The books I write search out *how*, over time, female sexuality, fertility, and maternity have provided opportunities for governments and other powerbrokers to institutionalize racism and white and male supremacy in the United States.

When my first book, *Wake Up Little Susie*, was published, I realized that the mostly academic, sort of turgid books I would spend my life writing would never be read by large numbers of people. I came to terms with the fact that writing is my main way of being an activist—and in fact, I like to believe, a legitimate form of activism—but also that I wanted to work in another non-classroom-based pedagogical form as well, a form that might reach more people. Since 1992, I have been working with artists to make exhibitions associated with the themes of the books I write.

Since I am a person who lives a sharply visual life, and am sharply concerned about the history and politics of representation (especially regarding race, class, and gender), I teamed up with a group of artists in the early 1990s to make the *Wake Up Little Susie* show. This room-size installation representing the structural, institutional forces that racialized single pregnancy in the US in the decades between World War II and *Roe v. Wade* traveled to fifty-six campus galleries, from Florida to Oregon and Maine to Texas, between 1992 and 2003.

As I began my work putting together exhibitions, I quickly realized that hosting a show gave gallery staff and faculty many opportunities to "interrupt the curriculum," to dream up pedagogical interventions associated with the issues represented in the show. For example, hosting the exhibition could be paired with a symposium, a film series, a lecture, a college community panel, and meetings with the local welfare authorities, all forms of public education. This is an old, old project: using images, using art to reshape and revitalize people's eyeballs, their hearts, their access to information, and their ideas.

Since the *Susie* exhibition, I have curated other traveling exhibitions, including *Beggars and Choosers: Motherhood Is Not a Class Privilege in America*, a beautiful and pointed exhibition of documentary photographs. This show, deeply rooted in RJ principles, presents the work of world-class and community-based photographers. Sixty images of women who occupy what I call "the reviled categories," that is, females who politicians and others define as too young, too poor, too gay, too not-white, too foreign, too disabled, too whatever, to be legitimate mothers. But in the photographs, these women are *being mothers*, with strength, dignity, and determination. This show opened at the Birmingham Civil Rights Institute in 2002 and traveled to more than twenty-five venues, doing what we'd now call reproductive justice work at each stop. For example, hosting the show stimulated full-day symposia on the politics of motherhood, new courses about welfare, and many other pedagogical interventions.

In 2006 *Interrupted Life: Incarcerated Mothers in the United States* opened inside the California Institution for Women (CIW) in Chino, a desolate place within the orbit of Los Angeles. As far as I can tell, this is the first time in US history that a major outside art exhibition has opened inside a prison. One reason *Interrupted Life* was allowed inside is that this prison, where about fifteen hundred women are incarcerated, was in the process of defining and implementing what administrators and others consider "gender sensitive" policies and practices.

Dawn Davison, then CIW's warden, explained why she thought the show met the special needs of female inmates: "Our hope is to strengthen the bonds between incarcerated women and their children. Ongoing contact with children is a key motivation for women seeking to rehabilitate their lives and survive the prison experience. The *Interrupted Life* exhibition explores the difficulties incarcerated mothers face as they serve their terms." Sister Suzanne Jabro, founder of the California prison reform organization Women and Criminal Justice and the Get on the Bus project that brings children to visit their incarcerated parents, created and sustained the bridge between the exhibition project and the CIW staff. The opportunity to bring the show inside the prison may have been greater because the exhibition project was funded by the Ford Foundation, a credential that could have lent dignity to the request.

I should underscore that the contents of the show were, in general, deeply and directly critical of the prison industrial complex. The radical and outright oppositional content of the exhibition did not seem to matter to the prison authorities, most of whom didn't seem to be examining the show's content very closely. But it must be said that the authorities we worked with appeared to cooperate with all matters associated with hosting the exhibition.

Interrupted Life had eight linked installation pieces. Its *Centerpiece* was made from the thousands of five-by-eight "art-cards" incarcerated women used to illustrate their experience that WAKEUP/Arts (the organization me and my coworkers function under) solicited from thirty-eight institutions around the country. Mostly we tried to make contact with women through writing, art, and parenting programs. We asked women to respond with visual art or otherwise to the prompt, "From where I sit, this is what being a mother means to me . . ." The yards and yards of two-feet-by-two-feet card-plaques in the *Centerpiece* suggest the system's power to constrain, diminish, and homogenize life. Yet each card reflects the intense individuality of its maker. The running lengths of cards suggest endless yet discrete and calculable time served, lives constrained.

The *Centerpiece* had a companion set of "shadow cards" or "Warrior Cards," ninety-eight cards that reported incidents and attitudes and activist events of *resistance* to the prison industrial complex. These cards documented the testimonies of incarcerated women, judicial decisions against prisons and in favor of the rights of incarcerated people, petitions, manifestos, legislative hearings, and other forms of interference with the system.

INSIDE/OUTSIDE, another installation piece, was a twelve-foot-long "corridor" made by a group of teenage artists in Columbus, Ohio, working all day every day for two weeks one summer. Some of these kids had incarcerated family members and friends. All of them met with activists and artists who know a lot about incarceration as they fashioned this piece. The panels that made up the corridor were painted on both sides: if you walked inside the corridor, you saw mother after mother, caged and variously enraged, dying, going nowhere, working on being alive. If you walked around the outside of the corridor, you saw the kids, variously stranded, wounded, sad, dying, and working on staying alive.

The other pieces in the exhibition include what maker and sound-artist Darryl Hell calls *Sonic Wallpaper*, a soundtrack of prison clangs and constant din, official verbiage, and first-person stories drawn from Paula Johnson's *Inner Lives: Voices of African American Women in Prison*. The show also included enlarged panels from the Real Cost of Prisons Project comic books—a fabulous source for *seeing* and grasping information about the finances of prison siting and building, imprisonment itself, the War on Drugs, and other matters. From Oakland, came images from the PhotoVoice project associated with Legal Services for Prisoners with Children, in which recently released women returned to the community from which they were arrested. They took photographs of what they saw there and, working with a graphic artist, inserted their own silhouettes into photographs and added their own commentaries, reflecting on the meaning of the content of the photograph. And the meaning and experience of reentry.

A totem-influenced piece called *Mapping the Lock-up* illustrated the explosion and distribution of prison building across the country. *The Rules*, the coldest, hardest, and most elegant piece in the exhibition, represented the rules governing the visits of children to their incarcerated parents. The rules are hard to read and impossible to avoid. They are, in totality, incomprehensible, often contradictory and illogical. For incarcerated women, however, these rules must be memorized and treated as watchwords; if not the consequences are harsh: "Violations of any visiting rule outlined in this policy may result in the termination of the visit, disciplinary action against the inmate, and restriction of any future visiting privilege." The rules include dicta about how many hugs and kisses a mother can give her child, who is not allowed, under any circumstances, to sit on his or her mother's lap.

At the entryway to the enormous gymnasium/auditorium where the *Interrupted Life* show was installed at CIW, we placed the piece called *Stretched Thin*, which is essentially about a girl's struggle to stay close to her mother doing time, and the mother's efforts to do the same. As usual, the mother is in a prison many hundreds of miles away from where her little daughter lives, making regular visits very difficult. This piece has several powerful elements, including twenty prison shirts hanging on metal clothes racks, with photographs, diary entries, and letters between the girl and her mother printed on the shirts. When dozens and then hundreds of women at CIW walked into the exhibition, their first encounter was with this mother and daughter and the imprinted prison garb. Sometimes it took a woman a good half hour to get past this first piece.

I want to say more about what happened inside the prison during the exhibition, but first I have to go back for a moment to the day that a group of incarcerated volunteers or assignees helped to unpack the crates. They were women who made art themselves and so were tapped to help install the show. Within a minute this group of five or six inmates was in charge. They positioned pieces and designed the space. They made decisions about how to improve the backgrounds, and in one case, a woman flawlessly stretched canvas over easels measuring twelve feet by four feet. Another woman spent several hours measuring, imagining, hanging fifteen pieces on canvas-covered easels as effectively as a seasoned gallery director. Women attended to electrical and lighting issues, assembly, nuts, bolts, everything. There was nothing left undone and everything was done with meticulous care. I stood around, expecting to be the boss, but it never happened.

One of the prison art teachers, having consulted with the women installing the show, proposed a companion show, an exhibition of CIW women's artwork in the vast space *Interrupted Life* had only half filled. In two or three hours, the teacher and women put together a selection of works and the whole event was further enhanced. All the women and prison staff flocked to the show, not just to see how outsiders represented incarcerated mothers, but also to see their own work and that of their friends and other incarcerated women.

There was a lot of crying. I do not know how much crying goes on at the California Institution for Women on an average day, but on the days I visited and stood in the midst of women walking through the pieces of *Interrupted Life*, I saw scores of women inside the corridor, crying, leaning on each other, whispering, and crying some more. I saw women who looked at each and every art-card in the *Centerpiece*, crying and seeming to think about what motherhood meant to them from where they sat. I saw many, many women gently shifting hangers, one by one, down the clothes racks, examining each prison shirt, honoring the efforts of the little girl and her mother to continue to know each other, and the willingness of these two to share their process with everyone who comes to see *Interrupted Life*.

When I try to imagine what was memorable about the exhibition, I think of the visibility. The claims. The voices. The attention being paid to truths about being an incarcerated mother. While I was at CIW some women told me that *Interrupted Life* is a way of getting the message out—out there. I wanted *Interrupted Life* to be a mechanism for amplifying the voices and the visibility of people who have been shut out and effaced. It was intended to object strenuously to invisibility and inaudibility and to the contemporary uses of prison.

After the exhibition at CIW, *Interrupted Life* traveled to college campuses all over the country. Faculty and students at every venue developed extraordinary curricular interruptions in coordination with hosting the show. *Interrupted Life* was a fragment of a massive project, involving communities of people objecting to and resisting the prison industrial complex. More generally, it is also part of the massive effort to perform those acts of public education so crucial to a real democracy to offer a challenge to the prison industrial complex.

There are stories about community groups in the 1970s taking over the walls of laundromats for exhibitions of political art about neighborhood concerns, exhibitions made and consumed by women who washed their clothes. We've seen these kinds of appropriations of public space in our own time. A gallery show on a college campus is a fine way to draw in an audience that's already accustomed to being educated. But the walls are all around us. The artists are all around us. And the issues are about to overwhelm us. Reproductive Justice has made astounding progress since the mid-1990s, making its way to the heart of reproductive politics. Using art to amplify RJ's truth is one way to open up that heart for everybody to see.

Tubes Tied, Truly Child-Free at Last!

AARONETTE WHITE

The term "child-free" has been reclaimed by people like me who contend that not having children can be an active, positive, and fulfilling choice. I am a child-free and voluntarily sterilized African American woman. I had my tubes tied, despite the horrific history of sterilization in this country and persistent misconceptions about child-free women. This is an issue of reproductive justice.

Although I believe, as an adult, that I share some responsibility for looking after and caring for children (it does take a village to raise a child), I have never wanted to be a child's mother. I have never wanted to have children—meaning, to bear my own, adopt, or foster another human being as a parent. However, people kept telling me that I would change my mind.

I also felt that as an African American woman, I had enough to deal with alone. Having a child would only complicate the injustices I was already experiencing and fighting against in my everyday life, my academic profession, and the political activism in which I am engaged, both nationally and internationally. The racial, gender, and class inequalities embedded in our society's institutions offer very limited definitions of family, work, healthcare, social security, and public education; as a result, I gradually disengaged myself from other people's expectations for my personal life. Having a tubal ligation, to me, meant no children. Not today, not tomorrow, not ever.

Writing about the decision not to have a child makes me visible to women who may not even see childbearing as something you decide to do or not. Additionally, I want to challenge certain books about child-free women that say only white women make this choice. I write to demonstrate what it means to have the clarity and a heart strong enough to live with my decision, despite negative stereotypes and judgments. Women can have awe-inspiring and satisfying lives in addition to, and even instead of, bearing and raising children. We can address feelings of emptiness and/or establish our authenticity as women without the experience of pregnancy or giving birth, and the experiences of child-free women should be equally respected and honored.

My initial reasons for not wanting children have multiplied as a result of the ongoing pressures I have had to contend with regarding my decision. Women who choose to remain child-free are expected to justify themselves in ways that women who have children are not. Motherhood is still considered to be women's primary role; and most societies, regardless of economic, political, or cultural systems, value childbearing over childlessness. Voluntarily child-free women challenge (and threaten) cultural expectations because in addition to not *having* children, they do not *want* them. Voluntarily childless women have been criticized as selfish, immature, and irresponsible. In contrast, the *involuntarily* childless woman is considered worthy of sympathy, resources, and support. It is assumed that "no children" means "can't have children" or "hasn't found the right mate."

To my mind, we need to understand both childlessness and sterilization in new ways that respect the choice and life of a woman who refuses to have a child and who acts with self-determination to protect that choice. This calls for the development of alternative vocabularies for the issues involved.

Scholarly research on women who are intentionally childless consistently demonstrates that child-free women do not constitute a homogeneous group. Explanations and motivations for remaining child-free are multiple, complex, and sometimes as contradictory as the reasons women give for having children. Most important, empirical research has found that both women with and without children are oppressed, albeit in different ways, by male-dominant societies. One group is not automatically more marginalized than the other, and I reject the view that the interests of mothers and child-free women are at odds. Despite our different choices, we as women have to negotiate the meaning of our experiences in ways that focus on the connections between us. We all need to work together for common solutions.

Finally, I do not mean to devalue women who choose to be mothers part-time, full-time, or every time they become pregnant. I am not rejecting mothers. I am critiquing the notion that all women must become mothers. I am rejecting motherhood as a role for me. I am breaking the taboo against black women, in particular, speaking critically about the lives of long-suffering, self-sacrificing black mothers. I regret the reluctance of women of color to speak about voluntary sterilization as a liberating option, despite or because of this country's racist history of sterilization abuse. At this writing, my youngest sister is undergoing fertility treatments, and I applaud her for exercising her right to make that choice.

My perspective on reproductive justice is simply one of many, and to discuss all feminists' views is beyond the purpose of this very personal and political essay. I am simply sharing my story of exercising reproductive freedom after experiencing racism, sexism, classism, and heterosexism as an African American woman. Also, I lay out my objections to self-serving, masculinist notions of black women's identities. Our identity is not limited to a provider of sex, the eroticized or romanticized fertility figure, or a nurturer and power behind the throne. Rather than getting tired of feeling different, I want child-free women to be able to feel comfortable in their nonconformity, because remaining unapologetically child-free takes guts.

True Confessions

I have never felt driven to be married or to have children, although I've been married twice. I have had four abortions—all legal, thanks to the feminist movement. Two occurred during my marriages (stressful periods during which I was most pressured to have children by people outside my family), and two others while I was with men whom I considered marrying. I loved all of these men. However, that love did not translate into wanting to have a child with or for any of them.

The last man, who had a role in my fourth and final pregnancy, was wealthy, African American, and the true love of my life. Before I became pregnant I had taken the unusually bold, feminist initiative of proposing to him. We had been dating for two years, and I felt it was time to make a decision about the commitment level of our relationship. He seemed to be avoiding the matter. When I asked him to marry me, he refused. He loved me but did not want to be married at that point in his life (he was twenty-nine years my senior). Having a baby with him would have ensured my future wealth, as well as that of the child, but I did not want children nor did he. When I got pregnant, he agreed that the ultimate decision was mine. After all, it was my body that was pregnant. He contributed the sperm, but I contributed the egg, the womb, and the body. That's three to one, not counting the lifetime commitment, which primarily falls on the mother, having a child entails.

The Right to Choose: Contraceptives, Abortion, and Sterilization

If available by choice rather than coercion, abortion and sterilization, no matter how unpalatable they may seem, offer women opportunities to take control of their fertility. These two options were critical to the reproductive freedom I currently experience.

Every birth control method I have ever used has failed at least once since I began having sex at age twenty. I cannot explain it, some women, like me, just seem to be "fertile turtles." After a lot of wear and tear on my body and peace of mind, I grew weary of chemical contraceptives and the diaphragm. I had never been on the pill because I hated the idea of altering my hormone levels. When I first became sexually active, I liked the convenience of birth control suppositories, but the spermicides in them resulted in vaginal irritation and urinary tract infections. Birth control devices that required surgery for insertion and removal, like the IUD or Norplant, seemed too risky healthwise.

After my last abortion, I vowed to never become pregnant again. Although grateful I could choose abortion as an option, I was tired of getting pregnant and of the monthly dread and panic when my period was late. I had developed a deep-rooted fear of becoming pregnant and was slowly developing distaste for sex with men. I entertained several unrealistic fantasies: becoming lesbian, developing an asexual identity, and becoming permanently celibate. I actually did stay celibate for a number of years and claimed to be asexual during a time when the fear of becoming pregnant led me to question my sexuality. I was stunned to discover much later that other child-free women have entertained extreme fantasies and dreams, such as being in a car accident or having a rare disease, waking up in the hospital, and hearing a doctor say, "You'll live but you'll never have children," and shouting "Bless you!"

As I made the arrangements for my fourth abortion, I remember feeling pleased that gay and lesbian people were asserting their rights as parents. I also admired single women asserting their rights to have babies and adopt children solo. Grandmothers have raised their children's children for centuries, so I had no problem with women who were old enough to be grandmothers enjoying their right to give birth for the first time—after all, men old enough to be grandfathers have historically asserted their right to have children. However, despite maternal revivalism, campaigns to "save the family," and the concurrent rise of infertility treatments and new reproductive technologies, I wanted no part of the postmodern baby boom.

In my gut, I knew that after this fourth abortion and the failure of the diaphragm to protect me from my own fertility, I was going to seek permanent pregnancy prevention. Being pregnant made me so depressed that I became suicidal and experienced a chronic sense of panic. I sought comfort from a therapist, who assured me that I would survive the upcoming abortion and could look forward to becoming sterilized shortly thereafter.

To pass the time and to quell my anxiety, I researched various sterilization techniques for women on the Internet. I talked to two of my older sisters about their experiences of voluntary sterilization after giving birth to children. I also spoke to my mother about my plans. She told me she had wanted my father to have a vasectomy, and that he had refused. Later she opted for a hysterectomy. My sisters affirmed that sterilization was one of the best decisions they had made, and they and my mother encouraged me to follow my heart. I did not ask my father his opinion, and although he didn't volunteer one, he also did not discourage me. I was not postponing a decision about childbearing; I had made one that I was finally acting on.

To my dismay, my doctor informed me that because I had never had children and had also recently had an abortion, I had to wait three months before an elective tubal ligation could be carried out. That was her policy. I was livid! How could a doctor so easily deny my right to choose something I had wanted for years? She explained that studies have shown that women who were sterilized around the same time they ended a pregnancy were much more likely to regret the operation. However, she neglected to add that women who regret being sterilized are overwhelmingly women who *already* have children, not women who are determined never and under any circumstances to have children. My ability to answer all the "what if" questions (e.g., what if you get married, fall in love, change your mind) did not make a difference. The role of gatekeeper is an established and intrinsic part of any doctor's responsibility—even a pro-choice doctor—though it may be inappropriate under some circumstances. I was inconsolable. Finally, after an agonizing three months, I was sterilized.

Voluntary Sterilization: My Experiences

Among women of color, the word "sterilization" understandably evokes images of abuse. However, reproductive freedom has always been about a woman's right to choose what she views as best for her own body. If a woman can choose sterilization, it may be a liberating rather than an oppressive choice. A similar debate occurred among African Americans when the pill grew in popularity among black women during the height of the Civil Rights and women's movements. Black women were admonished by black men to "throw away the pill and hop to the mattresses and breed revolutionaries and mess up the [white] man's genocidal program."[1] As the late Toni Cade Bambara suggested, neither the pill nor voluntary sterilization intrinsically liberates women. They can only help by giving black women control over some of the major events in their lives and time to fight for liberation in other areas with their minds, not necessarily their wombs.

In a study of child-free women who actively chose to be sterilized, overwhelming relief was the most common experience after sterilization. Although these women were white and British, I could relate intimately to their stories. Like many of them, I knew at an early age that I did not want children. Like them, after difficulties with various contraceptives, I decided to have a tubal ligation. It was no spur-of-the-moment decision. In addition to two divorces and four abortions, I had worked as a babysitter during my teens, a child therapist during young adulthood, and the part-time caretaker of nieces, nephews, and godchildren. I liked other women's children well enough, but I knew I wanted none of my own. I looked forward to menopause; it just wasn't coming fast enough for me.

This very personal decision was shaped by race, gender, and class factors that interact in my social and professional life: great health insurance that covered my last abortion and tubal ligation, parents who supported my decision, and exposure to feminist ideas about constructing an identity as a child-free woman. In that sense, it was undoubtedly political, too. Being employed full-time at a university certainly increased the chances that I would have viable options. But not all health insurance policies cover both abortion and sterilization procedures. Clearly, all women need health insurance that supports their reproductive health decisions.

It helped that my parents respected my decision and weren't particularly upset by it. Three of my four sisters have provided them with five grandchildren, and my entire family is pro-choice. Being socialized in a pro-choice family was strengthened by feminist perspectives I acquired in graduate school. I watched my two older sisters parenting without much help from their ex-husbands, the fathers of their children. Although I applaud and admire my sisters, I did not want to experience the emotional and financial strain they experienced. Higher education exposed me to a wonderful feminist network of friends who supported my choices. My career path entails endless professional qualification processes, publication pressure, and time-consuming research—all of which I actually enjoy. Some women are happiest giving birth to ideas, art, women's organizations, new courses, and social-change-oriented research projects, rather than children.

The tubal ligation was a present to myself, to start the new millennium. It was done on January 3, 2000, when I was thirty-nine years old. A tubal ligation is a medical procedure that closes off the fallopian tubes, the site where an egg is fertilized by a sperm. When the tubes are closed, sperm cannot reach the egg, and pregnancy cannot occur. No glands or organs are removed or changed, and all female hormones will still be produced. Therefore, tubal ligations do not cause symptoms of menopause or make menopause happen earlier. The ovaries continue to release eggs after the procedure, and the eggs will dissolve and be absorbed by the body each month, like other dead and unused cells. Menstrual cycles usually follow their regular pattern, and the procedure does not affect sexual pleasure; however, some women have reported that their sex lives have dramatically improved afterward because they no longer fear pregnancy.

Sterilization is more than 99 percent effective in the first year. In following years, there is a limited possibility that the tubes may reconnect themselves, given the body's ability to regenerate. Up to one in one hundred women become pregnant each year after sterilization. About one in three of these pregnancies is ectopic (a fertilized egg develops in a fallopian tube, not the uterus) and may require emergency surgery. A tubal ligation provides no protection against sexually transmitted infections.

Today, under some circumstances, if a person is single or childless, as I was, sterilization may be difficult to arrange. Policies and practices vary with individual providers and hospitals, and from place to place. To avoid needless stress and getting the runaround, women can find the names of pro-choice doctors in their state on the website of Physicians for Reproductive Choice and Health. Although married women used to need a husband's consent before sterilization, that is no longer the case.

There are several techniques for performing tubal ligation: hysteroscopy, laparoscopy, mini-laparotomy, and laparotomy. I had a laparoscopy under general anesthesia. After the anesthesia took effect, my abdomen was inflated with an injection of harmless gas (carbon dioxide), which allowed my organs to be seen clearly. Then, the surgeon made a small incision near my navel and inserted a laparoscope (a rod-like instrument with a light and a viewing lens) to locate my tubes. In my case only one incision and one instrument were used (sometimes two incisions and two different instruments are used for opening and closing the tubes). It took about twenty to thirty minutes for the entire procedure. After the anesthesia wore off, I went home the same day. As a result of opting for general anesthesia, the procedure was entirely painless.

The next day, I woke up to the fresh smell of flowers from my lover with a card saying, "These flowers are where I wish I could be." Next to his bouquet stood a single long-stemmed rose in a vase from my surgeon and her staff. Beside the rose was a card from my parents saying, "We love you and are proud of you."

I felt no discomfort immediately after the procedure and had to use a magnifying glass to see the tiny incision inside my navel after removing the bandage the next day. However, one week later I developed light cramping due to adhesions (scar tissue), for which I had a hereditary predisposition. Massage therapy helped stretch the adhesions, and the discomfort ended after a two-week period.

Similar to my experience with the four abortions, I felt huge relief after my tubal ligation. In addition, I felt less vulnerable and more content, and I developed a renewed and relaxed ability to enjoy heterosexual activity, free from the fear of pregnancy.

Conclusion

Reproductive choices and access to certain reproductive technologies are often determined by a woman's race, class, education level, and other social factors. Thus, feminists address issues of reproductive choice by targeting sociopolitical conditions that limit choice. Women in many parts of the world, and even in parts of this country, are unable to exercise reproductive freedom and access the technologies that facilitate being child-free; the struggle continues to ensure that this choice is available to all rather than a privileged few. The feminist vision includes individual and collective power for all women by eliminating the hierarchies among women that systemic injustices have created. Feminists also believe power is created in multiple ways, and we must be willing to explore and find them. Liberation, not mere personal satisfaction, is the larger goal, and liberation is a collective project.

I support a woman's right to choose to have children or remain child-free as the reproductive justice movement demands, regardless of race, sexuality, marital status, religion, or economic status. The choice I made should be available to all of us, and the following 1989 black feminist statement regarding reproductive freedom has become my personal anthem:

> Choice is the essence of freedom. It's what we African Americans have struggled for all these years. The right to choose where we would sit on a bus. The right to vote. The right for each of us to select our own paths, to dream and reach for our dreams. The right to choose how we would and would not live our lives.
>
> This freedom—to choose and to exercise our choices—is what we've fought and died for. Brought here in chains, worked like mules, bred like beasts, whipped one day, sold the next—244 years we were held in bondage.... Somebody said that we were less than human and not fit for freedom. Somebody said we were like children and could not be trusted to think for ourselves. Somebody owned our flesh and decided if and when and with whom and how our bodies were to be used. Somebody said that Black women could be raped, held in concubinage, forced to bear children year in and year out, but often not raise them. Oh, yes, we have known how painful it is to be without choice in this land.... Reproductive freedom gives each of us the right to make our own choices and guarantees us a safe, legal, affordable support system.[2]

My mobile status—single, child-free, and financially independent—has allowed me to explore the aspects of life that venture far beyond a woman's womb. I have accepted the responsibility of living on the radical edge without burdening a child with that choice. To each her own. Let's live and let live.

Notes

1. Toni Cade, "The Pill: Genocide or Liberation," in *The Black Woman: An Anthology*, ed. Toni Cade Bambara (New York: Washington Square Press, 1970), 162–69.

2. African American Women Are for Reproductive Freedom, "We Remember," in *Still Lifting, Still Climbing: African American Women's Contemporary Activism*, ed. Kimberly Springer (New York: NYU Press, 1999), 38–39.

POETRY

Love Letters to the Queer Liberation and Reproductive Justice Movement(s)

Edited by INDRA LUSERO, CARA PAGE, and MIA MINGUS

With contributions from Indra Lusero, D Queen B, DuxFemFac/La'Tasha, Alexis Pauline Gumbs, Vanessa Huang, Sheila Isong, Mia Mingus, Cara Page, aya christie de chellis.

We are organizers, parents, activists, artists, lovers, builders, healers, teachers, warriors, poets, and dreamers. We are queer people of color working for queer liberation and reproductive justice, knowing that one cannot exist without the other and we wouldn't want it any other way.

We are at a historical moment in the RJ movement, as the framework and language has become a powerful movement to be reckoned with, tackling population control, eugenics, and right-to-parent battles that have historically been ignored by the pro-choice movement. And within the RJ movement, queer activists of color are at the forefront, pushing a deeper, more inclusive politic and understanding of queerness, sexuality, gender, family, sex, bodies, and RJ. Queer activists of color are working to bridge the LGBT, queer liberation, and reproductive rights, health, and justice movements. It is from the queer liberation and reproductive justice movements that the queer activists of color in this chapter write, many of whom who work and organize in both.

We asked queer and RJ activists of color to write love letters to the queer liberation and RJ movements. We asked them to write a short or long letter/poem/prose/recipe about our love, struggle, contradictions, and hope for the queer liberation and RJ movements. We wanted activists to reflect on how they want these movements to hold, embrace, and to love us, and how we want to love them back.

We have broken the chapter into two kinds of love letters: "How We Love Queer . . ." and "How We Want the Queer and Reproductive Justice Movements to Love Us Back . . ." The first is about us, unapologetically sexual and undeniably queer, loving who we are, our bodies, and each other. The second contains our visions for where we are going and how we want to reinvent our movements.

How We Love Queer . . .

Recipe for Compassion:

when you come to a slow rolling boil
let yourself float above
to look down on that no-good, hatable, violating
tuft of a human being who
rattles you so.
but as you swivel your head in disapproval,
catch a glimpse of all those folks
carrying-on above you
about just how much you have done wrong.
simmer in that space until you can see yourself
on all sides
and a new
loved self will inhabit your space.
(best ladled out warm among friends,
garnished with a cinnamon stick.)

—aya christie de chellis

■ ■ ■

I wanted to begin this letter to you naked. Why else would you come? And not for some prurient display. No. But because I know you have a hunch about this thing called truth. You've seen the fabric slip. Maybe you, too, have a mountain range under your skin.

I call it queer. This nakedness that I offer you, this thing called my life. Queer, because I can't deny lies and partial truths. Queer because I would rather live with the paradox than pretend that it doesn't exist. I want to take up all the little bits of truth that don't fit and live with them inside me, let them leech into my bloodstream, crystallize, give birth to something new.

It's funny how the truth gets made. I live. I function. I have friends. I go to work. I have a loving family. And mostly truth isn't an issue—it's something we take for granted and get some sense of comfort from imagining we share.

But half the time I'm lying. I'm lying about being from here. I'm lying that I speak this language. I'm lying that this flesh covers regular bones.

I don't mention where I'm really from, I rarely speak my native tongue, and I never, ever admit to what's beneath my skin.

That's how the truth gets made.

What we live with and wear and share between ourselves at gatherings in the backyard on summer evenings, with the gas grill flaming and kids giggling, is a truth of omission. It's fibers we've woven together to cover up our nakedness. Fibers of language; fibers of chronological time.

If one could dissect my living flesh they would certainly find a mountain range where they'd expect a spine. If they could do a CT scan to reveal the language that lives on the inside of my tongue they would certainly see an avian song. Have you ever looked into the eyes of a magpie and seen yourself there? If they could count the rings of my insides to see how long I have lived they'd find I stretch back to before time and keep going past it.

Which is not to say that I am unaware of the details of my day and age. I *am* from here. I *do* speak this language. I *am* decaying flesh and bones. I weave that intricate fiber of truth with the best of them; I take this strand, up and over and up and over in an elegant pattern tight against itself, carefully intersecting, flexible yet taut.

—Indra Lusero

■ ■ ■

Recipe for Determination:

lay bare the sass of your fleshiest dream
and rub in some coarse salts and torn sage.
as they say,
feel the burn.
you can take it, your sinews coming to life
under duress.
you are now ready to brave the roasting
while you silently meditate on desire
and humbly commit to sifting through the minutes
until you find that ripest moment.
(make sure to savor. each. bite.)

—aya christie de chellis

■ ■ ■

Dear Queer Liberation Movement (my family),

I haven't felt as sexy before as I do now. Funny how things work, my body weight has fluctuated over the years, battling borderline eating disorders at times, and even when I was a size nine, I didn't feel as sexy as I do now. I stood in front of a camera the other night, in a tutu and fishnets. I harnessed her in as photos were being taken. Without hesitation I told her I wanted to suck on her cock. It was purple and delicious. She licked my nipple without asking. The rush felt different, sexy, as if somehow even though boundaries were crossed, I wanted them to be crossed more. Her cock made me wet. Those photos affirmed me, validated how sexy I felt at that moment.

I wanted to share all of these feelings with you, the movement that has given birth to this space, the ability to feel whole and vulnerable and safe and liberated and empowered. You're like family to me. And to my family I say yes, the world is my fucking oyster. And I have officially fallen in love with seafood.

Sometimes I wake up, wet. Ingrained in waters of lust, I feel biotic, erotic, and fucking hot. I had been dreaming of wearing my harness and fucking my husband, now just life partner and best friend, on the desk in our bedroom. I realize as I awake, *fuck I am wet*, and that it wasn't a dream. I feel queerer at that moment with him than I ever have before. I like to top him, make him cum, validate his queerness. I haven't wanted his penis in a while, but I am turned the fuck on by how queer he likes it, and how queer I am standing there, giving it.

And Bell radiates energy from her entire being that runs shivers down my spine and between my legs. She and I make out sometimes, mostly we're just friends, but the kissing feels good. I have wanted to kiss her for a long time! The fact that my fantasy is coming true entices me to indulge in all of the other dreams I only write about in my journal. But mostly, I am in love with the way she listens. She has a way about her that allows me to feel safe, outside the bounds of her kiss.

Vulnerability is scary sometimes, but polyamory creates spaces where I can conquer that fear, and feel safe doing it. I wonder if she knows that I love her.

And I am not finished smiling from that overwhelming feeling, slightly hungover from beers and lip-locking with her, when the mail arrives. In this mail is a package from Indra. I have never felt her kiss, but the touch of her hands, her face against mine, the love and lust in the words she writes, the theory she produces, only makes me want to beg her for more. She doesn't know this yet, but I want her to be my guide, my midwife, that is, when I am ready. I want those hands to touch me, to guide me into giving light to a new being, I want her energy inside me. She heals mind-body splits on levels unrecognizable.

Later I had sex for hours with my trans lover. He fucked me with my purple dildo all night long and then, he let me fuck him. He had never let someone do that to him before. And I don't know where we will be a month or six from now, but I know that moments like this engrave themselves into my skin, like inked flesh. And he can ink into my flesh all he wants. I hit the pillow hard, into a deep sleep, a slumber of erotic juices dampening the sheets around me. Polly, our Jack Russell, came in and crawled underneath them. I am sure she fell in love with me right then too.

My affair, my lust, or intense love for my sexuality provides the air in which I breathe, the grain of sanity that keeps me going in the day, it's a light I never knew had a light switch before. I have only recently began to acknowledge this relationship I have. Yes, I am in deep. A deep love affair with my lust, my sex, my sexuality.

At times I feel the need to step foot into a Catholic church, even though I haven't known one for fifteen years. I have images of walking into a confessional and sharing my lust, my intimacy, my polyamory, my queerness, my wetness, my desire, and want to be touched all over. Then I wonder if I would just make the priest hot in the process. And it makes me want to confess even more. Did I tell you I once had oral sex behind a Catholic church? I knew right then that I wasn't meant for religion, but something more erotic, spiritual, libratory.

You can't tame a wild spirit. You can't box her in or control her in any way. She lives in the now, in the beauty of others, in the waters of lust, she is a wild spirit, riding into sunsets, crossing borders, creating hybrids, and soaking in hot springs. She cannot be tamed, boxed, labeled, controlled, regulated, or bound. So, I write and I love and I sex and I continue to chase after what I believe helps my body/mind/spirit be whole, because I am in lust, if not fully in love with my sex, sexuality, and the people who are written into my life. They are the blood that keeps my heart pumping, the wetness between my legs, the sugar on my lips, the curves on my body, the touches I feel daily, the smiles that radiate energy, the ink tattooed into my flesh. I am finally ready, spiritually, mentally, emotionally, politically, sexually, and the rest of my being, to embrace and accept this part of my identity I have been seeking and exploring for so long!

Sincerely,
Amor, Abrazos, y Revolución,
D Queen B

Recipe for Sexiness:

swish through your garden
and pluck out
equal parts wit and kindness.
slice those lovely colors and
lay them out for admiring.
spread on a generous sense of humor,
rippling through taut texture.
toss in passion, tucked in, just so,
for a subtle taste
that stays with you.
find the perfect tray to decorate—
you know the distinctive style, the
presentation all your own,
so good to look at that no one could possibly
imagine ruffling that beautiful dish for a bite—
almost.
(don't forget the chili and lime sauce.)

—aya christie de chellis

■ ■ ■

Dear World,

I don't want to leave her. I never do. And, if you were watching, you'd probably think we spend as much time fighting as we do loving. You might even misunderstand how we communicate or how we touch one another. You wouldn't understand how we love. We love hard and fast and deep. I never want to leave her and tonight is not any different. She sleeps. I write. This is partially due to my insomnia and partially due to the inspiration that our daily encounters prompt in me. You see, she's a beacon of hope. I tattooed an adinkra symbol on my left wrist. It balances me when I'm unsteady. She catches me when I fall. Things have been so rough, so depressing, so black and blue that I've lost the beautiful shades of black and brown that reflect off of our skin when we make love on her bed, in my car, in our dreams.

I do it big with love. I'm one of those believers. I give people a chance, hoping for the best. I figure you never know. I never knew. I never knew until I met her. It was so untraditional, so unintentional, so real. Some would frown. I haven't stopped smiling. Because if they knew how her brown mixes with mine, if they knew the wine that pours out of us, then they'd understand. Because I'm pretty sure I'd take a bullet for her, and for her grandmother too, even though I haven't met her. Because she pressured me into kissing her that day in her car. Because her hands shook when she tried to tell me. Because I was attracted to her the first time we went to dinner. Because she trusted me with her life, her future, her broken heart. Because when I look at her my heart smiles. Because her hand fits so perfectly in mine. Because she's emotional and so am I. Because she tries really, really hard. Because she deserves some sunlight in all her darkness. Because she trusts me. Because I trust her. Because she loves me just as hard as I love her.

To the love of my life I give you my vows: I vow to always value your feelings and thoughts. I vow to consider you before I consider myself. I vow to love you unconditionally. I vow to reach out and touch your heart every day. I vow to see things out of your lenses. I vow to always swallow my pride. I vow to love you unconditionally. I vow to try your taste. I vow to reciprocate. I vow to encourage and push. I vow to help you grow. I vow to relax. I vow to try new things. I vow to forgive and forget when necessary. I vow to love you unconditionally. I vow to give and receive. I vow to understand. I vow to hold you every night. I vow to have patience. I vow to love your light brown skin. I vow to tell you how beautiful you are every day. I vow to say please and thank you. I vow to believe in the unbelievable. I vow to love you . . .

Sincerely,
A Lover.
Sheila Isong

■ ■ ■

Recipe for Faith:

measure out memories of just how indifferent
the world can be.
and breathe.
feel the stirring in yourself of survival,
not despite the prickliness of the world,
but because you were destined to flourish.
(makes a hearty stew.)

—aya christie de chellis

How We Want the Queer and Reproductive Justice Movements to Love Us Back . . .

I am not afraid of love. I am not afraid of my whole self asking your whole self to join me in liberation. I am not afraid of love.

I am not afraid of difference. I have dreamt of you seamlessly weaving together, loving the places you reflect each other, and touching the differences that define you with admiration. You are the kind of beauty that is fierceness in pain, in laughter, in survival. What I mean to say is, we are too precious to turn away from one another. Too precious to think we can leave our work to our respective movements. Because the warriors, the people, who straddle the borders of fear know that we were never enemies. We were always kindred. We were always each other's gravity and air. Because when the fire comes, it comes to burn us all and your seeds blow over our fences and take root in our soil.

This is a love letter for RJ activists who are too afraid to publicly incorporate a queer politic into their work. A love letter for queer people who are complicit in reproductive oppression every day. A love letter for the heteronormativity and sexism that exists within the reproductive justice movement and the racism and misogyny that exists within the LGBT and queer movement. A love letter for our fears which seek to strangle us every day through criminalization, silence, and isolation. A love letter for repeating our histories.

This is for those of us who know that building intentional families, intentional community, intentional love, genders, and bodies can never be separated from justice; can never be separated from healing, from truth—and will always be transformative. This is for our desires lying down together outside of oppression, outside of ownership, outside of abuse.

This is a love letter for those who have come before us and never stopped pushing their way into the conversation, the family, the agenda. This is a love letter for those who will come after us and look back with pride and strength at how we wrestled our fears and hate to the ground and didn't stop until our bodies were whole, our children were free, and our land could breathe.

This is my love, out in the open, reaching a hand to you, asking you to join me in our liberation.

—Mia Mingus

■ ■ ■

Recipe for Curiosity:

tip
back
your head
and loll about in playful senses.
imagine each spice is a question
and the combination
changes everything.
the endlessness of potential—
imagine how this tea will taste under that sun,
or how long it will take the moonlight to ripen
that spirit.
(nibble after dinner.)

—aya christie de chellis

■ ■ ■

as I exist at this point and time in the Universe, I am eternally grateful for the blessing of authenticity. and the blessing of discovering you as my hope and inspiration to be completely who I am, knowing you intimately in joy and pain and loving you with my deepest passions and greatest desires.
each day you motivate me to BE my purpose and manifest all that the Universe has designed for my life. you remind me of the best parts of myself as I was birthed into this lifetime and called by my ancestors to be an activist, visionary, and leader. I carry your love, peace, and memory in my spirit.
you are my light out of the darkness of oppression, my peace in all my identities, and the powerful force that stirs my soul for justice.
it was love at first sight and I am still in love with you forever and a day.

your love,
DuxFemFac/La'Tasha

■ ■ ■

Recipe for Peacefulness:

clean off your counters

pushing every mess and stain to the floor
and climb up into the cupboards,
sharing space with the plates and dishes that
have served you so well.
settle into the spaciousness
of being a wisp of a secret
hidden among the ordinary day,
in that favored room
where just being is enough.
(chill and serve.)

—aya christie de chellis

■ ■ ■

love my sewn-up hand the hand of childhood uncloseting n desirous of connection home n love
love the stories n dreamin it holds so deep love the fingers excitin my nipples n paintbrushin my clit to ocean's edge
love the way my hair falls the way it dances its need for play its refusal to pass eyes surfing this immigrant body love us faggy dykes genderqueers n tranny fags n girls love all the parts of me n all the parts we missin love away trans n nontrans misogyny in one same breath love us labelless love us families whole
love my fierceness questions n push back
love my then need for quiet n rest

love why i built these walls as a kid whose daddy left n crossed the ocean a kid whose momma taught us to just trust your self n momma

love why i forget when herbalists grandmothers n their friends boy my queering body cuz i ain't fittin love why i cringe when you ma'am, lady, n girl me immigrant eyes surfing this immigrant body

love my discomforting sag of breast some braless nights love my arms crossed for reassurance love my puss n his n hirs our bound n unbound chests

love us full with possibility love to stretch upside down n sideways both love this boundless yearning

love my fear outta this vein n muscle
love these walls i built to bridges
love me truly open

love me tough n love me tender
love me soft n slow

love to imagine how we could be
not old n grayin not tomorrow
imagine us embodied
now

—*Vanessa Huang*

■ ■ ■

Recipe for Gratitude:

marvel at the elegance
of honey in a comb.
how modest the trees are
to lend their fruit.
take. eat. and think of me.
that was a line borrowed,
instruction from the mama.
she sighs and keeps on finding
new ways to make dew.
you must
patiently harvest hope,
long for the perfect foods,
conjure up symbiosis
that sustains your aspirations
in remembrance of her.
(share with imperfect strangers.)

—*aya christie de chellis*

■ ■ ■

I wake up wanting you. Fall asleep waiting.

You make my body into a space station and a time machine, a loving opening for ancestors and the unborn. Fill my pores with invisible partners for a world to be made.

Although everything about this feels natural, this mother-sister-daughter-love, past-present-future-love is taboo and illegal. For us, to create a girl, to be a girl, to love a girl, is to confront the totalizing logic of a world structured on rape. We live in a world in which it is impossible to love your mother, and we do it anyway. Where it is criminal to be a girl-mother or the mother of a girl. We live in a world in which it is impossible to love ourselves, but we do it somehow. We live in a world in which it is impossible to love creation, but I love you. That is the queer thing.

We ask for a justice that we call "reproductive." What we want is a way to sustain our communities, to survive these deadly times. We want our kids to grow up knowing that no one will beat them down and say they should never have been born because they look this way, move this way, love this way. We want this love to outlast our bodies and fill time. And that's where I want to lay down and rest with you. That's where I want to wake up in the morning.

But don't forget that our survival is a queer thing in a world that says we never should have happened. A world that works to steal and kill everything we create. The queerest most dangerous thing of all is that we are even here to say it: I love you. We were never meant to survive.

Our survival cannot be reproduced. Our survival requires we remake every single piece of life on this planet, especially us—explicitly what we mean when we say "we." There is something queer about the love between us. I am asking you not to pretend otherwise. I am pleading with you not to tame your love for me to barter acceptance. Not to pretend we're normal when it seems convenient. I am asking you to hold me in the grocery store like the part of the story when god knocks all of capitalism down and declares it unholy. I want you to scream my name like you know there is life waiting in its echo. I want you to introduce me to the whole family like thunder, breaking the table into a joyful excuse to build anew again.

Love me back.

I want a love that is queer and intergenerational, a radically transformed forever that means we never take each other for granted, for borrowed, or for sold. That means there is something (inter) between us that (generate) makes everything possible and that can make our whole world (queer) different than anything we've known.

Because they say you're too old for me, too old for me, not ready. But the queer thing is, here we are. Now.

—Alexis Pauline Gumbs

■ ■ ■

Love in Parts I & II

(Two haikus for the queer liberation & RJ movements)

I

come into my bed
love me/parts and particles
without owning me

II

mis/taken apart
body and geography
love me queerly/whole

—Cara Page

Brown Seed

GUADALUPE ANAYA CANO

"I am a woman,
like silk I was cut from a royal cloth that was on my father's back.
I am simply Gold not gold plated,
blood ruby red running through my veins, strength inherited from my mother who I often call a queen.
I am a brown seed buried by the gravel that holds up the wall inches away from my freedom.
I am a brown seed that is expected to grow. & so I'm doing just that."

—Monna

I Am KING!

GUADALUPE ANAYA CANO

Freeze! Hands in the air! I have no choice now but to give in.
Turn in my body, surrender my soul, give up my strength, and play my role. My mind keeps drowning I'm trying to swim, swallow my pride, that was shot down by him.
My inner woman just died. From men like you.
Men who in public parade me, yet behind close doors beat and degrade me, men like the ones who stole my mother's and grandmother's virginity, who did as they pleased willingly. Men who took turns drawing the negative perception of women artistically and believe our only role in society is fertility.
Now ain't that shit tyranny?
My inner woman just died at least that's what you see, silly men please try to keep up with me.
I am woman which makes me strong, and with strength I manage to break free from the handcuffs that tied my hands together. I am woman which makes me capable, and with capability I am no longer oppressed but the oppressor. I am woman which makes me royal, and with royalty knowledge and being powerful Is my only treasure.
I am woman, and being woman makes me KING!

Depression

SANDRA PONCE de CID

Depression.

It's not about always being sad,
it's mostly about guilt.
Guilt in a smile you didn't deserve,
guilt in praise you didn't earn,
guilt in the happy moments you can't fully appreciate.

Maybe you're not meant for joy.
Maybe this is as good as it gets.
Maybe no one is really happy.
Maybe they're faking it too.

Whatever you do,
don't take Prozac!
The shame,
the stigma.

What would your mother say?
Don't be so selfish,
so self-centered.

Americans have a pill for everything.
Tough it out!
You're Mexicana!
You don't have a psychological problem.

For her, and for her.

UMA RAO

This is the story of my survival, in four parts.

ONE.

The first time, I didn't really get to meet her.
She was gone before I knew it.
I knew she was smart, because.
She Escaped.

A man . . .
Who told me that if I said anything to anyone,
  he would hurt my sister.
I thought if I said a word,
  he would never stop coming in at night
  to watch me sleep.
Perhaps if I kept really quiet,
  he would stop coming in
  when I was about to take a bath.

I felt dirty For Years.
Every year,
  for four years,
  it was the same.
But the year that She Escaped,
  that's when
I Understood.

I refused to go back there.
My grandfather died a few months after the Escape.
My grandmother died a year later.
After that,
The Girl Who Escaped,
    she came to me and said,
    "Now, it's time to speak."
"Now."

TWO.

My mother was on her knees,
    grasping my leg,
    begging for forgiveness.
I could not predict my survival from day to day.
My father decided to travel there.

I think The Girl Who Escaped,
    I think she went with him.
When my father returned Home,
    we were his only family left.
He let all of them go,
    when they refused to stand with him.
He has been isolated from them ever since.

I still think sometimes,
    "Can I forgive myself, for doing this to my father?"

But The Girl Who Escaped,
She reminds me,
My father chose Me.

THREE.

The day I met another survivor.
She was a 72 year old black woman,
    who lived in Albermarle County, VA.
Over a glass of sweet tea,
    she told me the story of her survival, in one part.
It took her three minutes.

I poured myself another glass.

With each sip,
  I received a blessing.
I told her the story of my survival.
It took me thirteen hours.

FOUR.
More recently,
  I met *Her.*
When she came,
  I wasn't scared.
No pain.
No anger,
  not even a little bit of rage.
Not even a drop of guilt.

When she came,
  I was happy.
From indiscretion,
  from deviant behavior.
From joy.
From the very core
  of my sexual being.

This time,
No family.
Only Faith.

Amidst my conversations with God,
in a matter of days
she left before I knew her.

But now I know her.
She is *The Girl*
Who Gave Me Choice.

If You Were in My Shoes

SAFIRE
(NOW FORWARD TOGETHER)

Even though I am not old enough to vote,
  I make choices all the time.
I make choices for my family
  so that we can live a better life.

When I learned about the propositions on this year's ballot
  it seemed like some groups only want a better a life
    for some people but not everyone.

So I want to ask everyone . . .
  Do you know what it's like to be a youth nowadays?
  Do you know what it feels like when it seems everyone is against you?
  Do you know what I go through?
If you knew, what would you do if you were in my shoes?

If you try and try your best
  but fear disappointing others,
  would you still want the right to make decisions
  that affect your body at any age?

Would you want to talk to whomever
  you thought would be the most supportive?

Would you want support
  to help forget about past mistakes
  so that you could continue your education?

What would you do if you were in my shoes?

If you look up one day
and find yourself on the wrong path,
would you want support to make it right?

Or would you want to live in a world of blame,
shame, and no second chances
that puts even the youngest member of your family at risk?

What would you do if you were in my shoes?

If you were always taught to have an open heart,
but later told you couldn't marry whom you truly love
because of your sexuality?
First we can, then we can't, then we can,
and now maybe we can't again.
How do you think that feels to have your right to love be taken away?

What would you do if you were in my shoes?

When the world around you
wants to take away support from people
when they need it the most.
Wouldn't you do whatever you had to do to learn freely,
live freely, and love freely?

I would.

I may not be old enough to vote THIS YEAR,
but I am a strong young woman with a voice
dedicated to those not old enough,
not citizen enough, or not free enough.

And I believe if we come together,
we can push back these attacks
from groups that don't want liberty and justice for all.

So on Election Day,
think about if you were in my shoes,
even if it is just for a second.

And I hope that you vote NO on propositions 4, 6, 8, and 9.

Reproductive Justice for Women of the East

BONITA B. SHARMA

I am a mother, sister, and a daughter.
I live with my family, in my village.
I am most happy when I am
  with my mother and father,
  sisters and brothers,
  friends and relatives.

You tell me to stand up for myself,
  I do, but with my family.
You tell me to decide for me,
  I do, amidst my village.

I am like a tree in the middle of a forest.
I grew to this height under the surrounding trees
  that braced and provided me with sun and shade.
Yet, I grew to this height
  even when the other trees lashed at me
  with the harsh wind and the rain.

I don't want to be like an animal in the zoo,
  separated from my village and forest.
Another person deciding when or where
  I'm supposed to have my offspring.

Let me be, so I am a part of this forest.
Let me be a part of this family.
Let me be so I can be me.
Let me be me and foster me,
  to decide on my reproductive rights.

Contributor Bios

Madina Agénor is a social epidemiologist who uses quantitative and qualitative research methods to investigate the social and policy determinants of sexual and reproductive health inequities at the intersection of gender, race/ethnicity, socioeconomic position, and sexual orientation, with a particular focus on women and girls of color and LGBTQ populations of color.

Guadalupe Anaya Cano is a poet who, ever since she was young, often found herself writing about personal experiences and describes her writing as a form of healing.

Mary Lee Bendolph is a community memory keeper and perhaps the best-known Gee's Bend quilter. In 1999 she was the subject of "Crossing Over," the *Los Angeles Times*'s Pulitzer Prize–winning article about the effort to reestablish ferry service across the Alabama River. Bendolph's work has been shown at US embassies around the world.

Erika Derkas is a professor of sociology and women's studies and codirector of the women's studies program at New Mexico Highlands University. She is an active researcher in the area of reproductive justice, particularly international sex worker organizing, population control, and sterilization abuse among poor women and women of color.

Mary Krane Derr, a poet and pro-life ecofeminist activist best known for coediting *ProLife Feminism: Yesterday and Today*, passed away at age forty-nine on November 12, 2012.

Dázon Dixon Diallo, DHL, MPH, is a national and international sexual and reproductive justice advocate, activist, and lecturer with a special focus on HIV and other sexually transmitted infections.

Forward Together, formerly SAFIRE, is a multiracial organization working with community forerunners in order to transform culture and policy to catalyze social change, and seeks to ensure that women, youth, and families command the power and resources needed to reach their full potential.

Marlene Gerber Fried, a long-time activist and scholar and faculty director of the Civil Liberties and Public Policy program at Hampshire College, was founding president of the National Network of Abortion Funds and is currently on the board of Our Bodies Ourselves and working internationally with Women Help Women.

Lucia Leandro Gimeno is an Afro-Latinx, transmasculine femme bruja and organizer based in Seattle and director of the Queer & Trans People of Color Birthwerq Project, an organizing project to increase access to birth education for trans, gender nonconforming, and queer people of color.

Laura Jiménez has worked with women of color organizations across the country on issues of reproductive justice, including the National Latina Health Organization, the Dominican Women's Development Center, and SisterSong; and is currently executive director at California Latinas for Reproductive Justice.

Kierra Johnson, executive director of URGE: Unite for Reproductive & Gender Equity (formerly Choice USA), heads the leading pro-choice organization working to mobilize and provide ongoing support for the diverse, upcoming generation of leaders who promote and protect reproductive choice both now and in the future.

Toni M. Bond Leonard, one of the founding mothers of the reproductive justice movement, is an RJ activist and womanist ethicist completing her PhD in religion, ethics, and society at Claremont School of Theology.

Indra Lusero is a reproductive justice attorney, entrepreneur, and parent. As founder of Elephant Circle and president of the Birth Rights Bar Association, Indra is dedicated to defending clients and advocating for policy change that supports families and honors our physiological well-being.

La'Tasha D. Mayes is the founder and executive director of New Voices for Reproductive Justice, a native of West Philadelphia, and believes in the indefatigable spirit and infinite power of black women, femmes, and girls.

Caroline R. McFadden is an anti-racist feminist writer and activist located in Ann Arbor, Michigan.

Mia Mingus is a writer, educator, and community organizer for disability justice and transformative justice.

Benita Miller, executive director of the NYC Children's Cabinet in the Office of the Mayor, previously served as founder and executive director of the Brooklyn Young Mothers' Collective and lives in Brooklyn with her daughter, Memphis.

Katie O'Connell is a queer disabled femme and dog mom committed to compassionate and radical organizing that amplifies the voices of those marginalized in social justice movements.

Anna Ochoa O'Leary is head of the Department of Mexican American Studies and codirector of the Binational Migration Institute at the University of Arizona in Tucson.

Cara Page is a black, queer, feminist cultural worker, practitioner, and organizer building movements, collective safety, and wellness rooted in black ancestral traditions of resistance and resilience.

Whitney Peoples is an Instructional Consultant with a focus on race and ethnicity in the Center for Research on Learning and Teaching at the University of Michigan. Her work has been published in books such as *No Permanent Waves: Recasting Histories of U.S. Feminisms* and *A History of African American Autobiography*, as well as in several journals.

Sandra Ponce de Cid is a passionate fluid Chicanx feminist who hails from Canoga Park Cali and is a lifelong aficionadx of Frida Kahlo; her poetry "*es puro al alma y corázon*."

Uma Rao is a one-and-a-half-generation American desi femme who has survived violence with gratitude to her family (bio and chosen) and because of divine grace.

Lynn Roberts, an assistant professor of community health and social sciences in the CUNY School of Public Health, examines the intersections of race, class, and gender in adolescent dating relationships, juvenile justice, and reproductive health policies, as well as the impact of models of collaborative inquiry and teaching on civic and political engagement.

Diana Romero, associate professor and chair of community health and social sciences in the CUNY School of Public Health, conducts research at the intersection of social policies and women's reproductive health and well-being with an emphasis on historically disadvantaged groups.

Loretta J. Ross cofounded and served as National Coordinator of SisterSong until 2012. Ross is the coauthor of *Undivided Rights: Women of Color Organize for Reproductive Justice* and has written extensively on the history of African American women and reproductive justice activism.

Rachel Roth is a writer, consultant, and activist. She is a blogger for MomsRising, author of *Making Women Pay: The Hidden Costs of Fetal Rights*, and former director of the Massachusetts Anti-Shackling Coalition.

Bonita B. Sharma is currently an adjunct practice faculty at the University of Texas at Arlington's School of Social Work, where she specializes in gender equality and empowerment.

William Paul Simmons is a professor of gender and women's studies and director of the fully online master's degree in human rights practice at the University of Arizona in Tucson.

Monica Simpson, named a new civil rights leader by *Essence* in 2014, is a black, Southern, queer artivist and doula who serves as executive director of SisterSong, where she brings nearly two decades of grassroots organizing experience and a deep passion for human rights, birth justice, art activism, and black liberation.

Alice Skenandore, one of the foremothers of SisterSong, is an Oneida and Green Bay community member, a traditional midwife, and founder of Wise Women Gathering Place who has practiced the womanly art of cradle-to-the-grave home-birth midwifery for more than 750 babies over twenty-nine years.

Andrea Smith is a cofounder of INCITE! and teaches in ethnic studies at University of California, Riverside.

Rickie Solinger is a historian, author or editor of eleven books, and curator of seven social-justice-themed art exhibitions that have traveled to over 150 college and university galleries.

Rachael Strickler found family in the Civil Liberties and Public Policy program at Hampshire College and mentors/mothers in Loretta J. Ross and Marlene Gerber Fried; after graduating with a degree in reproductive justice and the carceral state, she is excited to continue a lifelong journey toward justice.

Pamela Bridgewater Toure, an activist lawyer and legal scholar specializing in issues related to reproduction, sexuality, identity, poverty, and women's health, passed away on December 27, 2014, in Washington, DC, with her husband by her side.

Beverly Yuen Thompson is an associate professor and department chair of sociology at Siena College in Loudonville, New York.

Aaronette White was professor of social psychology and associate dean of equity and social responsibility at the University of California, Santa Cruz, who wrote and spoke widely about issues of race and gender until her transition to a deeply beloved ancestor on August 13, 2012.

Permissions

Beyond Pro-Choice versus Pro-Life: Women of Color and Reproductive Justice by Andrea Smith (p. 151). This article was originally published in *NWSA Journal*, vol. 17, no. 1, 2005. Reprinted with permission.

"She Doesn't Deserve to Be Treated Like This": Prisons as Sites of Reproductive Injustice by Rachel Roth (p. 285). This essay is updated and reprinted from *Reproductive Laws for the 21st Century Papers* (Washington, DC: Center for Women Policy Studies, 2012). For a complete version of this essay with full endnotes and references, see the Prison Policy Initiative Research Clearinghouse at https://www.prisonpolicy.org/research/women.

HIV Prevention and Reproductive Justice: A Framework for Saving Women's Lives by Dázon Dixon Diallo (p. 340). This article was originally published by the National Women's Health Network in *Women's Health Activist*, May/June, 2008. Reprinted with permission.

Making Art for Reproductive Justice by Rickie Solinger (p. 397). A version of this chapter originally appeared as "Interrupted Life: Incarcerated Mothers in the United States: A Traveling Public Art Exhibition" in *Meridians*, vol. 7, no. 2, 2007. Reprinted with permission.

Acknowledgments

As the editors of this anthology, it would be impossible to list all of the people who helped bring this dream to fruition. Nor can we list them in order of importance, but our sincere thanks go to each of them. We'd particularly like to thank Pamela Bridgewater Toure, Aaronette White, and Mary Krane Derr, who trusted us with their submissions but passed away before they could see their work in print. Thanks also to Gabriela Moreno for her assistance reviewing the poetry section. We are particularly grateful to the SisterSong family, current and past members of the Board of Directors, and particularly SisterSong founder Luz Marina Rodriguez-Cintron, for allowing us to assemble this offering of love. Thanks are also offered to the authors included in this book.

Loretta J. Ross would like to thank the following: Blue Mountain Center—Harriet Barlow and Ben Strader—Darcy Buerkle, Sonja Dolinsek, Joyce Follet, Alexis Pauline Gumbs, Elizabeth Hackett, Kia Hall, Lokeilani Kaimana, Carrie Lee Lancaster, Lara Matta, Anne McClintock, Rob Nixon, Karen Pittelman, Grace Ramsey, Sherrill Redmon, Stephanie Rosen, Nayiree Roubinian, Jeanine Ruhsam, Barbara Smith, Kerry Spitzer, Gloria Steinem, Banu Subramaniam, Rosemarie Garland-Thomson, and Isa Williams.

Lynn Roberts thanks Dulari Gandhi for volunteering her time to get the editors organized in the beginning with invaluable clerical support, and Kweku Toure and Lisa Diane White for their gracious support and permission to include their beloved wife and sister in this volume. She is especially grateful for the life and forbearance of her ancestors, the grace and wisdom of her mother, Constance Lovell Gates, the constant friendship of her sister Pamela Baker, and all the joy and hope derived from her children Keely, Thaddeus, Laneé, and Cameron, and grandchildren Isaiah, Jonah, Jada, and Naiella.

Erika Derkas would like to thank Kristie Ross for her unyielding support, belief, and friendship: "Her overall spirit continues to inspire and guide and for this I am eternally grateful." Special thanks to Mia Ramirez for her clerical support and eye for detail.

Whitney Peoples would like to thank Erika Derkas, Lynn Roberts, Loretta J. Ross, and SisterSong for bringing her into the important and affirming work of this anthology. She is also grateful for Dr. Moya Bailey's role in bringing her to this project. She extends special thanks to the students in her Fall 2016 reproductive justice seminar for their enthusiasm and excitement for this book and for wholly embracing the invitation to become reproductive justice scholars and advocates in their own right.

Index

A

B

E

F

G

Q

R

S

T

U

V

W

Y

Z

The Feminist Press is a nonprofit educational organization founded to amplify feminist voices. FP publishes classic and new writing from around the world, creates cutting-edge programs, and elevates silenced and marginalized voices in order to support personal transformation and social justice for all people.

See our complete list of books at
feministpress.org